HISTORY OF OLDHAM VOLUNTEER CORPS 1798 – 1908

By Iain Wilkinson

Iain Wilkinson

1 Dec 2009.

JAGI PUBLISHING

Published by:

JAGI PUBLISHING

ISBN 978-0-9564140-0-7

Acknowledgements

Staff at Oldham Local Studies, Garry Smith at the Museum of Manchester Regiment, Dr Stephen Bull at the Museum of Lancashire, Robert Bonner, Simon Butterworth, Bill Mitchenson, Colin McInnes, John Cleverley, David Rodger MBE and the Trustees of 10th Bn MR & 40/41 RTR Trust, Carol Hyde of Oldham Mayor's Office.

For sparing their valuable time to proof read the draft manuscript, Mary Howarth, Mary Pendlebury, Ben Townsend and Mandi Wilkinson.

Painting of the Oldham Local Militia Officer and Oldham Local Militia Colours by Alix Baker. Painting of the Oldham Troop of Yeomanry Cavalry guidon by Mandi Wilkinson. Painting of the Oldham Rifle Volunteers by Ray Kirkpatrick.

To

Mary Howarth for setting me off on this journey,

&

Jane, Amy and Gemma for putting up with me.

Volunteer Origins

The origins of the Volunteer Corps and Yeomanry Cavalry can be traced back to the end of the Eighteenth century when, on 1st February 1793, the new revolutionary government of France declared war on Britain. This immediately sparked off offers of voluntary service from persons mainly residing on the south coast of England, those who saw themselves most closely under threat from any invading French army.
The British government granted permission to these requests to form volunteer corps and gave them assistance by issuing them with arms and accoutrements. During this period the government also feared civil disorder on the home front from working class disaffection and as a large part of the regular army was committed overseas, the government had only the under-strength and poorly trained Militia available for use in home defence and policing during civil disturbances. On 5th March 1794 the Prime Minister, William Pitt the Younger, proposed several measures to the House of Commons to establish some control over the new volunteers and strengthen the internal defence of Britain in anticipation of any French invasion.

The Volunteer Act of 1794[1] was the first of a number of Acts of Parliament intended to encourage men to volunteer for the defence of their counties and towns and, if necessary, for the defence of Britain.
This Act authorised the raising of Volunteer Corps of all arms that could be used for home defence and policing duties within the counties. Clause 31 of the Act aimed:

> *'to encourage and discipline such corps and companies as should voluntarily enrol themselves for the defence of their counties, towns, coasts, or for the general defence of the Kingdom'*

At the same time as this new Act a new ballot system was introduced to the Militia to try to augment its numbers. These two measures are inter-related due to the fact that members of volunteer corps were exempt from Militia service if balloted. This had the effect of increasing the numbers in the volunteer corps at the expense of the Militia.
By May 1794 the volunteers had increased to 32 mounted corps and 72 companies of infantry and artillery volunteers.
No Volunteer Corps formed in Oldham at this time but one was formed nearby in Rochdale. On 28th May 1794, the *Rochdale Volunteers* were formed consisting of four companies commanded by Lieutenant-Colonel John Entwistle.
Towards the end of 1796 the general feeling within government was that a French invasion was very likely and was keen to increase the military force available for home defence. The government sanctioned the creation of a Supplementary Militia and a Provisional Cavalry. The Supplementary Militia did not quite achieve the proposed

---

[1] Act 34, Geo II, Cap 31

strength of 60,000 men, but was deemed a success by government. The Provisional Cavalry was not as successful. The raising of this force was based on a levy, of one horse in ten, from all those who paid the horse tax. The Provisional Cavalry proved difficult to raise and train. In February 1797 the furore caused by a small French force landing at Pembroke caused a new wave of volunteering. In March 1797 the government encouraged each parish to form an *Armed Association* for local defence and security. A year later, in April 1798, the threat of a French invasion meant that anxiety was reaching fever pitch throughout the country.

The French were engaged in building up fleets of barges in preparation for the invasion of England, General Bonaparte's *Army of England* was gathering on the French coast, this caused the Government to contemplate arming every able-bodied man in the Kingdom.

The government passed the Defence of the Realm Act[2] in 1798 which required each county Lord Lieutenant to compile lists of all able bodied men between the ages of 15 and 60, together with details of their occupation and stipulating the type of service, combatant or non-combatant, which they were capable of performing in time of emergency. This act resulted in the formation of more *Armed Associations* in which persons so registered in a community could unite to form bands of 50 men under the command of an elected commanding officer for the purpose of local defence. These *Armed Associations* could be in the form of infantry or cavalry. The essential difference between units of the Volunteer forces and the *Armed Associations* was that the latter received no pay and normally confined their services to the defence of a specific town or small locality. The Government could provide assistance in the way of providing these volunteer corps with an issue of arms and accoutrements, but quite a number of Associations equipped themselves. They also made use of the non-combatant element – men who by reason of age or other cause, could not, or did not wish to bear arms. Those men were made constables, responsible for marshalling civilians, organising transport and herding together livestock in the event of an invasion. Others became beacon watchers, lookouts, pioneers and drivers of requisitioned wagons.

It is this type of Volunteer Corps that makes its first appearance in Oldham.

The raising of the volunteer units was normally organised by an individual or a small group of like-minded individuals. A public meeting would be organised to try and gauge the reaction of the local populace and then, once sufficient support had been obtained, regulations would be fixed and subscriptions would be raised. Subscription books were normally made available in public buildings so that people could make their pledges.

Expressions of loyalty to the local volunteer corps could be expressed in two ways, either by joining the corps or by subscribing to the financial support of the corps. It was not expected that all propertied men join the volunteers but it was expected that they gave some kind of financial support.

[2] Act 38, Geo II, Cap 19, 27 & 38

The Oldham Horse and Foot Association (Oldham Loyal Volunteers), 1798-1802

Unfortunately very few records relating to the organisation and activities of the early volunteers remain. Local archives in the form of the Oldham diarist, Rowbottom, make some mention of them; otherwise the only other information relating to them reside at the National Archives at Kew amongst the correspondence of the Home Office and War Office.
On 18th April 1798 a meeting was held to raise funds for clothing and equipping volunteers in the town of Oldham and two bodies of volunteers were raised known as the *Oldham Horse and Foot Associations*. The meeting was probably organised by John Lees, a local businessman who had interests in a number of concerns including cotton spinning and coal mining; he resided at Church Lane, Oldham. Normal practice was for a committee to be formed for the purpose of regulating the admission of members into the Association based on government guidelines, especially regarding the choice of officers.

The government was very keen to ensure that only trustworthy men would be allowed to become volunteers. This was mainly achieved by trying to ensure the officers appointed were loyal and respectable gentlemen. A landed qualification with an income of at least £50 per year from property was required for a commission in an *Armed Association*, though this was not essential for a commission in a volunteer or Yeomanry corps. The Lord Lieutenant (in the case of Lancashire, this was Lord Derby) would also be responsible for carrying out informal enquiries about any potential officers to ensure their suitability and that they were not connected with any of the political reform societies.

In addition to the raising of the volunteers within each town, Lord Derby was also interested in gathering together men who were skilled shots who could in the event of an invasion be issued with rifles and act as sharp shooters or riflemen. They would stay and train within their existing volunteer corps and only in the event of an invasion would they be called for their special duties.

(See proclamation on following page.)

TO THE

GAME-KEEPERS

OF THE COUNTY OF LANCASTER.

IN Obedience to his Majeſty's Commands, ſignified to me by the Right Honourable the Earl of *Derby*, the Lord Lieutenant of the ſaid County, and in Compliance with the Directions given to me by his Lordſhip, I have made a Return to Government of a Liſt of all your Names; and by the ſame Authority I am directed to inform you, and all Perſons ſkilful in the Uſe of Fowling-Pieces, who (it is thought by his Majeſty's Miniſters) might be of eſſential Service in Caſe of actual Invaſion, to act as Sharp Shooters, or Rifle-Men, that ſuch of you as are willing to come forward at this important Criſis are deſired without delay to make a Return at my Office of ſuch Arms as you now poſſeſs, ſpecifying whether it is your Wiſh to receive a Rifle from Government. If any of you are now attached to any local Corps of Volunteers, it is not intended to call you from it, or from your reſpective Place of Reſidence or Occupation, unleſs an Enemy ſhould have actually landed; in which Event it is conſidered the great Advantage that might be expected in that Emergency, from your being collected to act as a ſeparate Corps under proper Officers, who would then be pointed out for this Purpoſe. I have it in command further to collect your Sentiments on this Propoſal, and to give you diſtinctly to underſtand, that you will not be called forth except in the Caſe of actual Invaſion, and then only within the Military Diſtrict to which the County of *Lancaſter* belongs.

By Order of the Lord Lieutenant.

Office at LEIGH, May 3, 1798.

JAMES TAYLOR,
Deputy Clerk of the Peace for the ſaid County.

The Oldham Horse and Foot Association (Oldham Loyal Volunteers) 1798-1802

The overall command of the *Oldham Association* was in the charge of John Lees. The command of the *Oldham Horse Association* was entrusted to Mr Ralph Kershaw, of Copster Hill, Oldham.[3]
On 2nd May 1798 John Lees made a request, via the Lord Lieutenant, for allowance support from the government but as the terms for the formation of the *Oldham Association* had been that they would only be used in the immediate local area, the Home Office rejected this request. In a letter to Lord Derby from Henry Dundas, Secretary of State for the Home Office, on 17th May 1798, a number of volunteer corps of cavalry was accepted, including Oldham. A specific mention was given to the Oldham volunteers.

> '*I am also desired to signify to your Lordship, His Majesty's gracious acceptance of the very public spirited proposal from the town of Oldham.*'[4]

On the 11 June 1798 a letter confirmed the King's acceptance of the gentlemen proposed to be officers in the *Oldham Association* and three companies were now formed.

> '*... recommending several Gentlemen to be officers in the Loyal Association of the Town of Oldham. I have the pleasure to acquaint your Lordship that His Majesty has been pleased to approve thereof and commissions will be prepared and delivered to those Gentlemen or their agents at my office, on paying the Public stamps for the same.*'[5]

The following day commissions, all dated 12 June 1798, were issued to the following:

> '*John Lees Esq. Commandant of the Loyal Association of the Town of Oldham and its neighbourhood*
> *James Lees Esq. Captain*
> *Edward Lees Esq. Captain*
> *John Booth Gent Lieut.*
> *John Wright Gent Lieut.*
> *Henry Fletcher Gent Lieut.*
> *James Cocks Gent Ensign & Surgeon.*
> *James Clegg Gent Ensign.*
> *James Fletcher Gent Ensign.*
> *William Chippendale Gent Adjut.*
> *Wm Winter Chaplain.*'

[3] Rowbottoms Diary
[4] WO6/197
[5] HO51/105

John Lees, as commander of the *Oldham Foot Association,* was granted the commission of Major.
Within a few weeks of the commissions being granted to the *Oldham Foot Association* the commissions were duly appointed for one troop of the *Oldham Horse Association.*

> *'Having laid before the King your Lordships letter of the 17th Inst recommending three Gentlemen to be officers in the Oldham Troop of Associated Cavalry. I have the pleasure to acquaint your Lordship that His Majesty has been pleased to approve thereof and commissions will be prepared and delivered to those Gentlemen or their agents at my office on paying the Publick stamps for the same.*
>
> *Ralph Kershaw Esq. Captain (Cavalry) ... dated 27 June 1798*
> *John Twemlow Gent Lieut. ... dated 27 June 1798*
> *John Dunkerly Gent Cornet ... dated 27 June 1798'*[6]

Before the commissions were granted, the *Oldham Horse Association* had already started training and they had been observed on Northmoor, Oldham on 18th June.[7]
At some stage in the short history of the *Oldham Horse Association* Captain Ralph Kershaw retired and John Twemlow took over as Captain and commander. It is possible Ralph Kershaw retired due to ill health, as he died at the young age of 46 in 1809.
By the end of 1800 twenty volunteer infantry corps and four volunteer cavalry corps had been established in the county of Lancashire.
A canvas of the population in Oldham was carried out in 1799 of people aged between 15 and 60 to determine who was eligible for military service. The canvas lists 224 persons of which 51 are infirm or unfit and 43 are stated as serving with the *Oldham Loyal Association* with no distinction as to if they served with the Foot or Horse, there are also two persons listed as serving in the Yeomanry Cavalry so these could have been members of the *Oldham Horse Association.* This seems to be the only record we have of some of the rank and file of the *Oldham Foot and Horse Association* as no official returns are held in the Home Office and War Office records. A full list of these members of the Association from the 1799 canvas can be found in Appendix 1.

There seems to be no shortage of volunteers and some of the notes from this canvas make interesting reading and show the true Oldham pluck:

> *"James Gartside, very lame, but willing"*
> *"Jesse Jackson, one eye but willing"*

---

[6] HO51/105
[7] Rowbottom's Diary

The Oldham Horse and Foot Association (Oldham Loyal Volunteers) 1798-1802

The canvasser also had a sense of humour as the note written against John Bury says:

> *" very bad windy complaint, and mostly in the head"*

On June 24th 1799, the *Oldham Association* were presented with their colours, which were consecrated by the Rev Mr Winter. Miss Lees, the daughter of Major John Lees presented the colours. Miss Lees was to later marry the adjutant of the corps, William Chippendale.
Tradition says that the Oldham ladies subscribed for these colours. Major Lees was a man of great loyal public spirit and made an extraordinary speech on receiving the colours:

> *'Ladies, we receive these colours wi' gratitude. We'n defend um wi' fortitude, an' if th' French shooten th' rags away we'n bring th' pows back.'*

In celebration of the formation of the Oldham Volunteers a song was written by Mrs S Lees of Greenacres Moor, Nr Oldham, and sung to the tune of *Rule Britannia:*

See, nobly daring, hand in hand,
The volunteers of Oldham stand;
And vow united, united to defend
Their King and country to the end.
Chorus
So now dispel, now dispel at once your fears,
Success to Oldham Volunteers

They swear that wheresoe'er they go,
They'll hurl destruction on the foe;
And each blue bullet, blue bullet from their guns,
Shall drop at least one Gallic son,
Chorus

For what they've spoke they will make good,
Or seal the promise with their blood;
With heaps of slain, heaps of slain they'll strew the ground,
And largely deal grim death around.
Chorus

For, damme, if the monsieurs come,
Our volunteers will charge them home;
And with fix't bay'net, fix't bay'net or with gun,
Give them a taste of *English fun.*
Chorus

In November 1799 the decision was taken to extend the service of the *Oldham Foot Association* so that they could be called out and used in the whole of the Military district. The advantage of agreeing to extend their service is that they could now claim allowances for clothing from the government and they would also receive pay when called out or when training:

> *"I have had the honor of laying before the King, the letter, addressed to your Lordship by Major Lees, and transmitted to me in your Lordships of the 18th instant, containing an offer of extending the service of the Oldham Volunteer Association to the whole extent of the military district, under the usual regulations and conditions, and I have the honor to acquaint your Lordship, that His Majesty has been graciously pleased to approve of this extended offer of service."*[8]

From this point onwards, official documentation refer to them as the *Oldham Loyal Volunteers,* but Rowbottom still sometimes refers them to as the *Oldham Foot Association* in his diary.

From the monthly pay list and return for the period of 24 December 1799 to 24 January 1800[9] the *Oldham Loyal* had four days training, for this training they received the following daily rates of pay:

Major: 14s 1d
Captain: 9s 5d
Lieutenant: 4s 4d
Ensign: 3s 5d
Adjutant: 3s 9d
Sergeant Major: 1s 4d
Sergeant on Permanent pay: 1s 6¾d
NCOs & Privates: 1s 0d

From these first official returns we can see that three companies were formed, the first company commanded by Captain Edward Lees (the son of John Lees), the second company commanded by Captain James Lees and the third (or Majors) company by Lieutenant John Booth.
By the beginning of 1800 Captain James Lees had resigned and John Booth had been promoted to Captain in his place. Lt John Wright then assumed command of the Majors Company in place of the promoted John Booth.

[8] WO6/199
[9] WO13/4419

The Oldham Horse and Foot Association (Oldham Loyal Volunteers) 1798-1802

Each company within the *Oldham Loyal* consisted of its officers, a sergeant on permanent pay, two non-permanent sergeants, three or four corporals, two drummers and around 60 privates. A drill sergeant and drummer were also appointed to the corps who were on permanent pay, the allowances claimed for these two permanent staff did not cover their costs and their pay was subsidised from the subscription fund.

The following men were appointed on the permanent staff of the Oldham Loyal:

Adjutant: William Chippendale
Sergeant Major: James Mellor
1st Company Sergeant: John Winterbottom
2nd Company Sergeant: John Travis
3rd Company Sergeant: Robert Marlor

During March 1802 the *Oldham Loyal Volunteers* were mustered for eight days training, by this time the numbers had slightly reduced to around 50 privates per company.
The Oldham Loyal Volunteers were entitled to an issue of arms with the Ordnance Department supplying them with 195 muskets and bayonets, six sergeants' pikes and three drums. [10]

Being a member of *Oldham Loyal Volunteers* did have some benefits. As long as the volunteer remained a member and they attended the required number of days training they were exempt from the Militia ballot. Being a volunteer did not require any commitment to a minimum term of service, the volunteer was free to quit the corps at any time he liked, but if he did quit, then he would then, once again, be liable to be included in the Militia ballot.
The Militia was a limited form of conscripted service. Service in the Militia was full time with the conscripts serving for five years, all men aged between the ages of 18 and 45 years old were eligible to serve. Each county was bound by statute to raise men for the county militia according to a quota fixed by the Government. Registers were kept of all men who were eligible for service and ballots were held to determine who was to serve. Substitutes could be provided but they had to be paid by the individuals for whom they were standing substitute. The price could vary depending on how desperate the times were.
On 30 January 1797 lots were drawn for the Supplementary Militia. The ballot for the Hundred of Salford, which included Oldham, was drawn in Middleton. The following quotas were required in the Oldham area:

Oldham –	89	Chadderton –	29
Royton –	30	Crompton –	29.

[10] HO57/76

For the whole of Lancashire the requirement was for 5150 men. For those who did not want to serve, substitutes could be obtained for a price of between four and ten guineas.[11]
Militia regiments were sent on duty for months at a time in various parts of the United Kingdom and service in the Militia was very unpopular.
Initially there was just one regiment of Militia in Lancashire but 1797 brought big changes and four supplementary battalions were formed. By 1799 they were known as the *Royal Lancashire Militia* with five regiments in all.

> 1st Royal Lancashire Militia, commanded by Colonel Thomas Stanley
> 2nd Royal Lancashire Militia, commanded by Colonel Edward Lord Stanley
> 3rd Royal Lancashire Militia, commanded by Colonel Sir Henry Philip Hoghton, Bart
> 4th Royal Lancashire Militia, commanded by Colonel Le Gendre Pierce Starkie
> 5th Royal Lancashire Militia, commanded by Colonel Peter Patten

Civil Duties and Unrest

Under the terms of the Volunteer Act the local magistrates, to aid them in the case of civil unrest or tumult, could call out the *Oldham Loyal Volunteers*.
An example of how they were used by the local civil authorities is related in Edwin Butterworth's '*Historical Sketches of Oldham*'. In 1800 the country was faced with difficult times, food was scarce, prices were high and food riots were frequent. The price of food had risen by around 150% from the levels of 1799; it was reported that nettles were being sold in Oldham for 2d a pound. On 19th May:

> *"two magistrates of the district, Sir Watts Horton and the Rev W.R. Hay attended by the Oldham Horse and Foot Associations, and some light horse from Manchester, assembled here in order to prevent outrage, but fortunately no riotous movement occurred, with the exception of a few stones thrown by women and boys."*

One of the first civil duties of the Oldham Horse Association was on 10th August 1798, and that was to escort John Entwistle Esq., of Fox Holes, Rochdale, for about 2 miles out of Rochdale on his going to the assizes at Lancaster. The *Rochdale Volunteers* accompanied the *Oldham Horse Association*.[12] They were carrying out the same duties the following year on 25th March 1799 but this time they were escorting Joseph Starkey Esq., the High Sheriff, as he set out from his house in Royton, this time the escort was accompanied by a band of music.[13]

---

[11] Rowbottom's Diary
[12] Shaw Annals
[13] Rowbottom's Diary

The Oldham Horse and Foot Association (Oldham Loyal Volunteers) 1798-1802

In these difficult times there was still a high degree of loyalty towards the cause of the protection of the Country and any acts of disloyalty were not taken kindly. Instance the following taken from the Manchester Gazette, April 25, 1800:

> *'a gentleman of the Oldham Cavalry, an honest butcher, goaded by the pinching poverty of the times, lately seceded from the corps and sold his horse. For this act of disloyalty some of the wise Oldhamites, alias Gothamites, burnt him in effigy.'*

Peace Treaty of Amiens

On 28th March 1802, the Peace Treaty of Amiens was signed and the war against the French Republic temporarily came to an end. The Government in an effort to save costs, set about reducing the Volunteer forces. Effectively the Militia and the Volunteer Corps were stood down. On 22nd June 1802, an Act (42, GIII, C66) was passed to enable His Majesty to avail himself of the offers of certain Yeomanry and Volunteer Corps to continue their services. This Act enabled the King to accept the services of any corps who wished to continue; some of these corps continued to be paid, but most others volunteered to continue to serve without pay or allowances. The *Oldham Horse Association,* along with many of the Volunteer forces, did not take up this offer and disbanded around this time.
The Lord Lieutenant of Lancaster, Lord Derby, informed the Home Office on 10th July 1802 that of the four Horse Associations so far asked in Lancashire only one had signified its willingness to continue.[14]

> *"Loyal Blackburn Ass. Capt W. Fielden – decline-*
> *Oldham Cav Ass. Capt J. Twemlow – decline-*
> *Bury Cav Ass, Capt E. Gates – decline-*
> *Ashton Cav Ass. Sir W Gerard – continue –"*

In addition to the *Ashton Horse Association,* two other Lancashire Volunteer cavalry units continued service; these were the *Liverpool Light Horse* and the *Bolton Light Horse*. The *Manchester & Salford Light Horse* also declined to continue.

On 11th March 1803, with the prospect of hostilities resuming with the French, orders were issued to re-embody the Militia. On 31st March, the Lord Lieutenant's were instructed to encourage the formation of Volunteer Corps again under the terms outlined in the Volunteer Act of 1802. On May 12th 1803 war again broke out between

[14] HO51/103

Great Britain and France and those recently disbanded volunteers started to be re-formed and new ones established.

On 21st July the French had mapped out plans for the invasion of England with an ambitious plan of building two thousand vessels to bring the French army across the channel via a number of routes. This proved to be an impossible plan for the French; by the spring of 1804 little more than three-fifths of the vessels were ready. There were problems with the suitability of the vessels being built and also it would have proved too difficult for the vessels to all set sail at once and therefore the ships would have to be deployed over a number of tides. This would leave them open to attack by the Royal Navy and the French Navy was unlikely to prove strong enough to protect the invasion flotilla.

The arms and accoutrements for the *Oldham Loyal* had been held in storage by Major Lees, he must have expected that a volunteer corps would be reformed in Oldham with the war now back on with France. The Home Office requested that he return the arms in his possession for use by another corps. Major Lees wrote[15] back on 3rd September 1803 requesting that he retain the arms due to his conviction that another volunteer corps would be formed in Oldham shortly.

Major Lees listed 180 muskets and bayonets in his possession, a deficiency of 15 from the original issue. This discrepancy he explained was due to:

> *'some of them bursting when fired and by others being rendered unserviceable by various unavoidable accidents'*[16]

He also had a surplus of sergeants pikes, the *Oldham Loyal* was originally issued with six pikes and now held 12 which:

> *' where furnished at the expenses of the corps'* [17].

Major Lees expectations for a new corps were correct, by 19th September 1803 the newly reformed *Oldham Loyal Volunteers* were being:

> *'assembled for the first in order to there being trained and exercised them having being accepted by His Majesty'*[18]

---

[15] HO57/76
[16] HO57/76
[17] HO57/76
[18] Rowbottom's Diary

Oldham Loyal Volunteers 1803-1808

A committee was formed in Oldham to officiate over the re-raising of the volunteers and to manage a subscription fund for the equipping of the Oldham volunteers. The government on 6th September 1803 officially accepted the *Oldham Loyal Volunteers.* This time the Oldham volunteers consisted of infantry only, with no offers being put forward from Oldham to form a cavalry corps. The renewed threat from France had sparked even greater concern from the population, it was seen that the threat of invasion was very real. This increased threat was reflected in the increased number of volunteers throughout the country and Oldham was no exception. The Oldham volunteers increased from the original three companies to five companies. The *Oldham Loyal Volunteers* were now large enough to merit the appointment of two field officers. In the first returns the *Oldham Loyal Volunteers* consisted of two field officers, five Captains, 12 subalterns, three staff officers, 16 sergeants, 20 corporals and ten drummers. Each company had 60 privates per company giving an effective total of 300 men.
John Lees was once again the commandant of the corps but now with the rank of Lieutenant Colonel, with second in command Major Edward Lees.

Those Volunteer Corps that formed within the first few months of the start of hostilities with France, would receive training pay for two days in the week from Lady Day to Michaelmas and for one day of muster in each month when present under arms.

Sergeants: 1s.6d
Corporals: 1s.2d
Drummers & Privates: 1s.0d

And an annual clothing allowance of:

Sergeant: £3.3s.9d
Corporal: £1.11s.3d
Drummer: £2.3s.6d
Private: £1.10s.0d

An annual allowance was made to each company in lieu of all contingencies, £25 for companies of 50 private men with an additional £5 for every ten men beyond that number. Field officers and adjutants were exempted from the tax on one horse. All volunteers were exempt from paying duty on hair powder and from being balloted for service in the Militia. These terms were known as the *June Allowances* and units accepting them were allowed pay for up to 85 days training per annum. In return they agreed to serve as required in any part of the military district. These allowances did not entice as many offers to form volunteer corps as the government expected, in

Lancashire only 18 infantry and four cavalry volunteer corps formed under these June allowances. A short while later the *Levée en Masse Act* was introduced, this act gave power to the government to drill every able bodied man whether he liked it or not, but the government promised not to enforce this part of the Act if enough volunteer corps were raised. The *Levée en Masse Act* also had a clause, which stated that no further exemptions from the Militia ballot would be granted to any man whose name did not appear on the muster roll of a corps prior to 22nd June 1803.

To minimise expenditure, the Government agreed to provide those corps accepted for service after 22nd June with pay for only twenty days annual training, furthermore, they were required, in the event of an invasion or national emergency, to march to serve in any part of Great Britain, these terms were obviously a lot less favourable than those volunteer corps on the *June Allowances*. The government delayed the acceptance of a great many of the volunteer corps until the new acts had come into effect. On 31st August 1803 the Government accepted the services of all additional corps, hence the new terms became known as the *August Allowances*. In Lancashire there were 147 infantry, three cavalry and six artillery volunteer corps on the *August Allowances*.

Some people would come to the conclusion that the large rush of volunteers was not due to patriotism, but more likely that the motivation was to beat the June dead line and thus gain exemption from the Militia ballot. The *Oldham Loyal Volunteers* were not accepted until after this deadline but probably applied along with many others to beat the deadline.

The increase in volunteers undoubtedly had an effect on the strength of the Militia; at the beginning of 1804 the *Lancashire Militia* was deficient by some 360 men. A Home Office circular sent to the Lord Lieutenant of Lancashire urged for the completion of the Militia quota.

> '*In the present most important and critical conjuncture of public affairs, when an immediate and formidable attack upon our independence and existence as a nation is threatened by a powerful and implacable enemy, I think it my duty most earnestly to call again upon your Lordship to use your best endeavours, and to exercise your utmost influence to provide for the completion of the full quota of the County of Lancaster with the least possible delay*'[19]

This does not mean that their sole driving factor for forming volunteers was to beat the Militia ballot, the *Oldham Loyal Volunteers* desire to defend their King and country is amply shown in a hand written note by Lt-Col John Lees on the first returns.

> *'From the time of its Imbodiement to the end of the year 1803 the corps of Oldham Loyal Volunteers had sixty one drills. None of those volunteers who are charged 20 days have attended less than forty and the chief part of these more than fifty. Where any volunteers has attended less than forty days it has been*

[19] HO50/110

> *occasioned by the late period of his involvement except in a few cases for which no charge is made, on that account such as are charged less than 20 days.'*[20]

Sixty-one drills in its first 116 days is strong indication of the Corps' commitment and the threat that the people of Oldham felt they were under from an invasion by France.

The volunteer corps structure was such that each of the companies were not to be less than two sergeants, two corporals, one drummer and 50 privates each with one Captain, one Lieutenant, one Ensign, the flank companies had two Lieutenants. Each company was to consist of at least 80 privates, no company to have more than 100 privates. For a corps consisting of 300 private men and upward then an adjutant and Sergeant Major was allowed. For corps of 150 to 300 then only a Sergeant Major was allowed.

The five companies of the *Oldham Loyal Volunteers* drew their officers from the original pre-1803 officers plus other prominent Oldham residents:

> '*List of gentlemen nominated to serve as officers in the Loyal Oldham Volunteer Corps of infantry. Commission to be dated as 6 September 1803.*
>
> > *John Lees Esq. to be Lieutenant Colonel Commandant*
> > *James Lees Esq. to be Major*
> > *Edward Lees Esq., John Booth Esq., Thomas Barker Esq. and John Wright Esq. to be Captains.*
> > *William Chippendale, Gent to be Captain Lieutenant.*
> > *James Fletcher, James Cocks, Henry Fletcher, Henry Barlow, Gentlemen to be Lieutenants.*
> > *James Clegg, Joseph Travis, James Mellor, John Winterbottom, Thomas Wilkes Wnett, gentlemen to be Ensigns.*
> > *William Chippendale, gent to be Adjutant.*
> > *James Cocks gent to be surgeon*
> > *The Rev William Winter to be Chaplain.*
> > *Arthur Clegg gent to be QuarterMaster.*'[21]

Perhaps the demands being made by Lt-Col Lees on the amount of training being carried out by the corps were too much for some of the officers. Volunteer duties were taking up too much of their time and taking then away from their businesses, because within four months there were seven resignations, but there seemed to be no shortage of gentlemen willing to take their places:

---

[20] WO13/4419
[21] HO50/76

A list of resignations:
James Lees Esq. – Major
John Booth Esq. – 2nd Captain
Thos Barker Esq. – 4th Captain
John Wright Esq. – 5th Captain
James Fletcher – 2nd Lieutenant
James Mellor – 2nd Ensign
Thomas Wilkes Wnett - 5th Ensign
NB No appointment was originally made to the 3rd Captain nor the 6th Lieutenant.

Promotions and appointments
Major Edward Lees – late 1st Captain
To the 1st Captain Wm Chippendale - late 1st Lt
To the 2nd Captain James Cocker - late 3rd Lt
To the 3rd Captain Henry Fletcher – late 4th Lt
To the 4th Captain Henry Barlow – late 5th Lt
To the 5th Captain James Clegg – late 1st Ensign (Light Company)
To the 1st Lt Joseph Travis late 3rd Ensign
To the 2nd Lt John Winterbottom late 4th ensign
To the 3rd Lt Arthur Clegg late Quartermaster
To the 4th Lt Samuel Mayall
To the 5th Lt Joseph Jones
To the 6th Lt George Booth
To the 1st Ensign James Duncuft
To the 2nd Ensign Thos Whittaker
To be Quarter master Thos Whittaker [22]

By December 1803 the county of Lancashire had increased its volunteer strength to 176 infantry companies consisting of 13,710 men, 8 cavalry troops of 586 men and 5 artillery companies of 560 men.[23]

It is worth mentioning at this point the position held in Oldham society by the commanding officer. John Lees was the son of Daniel Lees, of Barrowshaw, a farmer. John had started his business in cotton manufacturing, with a small concern at the bottom of Church Lane around 1775. This business was further developed over the years and he built Church Lane mill in 1780. By 1795 he had acquired great wealth through his business and he was able to acquire the title of 'Lord of the Manor of Oldham' by buying Werneth Hall for £30,000, an amount that in today's terms would relate to around £1.3 Million[24]. Along with the Jones family and the Lees family of

[22] HO50/110
[23] WO70/34
[24] Based on calculations from House of Commons research paper 02/44 dated 11/7/2002

Clarksfield, John Lees secured mineral rights in the Oldham area and achieved considerable wealth from the right to work coal.

John Lees had continuous grievances over failure of the Home Office to pay allowances for his regiment. In 1804 he failed to gain an allowance for repairs to arms due to government red tape:

> *'I shall take this opportunity of repeating that I have lost the allowance for the year 1804, which was denied me upon grounds that I then thought and must state consider very unsatisfactory. Owing to the neglect of the Deputy Lieutenants to whom I applied upon the occasion my arms were not inspected within the period specified by the act. Two different days were fixed and my corps was actually drawn out twice for the purpose, but no Lieutenants attended. On application for the allowance it was refused me for want of necessary certificate and I suffered the loss of £100-0-0 thro the omission of Gentlemen over whom I had no control and whose attendance I had no authority to compel. The expenses of that year were considerably more than the allowance,...'*[25].

In 1808, when the *Oldham Loyal Volunteers* were being disbanded and the Local Militia were being formed, the volunteers had already completed their 26 days exercise for the year yet the Home Office would only allow three quarters of the amount claimed as the Volunteers were being disbanded before the end of a complete year. In all cases where the allowance was not enough to pay the men or for repairs to equipment then John Lees would have paid this from the subscription fund or from his own money if the subscription fund were empty.

James Clegg
(Captain of the Light Company)

All of the officers in the volunteers were leading citizens from the Oldham area with business interests in coal, cotton and hatting. James Clegg of Bent Hall was one of the leading local hatting manufacturers and Joseph Jones with his brother William were heavily involved in the coal mines around Oldham.

---

[25] HO50/224

A full list of the officers and their service in the *Oldham Loyal Volunteers* can be found in *Appendix 2.*

Arms, Accoutrements, Colours and Uniform

SERGEANT'S PIKE, 1791–1830

On 6th May 1804, the *Oldham Loyal Volunteers* were presented with their colours. Again Lt-Col Lee's daughter, made the presentation, who by this time was Mrs Chippendale, and the sermon preached to the corps was conducted by Rev William Winter. Rev Winter was also the minister at St Peter's church.
The uniform of the *Oldham Loyal Volunteers* was a red jacket with blue facings with silver lace for the officers and was worn with white breeches.[26] The headdress was likely to have been a stovepipe shako for the rank and file with the officers wearing bicorn hats.

Arming the volunteers was a major headache for the government. Within a few months the volunteers in the country had increased from virtually none to 380,000 men. Many corps complained of receiving no arms. Oldham were luckier than most; despite the government requesting the return of the arms, originally issued in 1799, in order that they could be issued to other corps, John Lees had managed to hold on to them, until the new *Oldham Loyal Volunteer* corps were formed in Sept 1803, and they were thus retained for this new corps. In August the War Office directed Lord Derby to encourage the formation of volunteer corps:

> *'..to be armed with pikes and if by "any other weapon than those generally made use of" your Lordship means Fowling pieces and private arms not precisely military, I think they might be certainly be mixed with good effect with pikes.'*[27]

On 26th Sept 1803 Lord Derby was informed:

> *'.. Upon the subject of Arms, I have the honour to acquaint your Lordship, that the Board of Ordnance has been directed to issue on your Lordship's application, a supply of arms equal to one half of the quota of volunteers for the county of Lancaster, exclusive of those in possession of the Oldham and Bolton volunteers. I must at the same time acquaint your Lordship, that no further supply of arms, with the exception of pikes, can be issued at present, and that your Lordship is requested to make a proportionate distribution of*

[26] Wilson's Volunteer Chart of 1806
[27] WO6/202

> *those directed to be issued, among the several volunteer corps in Lancashire.'*[28]

The *Oldham Loyal Volunteers*, along with most volunteer corps were armed with the *Brown Bess* musket.

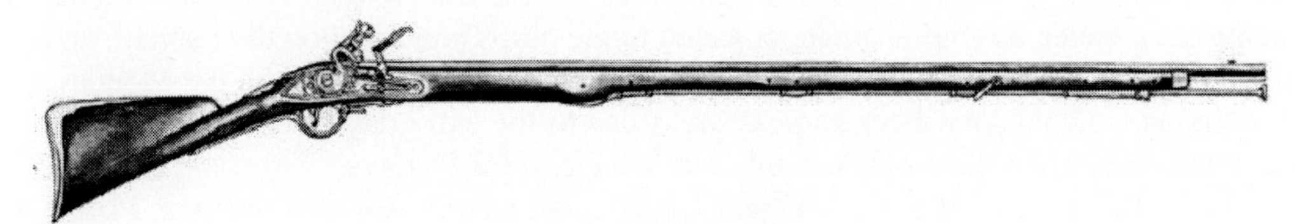

Brown Bess Musket

Brown Bess was the nickname given to the British Army's Land Pattern Musket and its derivatives. The British Army and its Empire armies used these muskets, all 0.75 calibre flintlocks, for more than 100 years, from 1722 until 1838. Some of these various versions include the Long Land Pattern, Short Land Pattern, India Pattern, New Land Pattern Musket and Sea Service Musket.

In addition to the 180 muskets originally issued to the pre-1803 Oldham volunteers, which were retained for the new *Oldham Loyal Volunteers*, an additional 120 muskets and 120 sets of accoutrements were purchased at the expense of the corps out of the subscription fund. In 1805 the subscription fund also paid for the volunteers to be furnished with great coats and knapsacks, as the government provided no allowance for these items. Unfortunately this expenditure exhausted the subscription fund and left them with no money for contingencies. Colonel John Lees requested through the Northern area inspecting field officer, Lieutenant Colonel Baillie, a request for assistance with the funds, in particular for an allowance for the 120 muskets that had been privately purchased. He noted that all volunteer corps in the neighbourhood had been furnished with all their arms from government, except for Oldham, and under regulations Oldham should have an allowance for these arms.[29]

In addition to the issue of arms, the government also issued haversacks, canteens and billhooks[30]. The haversack was a white linen bag carried over the shoulder and used for carrying bread and other food.

Training and Discipline

Within a week of being accepted the newly formed volunteers had mustered and were practising drill. This was carried out in earnest to bring the volunteers up to an acceptable standard. In the first four months of its existence the volunteers were mustered for training and drill an average of four times per week.

---

[28] HO51/75
[29] HO50/137
[30] HO51/79

The corps first training camp was held at Preston for 14 days. On their march out of Oldham on 11 June 1804 the 20 officers and 345 NCOs and Privates were accompanied by a large concourse of people and on their return, according to Rowbottom, they were greeted in Oldham by church bells and universal acclamations of joy. This 14 day training ended up being 15 days owing to the fact that the return marching day fell on a Sunday and the Field officer for the Northern district, Colonel Thompinson, being a religious man, objected to the corps marching on the Sabbath and therefore the volunteers had to halt at Bolton and continue their march on the Monday. This caused Colonel John Lees some distress due to the extra day of costs, which was due to the men, when the corps had only put in a claim for 14 days.[31]

The following year in 1805, the Oldham Loyal again went to Preston for their 14 day annual training. Besides Preston the corps is also known to have trained at Bolton.

During training camp the volunteers would practice drill and tactics nearly every day. One of the five companies was a light company; once this company was proficient in line company drill then it would carry out extra training based on light company tactics, which included skirmishing in front of the main infantry line and protecting the flanks.

In addition to the annual training the corps also mustered for parade once per month on a Saturday.

As a volunteer could resign from the corps at short notice it was difficult to enforce any serious discipline on the men. Take the instance of the drummer boys: Lieutenant-Colonel John Lees had a problem with the disobedient conduct of his drummers. From the beginning of the formation of the *Oldham Loyal Volunteers* a Drum Major had been permanently employed, being paid from the subscription fund, to train the drummers:

> *'boys have been trained, who from some slight cause of offence, such as reproof from the adjutant or Drum-Major, have in succession left the Corps after receiving several months instruction, and on Sunday morning last, in consequence of a frivolous dispute with the drum major, whose conduct on the occasion was by no means blameable, one boy only mustered for duty.'*[32]

Lees struggled to enforce discipline on the boys and suggested to the Home Office that one drummer per company be placed upon permanent pay, in the same manner as Sergeants, so that it might encourage them to stay. This idea does not appear to have been adopted.

---

[31] HO50/137

[32] HO50/137

Civil Disturbance

As with the previous Oldham volunteer corps the *Oldham Loyal* could be called out to aid the civil authorities. 1808 was once more a time of distress and rising food prices; weavers were again suffering and campaigning for a minimum wage. On 19th May, a bill to regulate wages was withdrawn and the starving weavers showed their discontent throughout Lancashire. On 25th May, a reported 10,000 people attended a meeting in Manchester. Troops were called to disperse the meeting, resulting in one man killed and several wounded. A meeting was held in Royton, near Oldham, by the weavers and other inhabitants of Royton and a statement for the general public was printed on the 30 May 1808 stating that the current poor state of their circumstances was owing to the war with France but called for the current rioting to cease as it could only lead to further distress and suffering. Parts of the statement read:

> *'While we lament the general distress, we beg leave to suggest that it is our opinion your proceedings are not likely to obtain you relief; for that distress can only be removed, by removing the cause; which cause we have no hesitation in pronouncing is the WAR:- to prove which we need only to refer to our dependence upon commerce, and how it is obstructed by the war; and it is our humble opinion that it is impossible for either the legislature or commercial characters to remedy the evil by any other means than that of the restoration of peace.'*
> *'Yet not withstanding, we are ready at all times to forward, in any constitutional manner, that which is likely to be productive of the good we all aim at. But will never lend our aid to any illegal measure; therefore by your permission, we will advise you to desist from your present proceedings – return to your families and respective employment's, as the neglect to do so, will, we fear, only tend to your misfortune and distress.'*[33]

The notice did not have the desired effect for on that very same day rioters in Rochdale broke into the private houses of weavers, carried off their shuttles and other implements of weaving[34], in the evening of the same day the Police Office was attacked with large stones thrown at the windows narrowly missing the magistrates who were in sitting there. After the attack on the Police Office the rioters moved on to the prison, which was broken open and then burnt to the ground. There were also reports of the rioters extracting money from individuals by threat of burning down their houses or factories. The civil authorities could do nothing and the situation was only brought under control by the appearance of half a troop of cavalry from Manchester and the Halifax volunteers.

---

[33] HO42/95
[34] HO42/95

There was also unrest in Oldham but not quite as severe as that in Rochdale. A few houses owned by persons obnoxious to the populace had their windows broken[35]. The Oldham civil authorities called out the *Oldham Loyal Volunteers* to quell the unrest. They were called to muster by the beating of drums. Around 80 mustered at the designated place, the Royal Oak on Maygate Lane. They were marching along Rochdale road when a large crowd confronted them and the men of the *Oldham Loyal Volunteers* were pelted with mud and stones.
On 1st June a large mob assembled on Oldham Edge and then proceeded into Oldham town where they took out some of their anger by breaking the windows of William Lees of Church Lane, most likely a relative of Lt-Col John Lees. It took a large military force to eventually calm the situation in Oldham and surrounding neighbourhoods. The *Oldham Loyal Volunteers* were called out for duty for three days, being stood down on 2nd June. The majority of the *Oldham Loyal Volunteers*, 223 rank and file, were on duty for the 3 days, each private being paid a shilling per day during the call out period.
The local authorities made requests to the government for adequate protection in the towns and by July a troop of the *6th Dragoon Guards* and several companies of the *Hereford Militia* were stationed in the area.

In readiness for invasion, every corps within its district would identify wagons and horses that they could commandeer to transport baggage and stores in an emergency. Commanding officers were informed of the routes of march and concentration points to which they would march to in case of invasion. Despite all these preparations the Volunteer Corps were not to be put to the test, as the French could not gain control of the English Channel and Napoleon's invasion plans were abandoned.

After the Royal Navy and Lord Nelson had defeated the French at the *Battle of Trafalgar* on 21st October 1805, the main threat of invasion from France had subsided owing to Britain's complete control of the seas, but the government was still keen to have an efficient and effective force purely for local defence. By 1806 it was estimated that the volunteers were costing the government around £5M per year and the level of efficiency and effectiveness of these volunteers, or otherwise, was solely down to the competence of the officers of the individual corps. In December 1807 Viscount Castlereagh proposed that the Regular Militia would provide 80,000 men and 200,000 men would be raised by the establishment of the Local Militia. On 30th June 1808, in order to bring the volunteers under more government control, the *Local Militia Act* was introduced.[36]
Enlistment into the Local Militia was initially to be voluntary and the intention was that all volunteer corps would transfer their service. If there were insufficient volunteers then the ballot could be used to bring any deficient regiments up to strength. The ballot would be applied to men aged between 18 and 30. Unlike the normal militia,

[35] Butterworth's History of Oldham
[36] 43 GIII C111

were substitutes could be used, there would be no substitutes allowed if a person were balloted for the Local Militia.
All Volunteer corps were invited to transfer their service as a body into the new force in return for a bounty of two guineas per man. By 1809 the bounty was abolished and in June any volunteer corps that had not transferred their service were given further encouragement by being told that they could expect no further clothing allowances from the government. One year after the act there were 250 Local Militia Regiments formed consisting of over 195,000 men, approximately 125,000 of these men had transferred from the volunteer corps.

Oldham Local Militia 1808-1816

On 5th July 1808, Lieutenant Colonel John Lees received a letter from the Home Office requesting to be informed whether it was the intention of the *Oldham Loyal Volunteers* to transfer its services into the Local Militia under the provisions of the new *Local Militia Act*. On 9th July the *Oldham Loyal Volunteers* were mustered and John Lees explained to the men the terms of the proposed transfer. At the end of the muster parade each man was requested to signify his acceptance or not of the transfer. Nearly the whole strength of the corps signified their acceptance excepting two officers and 21 privates. The two officers Captain James Clegg and Lieutenant John Wright were not at the muster; Clegg was out of the county on business and Wright in America on urgent business. On their return, only James Clegg declined to transfer into the Local Militia. Lees explained the decision of the 21 privates:

> *'The 21 privates are men who could not, from the nature of their occupation render themselves liable to march from Home for the time required by the act without putting themselves and families to much inconvenience and I have not the smallest doubt but they will be immediately replaced by men who are willing to transfer their services with the rest of their corps.'*[37]

The *Oldham Loyal Volunteers* were not large enough to form a Local Militia Regiment on their own. The *Local Militia Act* required that a regiment should be no less than 700, and no more than 1200 privates, as far as circumstances permitted, and dividing the county into suitable divisions for the maintenance of each regiment according to the provisions of the 5th clause of the *Local Militia Act.*

If there were not enough volunteers to make up the minimum of 700 then there was provision in the act that the strength could be augmented to the required strength by use of a new levy. It was the responsibility of the parish to ensure that the strength was maintained, and if no volunteers were forthcoming then the parish had to call a ballot to augment the numbers. If vacancies were not filled up by 14th February in each year then a fine of £15 shall be imposed for every man deficient. It was therefore for the parishes, in which such deficiencies may arise, to consider whether they would prefer balloting the men, rather than incurring the fine. A ballot could be called at any time, to fill vacancies arising in the Local Militia due to death, discharge, desertion or enlisting in the regular army, provision for this ballot was stated in the acts of 48, GIII, CIII, S46 and 49, GIII, C40, S7 without any warrant or order from his Majesty.[38]

The government had set a quota for Lancashire in that it had to provide 14,634 private men.[39]

---

[37] HO50/196

[38] HO51/45

[39] HO51/42

A suggestion was made by Lt-Col Lees that his corps came together with the *Newton and Failsworth Volunteers*, who were under the command of Lt-Col Heymer. His argument being that once combined with this corps,

> *'..both corps consist of the same number of companies and the same number of men in each company, and when united will form a compact battalion of 10 companies, constantly organised for Field Duty without disturbing the standing order of either corps. The two corps are raised in adjoining parishes, both officers and men are upon terms of intimacy and a constant exchange of intercourse and of similar habits. Circumstances which I conceive are of some importance, as they are likely to conduce to a cordial co-operation.'*[40]

Unfortunately one of the problems with this suggestion was that the combined numbers of these two corps only came to 600 and this was not enough to meet the minimum requirement of 700. This should not have been a major problem as it would not have been too difficult to raise an additional 100 men, but this union did not take place so other factors must have precluded the merger. It should be noted that the *Newton & Failsworth Volunteers* formed their own Local Militia titled *Newton and Failsworth Regiment of Local Militia*, so it has to be assumed that the numbers were made up with volunteers from the local areas.

Instead of merging with the immediate parish to the south of Oldham it was the parishes to the north that made up the numbers to battalion strength. Volunteers were raised in the Rochdale and Todmordon areas.

The process of implementing the new *Local Militia Act* and transferring volunteers into Local Militia regiments took some organising in Lancashire. In most cases, like Oldham, the volunteers were not large enough to form their own regiment and therefore it was a case of agreeing to which volunteers would join together. If they were not prepared to join together then they would have to discontinue. In the case of the *Pendleton and Swinton Volunteers* only some of the volunteers transferred their service the rest wishing to remain as volunteers, but this was denied. A meeting of the Deputy Lieutenants of Lancashire took place at the Bull Inn, Preston[41] on 18th January 1809 to discuss and resolve the act of forming the Local Militia Regiments for Lancashire with the required number of men. The quota for Lancashire was determined to be 14,634 men to serve in the Local Militia. With the transfer of the volunteers into the Local Militia it was determined that there was a deficit of 6,887 men. It was resolved that this deficit in men should be tried to be made up by volunteers initially and if the numbers had not been made up by 7th February, then a ballot would take place on that day to make up the numbers. Each of the subdivisions of the county was allocated a quota. The sub-division of Middleton was required to find 1,799 men to serve in the Local Militia, these men were to be found from 4,454 men in the Middleton sub-division who were liable to serve, equating to around 40% of eligible

---

[40] HO50/196

[41] HO50/224

men who would have to serve. This figure was similar over the other sub-divisions. For the whole of Lancashire there were 36,222 eligible men to fill the 14,634 places equating to around 40%.

The sub-division of Middleton was spread over three regiments with a small allocation of 97 men allocated to the *Newton and Failsworth Local Militia* and the remainder split evenly between the *1st and 2nd Middleton Regiments.* By February 1809 the number of Local Militia Regiments was fixed and the officers appointed.

The process of change from Volunteers to the Local Militia was an opportunity to get rid of officers who were not deemed suitable; a letter from Hakebury at the Home Office to Lord Derby plainly highlighted this;

> *'With respect to those corps which are commanded by persons whom your Lordship sees not deemed fit to entrust with the command of a regiment of Local Militia, as well as those which are commanded by persons of inferior stock they must submit to be incorporated with other corps and placed under another commandant.'*[42]

The following Local Militia regiments were formed in Lancashire along with its initially proposed commander and headquarters:

Name of Regiment	Commander	Headquarters
Amourdness	Lt-Col Nicholas Grimshaw	Preston
Bolton	Lt-Col Ralph Fletcher	Bolton
Blackburn Higher Division	Lt-Col John Hargreaves	Burnley
Blackburn Lower Division	Lt-Col Henry Hulton	Blackburn
1st Manchester	Lt-Col John Silvester	Manchester
Trafford House & Hulme	Lt-Col James Cooke	Salford
Newton & Failsworth	Lt-Col Robert Keymer	Culcheth-Newton
1st Middleton	Lt-Col John Lord	Ashton under Lyne
2nd Middleton	Lt-Col John Lees	Rochdale
Lonsdale	Lt-Col Marston	Lancaster
Liverpool	Lt-Col William Earle	Liverpool
Leyland & Ormskirk	Lt-Col Sir Thos D Hesketh	Ormskirk
Prescot	Lt-Col James Fraser	Prescot
Warrington	Lt-Col John I Blackburne	Warrington
Wigan	Lt-Col Thomas S Standish	Wigan

On 12th February 1809, Lord Derby transmitted the list of officers for the newly formed *2nd Middleton Regiment of Lancashire Local Militia*, the creation of this new force meant instant promotion for most of the Oldham Volunteer officers.

[42] HO51/42

Oldham Local Militia 1808 - 1816

Lt-Col Commandant John Lees Late Oldham Volunteers
Lt-Col Edward Lees (Late Oldham Volunteers)
Major Henry Barlow (Late Oldham Volunteers)

Captains:
Joseph Travis, late Captain Oldham Volunteers
John Winterbottom, late Captain Oldham Volunteers
Arthur Clegg, late Captain Oldham Volunteers
John Beswick
Samuel Mayall (late Lieutenant Oldham Volunteers)
Joseph Jones (late Lieutenant Oldham Volunteers)
James Duncuft (late Lieutenant Oldham Volunteers)
John Lees (late Lieutenant Oldham Volunteers)
John Crossley
John Crompton

Lieutenants:
John Wright, late Lt Oldham Volunteers
Thos Hollinworth, late Lt Oldham Volunteers
Joshua Robinson
Abraham Billott
John Taylor
John Travis
Joshua Winterbottom
5 vacant

Ensigns: 8 vacant

Adjutant with brevet of Captain, Wm Chippendale late Volunteers
Surgeon Abram Billott
Quarter Master Thomas Whittaker

Over the next three months the following additional officers were commissioned:
Thomas Bale – Gentleman to be Lieutenant
Abraham Milne - Gentleman to be Lieutenant
John Travis - Gentleman to be Ensign
Edward Clegg - Gentleman to be Ensign
Robert Hardman – Gentleman to be Lieutenant
John Eastwood – Gentleman to be Lieutenant
Jack Horsfell – Gentleman to be Ensign
William Sutcliffe Esq. to be Captain due to death of Captain Mayall[43]

[43] HO50/224

Initially the Oldham regiment was known as the *2nd Regiment of Middleton Division Lancashire Local Militia,* the first Regiment of Middleton covered Ashton and surrounding parishes. According to an assessment that was carried out in April 1805 under the act of 44 GIII C5 the following townships are listed in the Middleton division:
Ashton under Lyne, Butterworth, Castleton, Wardleworth, Wuerdle & Wardle, Blatchinworth & Calderbrook, Thornham, Birtle cum Bamford, Ainsworth, Oldham, Royton and Spotland.[44]
In the initial correspondence, in early 1809, from the Home Office it shows the Headquarters for the Second Middleton as being in Rochdale. On 13th April 1809 Lord Liverpool at the Home Office informed Lord Derby that

> '.. *requesting that the 2nd Middleton Regt of Lancashire Local Militia should in future have the title of the Oldham Regt and I have the satisfaction of acquainting your Lordship that His Majesty was graciously pleased to consent thereto.*'[45]

It is highly likely that Lieutenant Colonel John Lees instigated this change, after all, he was the commanding officer and the majority of the trained men had come from the *Oldham Loyal Volunteers*, he also had the headquarters for the regiment moved to Oldham.
The *Oldham Local Militia Regiment* was composed of ten companies, a Grenadier company under the command of Captain Arthur Clegg, a light company under the command of Captain John Winterbottom and a further eight line companies. Both the Grenadier and light company had two Lieutenants each, whilst the other companies had one Lieutenant each.
The Grenadier Company would have consisted of the taller and more robust men and their role would be to lead assaults in the field of battle. The light company would consist of the quicker and more intelligent men. The role of the light company was to work in open order and be able to think for themselves. They were to operate in pairs ahead of the main infantry, which were bunched in close formations, these men had to think for themselves and not rely on being told when to fire, when to march, when to stop.
Initially the regiment consisted of 35 sergeants and 35 corporals; half of each rank was on permanent pay. 32 drummers and 815 privates made up the strength of the regiment. The number of men on permanent pay was drastically reduced from 25th December 1809, so that no corporals were to be on permanent pay and only one sergeant per company, including the Sergeant Major would receive permanent pay. In addition one drummer per two companies would be employed on permanent pay, inclusive of the

[44] HO50/137
[45] HO51/43

drum major. As the regiment was over 800 strong then it was entitled to two Majors and in June 1810 Captain John Beswicke was promoted to the position of 2nd Major. John Taylor Esq. was initially appointed as Lieutenant Surgeon for the regiment, but the authorities suspended his commission, as he had not passed his medical exams. However in November 1810 he passed his exams at the College of Surgeons and his commission was re-instated.[46]
With around 320 men coming from the *Oldham Loyal Volunteers*, these men would have formed the foundation of the *Oldham Local Militia* with most of the Non-commissioned officers coming from these men. Promotion of a corporal to sergeant was not done on seniority; promotion was to be given to those

> *'such as have manifested a strict and active attention to their duty will always be preferred.'*[47]

The permanent non-commissioned officers were normally men with regular military experience, for example Sergeant Thomas Handforth; a native of Oldham, at the age of 16 either joined or was balloted into the *1st Royal Lancashire Militia* in 1783 with whom he served as a private until 1787. He joined the regular army in 1793 and served with the *20th Regiment of Foot* for nine years, three of these as a corporal. The *20th Regiment of Foot* served in Egypt and fought against Napoleon in 1801, so it is highly likely that Thomas saw action on this campaign. When the *Oldham Loyal Volunteers* formed in 1803 he joined them as a Sergeant and continued as a Sergeant in the *Oldham Local Militia* until their discontinuance. In total he served for 33 years, retiring from military duties at the age of 49.
By 1812 when the government was asking for the Local Militia to extend their service by a further four years, some of these original volunteers were becoming discontent and made suggestions to Lieutenant Colonel Lees that for the next four-year period the regiment:

> *'..ought to consist of entirely new men with a view that the whole of the population might be instructed in military duties in the speediest way possible. This it was contended was one of the original objects of the existing act..',*[48]

But Lees did not agree with the arguments of his men

> *'..I am of the opinion that the Local Militia should extend their service without restrictions whatever. This would encourage those of bad behaviour and not suited to military discipline to leave the regiment and leave only the best men. This would give a core foundation to the regiment and enable the training of*

46 HO50/244
47 Standing Orders of Oldham LM
48 HO50/285

> *the new recruits. It is surely better to have such companies with this core of experience than to have companies of entirely new recruits...*'[49]

The *Oldham Local Militia* drew its men from quite an extensive area including Oldham, Chadderton, Crompton, Royton, Thornham, Castleton, Spotland, Wardleworth and Todmordon. There were also men in the regiment who lived at Ainsworth and Cockey Moor (between Bolton and Bury)
The men for the companies being formed at Rochdale, Wardleworth and Todmordon would have comprised of mainly new recruits, as Rochdale had not had its own Volunteers since the Peace Treaty of Amiens in 1802. Prior to that date Rochdale had its own volunteers, which was formed in 1794 under the command of Lieutenant Colonel John Entwistle. Unfortunately an incident in 1795 put the Rochdale volunteers into great disrespect with the public of Rochdale. Some of the Rochdale volunteers, when assisting to calm a riot in Rochdale, fired their muskets over the heads of the crowd and unfortunately killed two old men who were innocently watching the riot some distance away. This event probably contributed to no further Rochdale volunteers being formed in May 1803 when war again broke out with France.

Arms, Accoutrements and Uniform

The arms and accoutrements of the *Oldham Loyal Volunteers* were transferred across into the *Oldham Local Militia*, any of the arms that were found, upon inspection, to be unfit for service were exchanged by the government.
The uniform for the Local Militia now had to conform to government regulations:

> *'Sealed patterns of the several articles of clothing are lodged in the charge of Mr Trotter, the government storekeeper general, Duke street, Westminster, who will deliver, or forward the upon your requisition, for the guidance of such clothier as you may think fit to employ; these patterns are not intended to govern you in regard to the colour of the facings, figure of the Lace or buttons; upon these points you are to conform precisely to the uniform of the Militia of your county*'[50]

If the volunteers had previously worn white leather accoutrements then these could be re-used providing they passed inspection, if they were black then they had to be changed to white. The new uniforms were quickly ordered and the regiment was clothed by June, the clothing was inspected on 11th June 1809 and was found to conform to the patterns.[51]

---

[49] HO50/285
[50] WO70/34
[51] WO13/3538

In August 1809 Lt-Col Lees paid for the following accoutrements to Hebden & Co:

Qty	*Item*	*Cost*
855	Pouches	6s.10d
555	Pouch Belts	4s.6d
555	Bayonet Belts	4s.8d
855	Gun slings	7s.10d
555	Belt Plates	8d
26	Sergeants Sword Belts	6s.6d
41	Sergeants Sword knots	1s.6d
26	Sergeants Belt Plates	4s.6d
850	Brushes & Prickers	6d
18	Drum Sword belts	5s.6d
18	Drum Belt Plates	8d
11	Drum cases	5s.6d
17	Drum Carriages	6s

It would appear that the privates and drummers had a simple belt plate as it only cost 8d, and was an engraved brass plate, yet the Sergeants had a plate that was far more expensive and was probably cast with the regimental name on it, like those of the officers.
The full dress uniform of the *Oldham Local Militia* regiment was red jackets with blue facings, white trousers, black gaiters, black shoes, white leatherwork and on their head a stove pipe shako. Besides the red regimental jacket the men were also issued with white jackets (undress), which were used when training and drilling. These white jackets were also sometimes worn when marching out to Bolton for their training weeks.

In July 1813 there is a record of the regiment changing from white to grey trousers.[52]
A surviving example of an officer's uniform exists in the archive of the National Army Museum and aided by this and further uniform details found in an original copy of the *Oldham Local Militia* Standing orders has enabled an accurate illustration of an *Oldham Local Militia* officer to be made.
As with the *Oldham Loyal Volunteers* the *Oldham Local Militia* were armed with the Brown Bess musket. Sergeants and drummers were issued with swords and the sergeants were also issued with halberds. Drums were also issued from government stores.

[52] WO13/3538

Officers Belt Plate

Ordinary ranks Belt Plate
(by kind permission of Richard Boniface)

As the cost of arming and clothing the *Oldham Local Militia* was borne by the government; there was now no need for local subscriptions to be raised. If we take the stated insurance values of the equipment and the actual cost of the uniforms, then to clothe and equip approximately 900 men would have been around £3,800. This would equate to a year 2000 equivalent cost of £165,680.[53]

Values of some of the equipment were:

Musquets per stand £2 2s 0d
Carbines per stand £2 0s 0d
Serjeants Spears each 10s 0d
Serjeants Swords each 9s 0d
Drummers Swords each 7s 6d
Drums, with sticks each £1 6s 0d
Ticken cases each 6s 9d
Colours, pair £20
Ammunition 100 rounds of ball 5s 3d
Ammunition 100 rounds of blanks 3s 9d
Accoutrements for rank and file allowed by ordnance per 10s 6d, allowed by war office 8s, total 18s 6d.[54]
Uniform costs to clothe the regiment was £1922 9s 10d.[55]

---

[53] Based on calculations from House of Commons research paper 02/44 dated 11/7/2002
[54] WO70/34

Regimental Button Oldham Local Militia

The officer's coatee had 38 buttons of gilt metal 7/8" diameter and 6 of gilt metal 5/8" diameter regimental buttons of the style shown above.

---

[55] WO13/3538

Officer of the Oldham Local Militia c1812

Oldham Local Militia Colours

Each Local Militia Regiment was given the option that either the government could supply the colours of the regiment or an allowance of £20 was granted to allow purchase of their own colours, Oldham went for the former option. Unfortunately the colours for the regiment do not appear to have survived but there is a record of what they looked like from the flag maker's sketchbook held in the National Army Museum. This sketchbook and inspection of the surviving colours for the *Newton Heath and Failsworth Local Militia* enabled an accurate depiction of the *Oldham Local Militia* colours to be made.

Training

According to the *Local Militia Act*, training was to be limited to 28 days per year and the period of the year that training was to take place could be chosen by the regiment so that it was the most convenient with the course of the type of industry or cultivation of the area. 28 days was a long time for men to be away from their place of work and it would undoubtedly have been unpopular with their employers, therefore the training was split into two separate training camps.
In May 1809 the *Oldham Local Militia's* first training was approved for 14 days, starting 29th June, then 14 days starting 2nd October, both these training camps to take place in Manchester, but the first one was rescheduled to 12th June and the place changed to Bolton-Le-Moors.
Training of the men consisted of learning the same exercises and drill as the regular army, officers had to acquaint themselves with these exercises. The first paragraph in the *Oldham Local Militia Standing Orders* states that :

> *'Upon being appointed to the Regiment, all officers are to provide themselves with the Standing Orders of the Regiment, and the last Regulations for the Exercise of his Majesty's Forces, and to make the Adjutant acquainted with their Address.'*

Every officer who joined the regiment had to attend instruction with the Sergeant Major every morning until he had learnt manual and platoon exercise, the sword salute and all necessary parts of his duties.
The first training did throw up an issue about assembling the men prior to the official start day. As the *Oldham Local Militia* was spread over such a wide area it was necessary for those companies and men in the Rochdale and Todmordon area to be assembled and marched to Oldham a day earlier than the other companies and men. To accompany them a drummer and two fifers were sent to Todmordon and also a drummer and a fifer to Spotland to march with these detached companies. Thus a claim for extra pay was made for these men that was disputed by the Home Office. The Home Office had already paid the claimed money based on Lt-Col Lee's submission, which included the extra marching day, but then they tried to reclaim the money. As the money had been paid out to the men and the company officers refused to pay back the money themselves, the Home Office eventually dropped the claim.[56]
Once mustered the men were issued with their uniforms, accoutrements and muskets, all these items had to be returned to stores at the end of the training period, the only item that the soldier kept was the shoes as it was deemed that these items were not suitable for storage and would be best kept in the care of the soldier, who had to bring them back in a serviceable condition at the next training.

---

[56] HO50/224

The march out of Oldham Town must have been quite a spectacle for the locals; the marching column consisted of nearly 800 men, officers on horses and the baggage being carried by 17 mules.
During the training at Manchester in October 1809 the *Oldham Local Militia* carried out parades in Piccadilly, St Anne's Square and Lever Street, whilst field exercise was taken on Kersal Moor.
Whilst assembled for training the officers and men were entitled to pay and allowances, the following daily rates of pay were claimed:[57]

Lieut Colonel: 13s.11d
Major: 14s.1d
Captain: 9s.5d
Lieutenant: 6s.6d
Ensign: 5s.3d
Adjutant: 8s.6d
Surgeon: 11s.4d
Quarter Master: 6s.6d
Sgt Major: 2s.¾d
Sergeant: 1s.6¾d
Corporal: 1s.2¼d
Drum Major 1s.6¾d
Drummer or Fifer: 1s.1¾d
Private: 1s

The Chaplain claimed an allowance of 10s for each Sunday that he provides a service.
The NCOs and privates were also allowed an allowance of one penny per day for beer money, one halfpenny per day when in stationary quarters and five pence per day for food whilst on the march. The allowance was such a small amount when in stationary quarters because it was given to the inhabitants of the house that the men were billeted in. Generally the men would be lodged in public houses and the landlord would receive 9d per week per man to cover the expense of providing lodging and food.

In 1810 the training was again at Bolton but this time for 20 days, the training period had been reduced for all Local Militia regiments by the government to try and reduce the costs. They marched out on 1st May, with the recruits mustering the week before on 23rd April to receive extra training.
The local inhabitants, especially the innkeepers, were given a warning once the Regiment arrived at their destination:

> *'a drum, with a serjeant, is to be sent round the town, to acquaint the inhabitants, that they are not to trust the Non-commissioned Officers,*

[57] WO73/34

> *Drummers or Privates; this being done, Officers commanding companies are not liable to any debts that may be contracted.'*[58]

Whilst at Bolton the regiment was billeted in the local inns. Whilst quartered in the inn the innkeeper was required to provide each man with one hot meal per day, consisting of 1 ¼ pounds meat, 1 pound bread, 1 pound potatoes or an equivalent of other vegetables and also two pints of small beer. During this training period there were reports of the men being drunk. In the daily order for 20th May 1810 the following appears:

> *'Col Lees cautions the men against appearing drunk upon parade, at evenings muster, many shameful instances of drunkenness that occurred on Sunday last, was extremely disgraceful to the regiment, and if any men appears affected by liqueur tomorrow, he will be punished with the utmost severity.'*[59]

Despite this when the regiment was inspected by the inspecting field officer, Col Sleigh, he stated how satisfied he was with the regiment and '*respecting the discipline of the regiment he was pleased to say that he should think it his duty to report it fit for any service'*. It would appear that the acts of drunkenness did not reach the ears of Col Sleigh.
In 1811 the training period had been reduced again, this time to 14 days. The 1811 training period started on 15th August. Lt-Col Lees explains the choice of date and venue in a letter to the Home Office:

> *'..the month best adapted to this purpose will be August and the precise period of that month, the 7th for the weeks previous training of the recruits, and the 14th for the rest of the Regiment. The town of Oldham is the Head Quarters of the Regiment, but not being sufficiently large enough to contain so numerous a body of men as the whole consolidated, it will be necessary to march out and Bolton is the town I have fixed upon for quarters. With a wish to occupy as little of your time as possible, I nevertheless think it necessary to trouble you with a few remarks upon the proceeding arrangement. My reason for making choice of the 7th August as the commencement of the service, is to avoid interfering with the conveniences of agriculture, which I conceive will thus be effectually accomplished, as the hay harvest will be over before that period, and the duty will terminate before the commencement of the corn harvest. With respect to Bolton, I have already occupied that town in 1809 and 1810 and have found it a quarter exceedingly well adapted to the accommodation of my Regiment. The number of public houses is well calculated for the entertainment of the men and the distance by being sufficient to detach them from their homes is very favourable to discipline, there is also another circumstance calculated*

[58] Standing Orders of Oldham LM
[59] Regimental Daily orders of Oldham LM

to insure your approval of it, that it is but one days march from head Quarters..'[60]

The recruits training for the week prior to the main training was under the control of the Adjutant, Captain Chippendale. It was his job along with the drill sergeants to get the new recruits up to a good enough standard for them to be able to train with the rest of the regiment. A typical day for these new recruits in the first week would be; awakened by the beating of the drum at 4.30 am to be ready for their first session of drill by 5 am. The first parade was at 8 am at Cowcrofts with another one in the afternoon at 4 p.m. In between these parades would be further drill practice. At the end of the day the recruits would then be confined to their quarters, which would have been the local inns in Oldham around the Regent Street area.
To ensure that they did not wander the streets:

'A picquet consisting of eight privates two non-commissioned officers will parade in Regent Street at ½ past 9 o'clock and the men will be cautioned not to leave their quarters after tattoo, as any person found in the streets after that time will be taken in the guard house.'[61]

At the end of the week the rest of the regiment would start to muster and collect their uniforms, accoutrements and arms from the Regiment store. On the day of the march to Bolton the regiment paraded at 4.30 am in white jackets and in full marching order, formed up on Middleton Road opposite the Westwood Inn. The private soldier had to carry all his belongings on his back in a knapsack, the only persons allowed to put baggage on the baggage cart were the Sergeant Major, Drum Major, pay sergeants, adjutant, quartermasters clerks and servants of the officers.
Whilst at Bolton parades took place on the Flash and field training on Dean Moor, which was normally a full day's event with the men taking their food with them for the day, already cooked. During the day there would also be extra drill practice for the 'ackward squad', this was a squad consisting of new recruits being brought up to standard, it was also used as punishment to place fully trained men in this squad if they had been disciplined.
When marching back to Oldham the regiment mustered in the Market place and had one final parade in Deansgate before marching home via Bury.

In 1812 again the choice of venue for training was Bolton, and was proposed to take place on 18th June returning to Oldham on 4th July, with the recruits mustering one week before for additional training. The regimental orders for 18th June were that the men were to form parade in undress and full marching order on Northmoor with the

[60] HO50/267
[61] Regimental Daily orders for Oldham LM

Grenadiers company facing the Westwood Inn, Captain Duncuft being the Captain of the day and Lieutenant Hollinworth the subaltern for the guard.[62]
The final training camp for the *Oldham Local Militia* was in 1813 for 14 days, marching out to Bolton on 5th August. The 1813 training went without incident until the march back to Oldham when Jonathan Nield, a private in Captain Sutcliffe's company was charged with desertion. Nield had been ordered to duty with the rear guard on the march back to Oldham, whilst stopped at Bury he was given orders by Corporal James Whitehead to relieve the baggage guard, on arrival at Oldham on 20th August. Nield failed to turn up for duty and was consequently arrested and placed under guard in the *black hole* at the depot.
At the court martial proceedings, held at the Crooked Billet in Oldham, Corporal James Bradley, who was Corporal of the guard, explained what happened:

> *'– says that on Saturday evening the prisoner Jonathan Nield escaped from the guard house – says he had two Grenadiers, one sentry, told them not to let any person out whatever without his leave or the sergeants, and whilst Sgt Bradley and he were talking to their Captain at the door, the prisoner asked one of the guard to go with him to ease himself, and the prisoner suddenly jumped over the wall and bid the sentry good night saying he should come no more. The sentry then came and informed them he was gone.'*[63]

A regimental order was issued:

> *'Private Jonathan Nield of the 5th company having broken his guard and deserted, every possible exertion will be used for his speedy apprehension, and Captain Chippendale will arrange the permanent staff in such a way that his fathers house and his usual places of resort, will be constantly watched night and day till he be taken.'*[64]

Two days later, Sergeant James Mills apprehended Nield, and the court martial took place on 24th August under the Presidency of Captain Jones with Lieutenants Travis and Crompton assisting. Nield had two charges read against him:

> *'1st for absenting himself from duty on Friday the 20th day of the present month of August when ordered for guard.*
> *2nd for deserting on the evening of Saturday the 21st of August and neglecting to join his regiment before the expiration of the training period.*
> *Contrary to the fifth art. of the 14 sect. and to the fourth art. of the 6th sect. of the articles of war, and to the prejudice of good order and military discipline.*

---

[62] Regimental Daily orders of Oldham LM
[63] HO50/299
[64] HO50/299

Captain Jones sentenced Nield: 'after examining the witnesses produced against the prisoner and hearing his defence we find him guilty of both of the above charges and therefore sentence him to fourteen days imprisonment to be reckoned from the 24th day of August 1813 in the New Bailey prison Salford. Signed Joseph Jones , Captain & President.
Approved by John Lees'[65]

One other instance of a court martial is recorded in the Regimental daily orders of 3rd February 1813. Three charges were made against Drum Major Robert Whitehead[66] and Drummer John Crompton:

1- For getting drunk on Wednesday the 27th when on duty at Rochdale
2- For behaving in a riotous and disorderly manner at the house of Daniel Nield the sign of the Blue Ball, Packer Street in Rochdale on the day above mentioned.
3- For being absent from head Quarters till five o'clock on Thursday evening the 28th without the authority of the commanding officer.

The evidence was heard and the Drum Major was found guilty of the third charge only and John Crompton was found partially guilty of the second charge and guilty of the third charge. For these crimes the Drum Major was sentenced to be reduced to the rank of private for 14 days and John Crompton reduced to the rank of private for 28 days. So effectively they were only punished in the pocket and dignity.
At the same court martial Sergeant Major Edward Barlow was charged;

1- For being drunk on duty at Rochdale on Wednesday the 27th
2- For entering the room where the Lieutenants were assembled in a state of intoxication and in the presence of these gentlemen and in that disgraceful condition going up to shake hands with Col Lees and Major Beswick with an indecent and unbecoming familiarity towards officers in Rank so much above him.
3- For neglecting to muster the Non-commissioned officers of the staff and march them back to head quarters as ordered by Quartermaster Whittaker his superior officer.
4- For being absent when required to take the oath prescribed by the act of Parliament viz G52 Cap35 sect 82.
5- For neglecting to return to headquarters on Thursday the 28th at 5 o'clock in the afternoon....

He was found guilty and sentenced to be reduced to the rank of private for 14 days and be severely reprimanded.
Two other Sergeants, Samuel Street and Edward Barlow were also charged with being drunk on this day and both received the punishment of being reduced to the rank of private for 14 days.

---

[65] HO50/299
[66] Died May 1819 of consumption

Civil Disturbance

The main employment in Oldham and for that matter, most of Lancashire was that of handloom weaving. The golden age of handloom weaving was starting to come to an end. During the period 1790 to 1812, entire families were involved with the trade. Many men who had once worked the land turned to weaving, and immediately prospered. With a four- day week, high status as skilled craftsmen, and a wage that allowed them to live in comfort, the weavers were the elite of the burgeoning working class. However, things were changing; a series of inventions followed one upon the other that at first assisted the weavers, allowing for the production of larger quantities of finished cloth, but ultimately would replace them.

The years of 1811 and 1812 saw the rise of the so called *Luddites*. In the early months of 1811 the first threatening letters from General Ned Ludd and the Army of Redressers, were sent to employers in Nottingham. Workers, upset by wage reductions and the use of unapprenticed workmen, began to break into factories at night to destroy the new machines that the employers were using. In a three-week period over two hundred stocking frames were destroyed. In March 1811, attacks were taking place every night and the Nottingham authorities had to enrol four hundred special constables to protect the factories. Luddism gradually spread to Yorkshire, Lancashire, Leicestershire and Derbyshire.

In February 1812 the government proposed that machine breaking should become a capital offence. Parliament passed the *Frame Breaking Act* that meant people convicted of machine breaking, could be sentenced to death. As a further precaution, the government ordered 12,000 troops into the areas where the *Luddites* were active.

In addition to the *Luddite* rising against the introduction of power looms, wheat prices soared in 1812, bad harvests and the fluctuating price of staples such as bread and potatoes, left many families in dire need. Unable to feed their families, workers became desperate. There were food riots in Manchester, Oldham, Ashton, Rochdale, Stockport and Macclesfield.

In mid April 1812 rumours were reaching the Oldham authorities that a plan was being formed for seizure of the Arms of the Local Militia. This was obviously of great concern to Captain William Chippendale, as the adjutant of the *Oldham Local Militia* he was responsible for the stores and arms of the regiment. The store for the arms was no more than a:

> *'common dwelling house for my depot, not so much as an iron bar or a shutter to the windows which, to make the matters worse were very large, nor any better security for the door than one common lock.'*[67]

Chippendale had gained information that an attack was planned for the morning of Monday 20th April, on the Sunday he got together:

---

[67] HO42/122

'ten sergeants and got two mechanics in to the place and immediately began to fortify. By noon I was in a respectable state of defence. My door was quite secure, my windows well barricaded, loop holes broken into the walls at all practicable points of defence, my sergeants had each firelocks ready loaded..'.[68]

The following day Chippendale and his men prepared themselves for the worst:

'On Monday a numerous body of people collected in Oldham mainly from Saddleworth and Hollinwood, from the latter place almost all colliers which when united with the savages of Saddleworth formed an assemblage of the most desperate .. that can be imagined. These first operations were directed against the meal warehouses and provisions shops.'[69]

The rioters forced the shopkeepers to sell the food at what they believed was a fair rate, if they did not comply then they were threatened with the burning of their buildings and all its contents. As there was no military in the town and the only two constables for Oldham were nowhere to be seen, then the shopkeepers had no choice but to comply. Chippendale writes:

'Resistance was vain and all the meal flour and potatoes in the town and adjacent hamlets were quickly distributed at the above prices ... necessary to observe that if the constables had appeared the strength of the rioters was far beyond the control of the civil power. After finishing with the provision shops they found themselves much augmented in numbers and constantly increasing. A consultation was held whether they should attack my depot and procure arms.'[70]

The rioters made a number of inspections of Chippendale's arms store and decided that it was well fortified and too dangerous to attack it. The rioters then left Oldham and proceeded to Middleton to join others already there. The situation was far more serious at Middleton, the rioters had gathered outside Mr Burton's mill. Daniel Burton, who knew that the power-looms installed in his mill had upset local handloom weavers, had armed some of his workers to defend his mill. Several thousand gathered at Burton's mill with the intent to destroy his power looms, the men in the mill opened fire on the rioters, four young men were killed and a number were wounded. Two of the dead men were from Oldham, Daniel Knott, 20 years old, had been shot under the left eye and Joseph Jackson, 16 years old and a hatter by trade was also killed.
The following day, Tuesday 21st April, the rioter's again assembled, Chippendale writes:

[68] HO42/122
[69] HO40/1/1
[70] HO40/1/1

> *'About ten o'clock on the Tuesday the town was thrown in to the utmost consternation by a body of rioters almost all colliers. Part of them arrived with fowling pieces, pistols, swords and about five muskets, and the rest amounting to several hundreds with their picks in their hands. They headed directly to the depot,'*
> *'My ten brave fellows shook hands and swore to defend the place as long as brick stood upon another and Capt Whitaker, .. was all games.'*[71]

The rioters again decided that it was unwise to attack the *Oldham Local Militia* store so they:

> *'contented themselves with visiting all the shops that sold gun powder of which they took forcible possession where they found any. They then proceeded to Middleton where they were joined by an immense concourse from other parts of the country.'*[72]

Again the target for the rioters was Daniel Burton. Infantry of the *Cumberland Militia* had reinforced the mill, this left Mr Burton's home unprotected and the rioters set fire to this and a barn and then proceeded to the mill. The Manchester garrison commander writes:

> *'at 2 o'clock p.m. I detached an officer and 30 of the Scots Greys to their assistance. On the appearance of the cavalry the mob fled to the church yard and some other high grounds and commenced firing on the troops. They were immediately dislodged from the former position by a party of the Cumberland Militia leaving 5 of their people killed or wounded on the spot. The dragoons then drove them from every point they occupied and .. dispersed them, killing one of them and wounding severely another. The man killed was in the act of firing at a sergeant of the Greys who instantly shot him dead, some of the military were hurt.'*[73]

One of the men killed was another Oldham man, John Johnson. Reputedly Johnson had not taken part in the riots and was simply standing in Middleton churchyard reading a gravestone inscription when a Sergeant from the *Cumberland Militia* purposely took aim at him and shot him through the neck. Other Oldham men were also wounded.
By the Wednesday, Chippendale deemed it safe enough to leave the arms store, by then he, Quarter Master Whittaker and the ten sergeants, had remained holed up in the store for a total of three days and three nights.

---

[71] HO40/1/1
[72] HO40/1/1
[73] HO42/122

Intelligence reports were coming in to the local authorities in Lancashire that a major uprising was planned for 4th of May. This gave great concern to them as they felt that there was not enough military in the area to be able to control the militants.
People continued to gather over the following days and riot was continually threatened. The Deputy Lieutenants and magistrates acting in and for the subdivision of Middleton issued a letter on 27th April calling out 200 men of the *Oldham Local Militia* and 200 men of the *1st Middleton (Ashton) Local Militia* in order to suppress rioting in those districts.[74] They were called out for 14 days permanent duty.
The regimental orders issued for this day read:

> *'20 men from each company will be assembled at Head Quarters with all possible dispatch the following officers will be attached to this force whilst it remains embodied, namely Captain's Clegg, Travis and Winterbottom, Lieutenants John Travis L Infantry Hardman and Travis 4 company who takes Mr Hollingsworth's duty, a sergeants guard will mount at the depot.'*[75]

The 20 men from each company were then formed into three companies with Captain Clegg in charge of the first company, which consisted of his men from the Grenadiers Company and men from three, four and six company. The second company was placed in the charge of Captain Travis and consisted of men from the first, second, fifth and sixth companies. The third company under the command of Captain Winterbottom consisted of the men from his Light Company, sixth, seventh and eighth companies. In addition to the above the Sergeant Major, the Drum Major and four drummers were also called out. In addition to the calling out of the *Oldham Local Militia* a meeting was held at the Spread Eagle in Oldham where magistrates swore in a large number of constables on a temporary basis, this would have probably consisted of owners and workers of the local mills so that they had the authority to protect their properties from any rioters.
On 1st May a meeting of the Lieutenancy of Lancashire was held at The Bull Inn, Preston. The subject of calling out the Local Militia was the main topic of discussion, a number of resolutions on this subject were discussed, and one of these was:

> *'Is not the utmost Vigilance and Exertion necessary to prevent Evil-disposed Persons from contriving, raising or abetting Riots and Turmolts, and to oppose the first Appearance of Disorder; and can any Means for those Purposes, in the present Conjuncture of Affairs and inflamed State of the County, be more efficacious, than calling out the Local Militia of the county?*
> *Resolved unanimously, That Measure is the best'*[76]

---

[74] HO50/285
[75] Regimental daily Orders for Oldham LM
[76] HO50/285

A letter was sent to all commandants of the Local Militia in Lancashire to call out and assemble such parts of the Local Militia on Monday 4th May, at Nine o'clock in the morning, all 15 regiments of the Local Militia in Lancashire were required to assemble four companies each.
The *Oldham Local Militia* already had 200 men out on permanent duty since 27th April and to comply with the request a further 120 men were put on duty on 4th May to make the strength up to four companies.
The expected uprising on 4th May did not occur, but the *Oldham Local Militia* were on constant alert, by 9th May Oldham was re-enforced with a contingent of men from the *Stirlingshire Militia* and between them and the *Oldham Local Militia* they provided a presence in the town and surrounding areas that curtailed any further gatherings of people. A guard was mounted in the town at the Regimental stores consisting of one sergeant, one corporal and 24 privates from each of the regiments.
By 25th May a military camp was being set up on Kersal Moor, which consisted of the *Buckinghamshire, Louth* and *Stirling Regiments of Militia* along with some artillery. With the Oldham area now effectively under military control the authorities were keen to bring as many of the rioters to trial as they could find, and over the following few weeks officers of the *Oldham Local Militia* were involved in tracking down and arresting the suspects. Major Henry Barlow took into custody Isaac Midgly, of Hollinwood and Jas Taylor of Oldham who were both wounded and also James Ashworth of Hollinwood. A few days later, Captain Chippendale and Quartermaster Whittaker along with a constable and a large number of soldiers went to Mossley and apprehended four men on a charge of being involved in the riots. Joseph Nadin, the deputy constable of Manchester also made arrests in Oldham and Royton, he was accompanied by a contingent of *Scots Greys* to help with the arrests. Trials of those arrested throughout Lancashire took place during the summer of 1812 with the result that eight men were sentenced to death and thirteen were transported to Australia.

The final years

By 1813 the threat of invasion of England by Napoleon was non-existent; the French were beginning to be defeated on the continent and on the Peninsula. Wellington was winning battle after battle and slowly pushing the French army back to France.
The 1813 training in Bolton was to be the last official training for the *Oldham Local Militia.* The men assembled at the beginning of 1814, but this was only for the purpose of extending their services as per the Act of 54th, GIII, Cap 19. They assembled on Lord Street, the officers in full dress uniform but the non-commissioned officers and privates in civilian clothing. At this assembly the regiment consisted of two Majors, eight captains, nine lieutenants, 32 sergeants, 29 corporals, 19 drummers, 696 privates.

This assembly was a troublesome one for Lt-Col Lees, he had expected all the men to volunteer to extend their service but on the initial request many men refused, he claimed that:

> *'some evil disposed persons .. mistelling doubt and distrust into their minds with respect to the nature and object of the extended service'*[77].

After some re-assurances by the officers and non-commissioned officers a lot more were convinced to extend their service, but still in the end 156, mainly privates, refused to extend their service. On the 1814 returns there are listed a number of men who had enlisted in the regular army, thus showing that the *Oldham Local Militia* had been able to partially train and inspire some men to go and fight for King and country against Napoleon. Some of the regiments the men enlisted into were; *1st and 2nd Life Guards, 21st Light Dragoons, 23rd Regiment of Foot* and the *95th Rifles.*
The government gave orders for discontinuance of all Local Militia regiments in April 1816, all allowances were stopped and the return of government equipment had to be complete by 24th August 1816.
The final public gathering for the *Oldham Local Militia* was to celebrate the defeat of Napoleon at the Battle of Waterloo, when they paraded in Oldham the day after the defeat of Napoleon. This occasion was remembered by a Mr C.P. Brierley, an Oldham man who later emigrated to New Zealand and drew the scene from memory.

---

[77] WO13/3538

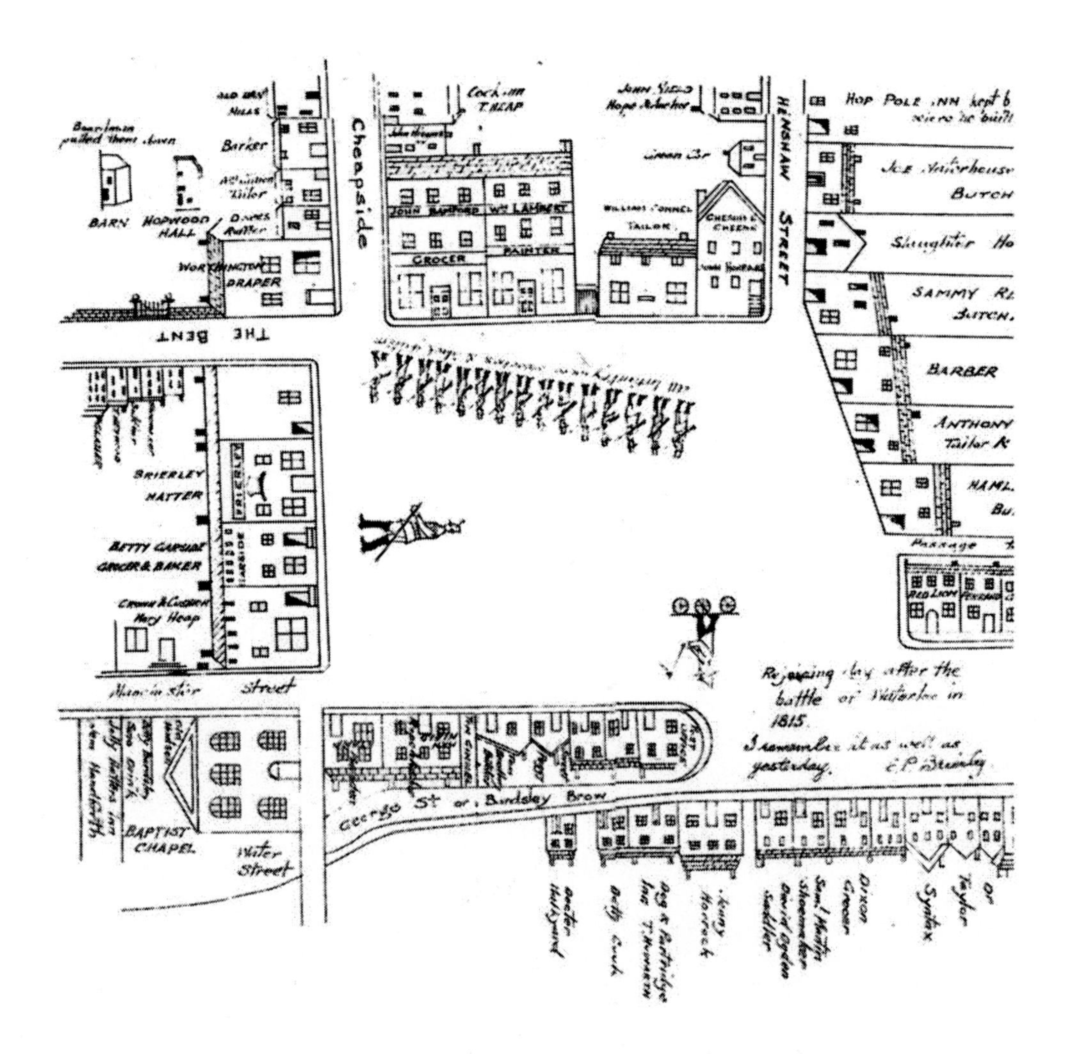

By kind permission of Oldham Local Studies

Oldham Troop of Yeomanry Cavalry 1817-1828

By the end of the Napoleonic wars, culminating in the defeat of Napoleon at Waterloo, the state of the country was one of exhaustion and decline. The economy was static, with trade at home and abroad at a low ebb. Prices and wages were greatly reduced. In Lancashire the weavers, hatters and other workers within the manufacturing industries were in a desperate situation, with many of them in a starving state. Most of the working classes blamed the politicians for the poor state of the country and a radical reform of the constitution of the House of Commons was demanded. Many political associations were beginning to form and this call was extremely strong in the manufacturing towns of Lancashire, including Oldham.

There is a record of a public meeting of the reformers in Oldham on 23rd September 1816 at Bent Green; speakers from Oldham and one from Bury addressed the gathered group. One of the main causes of concern was the Corn Bill of 1815, which was blamed for the high prices of food. In December 1816 Captain Chippendale wrote a number of letters to the Home Office informing the authorities of the current situation in the area. In one of his letters, Chippendale was concerned that the reformers appeared to have accurate information about the number and description of troops[78] at Chester Castle and that there were 39,000 muskets stored there. On 3rd January 1817 another large radical reform meeting took place on Bent Green, this time banners and a band playing music added to the effect of the meeting.

By now the authorities were becoming increasingly alarmed at the growing political unrest and also concerned that the reformers may resort to something less peaceful than a meeting to pursue their political reforms. In anticipation of another reform meeting on Bent Green on 10th February the local magistrates swore in special constables two days prior to the meeting, fortunately the meeting passed peacefully. Still concerned, on 8th March, the authorities stationed 104 soldiers from the *54th Regiment of Foot* in temporary barracks on Fog Lane.

During March 1817 three radicals- John Johnson, John Bagguley and Samuel Drummond - persuaded the area's starving workers to carry a petition to the Prince Regent in London, calling on him to help alleviate their distress. As they planned to sleep rough, the marchers were to carry rolled up blankets or overcoats on their shoulders, to keep them warm at night, hence they were known as the Blanketeers. This was effectively the world's first hunger march.

In the early hours of 10th March a party of reformers from Oldham gathered, with their blankets around their shoulders, ready to march to Manchester to join up with the other reformers. The special constables, the *54th Regiment of Foot*, and also a troop of the *13th Light Horse*, which had arrived from Huddersfield, were all on duty, but no interference was made to the Oldham Blanketeers and they were allowed to march to Manchester.

---

[78] HO40/3

St Peter's Fields was chosen as the starting point for the march and up to 10,000 people gathered to see the Blanketeers off.
But while Bagguley and Drummond were still talking to the gathering, the magistrates, whose spies had warned them of possible violence on the march, read the *Riot Act* and then sent in the *King's Dragoon Guards*. Bagguley, Drummond and 27 others were arrested. Johnston and fellow radical William Ogden had been apprehended the previous day and had spent the night in jail. In the confusion, many men decided to begin the march anyway.
When the magistrates realised this, they despatched soldiers and special constables after them. One group was overhauled about a mile out of the city, while the main group was hunted down at Lancashire Hill in Stockport.
The military weighed into the marchers with sabres and muskets. Several were wounded, an innocent bystander was shot dead and several hundred were arrested. A few managed to get as far as Macclesfield and even Ashbourne, but only one - Abel Couldwell of Stalybridge - made it to London to hand over his petition.

On 27th March 1817 Captain Chippendale reported to the Home Office that:

> *'crisis approaches, have clearly ascertained that those men who are to be the Chief Actors in the first assault are casting bullets and preparing other weapons.'*[79]

He went on to urge that the roads to Manchester should be watched to determine how many of the known reform leaders came into town. Without waiting for authority Chippendale placed a *trusty man* on each of the Oldham, Ashton and Blakely roads and arranged for them to report back in the afternoon what they had observed. The following day Chippendale along with Quarter Master Whittaker and Lieutenant Colonel Edward Lees went to Ardwick Bridge where a meeting was expected of the reformers, they went with the purpose of trying to identify who the leaders were.
It is more than likely that as a direct result of the Blanketeers march and the growing unrest in Oldham from the radical reformers, that the prominent manufacturers in Oldham decided that more of this behaviour was likely and the possibility existed of the radical reformers targeting Oldham businesses. A meeting was held to determine the possibilities of a troop of Yeomanry Cavalry being formed to protect the factories and businesses of Oldham. Only 3 weeks after the Blanketeers march a letter, dated 3rd April 1817, was sent by John Taylor Esq., a local Oldham Hat Manufacturer, to Lord Sidmouth, the Secretary of State at the Home office:

> *"My Lord,*
> *I have the honour to address your Lordship that a meeting has been held in Oldham for the purpose of taking into consideration the possibility of forming a Troop of Yeomanry Cavalry. Previous to however to coming to any final*

[79] HO40/5/4a

determination upon the subject, I am directed as chairman of the meeting to make inquiry of your Lordship what facility will be afforded by the Government in aid of the disciplining and forming a Troop of that description and also what pecuniary allowances will be made towards defraying the contingents expenses. An adjourned meeting at an early day having been appointed to consider your Lordships answer; I beg leave to solicit a reply at your Lordships earliest convenience.

I have the honour to be, My Lord

Your Lordships man and obedient and able servant

John Taylor"[80]

The reply from the Home Office advised Taylor of the entitlements and numbers of men required for the formation of a troop of Yeomanry Cavalry as per the requirements of the *Volunteer Act (44. G.III. C.54)* passed by parliament on 5th June 1804.
The Home Office advised that an allowance of 1s 10d per man usually for clothing and the same sum for contingencies and that these allowances will be issued to Corps when first established. A troop may consist of no less than forty and no more than one hundred rank and file. The troop would also be allowed one sergeant and one corporal to every 20 men, along with one trumpeter and one quartermaster for the troop.
After this letter all correspondence was then routed through Lord Derby, the Lord Lieutenant of the County of Lancashire. It is interesting to note the Government's concern regarding the political threat by radicals in Lancashire; in a letter to Lord Derby from Lord Sidmouth regarding provisional acceptance of the Yeomanry Cavalry in Oldham a note at the end of this letter reads:

"I beg hence to add that the establishment of an effective Yeomanry force in the county of Lancaster is considered by Government to be the object of considerable importance and it would afford me great satisfaction at the present juncture to secure any further offers of service."[81]

Once the details were known for establishing a troop of Yeomanry Calvary a committee was formed and a subscription fund opened for the purpose of raising, funding and training an Oldham troop.
On 24th June 1817, a letter to Lord Derby confirmed the acceptance and appointment of the officers of the *Oldham Troop of Yeomanry Cavalry* and so must be taken as the official date for the formation of the *Oldham Troop of Yeomanry Cavalry* (*OTYC*).

"My Lord,
I have laid before the Prince Regent your Lordships letter of the 19th inst. and I have the satisfaction of informing your Lordship, that His Royal Highness, in the name and on the behalf of His Majesty, does not disapprove of Mr John Taylor to

[80] HO50/359
[81] HO50/89

the Captain, Mr Richard Clegg to the Lieutenant and Mr J M Taylor to the Cornet in the Oldham Volunteer Cavalry.
Lord Sidmouth"[82]

So begins the process of actually establishing the troop, it was clear from John Taylor's letter of 3rd April 1817 that a meeting had been held with a number of people already willing to be part of the Yeomanry Cavalry. Most of the people at this meeting would have had a vested interest in protecting their own factories and businesses.
The three nominated officers of the troop were all involved with hat manufacturing. It should be noted that Oldham during this period was not only prominent in the cotton industry but it was also a substantial producer of hats. Oldham in 1817 had 22 hat manufacturers producing over 1,000 hats per week.

John Taylor was in partnership with Thomas Barker; (for a short period in 1803 Barker was a Captain in the *Oldham Loyal Volunteers*) they had a factory on Henshaw Street, Oldham. This was the former factory of Thomas Henshaw, the benefactor of Oldham's Blue Coat School. John Taylor came into the hatting business when his mother, Sarah, married Thomas Henshaw. Sarah Taylor was the widow of Joseph Taylor of Crumpsall. Taylor and Barker lived in large houses close to the factory. James Mayers Taylor, born in 1789, was the brother of John Taylor and was also involved with the business.

The Clegg family had been established in the Oldham area since the early 17th century and had acquired large amounts of land in Oldham and surrounding areas. Richard Clegg, born in 1782, was the second son of James Clegg (also a Captain in the *Oldham Loyal Volunteers*) but he became the heir when his older brother, John Taylor Clegg, came to grief. Rowbottom writing in his diary on 5th January 1815 comments:

> *"died at Edenburgh John Taylor Clegg Esq. of Lower Bent, Oldham, the fate of the young gentleman is pittable, he was seised with a fit on the 3rd and fell on a large fire where he was so miserably burned as to cause his death, his age 35 years".*[83]

James Clegg was married to Sarah Taylor the daughter of John Taylor of Crumpsall, this is assumed to be the same Taylor family of Captain John and Cornet James, and thus the troop was very much in the control of the hatting families of Oldham.

Initially the troop was formed with only 18 private men, including one farrier, two sergeants, two corporals, one trumpeter, one quartermaster a cornet, a Lieutenant and a

---

[82] HO51/71
[83] Rowbottom's Diary

Captain. The Home Office encouraged the Oldham troop to try to augment its numbers.[84]
By May 1818, James Clegg had gained a commission as quartermaster for the troop.[85] By the time of the first training camp in June 1818 the strength of the troop had risen to 36 men.

Joseph Mellor was engaged as the troop's trumpeter; Joseph was only 16 years old but had already had experience of being a trumpeter as he had previously joined his father, a bassoon player, in the *Life Guards*. He stayed with his father, also Joseph, for around two years before both returned to Oldham after the end of the Napoleonic wars.

An interesting poem was written, by persons unknown, to the secretary and troop member James Radley, it probably reflects the views of property owners and manufacturers in the district as to the roll of the *OTYC* as protectors against the increasingly radical element of the working classes.

On Political subjects the furies combine,
To heighten dissention, and havoc entwine;
Man's reason is flighty, and fickle his mind,
Till drifted by Fortitude's comforting wind.
The wind of the Cavalry,
Yeomanry Cavalry,
Daring defenders of old Liberty!

When WATERLOO'S trumpet proclaimed a Peace,
We fondly embraced the phantom of ease;
No sooner did limbo the tyrant entrap,
Than his vot'ries swore they'd recall little Nap.
Till napp'd by the Cavalry &c.

On blest Magna Charta an outrage they made,
Transform'd our Rights, Habens Corpus betray'd,
Then swift flew to gnaw down the pillars of state,
But gnaw'd their own fangs upon finding the meat
To be heroic Cavalry, &c.

Vile slander reports that the cavalry rose
The rich to befriend, to the peasants be foes;
O gross accusation! how fowl the report,
For if either, the poor man's cause they'l support,
Hail! Lenient Cavalry, &c.

[84] WO13/4008
[85] HO50/361

While fearless Yeoman our guardians will be,
From the horrors of slaughter old age will be free;
Modest Beauty may lay all her fears aside,
And dandle in safety her suckling pride.
O guardian Cavalry, &c.

May Fortune still favour old Albion's isle,
Each Briton live happy, and die with a smile,
Live long, and enjoy all the charms of the Fair,
Then gallop aloft and be Cavalry there.
Blest heavenly Cavalry,
Yeomanry Cavalry,
Daring defenders of old Liberty![86]

In aid of the Civil Powers

During May 1817 there was civil unrest at Saddleworth, where William Robert Hay reported on the incident and mentions the effective use of Yeomanry, at this time the *OTYC* had not yet formed but their potential worth was being highlighted. The military were present in force to keep demonstrations in check.
Extracts from Hay's report describes the day's events:

> '.. *cleared the streets a number of times with assistance from Kings Dragoon guards under the command of Cols Teesdale and Acklem, also from the Cheshire Yeomanry commanded by Lt-Col Townsend. The nearby attendance of the corps at a very short notice convinced to us the peculiar utility of corps of their description, at the same time that its exertions were a great support to us. The 85th under Col Thornton from Chester joined in the course of the day. The corps was not employed, but I understand that Col Thornton was personally very active and useful. He was with Sir John Byng., Capt Kirby at the head of a party of the 54th were of great assistance. Having stated tho' imperfactly how much we are indebted to the military in its several detachments I must not omit to mention how firmly and actively we were aided by the bodies of special constables, who attended throughout the day.*'[87]

Call out of 1819

The unrest of the working classes in the Lancashire area and Oldham in particular which had prompted the formation of the *OTYC* continued for most of the period that the troop existed. Despite the fact that the *Oldham Local Militia* had disbanded in 1816, the officers still took an active interest in the political unrest, especially Captain

[86] By kind permission of the County Archivist, Lancashire Record Office Ref DDX818/39
[87] HO40/5/4a

Chippendale who reported on seditious meetings and intelligence on radical leaders either directly to the Home Office or sometimes through Colonel Fletcher in Bolton.

By the summer of 1819 radical activity was increasing, on 19th July there was a report of men marching from Dry Clough to Oldham armed with pikes about two yards long, to join other men with pikes in a field.[88] On 1st August at 6 o'clock in the morning it was reported that around 2000 men had assembled on Tandle Hill, between Oldham and Rochdale. A soldier who had reputedly been at the Battle of Waterloo was drilling the men in regular marching exercises.[89] At this time there were already a large number of regular troops stationed in the area. In Oldham there were two troops of the *6th Dragoon Guards*, in Manchester six troops of the *15th Hussars* and six companies of infantry belonging to the *68th Regiment of Foot* and *71st Regiment of Foot* along with two 6 pounder cannons. Stationed at Ashton were two troops of the *7th Dragoon Guards* and at Rochdale two companies of the *68th Regiment of Foot.*
On the evening of 5th August there was a report of more men drilling; this time around 90 men had been spotted in a field belonging to Robert Bury in Failsworth.

> *'They had an awkward squad. The men had no firearms, but when the word fire was given they clapped their hands together. After drilling their commander informed them that the intended meeting was put off on account of their paper being illegal, but that would give them more time to drill. He said they must carry some colours and subscribe for them. He held out his hat for pennies and halfpennies. Some women were also close by and stated that he wanted twelve young ladies to carry the colours, for he was certain that there was a regiment of soldiers drawn up to oppose them, they could not find in their hearts to hurt them.'*[90]

In the early hours of the morning of 8th August around 2000 men again mustered on Tandle Hill:

> *'The front rank was said to be composed entirely of men who have been in the army, the pivot men of non-commissioned officers. There was a separate rifle company of about 85 young men who continued to practice the rifle movements, and what is remarkable there was a discharged rifle man in uniform upon each of the pivots.'* [91]

Much to Chippendale's consternation there were former members of the *Oldham Local Militia* in the ranks. One of the men by the name of Bardsley had been a Sergeant in the *Oldham Local Militia* for the first four years then served with another militia

[88] HO42/191
[89] HO42/191
[90] HO42/191
[91] HO42/191

regiment as a permanent sergeant. It was reported that the men had come to Tandle Hill from Manchester, Cheetham Hill, Middleton, Oldham, Rochdale, Ashton and Saddleworth. John Crompton, former Captain in the *Oldham Local Militia*, and Abraham Milne, former Lieutenant in the *Oldham Local Militia*, watched the men drilling on Tandle Hill and:

> *'particularly noticed one company of about 100 march in the wings under their leader, and advanced in wings, then the right wing advanced first, and the words of command 'firing front rank kneeling' and when the word of command 'fire' was given they clapped their hands. The leader then advanced the left wing in the same order. This was repeated several times. Mr Crompton being informed they were to assemble at Slattocks-in-Thornham, Abraham Milne and Mr Crompton placed themselves by the roadside in order to ascertain their numbers, when they past Milne and Crompton marching in military order 4 deep they counted 700 men.'*[92]

The day after this meeting the *OTYC* were placed on permanent duty. This meant that the troop would have mustered in uniform and billeted themselves in Oldham town and they were to be at the ready to be called out at short notice.
Reports continued of further gatherings and on 11th August a Mr Wriggley reported on the events in Lees:

> *'I have just witnessed a scene by the reformers collected in this village which has opened my eyes more than ever. They have parades through the village for two days with a large flag on a black ground with on one side 'No borough mongering, taxation without representation is unjust and tyrannical', on the reverse 'Unite and be free, equal representation or death', on one staff the cap of liberty on another, and the red (or bloody) flag on a third. Singing to some musik that most vile and infamous of all songs, called 'Green upon the caps', with green and pink ribbons in their hats, green is to be their colour, this song was the instigation of the Irish rebellion 21 years ago'*[93]

There was also a report of 200 radicals mustering at Rochdale parish church on 11th August and then marched off 4 deep to Milkstone in the district of Tandle Hill in Thornham.
All these gatherings and meetings were the prelude to the major demonstration and gathering being planned for the 16th August at St Peter's field in Manchester. On the morning of the 16th Chippendale reports:

> *'The muster at Tandle Hill having become too numerous for the accommodation, a separation has taken place and part of them have moved to*

[92] HO42/191
[93] HO42/191

> *the white moss. At both these places there was a muster yesterday besides another at Quick Edge in Saddleworth. Have not been able to obtain what I consider a correct account of the numbers at any of the parties except that which assembled at white moss which amounted to two thousand. (This number comes from Col Kenyon of the Newton & Failsworth Local Militia who was present and counted them himself).*
> *Two men who were present as spectators were extremely ill-treated by them, one of them was a Police runner from Manchester and the other a young man from the neighbourhood. They are nearly killed. I saw the party very distinctly from Edward Lee's garden with a telescope and heard the words of command quite plain. The Quick Edge party was much more numerous than any of them, and I judge .... the amount of all three at 8000. This is an amazing number to be assembled within 4 miles of Oldham.*
> *With respect to the meeting at Manchester, I have been particularly fortunate in obtaining correct information of the plans of the leaders. Orders have been transmitted from the .. at Manchester and conveyed to Royton to be from there circulated thro' this parish by confidential emissaries. This took place yesterday and my information was derived from the committee at Royton. The orders are not to break the peace on any account whatever. They are to leave any insult upon themselves or even to suffer any .. of their speakers to be taken from the stage without attempting resistance. They are ... not to bring any weapons of any kind whatever, and to keep flags furled till they receive orders from the committee to display them. It is impossible for me at this place to firm any idea of the probable numbers. The parties that have passed thro' this place in marching order amount altogether to about 864 with four flags from the following place vis Oldham, Royton, Lees and Saddleworth.*
> *A straggling stream of men not in the column followed. With the assistance of a friend he counted around 4000 marching towards Manchester.'*[94]

Despite being on permanent duty it does not appear that the *OTYC* were called upon to take any measures against the assembled reformers at Tandle Hill, they were left to march peacefully into Manchester to the gathering at St Peter's field. The actions of the military and Yeomanry at Manchester which led to this day being infamously known as the *Peterloo massacre* has been well documented and so will not be re-told in these pages as the *OTYC* had no part in its proceedings apart from keeping a watchful eye on the gatherings in the Oldham area prior to the march to Manchester.
The *OTYC* were stood down the day after *Peterloo* on 17th August. A day later Chippendale was writing to the Home Office:

> *'I have just been informed by a respectable inhabitant of Thornham in Middleton parish, that the reformers there abouts have prepared their scythes in a peculiar way, and mean to march this evening into Manchester, for what*

[94] HO42/192

> *purpose you need not long conjecture. These instruments were hid during this last night in the Pitts near Stakehill within Thornham.*'[95]

Unrest continued and more troops were brought into Oldham to try and calm the population down. The *7th Dragoon Guards replaced the 6th Dragoon Guards* and these were further reinforced with a detachment from the *32nd Regiment of Foot* who were later replaced by a detachment from the *85th Regiment of Foot*. Lord Sidmouth urged that all corps of Yeomanry Cavalry in Lancashire were to hold themselves in readiness to support and assist the Civil Authorities in case of necessity[96] and on 29th October urged the Yeomanry Cavalry to be ready for a possible attack on the Depot of the Arms of the Militia. By 11th December 1819 Oldham town was looking like a town under occupation, in addition to the cavalry and infantry, two pieces of cannon arrived at Oldham for the protection of the town.[97] On 12th December the *OTYC* was called out by the local magistrates, Samuel Taylor and Rev John Holme, they were placed on permanent duty until 16th December. Nothing significant appears to have happened during this period of duty.

The large presence of military in the town was putting a strain on the relationship between the populace and the military and fighting sometimes broke out between soldiers and local men. One such instance took place in April 1820 at the Bull's Head when some local men were reportedly singing disloyal songs and throwing beer around; they then got into a fight with five privates of the *7th Dragoon Guards*. Butterworth described this incident as a 'desperate contest'; one man was severely wounded with a fire shovel, a youth was wounded by a red hot kitchen poker, the furniture of the Bull's Head was completely demolished and the fight spilled out onto the streets with a further eighteen people being wounded. Captain Chippendale along with cornet White and Quartermaster Polity of the Dragoons managed to suppress the fight. A corporal also received a wound to the forehead with a carving knife. The *7th Dragoon Guards* had become unpopular in Oldham and were wisely redeployed to Carlisle.

A further incident took place in the Swan public house, kept by Mr Whittaker, on 20th July 1820. Three privates from the *5th Dragoon Guards*, William Norris, George Hamilton and Thomas Kenny were drinking in the Swan when an unnamed pensioner got up and said 'Here's a health to King and Queen'. Thomas Haigh said 'Here's to hell with the King and Queen' and then struck the other pensioner (a scuffle took place and Haigh was put out of the room) Haigh challenged to fight any man in the regiment. Haigh was under the influence of liquor.[98] Thomas Haigh was a pensioner and late of the *95th Regiment of Foot (Rifles)*, it is quite possible he was one of the rifleman

---

[95] HO42/192
[96] HO51/90
[97] Rowbottom's Diary
[98] HO41/14

observed drilling on Tandle Hill in August 1819 prior to *Peterloo*. For this affray Haigh lost his army pension and was sentenced to three months in prison.

Unrest continued in Oldham throughout 1820 and 1821 with Captain Chippendale providing intelligence reports to the Home Office on local gatherings, seditious meetings or names of possible radical leaders. During this period the authorities were on the lookout for any sign of gathering of arms, Chippendale reported that it had been discovered that pikes were being manufactured in Oldham by a young blacksmith whom was not under any suspicion. Chippendale had managed to acquire one of the three pikes that had been made.
In the same letter Chippendale mentions:

> *'A parcel was brought to Huddersfield yesterday morning by one of the coaches which the coach proprietor suspected to contain arms. He placed himself in ambush till it was called for and then seized the person who came for it and examined the parcel which was found to contain 1 sword, 2 brace of pistols, 2 bullet moulds, 3 bayonets and 2 musket locks. In addition to this he informs me that all the lead about the town that can be carried away is stolen and that many trees have been cut down on Murfield Head. Which it is presumed are for pike shafts.'* [99]

Chippendale continued to provide these intelligence reports right up to his early death, at the age of 50, on 10th March 1822.
An obituary in the *Manchester Chronicle* stated:

> *'His amiable disposition and unassuming manners gained for him the respect and veneration of all orders of society, which it is the lot of few men to obtain. He was an affectionate husband, a kind master, and a loyal subject. It may be truly asserted that by his death, his majesty is deprived of one of his most faithful subjects, and society of one of its brightest ornaments.*
> *To him when invasion threatened Old England, the volunteer regiment owed its organisation and its excellent discipline. Always acting up to his favourite motto 'semper paratus' he tendered during his life the same services to the local militia. He was a man of unshaken loyalty, and of a capacious mind, acute observation, and strong spirit of inquiry. His temper was social, his manners prepossessing, and his address easy and unassuming. He had a warm heart and liberal feelings. All who knew him respected his worth and deeply lamented his sudden loss.'*

It would appear that Chippendale was a well respected man, and we also have evidence of his sense of duty and honesty. Whilst Adjutant of the *Oldham Local Militia* he had received letters from two army contractors offering to pay him 5% of the total cost, if

[99] HO40/12

he placed the order with them for the new accoutrements. He reported them to Viscount Sidmouth at the Home Office:

> *'To enable the contractor to afford this allowance, it will be obvious to your Lordship that the articles in question must necessarily be finished 5 per cent worse in quality than the men have a right to demand, and thus the wages of corruption with which my dishonest services are intended to be purchased must be acquired by an indirect Robbery of the non-commissioned officers and private men.'*[100]

The military remained in force in the Oldham area until finally on 21st March 1821 the troops of the *1st Dragoon Guards* were the last of the soldiers stationed in the town to leave.

There was a request by a number of the Oldham mill owners to have a barracks permanently built in the town, but government gave no backing to this plan. In June 1821 a signed memorial was sent to the government to ask them to reconsider, signatures on this memorial included the magistrate John Hulme, the constables of Oldham and also all the officers of the *Oldham Troop of Yeomanry Cavalry.*

Call out of 1826

The situation for the hand loom weavers had become desperate by 1826, during this year there was a severe trade depression and many looms were idle or on half work. A weaver who formerly in the early 1800s would have earned six to eight shillings a day could not even earn six shillings per week, even working up to 16 hours per day. Rowbottom describes a desperate situation in his diary in April 1826:

> *'thousands unemployed in Oldham, parading the streets in a starving state, ranging the hills in search of nettles, docks, anything green, which they boil and mix with oatmeal.'*

The situation was the same throughout the manufacturing towns of Lancashire. In April, the Weavers Union Society of Blackburn wrote to the Home Secretary:

> *'Within the last eleven years we have experienced rapid reductions in the prices of labour: and often there was not the least reason, until at this time we cannot procure more than one or two meals a day. Our dwellings are totally destitute of every necessary comfort. Every article of value has disappeared, either to satisfy the cravings of hunger or to appease the claims of relentless creditors; our homes where plenty and contentment once resided, are now become the abodes of penury and wretchedness. This, however, is only a faint picture of the situation of those fully employed. No adequate idea can be*

[100] HO50/310

> *formed of the sufferings of those who are unemployed, of whom there are upwards of 7,000 in this town and neighbourhood. Were a humane man, sir, to visit the dwellings of four-fifths of the weavers and see the miserable pittance, which sixteen hours of labour can procure, divided between the parents and the starving little ones, he would sicken at the sight and blush for the patience of humanity'.*

On 24th April 1826 rioting began in East Lancashire and spread through the county over the following days. A day later at Haslingden, around 3000 weavers destroyed power looms in three mills, the military were summoned for the protection of further mills and 15 dragoons of *The Bays* and 20 men of the *60th Rifles* were deployed to the area, the riot act was read. Whilst protecting a mill at Chatterton, belonging to Mr Aitken, the situation got out of hand and six people were shot dead and many more wounded.

The riots in Lancashire was becoming of great concern to the authorities in Oldham as intelligence was being received that the same could occur in Oldham. On 28th April the local magistrate, Rev John Holme, swore in 113 men as special constables (*see Appendix 6*). These men were from all walks of life including shop keepers, tradesmen, mill owners and employees within the mills. On the same day Rev Holme wrote to Lieutenant Richard Clegg calling out the *OTYC* to aid the civil powers. The call out was sent to Clegg as Captain Taylor was away on business in London but was on his way back, Taylor eventually arrived back in Oldham on 2nd May:

> *'I think it highly expedient on account of the present disturbed state of the part of the county that every precaution should be used within our power to protect the property of our manufacturers and for the preservation of public tranquillity in the division of Oldham. With this view a considerable body of men have recently been sworn in as special constables, but as these, I concede, are not competent to the protection of so populace a district as their without the aid of military assistance, I desire you will assemble the Troop of Yeomanry Cavalry under your command in the course of the day that you may be in a state of readiness to assist the civil powers if requisits. Had you been in barracks, or in any situation ready to assemble on a short notice I should not have required this of you, but as your men and horses are scattered throughout an extensive neighbourhood and cannot be collected together in a very limited period, I see no alternative but that of adopting the measure I now do.'*[101]

The constables of Oldham, John Duncuft Esq. and John Radley Esq. were kept busy in gathering information on activities in the Oldham area, a messenger service was set up with the constables of Manchester so that they could keep each other informed if any

[101] WO13/4008

assemblage of people be collected in any part of the surrounding district, showing a disposition to disturb the public peace. [102]

In the early hours of Sunday 30th April 1826, people began to assemble on Tandle Hill, their numbers gradually increasing; reports ranged from as low as 600 up to as high as 3000. At 10 o'clock they marched to the closest mill that contained power looms, which was a mill owned by John Clegg at High Crompton, along the route a large part of the inhabitants came out of their homes to observe them when passing, but their demeanour appeared to be so peaceable, that there scarcely existed the smallest suspicion of their having assembled for a riotous purpose.[103] Once at the mill they broke down the outer mill door and then the inner door to the room containing the power looms, this was apparently done with hammers that some men had hidden in inside pockets of their coats. Whilst the rioters were breaking into the factory the nephew of John Clegg arrived, he tried to talk them out of their actions but in return he was pelted with stones and was compelled to make a speedy retreat. All twenty-eight looms within the mill were completely destroyed. After the looms were destroyed most of the rioters dispersed in various directions except for a small body of around 50 men who then proceeded on through Shaw towards the factory of Messrs Milne, Travis and Milne at Luzley Brook. One newspaper describes what happened next:

> *'These gentlemen, however, being by this time aware of the proceedings at Mr Clegg's has assembled all their work people, and had moreover obtained the assistance of a number of the inhabitants of the village; and the rioters finding that their force would not be adequate to carry the place by storm, thought it prudent to desist from the attempt altogether. They then directed their course to another factory at Luzley Brook, also belonging to the same gentlemen. This mill, however, was likewise stoutly garrisoned, and the rioters thus finding themselves anticipated in every quarter, dispersed soon afterwards.'*[104]

News soon reached the constables of Oldham, who immediately sent a messenger to Manchester asking for military assistance. General Harris, commanding the garrison at Manchester, ordered the *Rocket Troop* and a detachment of the *Cheshire Yeomanry* immediately to Oldham, John Norris, a Manchester constable accompanied them, they left Manchester around 2 o'clock in the afternoon.

By the time they arrived in Oldham the rioters had dispersed after the attack on the two mills and there was no sign of them or which way they had headed. Intelligence was received that the rioters would be assembling again on Tandle Hills at four in the afternoon and Norris with his military force stationed themselves at Tandle Hill remaining there until around 6 in the evening, but their presence obviously prevented any further gathering.[105]

---

[102] Giles Shaw MSS

[103] Manchester Courier

[104] Manchester Courier

[105] HO44/16

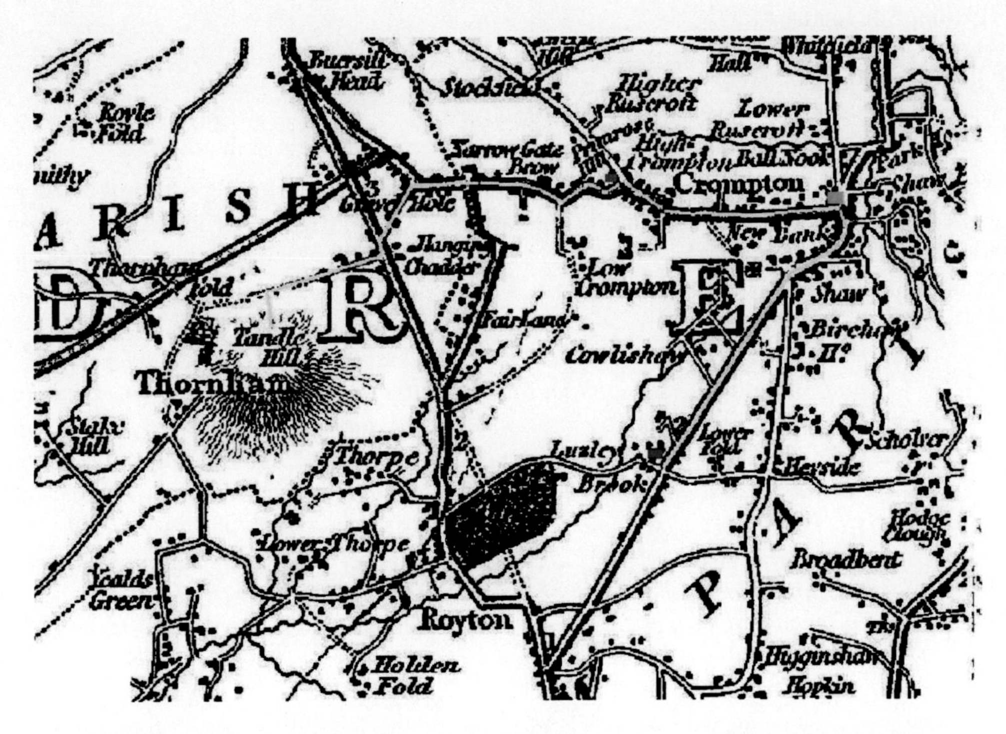

1829 map showing probable rout of machine breakers starting at Tandle Hill

The Oldham mill owners were now in great fear of further attacks on their properties and John Norris advised them:

> *'in the strongest terms to them the absolute necessity of defending their own mills which they appeared very sensible of and got a few arms in for that purpose last night. This system I hope secured our mills in Manchester for the present and is certainly the only one by which such property can in the first instance be defended.'*[106]

The mill owners took heed of this advice and were issued with arms by the Manchester constables. The following arms were issued to the special constables:[107]

	Guns	Pistols	Flints	Cartridges
Thos Wroe	4	6	10	100
Charles Walmsley	3	6	9	90
Josh Rowland	3	6	9	90

[106] HO44/16

[107] Giles Shaw MSS Vol XCII

Cussons & Co	4	5	9	90
Collinge & Lancashire	3	6	9	90
Jas Greaves	1	4	5	50
John Tattersall	1	3	4	40
	20	40	60	600

At around half past twelve, the Rev John Hulme had received the report on the riot at High Crompton whilst at his home in Hollinwood. He immediately rode to Oldham on horseback where the *OTYC* were quartered with the intention of proceeding to Crompton with the *OTYC*. Hulme describes his actions:

> *On my arrival at Oldham, I learnt that a messenger had been sent over from Crompton, with information that the mob, after destroying all the power looms in Mr Clegg's factory at High Crompton, and after an unsuccessful attack on the mills of Messrs. Milne, Travis and Milne, at the village of Shaw and Luzley Brook, had retired and that all was again tranquil in that neighbourhood. Satisfied that there was no necessity for the presence of the military in that quarter, and desirous of learning accurately every minutia of that mornings transaction, I rode on to Crompton, attended by a friend or two, and were learnt from enquiries at Luzley Brook and at Shaw, that the information I had received at Oldham, as far as it applied to these two places, was correct.'*[108]

The disturbance was also felt in Rochdale, one of the local magistrates requested the assistance of the *OTYC,* but was informed by Lieutenant Clegg that they had been told to hold themselves in readiness within the Oldham area by Rev Holme and therefore the services of the troop could not be depended upon at Rochdale.
The night of the Sunday was trouble free but the Monday was to bring more disturbances.
Rev Holme describes the day's events:

> *'About three o'clock on the afternoon of that day, as the officers of the Oldham Troop were at dinner, Mr Travis the younger rode up to the Angel Inn at full speed, with the greatest consternation depicted in his countenance, imploring immediate aid, as an immense body of men, as he stated, were moving from Tandle Hills in the direction of their factories at Luzley Brook and Shaw, and he was apprehensive they had at that time commenced an attack upon them. The Oldham Troop (much to their credit) immediately turned out, and I accompanied them to the spot where the depredators were imagined at that moment to be actually employed in the work of destruction. On our way however, we ascertained that the assemblage of persons on Tandle Hill had retired across the country to Oldham Edge, in the direction of Greenacres Moor where there are several extensive factories, in which are power-looms,*

[108] Wheelers Manchester Chronicle

> *and having satisfied ourselves that all was safe at Luzley Brook and at Shaw, we proceeded direct to Greenacres Moor, where we met with a crowd of some hundreds in the front of Mr Cocks's mill, who had attempted to get admittance and had broken a few squares of glass. At this moment a messenger from Messrs. Collinge and Lancashire, came to inform us that an attack was meditated upon their valuable mills, containing from three to four hundred power-looms, and requesting immediate protection. On our arrival at these mills we found no crowd, but were instantly followed by the concourse of people that we had just left, and in a few minutes the lane along which we had passed was completely blocked up, and some hundreds posted themselves in a field by the side of the lane. Exertions where used by the civil power to make them disperse, but without effect; nor was this accomplished until the Riot Act had been thrice read in different situations. With the exception of a few stones that were thrown, no actual mischief was done, and I have very reason to believe, that the major part of the crowd, who were inhabitants of Oldham, were led thither from more curiosity. It affords me great satisfaction to add, that no further disturbances has since taken place, and I do sincerely hope and trust now that the several mills are ably protected, and the civil and military powers on the alert, that those deluded men who have been the occasion of so much alarm to this neighbourhood, will see the folly of persisting in a system of outrage, which cannot possibly benefit themselves, but lead to their own destruction.'*[109]

The troop remained on permanent duty for a few more days and was finally stood down on 8th May. There must have been some incident with members of the troop, as the returns submitted for the period of the 'call out', show that four men were discharged during this period, one of them for disobeying an order, one for being absent without leave and the other two have no reasons stated. We can only speculate what happened to cause these men to be discharged.
With tension still running high the authorities posted regular infantry into the town, they were billeted into houses at not less than six in a house, in as central situation as possible[110], a guard room was also set up near to the Market Place.

As happened after the events in 1819 the subject of barracking soldiers in the town again came up. A meeting was held by the principle inhabitants on 15th July 1826 to discuss the establishment of a temporary barracks in the town. The officers of the *OTYC* were present at the meeting. The conditions stipulated by the government for having a temporary barracks in the town, was that the town was to furnish buildings for the accommodation of the infantry and government would provide the bedding, fuel and candles. The premises chosen were that of the Angel Inn. Some infantry from the *75th Regiment of Foot* were stationed in the town.

---

[109] Wheelers Manchester Chronicle
[110] Giles Shaw MMS Vol 92

Unfortunately some of the mill owners saw this as an opportunity to reduce the wages of the spinners. They argued that the wages of the spinners were higher in Oldham than the average wages for those in the rest of Lancashire. Consequently in September 1826, the workers from around 14 Oldham mills 'turned out'. This amounted to around 2000 people; in addition, some of the colliers also 'turned out' for similar reasons. The local magistrate, Rev Holme, disagreed with the action of the mill owners and believed them to be in the wrong for agitating a point at a time when trade seemed to be improving [111]. Despite the 'turn out' the mill owners were still able to find enough workers willing to work at the reduced wages. There were some 400 hatters out of employment, who:

> *'would be glad to obtain work on any terms, their earnings, just now, when in full work, do not amount to more than ten shillings a week, for a grown up person.'* For a hatter the wages of the spinners would have been very high, even at the reduced rate the spinners would '*earn from a guinea to twenty five shillings per week.*'[112]

The infantry were used to escort those workers who chose to work and they were on a number of occasions subject to attack from the 'turn out' spinners who threw stones at the troops and workers. On 7th November the 'turn-out' spinners managed to gain entry into the cotton mills of Collinge & Lancashire and also John Lees' mill at Greenacres Moor, and the new workers were targeted and assaulted. Despite Rev Holme's disagreement regarding the reduced wages he was still duty bound to keep the peace as the local magistrate. On this occasion he was accompanied by a number of constabulary and soldiers from the *32nd Regiment of Foot* and he was required to read out the riot act before order was restored.

By November 1826 the 'turn out' spinners had targeted most of the mills for attack and over 200 infantry and a troop of Bays were utilised in protecting the mills and workers. The 'turn out' disturbances continued into 1827 and by the end of January 1827 there was a desire for some of the workers to return to work, but they would not, due to threats of violence from those that would not go back.

Joseph Rowland, of Orleans House, a cotton-spinning manufacturer, wrote to the Secretary of State voicing his concerns and experiences. He claimed that most of his workers wanted to work and had no grievances regarding wages; the only reason they were not at work was because they were being intimidated and threatened by the 'turn-out' mob. He had managed to persuade twenty new workers to come and work at his mill and he would do his utmost to protect them as best as they could. On 17th January around 200 of the 'turn-out' men attempted to gain access to his mill and James Rowland (Joseph's son) went to investigate:

---

[111] HO40/20

[112] HO40/21

> *'.. he found a considerable number of men on the premises, and so soon as he approached them, he was attacked by a man who struck him a violent blow on the face, and he was kicked by several others who would have followed up their attack by worse usage but for the prompt assistance of a mechanic who came to his assistance. This man also got severely beaten and abused for his interference.'*[113]

The arrival of the military aided Rowland in ejecting the men from his factory. The 'turn-out' mob then took out their frustrations on those men who had been working at the mill:

> *'At the house of a spinner named Rhodes, the party proceeded to acts of violence. They forcibly entered his house in great numbers, broke the windows, and they threw the clothes out of the door, destroyed some and damaged other parts of the furniture and abused the family making use of very violent and threatening language.'*[114]

The mob returned two days later but were again dispersed by the military, during the same evening, after dark, two shots were fired into two dwellings of Master Spinners in the neighbourhood but fortunately without doing any damage to the family at either place who were in the room at the time the shots entered.[115]
A few days later there was a further clash when the workers at a few of the mills were compelled to leave work by the turn-out spinners, this time the head constable supported by *2nd Dragoon Guards* secured and arrested ten of the 'turn out' spinners. Over this period of disruption a total of 33 men were arrested and subsequently convicted at Lancaster.
The mill owners were highly reliant on the military and the under-secretary of state, Henry Hobhouse, in a letter to General Sir John Byng was critical of the Oldham mill owners:

> *'the backwardness of the mill owners to defend their own property and begs you will impress upon them the impossibility for the Guards to afford them an adequate defence, if they are not true to themselves.'*[116]

By the end of January there were still around 500 'turned-out', these men had now been away from work for 21 weeks, but by the beginning of February these men had also given in and gone back to work. Discontent still prevailed and a number of public meetings occurred over the next few months but all of them passed off peacefully. One such meeting was held on the 19th March on Bent Green, opposite the Hare and

---

[113] HO40/22
[114] HO40/22
[115] HO40/22
[116] HO40/22

Hounds public house. Two carts joined together with benches and an armchair placed within them, for the use of the chairman, speakers and press reporters. The purpose of the meeting was to discuss the poor economic state and its cause, draw up a number of resolutions, including a resolution calling for the total repeal of the *Corn Laws* and the resolutions to be printed and presented to both Houses of Parliament.
Throughout this latter period of disturbance the *OTYC* were not called out due to the large presence of the military force already in the town.

Training and Exercise

The period for training was a minimum of six days per year, initially Captain Taylor requested that the first training session in 1818 should be at Knutsford, Cheshire, but as it was outside of the county of Lancashire it was refused.[117] Instead it was proposed to train at Wigan from 24th June for six days and for two days marching to and from Wigan. They marched out of Oldham on 23rd June and Rowbottom describes them as:

> *'fine looking men commanded by Captain Taylor'*. On their return to Oldham *'they sat down to a sumptuous dinner at the Angel Inn where they were received with every demonsteration of joy by a numerous but select party of friends the bells ringing and demosterations of joy.'*[118]

Whilst being trained they were paid an allowance by the War Office of 2s per man and 1s 4d per horse per day.
The following year training took place at Preston, marching out from Oldham on 22nd June 1819, for six days training. On the march to and from training camp the *OTYC* travelled light, all their arms, accoutrements, clothes and other necessities were sent ahead of them on horse drawn carriages.[119]
In 1820, the *OTYC* again took their training at Preston, marching out on 14th June. The venue for training during the years of 1821 and 1822 was changed to Warrington, marching out of Oldham on 31st May and 20th June respectively. Again the training period was for six days. In 1823 they were back at Wigan for their training. In 1826 they went to Blackpool in June and the final training camp was held at Waterloo, Crosby in October 1827.
Besides the official training required by the government, training was also performed on a weekly basis, making use of the troop's riding school that had been constructed with money from the subscription fund.
The *OTYC* held a field day once a year; this was normally at Chadderton Hall Park. During this field day they would demonstrate the cavalry manoeuvres that they had been practising. Once a year they were inspected by an officer of the regular cavalry, during the inspection it would be put through the manoeuvres to the satisfaction of the

---

[117] HO51/89
[118] Rowbottom's Diary
[119] LRO- QSP/2754/218

inspecting officer. The inspections were also carried out in the park at Chadderton Hall. The inspections and field days were popular with the public and normally attracted a large number of spectators.

Uniform, arms and accoutrements

The *OTYC* was given an allowance for contingency, clothing and accoutrements and was applied to the Home Office, to cover a three year period. On 7th October 1817 these allowances were applied for to cover a period from 25th June 1817 to the 24th June 1820. For contingencies an allowance of £4.10s per man for the three year period was given. To cover clothing and accoutrements the same amount of £4.10s per man was allowed.[120]

In July 1817 the War Office issued the troop with 46 swords, 46 sword belts, 46 pistols, 46 sword knots and one trumpet. Captain Taylor made a request for the troop to be furnished with pistol pouches, belts and sabretaches as the subscription fund raised for the troop had been depleted due to:

> '*the erection of a Riding School, there being no building or other convenience in the Town that would admit of being adapted to that use. The money appended upon this object and the expense that must unavoidably be incurred in providing the building in question were not at all foreseen on the first establishment of the Troop and are now found to consume so large a portion of the fund subscribed for its formation and maintenance that it is deemed necessary to solicit you Lordships good Offices to procure a supply of the articles in question*'[121].

This request was denied due to no stocks of that description in the Government stores.[122]

The officers privately purchased blue and gilt 1796 pattern cavalry swords. The swords, purchased from Thomas Gill of Birmingham, where elaborately decorated, on one side of the blade is a mounted Hussar, a King George cipher with

[120] WO13/4008
[121] HO50/360
[122] HO51/89

Georgian Crown, a depiction of a flag and trumpet and lastly the cartouche of "OTYC".
On the other side of the blade it has drums and flags, the manufacturer's name "Gills" with the word "Warranted", a Royal coat of arms, an angel with horn and the name of the owner.
It is known that Captain Taylor, Lieutenant Taylor, Cornet Taylor and Quarter Master Clegg all had these swords with their names etched on them.

In July 1821, on the coronation day of King George IV, the *OTYC* took part in the celebrations. At 12 o'clock the procession formed in Lord Street and proceeded to Greenacres Moor, then to Hollinwood and back to Market Place where the National Anthem was sung and three volleys fired by the Royal Veterans and the Yeomanry.
The Yeomanry Trumpets, followed by a section of the Yeomanry, led the procession. The procession was formed and conducted by James Mellor of Manchester Street. Afterwards Captain Taylor treated the *OTYC* to a dinner.

There appears to be no information or records regarding the uniform of the Oldham Troop, the only possible indication we have is the sketch of a mounted Yeoman at the top of the poem written to the Secretary of the *OTYC* as a New Year's gift. It is not known if this is a generic depiction or a specific depiction of the *OTYC*.

Sketch of Yeomanry from a New Year's gift poem to the Secretary of OTYC[123]

[123] By kind permission of the County Archivist, Lancashire Record Office Ref DDX818/39

On 25th August 1825 the members of the *OTYC* mustered to acknowledge their Captain and:

> *'had a grand day on presenting their Captain Taylor with a superb silver cup, value £100 and a gold hilted sword. The day was very fine and a great deal of people of all denominations. There was ringing of bells and other demonstrations of joy, and a select band of music, which played several martial airs on the occasion.'*[124]

Guidon of the Oldham Troop of Yeomanry Cavalry

A guidon is a heraldic banner carried by cavalry regiments, the equivalent of the colours borne by regiments of line infantry. Up until the end of the 19th century, guerdons and colours were taken into battle as the distinguishing symbols and rallying points for fighting units.

The word derives from the Italian guidone meaning 'guide' or 'marker' and the Middle French corruption guyd-hommes; hence it is the focus for soldiers in battle. For a very long time, soldiers have given high regard to these talismans of identity, and so it is today.

Captain John Taylor's mother presented the guidon for the *OTYC* to the troop on 21st June 1819, the day before marching out to Preston for their annual training.[125]

We are extremely lucky in the fact that such a delicate artefact has survived to the present time.

The guidon previously hung in the west gallery of St Mary's Church Oldham, presumably placed there when the troop disbanded. It was left to rot and disintegrate and at some stage fell from the west wing and was eventually found in the late 1980s behind the altar in a number of pieces. The guidon was donated to the *Duke of Lancaster's Own Yeomanry Cavalry Museum*, who duly renovated it.

The guidon is blazoned on the obverse side with the Oldham coat of arms and with the words "OLDHAM TROOP OF" on the upper scroll and "YEOMANRY CAVALRY" on the lower scroll.

The shield is sable (black) with a gold chevron between three owls and a chief (upper part of shield) gold, the latter charged with three roses. The roses differ from the modern Oldham coat of arms, which has three red rings.

Either side of the shield are oak branches, which are traditionally a sign of loyalty. On the crest of the shield is a royal crown and to the left of the crown is a branch with a rose and the right side is a branch and thistle.

The motto below the shield is "Haud (pronounced "owd") Facile Captu" (meaning "Not easily caught" - a reference no doubt to the canniness of the local populace). This

---

[124] Rowbottom's Diary
[125] Rowbottom's Diary

motto is no longer used and the current motto is "Sapere Aude" (meaning "Dare to be wise" - the "Aude" also being pronounced "Owd").
On the reverse side is a very interesting Royal Coat of arms, as the guidon was presented in 1819 you would expect to see the coat of arms for George III, but the coat of arms depicted are those that were last used by Queen Elizabeth I. The shield is encircled with the Order of the Garter with its motto "HONI SOIT QUI MAL Y PENSE" (meaning "Evil be unto him who evil thinks").
The supporters are a chained antelope and a spotted heraldic panther and it could be that these are the badges of Henry VI. Maybe this coat of arms is being used to show some form of loyalty to the last Lancastrian monarch?
The motto underneath the Royal Coat of Arms is the usual "DIEU ET MON DROIT" (meaning "God and my right").

Guidon of the Oldham Troop of Yeomanry Cavalry
Original painting by Mandi Wilkinson

End of the OTYC

In December 1827 a letter from Lord Lansdowne (the Secretary of State for the Home Department) to Lord Derby drawing attention to the desirability of seeing that any Yeomanry Corps retained in the future should be at least three troops strong, and each troop to consist of not less than 50 men. A further letter suggesting the amalgamation of all corps whose strength were less than three troops followed a week or so later. In consequence of this, a meeting of the officers of the Bolton, Wigan and Furness Yeomanry was held at Preston in March 1828. Captain John Taylor did not go to this meeting as it had already been decided that the *OTYC* was not going to continue, in a letter from Robert Peel at the Home Office to Lord Derby he mentions a letter from Captain Taylor:

> *'It appears from Captain Taylor's statement that he entertains no hope of retaining his troop by any means wither by enrolment of new members, or by incorporation with other troops, to the standard prescribed in the circular letter...'*[126].

The purpose of the meeting at Preston was to adopt the measures of uniting the three corps of Bolton, Wigan and Furness into one regiment. On 18th April 1828, the amalgamation was approved and the *Lancashire Corps of Yeomanry Cavalry* was formed. This Corps eventually became known as the *Duke of Lancaster's Own Corps of Yeomanry Cavalry* in 1834.

It is likely that the demise of the *OTYC* is down to the fact that by the beginning of 1827 trade had greatly improved in the manufacturing districts of Lancashire, due to a demand in Europe for the low priced goods being produced in the area. In addition to this improved trade, an act was passed on 26th May 1826:

> *'An Act for paving, watching, lighting, cleansing, and improving the Township of Oldham in the County of Lancaster, and for regulating the Police thereof.'*[127],

The passing of this act appeared to have the desired effect in Oldham as a letter from the Home Office to the manufacturer Collinge and Lancashire states:

> *'that the workmen have returned to their labour and particularly that the provisions of the new Police Act have had so good an effect in accelerating that desirable event.'*[128]

[126] HO51/93
[127] GIV, Cap CXVII
[128] HO41/7

Perhaps it was felt that this improvement in the town's police reduced the need for a Yeomanry troop to be maintained in the town.

After the demise of the *OTYC* there is a period of 45 years before it makes its return to Oldham, when in January 1873 an Oldham Troop is formed as part of the *Duke of Lancaster's Own Corps of Yeomanry Cavalry*.

Oldham Rifle Volunteers 1859 – 1908

After the Napoleonic wars ended in 1815 there followed a long period of peace in Europe. With no threat of an invasion of England's shores then there was no real need for a volunteer force. Very few volunteer forces survived, the exception being the Yeomanry corps, but their main role was not defending against an external enemy but more for controlling an internal enemy. The only other volunteer units to survive were the *Honourable Artillery Company* and the *Royal Victoria Rifle Regiment.*

By the end of the 1840s affairs in Europe were beginning to change; revolutions within Europe were causing tensions throughout the continent. Napoleon III's coup in France in December 1851 prompted a number of offers from around the country to form volunteer corps, the government rejected most of these offers as they felt there was no real necessity for them. An offer was accepted by government in March 1852 from a group of middle-class citizens to form an Exeter and South Devon corps to protect the Devon coast. The formation of this corps seems to be an exception.

After a number of scares, matters came to a head in 1858. An Italian, Felice Orsini was involved in a bomb attempt on the life of Napoleon III on 14th January 1858 whilst on his way to the opera. Napoleon survived the attempt on his life, but the French discovered that Orsini had connections with England, he had associations with fellow refugees in London and the bomb was alleged to have been manufactured in Birmingham. Orsini's objectives were to gain a free and united Italy. There followed increased tension between England and France, with demands, mainly from French Army generals on their Emperor, to call England to account for harbouring and aiding the bomb plotters. In April 1859 France went to war with the Austro-Hungarian Empire in Italy and the French gained some quick victories. The Austrians were pushed out of Lombardy and Europe appeared to be on the brink of war. The war was averted through the treaty of Villafranca, but it did not stop the French from building up their naval fleet. In response England, under Lord Palmerston, the Prime Minister, began a programme of building coastal forts. This also sparked off calls, especially by the British press, for volunteer units to be raised for the defence of England. One of the arguments put forward was that the presence of volunteer corps would prevent the recurrence of invasion panics that the country appeared to suffer from every few years. In May 1859 *The Times* printed a poem by Tennyson entitled 'The War' which appeared to reflect on the mood of many of the public over the suspicion of Napoleon and France.

> There is a sound of thunder afar
> Storm in the South that darkens the day
> Storm of battle and thunder of war!
> Well, if it do not roll away,
> Storm, Storm, Riflemen form!
> Ready, be ready, against the storm!
> Rifleman, riflemen, riflemen form!

Let your reforms for a moment go!
Look to your butts and take good aims!
Better a rotten borough or so,
Then a rotten flesh and a city in flames!
Storm, Storm, Riflemen form!
Ready, be ready, against the storm!
Rifleman, riflemen, riflemen form!

Tennyson 'The War'

That month the government succumbed to public pressure and found the constitutional means of accepting volunteer corps by dusting off the original 1804 Yeomanry and Volunteer Act, which had never been repealed. The only other alternative the government had to the volunteers would be to re-introduce the Militia ballot to increase the home defence, but this would probably have been a very unpopular move. The biggest attraction for the government was that any volunteer corps that was raised would have to be funded by themselves, by way of public subscription, thus the volunteers would be a cheap alternative to the Militia.
On 12th May 1859, the Secretary of War sent a circular to all of the Lords Lieutenant of counties. This circular summarised the main provisions of this 1804 Act. This was the catalyst for public meetings throughout the UK to discuss the possibilities of raising volunteer units. A further circular was issued in July confirming the conditions of service.
Some of the provisions in the circulars were:

> *'In all cases of actual invasion or appearance of any enemy in force on the coast of Great Britain, or if rebellion or insurrection arising or existing within the same, or the appearance of any enemy in force on the coast, or during any invasion, but not otherwise, the services of the Volunteer Force will extend to any part of Great Britain.*
> *That members should not quit the corps when on actual service, but might do so at any other time by giving 14 days notice.*
> *That members who had attended 8 days in each 4 months, or a total of 24 days drill or exercise in the year, be entitled to return as effective.*
> *That all property of the corps be legally vested in the commanding officer and subscriptions and fines under the rules and regulations be recovered by him before a magistrate.'*

Establishment of a corps was fixed at one Captain, one Lieutenant and one Ensign for a company consisting of 60 to 100 men.
County precedence numbers were allocated according to the date of the first unit within a county offering its services to government. As a corps had been formed earlier at Exeter then Devonshire was given first precedence, with Middlesex second and

Lancashire was third. Within each county then corps numbers were also allocated generally on dates of acceptance but not strictly so. See *Appendix 10* for allocation numbers of the Lancashire Rifle volunteer corps.
By the autumn of 1859 there were around 60,000 volunteers and by June 1860 the number of volunteers had reached 130,000.
The *Oldham Chronicle* reported on the poem by Tennyson and suggested that it might have been written to order by the government, the *Oldham Chronicle* looked on the formation of rifle volunteers suspiciously and felt that the current invasion panic was one of those that seemed to affect the country periodically.

> *'The last phase of the mania is the formation of rifle corps to consist of gentlemen volunteers who can pay for their own equipments, and who will submit to be under the control of the War Office, but they will have the satisfaction of playing at soldiers and may perhaps cheat themselves into the belief that they can beat back the grim invasion spectre that has glared so ominously on our national prospects for some time past.'*[129]

The *Oldham Chronicle* felt the formation of volunteers was a device of the Tory government for the suppression of liberalism and made references to previous volunteers such as the Yeomanry and their actions at *Peterloo.*
There were reports in July that:

> *'the greatest activity prevails all along the French coast, the channel coast especially being fortified; and from Cherbourg to Dunkirk earth batteries are being constructed every 3,000 yards.'*[130]

In July the *Oldham Chronicle* was still claiming it was a Tory device to impede parliamentary reform and was even stating that the rifle corps movement has proved to be a failure, as it had not attracted the numbers expected as yet.

Raising of the Oldham Rifle Volunteers

The raising of a Rifle Volunteer corps in Oldham was by no means an easy affair, they were certainly not one of the first to be raising a unit, but they were far from last. Arguments were raised in the local Oldham press via readers' letters to the merits and motives of such a force. A typical letter in favour of the volunteers:

> *'I cannot but think that Oldham has been somewhat tardy in this matter, although no one can suppose that we are a whit less loyal and patriotic than our neighbours. I hope, Sir, that the public meeting which I believe is to be called next week will be attended by men of all sorts and conditions, actuated*

[129] Oldham Chronicle
[130] Oldham Chronicle

by a right and proper feeling, and not by a mere love of display; men who will be ready to take their places in the ranks, caring nothing whether their front rank man be a millionaire or a man with an income only large enough to keep his head above the water, whether his right hand man wear broadcloth or fustian. Above all, let us beware of making that mistake which so nearly proved fatal to the movement in Manchester. I mean the keeping of the affair "select". I think the working men of Oldham are quite as fit to be trusted with a rifle as their more fortunate brethren, many of whom live in ease and luxury through no exertion of their own. If this letter has merely the effect of inducing a few to attend the public meeting who might have stayed away it will not have been written in vain. I remain Sir, yours respectfully, A THOROUGH BRITON'[131]

It was not until 17th November 1859 before a meeting was called to discuss forming Rifle Volunteers in Oldham. A second meeting was held in the Masonic Hall of the Angel Inn on 24th November, and was called to consider the propriety of establishing a volunteer corps for Oldham. John George Blackburne, a local civil engineer, chaired the meeting. The cost of establishing a corps of Rifle Volunteers Corps was a main discussion point. At this stage the government had now agreed to supply the volunteers with 50% of the rifles and it was very likely that the government would agree to supply 100% of rifles soon. It was estimated that the cost of the uniform and accoutrements would not be more than £3, with an annual expense of around £1 per man. They believed that they would be able to obtain a suitable room for the purpose of drilling for very little cost. There was an effort by Blackburne to try and ensure that the corps was not just for those who could afford the fees:

'There might be parties willing to become members of a rifle corps in Oldham able to pay for their uniform and accoutrements, but he should suggest that every one should subscribe to one fund for the purpose of providing uniform and accoutrements. A man willing to provide his own could put that amount into the common fund, and let all have their uniform out of the general fund, which would do away with invidious distinctions, and would make all the members as equal as possible. Those parties willing to serve in a volunteer corps, whose means would not justify them in finding all their accoutrements, were as entitled to honourable notice as the man who found everything; in fact, there was greater credit to them for coming forward. On that account he would subscribe to a general fund, and all the cost of clothing and accoutrements to be paid for out of that general fund; and not let one say, "I will find myself", and others say, "I require some assistance."' [132]

---

[131] Oldham Chronicle
[132] Oldham Chronicle

The meeting also discussed in what capacity the volunteers could be used by the government and it was made clear that the volunteers could not be called together by government for civil disputes, neither be called to Ireland. The only purpose they could be called is for actual or imminent invasion.
At the end of the meeting Mr J.W.Mellor made a proposal:

> *'That it is the opinion of this meeting that it is desirable that a rifle corps should be formed in Oldham upon economical working principles, and that a deputation be appointed to wait upon the Mayor to convene a public meeting for the purpose of calling the attention of the inhabitants of the borough to the rifle corps movement" (Applause). Mr John Bamford seconded the motion.'* [133]

By the end of the meeting 30 persons had put forward their names to be volunteers.
On 30th November a public meeting was held in the town hall presided by the Mayor, Abraham Leach. There was a very large attendance, the town hall was densely packed and a large number of people were left outside unable to get in. The Mayor outlined the reasons for forming a volunteer corps, mainly that France over the last two years had been busy building up its army and especially its navy and that it was natural for England to feel alarm because France had but few colonies to defend, and there had been some fear on the part of the English that the French navy might be employed against England.
John G Blackburne then proposed a resolution:

> *'That this meeting is of opinion that it is desirable to aid in the national defence of the country, by forming a volunteer rifle corps in this borough'.*

Blackburne argued that the force was a force truly belonging to the people. It was a force especially for the preservation of peace, and it was not in any way connected with war. He was not of opinion that there was any probability of a war; he thought there was no occasion to fear any war, but he thought at the same time there was a possibility of war, and he thought this country should not be in the risk of a possibility. Mr W.E.Rudolph seconded the resolution.
Besides there being a great many in favour of the formation of the volunteer corps, there was also a large number who were against it. Mr James Schofield, proposed an amendment to the resolution, which he said was supported by gentlemen of great ability. The amendment was:

> *'That in the opinion of this meeting, the agitation for volunteer rifle corps to repel an invasion, is uncalled for and useless, and is resorted to as a means of diverting the people from those great reforms of representation and taxation which the condition of the working classes so urgently demands at the present time.'*

---

[133] Oldham Chronicle

Schofield argued that the rifles were not intended to defend the rights of the people, but to be used as the rifles were during the French war and *Peterloo* agitation. His firm opinion was that, if they allowed rifle corps to be foisted on them, the condition of the people would never be ameliorated; but if they first got their grievances redressed, then, like the Americans and Swiss, they would use one rifle because they had one vote. G.H.Fea seconded the amended resolution. John W Mellor then rose to support the first resolution, but explained that his politics were those of the radical, he was old enough to witness the deed of *Peterloo* and had been a radical at heart ever since. He believed in vote by ballot, equal electoral districts and no property qualifications. In spite of this he believed the volunteer movement would be carried on with honest English spirit, honest English hearts would be able to defend their hearths and homes, their liberties and rights, their wealth and privileges, their wives and children. Mellor's speech caused great applause and confusion within the hall and the next speaker could not be heard. The arguments continued for some time, many of those against the volunteers argued that the volunteer rifleman could be used to suppress the populace, but Blackburne assured them that the rifle volunteers were not the same as the Yeomanry:

> *'Peterloo and all those places which had been mentioned were things of the past and now met with universal reprobation and had nothing to do with the rifle corps, which could not be called out in civil disturbances'*

The Mayor then put both resolutions to the hall, but no decision could be made either way, so they were put to the hall again. It was difficult to determine which had won, in the body of the hall the amended resolution appeared to have a very slight majority but when they took into consideration the platform, it appeared there was a slight majority in favour of the original resolution.
Nathan Worthington Esq. then moved:

> *'That a public subscription be raised to assist in arming and equipping such volunteers as may enrol themselves in accordance with the preceding resolution.'*

The meeting had lasted nearly three hours and ended with Mr John Bamford saying of the public meeting that:

> *'the motion had been fairly won, and after the fair expression of opinion they had heard that night, he felt prouder of Oldham than ever.'*

It was a narrow victory for the supporters of the rifle volunteers; the meeting was a sign of the ill feelings the volunteers would have to endure in their early days from those who considered them as a Tory political device to divert attention from political reform. Similar objections at a public meeting in Rochdale were also shown to the raising of rifle volunteers. By 1861 the government made a deliberate effort to distance the Rifle Volunteer Corps from politics by banning volunteer meetings and drill at election times.

Now that the formation of a rifle corps for Oldham had been agreed the next step was to swear in volunteers and choose the officers. On 10th December a meeting was held at the Masonic Hall, Chapel Street at which Nathan Worthington, Esq., Deputy Lieutenant was present for the purpose of swearing in the volunteers. The form of joining consisted of taking an oath of allegiance to the sovereign:

> *'I A.B. , do make oath that I will be faithful and bear true allegiance to Her Majesty, her heirs and successors; that I will, as in duty bound, honestly and faithfully defend to Her Majesty, her heirs and successors, in person, crown, and dignity, against all enemies, and will observe and obey all orders of Her Majesty, her heirs and successors, and of the generals and officers set over me. So help me God.'*

Worthington explained that he had written to Lord Sefton the Lord Lieutenant for Lancashire, regarding the formation of the Oldham Volunteer Rifle Corps. Lord Sefton had written back and advised that before he could ask for Her Majesty's approval and acceptance of the corps he should have to be informed (in compliance with the War Office memorandum) that the corps had obtained the necessary range for ball practice of at least 200 yards, a safe place of custody for the arms, and a competent person to take charge of them.[134] If this information had been provided with the initial request perhaps Oldham would have been designated with a lower number to the one that was eventually allocated.

The rules for the corps were discussed and agreed and an election of the officers was made. The following appointments were made: - Captain, Mr J.G.Blackburne; Lieutenant, Hilton Greaves; Ensign, William Blackburne; Paymaster (position later changed to treasurer), Mr J.W.Mellor. By the end of the meeting the total sworn in as volunteers was 58. By 17th December the total of those attested stood at 72 with a further 20 having given in their names but not yet attested.

One of the rules of the corps was that a committee of management should be formed; this was to consist of the Captain, Lieutenant, ensign, four volunteers and the paymaster. The four volunteers appointed were Messrs Samuel Murgatroyd, Christopher Brakell, Humphrey Goodwin, and G.F.Bradley. Mr J.F.Tweedale was appointed as Honorary Secretary.

Immediately after the public meeting subscription books were opened at the District and Saddleworth banks in Oldham for those wishing to subscribe to the Oldham Volunteers. For those that wished to support them, but did not want to be an active member, then they could become an honorary member of the 1st company if they subscribed 5 guineas or more. By the end of January 1860 the subscription fund stood at £420 and by the end of 1860 it had reached £907.19s.6d.

---

[134] Oldham Chronicle

The newly formed Oldham Rifle Volunteers wasted no time in attempting to get themselves organised, by the middle of December 1859 the uniform was more or less decided upon and they were carrying out drill practice three evenings per week in a room at Mr Gillham's hat factory on Henshaw Street. Sergeant Major Holt was conducting the drill practice.
With the officers selected the next process was to select and appoint non-commissioned officers (NCOs). These appointments were the privilege of the commanding officer, Captain Blackburne, but he decided to waive his right and allow the men to elect their own. Mr George Hamilton was appointed chairman. The number of NCOs, to be appointed was nine, consisting of four corporals, four sergeants and a sergeant major. It was decided that the votes should be taken by ballot, the nine who obtained the highest number of votes to be the non-commissioned officers, and the votes to be taken again to determine their grade. The result of the voting was that the following gentlemen were selected: Messrs Schofield. King Mowbray, G.B.Nield, H.Tipping, S.Murgatroyd, James Whitehead, Bradbury, J.F.Tweedale, and J.Waterhouse. Mr Tweedale and Mr Whitehead thanked the corps for the honour they had received in being selected as non-commissioned officers, but for sufficient reasons declined to serve. Mr William Wild, and Mr Joseph Gillham, was selected to fill the vacancies caused by the resignations, and the votes were then openly taken on the question of sergeants and sergeant major. The result was that Mr T.F.Schofield was appointed Sergeant Major, and Messers King Mowbray, H.Tipping, G.B.Neild and S.Murgatroyd, sergeants. The rest of the gentlemen selected by ballot were appointed corporals.
Captain Blackburne had set a precedent by allowing the NCOs to be chosen under a ballot by the men and when a couple of months later a position for sergeant arose and he appointed a man of his own choice, it led to complaints of undue partiality.
It took another month for the choice of the ground for the firing range to be finalised and inspected. The chosen ground was Chadderton Park where a government representative inspected a rifle practice ground of 350 yards. The place chosen as a secure place for the rifles was the Town Hall. With these two places now settled, the official approval of the corps could now be granted and this was done on 1st February 1860 and the corps was given the designation the *31st Lancashire Rifle Volunteers*.
In celebration of the raising of the *31st Lancashire Rifle Volunteers* a song was published in the *Oldham Chronicle*, sung to the tune of 'The British Grenadiers'.

Some sing of love and beauty,
Of rosy cheeks, bright eyes –
Some sing of war and duty,
The path where honour lies;
But I sing of a noble band
Of hearts that know no fears-
An honour to the native land,
The Rifle Volunteers!

Chorus:
Then Come! Arouse ye! While ye may,
And give three hearty cheers,
Hip, hip, hurrah! hurrah! hurrah!
For the Rifle Volunteers.

Our ancestors have striven
A noble name to bear,
And to their sons have given
The laurel wreath to wear.
Then I ask, will they abuse it
With girlish doubts and fears?
There are some who ne'er will loose it,
The Rifle Volunteers!
Chorus

If Frenchmen dare attack them,
And prove a false ally;
A lovely Queen to back them
They'll either win or die.
Fight well, too, for their country's weal,
Their English homes, and dears,
With "hearts of oak" and arms of steel,
The Rifle Volunteers!
Chorus

Long may they live to cherish
The fondest hopes they've made,
And never see them perish
In sunshine or in shade;
But, as they gently glide along
Adown the vale of years,
But this the burden of their song,
The Rifle Volunteers!
Chorus

OLDHAM - M

It appears that this song was not adopted as the Corps official song; in the early years the *31st LRV* adopted song was '*A sound was heard on England's shores*'.

The early years

Raising the numbers of the Corps progressed steadily and by August 1860 it had its full complement of 100 men and with still more wishing to join, motions were set in place to raise a second company. With the subscription fund continuing to grow and as an inducement to recruit more men, the entrance and subscription fees were reduced. Terms of admittance were: Entrance and subscriptions £1.10s. Volunteers to pay one-third on enrolment, and the remainder by instalments of not less than one shilling per week, and a yearly subscription of £1.1s to be paid at the commencement of each year, or not later than the 31st March.
In the first 18 months of the *31st LRV*'s existence they were still being met with opposition from a section of the Oldham public, quite often volunteers walking the Oldham streets dressed in uniform would be met with 'offensive epithets'. The local nickname given to the Oldham volunteers was 'Saturday neet sodgers'[135]
By September 1860 the second company was large enough to appoint its officers; Thomas Evans Lees Esq. of Hathershaw House to be Captain. Daniel Greaves of Derker to be Lieutenant, Joseph Rowland, Jun, Esq. of Rushbank to be Ensign, and by the end of October the second company was complete and the raising of a third company was in place, with a renewed appeal to the public for subscriptions to help clothe and equip them. By the end of 1860 the third company was nearly complete and appointed as their Captain was Dr Samuel.H.Armitage. John.W.Mellor was appointed as Lieutenant and James Frederick Tweedale as Ensign. Officers' appointments were proposed by the corps commander to the Lord Lieutenant, and ultimately the appointment of all officers was vested by an Act of Parliament in the Lord Lieutenant, subject to the Queens approval.
To be an officer in the Corps required a man of some wealth or a very healthy income and was certainly beyond the means of most. In addition to the subscriptions the officers were obliged to pay more towards the funds of the Corps and the following resolutions were made:

> *'Contributions by the officers to the funds of their respective companies, namely-*
> *Captain £20, Lieutenant £15, Ensign £10. Sergeants to pay £3 and corporal 30s (The privates paying 21s according to the rules)*
> *2. That the following officers contribute annually to the regimental fund, the undermentioned sums – namely:*
> *Major £40, Captain Commandt £5, (in addition to his contribution of £20 to his own company fund) Surgeon £5 5s and Chaplain £3 3s.*
> *3. That the regimental fund be applied to the annual payment for the band – the expenses of drill ground, drill rooms and practice ground as well as all other similar general expenditure.*

[135] Oldham Chronicle

4. That each company contributes in equal proportions to the general regimental fund out of their respective companies, the first call being based upon an estimate of the whole expense and the second call upon the actual cost of the year.
5. That the fees and subscriptions appertaining to the three companies be placed into Saddleworth Bank to the credit of their respective captain and that all cheques be signed by them and countersigned by the treasurer of the corps.
6. That the regimental fund be paid into the same bank to the credit of the commanding officer and that the cheque be signed for by him and countersigned by the treasurer.'[136]

In addition to the above subscriptions the officers were also expected to contribute prize money towards the Corps shooting competitions. Officers' drill night was Wednesday and to encourage high attendance a fine of 1s was inflicted for non-attendance.

Fund raising also played an important part for the corps in the early years, raising money from subscriptions alone was not enough, as money was also needed to be raised for the erection of a suitable armoury and drill ground. The Corps organised various events to raise money. A large crowd paid to watch the first event on 21st April 1860, a concert review with music by the newly formed corps band and other musicians. A patriotic song called 'Come who dare' written by the Corps' treasurer, John.W.Mellor was also sung. The Corps also raised its own amateur dramatic group and performed the 'Three Musketeers' to a packed audience in the Working Men's Hall. The following year the Corps amateur dramatics group put on more performances, this time at the Theatre Royal. One of these performances was a comedy called 'The Wonder!, A woman keeps a secret'.
In January 1861 and February 1862 a 'Volunteers Ball' was held at the Town Hall, which attracted many of the high society of Oldham and surrounding areas. A room in the Town Hall was highly decorated with royal coats of arms, rifles and cutlasses. The floor of the hall was covered in cloth; the outside steps at the front of the hall were carpeted. About 200 ladies and gentlemen attended the event. Volunteers were present from Ashton, Saddleworth, Manchester, Salford, Macclesfield, Sheffield, Liverpool and Heywood. Entry to the ball was 10s for gentlemen, 5s for ladies and 7s 6d for volunteers in uniform. Proceeds from the Volunteers Ball went into the regimental fund. During these early years the social activities of the volunteers was an important part for many of the members, in July 1860 a social outing was arranged to Lyme Park for the members along with their Lady friends, the day was marred by rain but a good time was had in a local pub, on returning to Oldham an impromptu ball was held at the Angel Inn. The following year the excursion was to Worsley Hall, there were around 100 on the trip, around 60 of them volunteers in uniform, plus a large number of ladies. The volunteers were met by the band belonging to *Duke of Lancaster's Own Yeomanry*

---

[136] Minutes Book of 31st LRV held at Chetham's Library

Corps; they then toured the buildings and grounds of Worsley Hall. Dinner was served in the town hall.

Drill for the *31st LRV* was organised in any room that could be made available, which included the Parish School and rooms of local manufacturers. Drill instruction was under the care of Sergeant Major Holt, late of the *6th Dragoon Guards*. This situation could not continue indefinitely and the corps was now well enough established to warrant its own facilities.
By June 1861 the *31st LRV* had secured a 900 year lease on a plot of land on the Intake for the purpose of erecting an armoury, drill hall and drill ground. Issuing £700 of shares at £1 per share raised part of the capital. The armoury was also to include a dwelling for the drill sergeant.
The indoor drill room was to be a modest 71 feet by 33 feet and the outside drill ground was 165 feet by 144 feet. A plot of land was also reserved for the building of a gymnasium.
The construction of the armoury and drill room was done in such away that they could be easily converted into dwellings, just in case the volunteer movement came to an end, an indication that the officers of the *31st LRV* were astute businessmen.
Construction began in September 1861 and the volunteers were using the new indoor drill hall in February 1862.

Interest in the rifle volunteer movement continued to grow in Oldham and there was a large interest from the local Irish immigrant population. By July 1862 plans were in motion to raise a fourth company and due to the high proportion of Irish in this company, it was for a while known as the Irish company. Within a month, enough recruits had been obtained for the fourth company and Captain Blackburne offered its services to the Lord Lieutenant. This increase in strength of the Corps to four companies also enabled Captain Blackburne to be promoted to Major Commanding, thus leaving him to concentrate his duties on the overall command of the Corps, as the first company was now in the charge of the newly promoted Captain Abraham Crompton.
The recent building of the armoury and drill ground still had to be paid for and in August 1863 a bazaar was organised, mainly by the ladies of Oldham, to try to liquidate the debt. The bazaar was held at the armoury and included:

> *'marionettes, a small tent for photographic portrait gallery, shooting gallery, a piping bullfinch, large set of 'dobby horses', one corner of the ground was devoted to the renowned 'Aunt Sally', dressed in her holiday garb, and who appears to withstand any amount of blows from those who are disposed to have a try at her.'*[137]

The bazaar was a success and raised £500 towards paying off the debt.

---

[137] Oldham Standard

In 1862, the numbers of Volunteers in the country stood at 162,000. The government carried out a review of the state of the Volunteer Force and a commission was set up to interview respected commanding officers of Volunteers, from around the country. Captain Blackburne was one of the 51 officers and witnesses invited to London, to be interviewed by the commission. In his interview Captain Blackburne expressed his opinion that, with the exception of one or two Corps in Lancashire, he believed that the Volunteers would need financial support from government to continue, they could not continue to rely on monetary support from the public and honorary members. He also believed the Volunteers:

> *'certainly never can be placed on a solid foundation so long as you have to obtain subscriptions from the men in addition to the time they devote to drill'.*[138]

Considering the objections made by certain sections of the Oldham public when the Oldham Volunteers were being formed, it is interesting to note that Captain Blackburne now considered that:

> *'the volunteer force now is a popular force in Oldham, and any small thing that is done by way of recognition of it always meets with the support of the public.'*[139]

Many recommendations were made from this report, the important ones being that the government should give financial support, and smaller Corps be consolidated into battalions, with a paid adjutant to each battalion.

Consolidation and Government support 1863 to 1882

The object of the forming an administrative battalion was to unite the different corps composing it, under one common head, to secure uniformity of drill among them, and to afford them the advantage of the instructor and assistance of an adjutant, but it was not the intention to interfere with the financial arrangements of the separate corps, or with the operation of their respective rules, or to compel them to meet together for battalion drill in ordinary times, except with their own consent.
So it was that in November 1863 the *31st LRV* and the *23rd (Ashton) LRV* formed the *7th Administrative Battalion*. Unfortunately, as far as Oldham was concerned, the head quarters for this new administrative battalion were in Ashton and the single adjutant for both corps was also based there. Ashton was probably chosen because at the time despite being a smaller town than Oldham, their Volunteers were the larger of the two

[138] 1862 (3053) Royal comm. to inquire into condition of Volunteer Force
[139] 1862 (3053) Royal comm. to inquire into condition of Volunteer Force

with four companies and 300 men compared to Oldham's three companies and 220 men. (As per the returns of 1 April 1862 submitted for the Royal commission)
The two Corps remained independent and retained their original titles of the *31st LRV* and *23rd LRV* and only came together four or five times each year to practice battalion drill and for the annual inspection. The overall command of the *7th Administrative Battalion* was given to Colonel Mellor of the *23rd LRV*. This administrative arrangement with Ashton was the subject of dissatisfaction in Oldham for many years and Major Blackburne made many attempts to have it changed, and for Oldham to have their own adjutant. In a speech by the Mayor of Oldham at the 1873 annual prize presentation, he echoed the views of the Oldham volunteers, he was:

> '*sorry they were still connected to the Ashton administration battalion, as he believed they should have an adjutant of their own, (cheers). He never liked to see Oldham play second fiddle to any other town (cheers). The late Lt-Col Blackburne tried very hard to get Oldham their own adjutant but did not succeed.*'[140]

1863 saw two major changes for the *31st LRV*, besides being associated with the *23rd LRV* the government introduced in this year allowances for all Volunteer Rifle Corps. Providing a volunteer made himself efficient, by attending a minimum numbers of drills per year, and he obtained the necessary skills in drill and shooting, then the corps would be entitled to 20s per man who was efficient. This 20s would be used to offset against that man's annual subscription. If the volunteer did not achieve the minimum levels to qualify, to be called efficient, then he would have to pay the 20s himself in full. An additional 10s could be earned for extra efficiency, to be entitled to this extra grant, the volunteer simply had to fire an extra 60 rounds at a target.
One of the consequences of being linked with the *23rd LRV* was that both corps should have the same uniform, after much deliberation this was finally achieved and the corps were completely re-clothed by August 1865 in time for a public display of the *31st LRV* at the opening of Alexandra Park in Oldham.
Interest in the *31st LRV* was still high in 1863, with young men applying to join, but the four companies had their full complements, so they had to be turned away, it was not until 1867 that it was decided to raise a further two companies of the *31st LRV*. One was to be raised in Royton and the other in Oldham.
In November 1867 a meeting was held in the village school, Royton:

> *'The Drum and Fife band plus 50 members of 1st company in uniform marched to the village school. Henry Whittaker of Brooklands was appointed chairman. Aim of the company was to be drilled in Royton and allied to 31st. It was stated that persons joining would be put to no expense in the shape of uniform or travelling expenses, and he hoped the young and able men of Royton would come forward. He had often witnessed the careless and slovenly manner a*

[140] Oldham Standard

number of them carried themselves, and it was, to say the least, disgusting to see their arms dangling any way and their chins down on their stomachs. Drill would alter that.
John Kershaw Jun seconded the motion for raising a company and it was carried unanimously.
Ensign H Clegg informed them that if formed at Royton it could drill there and only called upon to attend battalion parade at Oldham or Ashton, expenses would be borne by government. Colour Sergeant Shaw gave a speech. He concluded by saying that in Oldham a man had to be proposed before he was allowed to join. They did not take any character, but those only that were worthy to sit and associate with intelligent and respectable company.
Preparations for taking down names were made and the first man approaching the table was loudly cheered. About 40 entered their names before leaving the school.
Ensign Clegg then invited all those who had put down their names to adjourn to the Spread Eagle Inn, and to take a glass with Lieutenant Redfern and himself, and those who wanted to enter could do so there. A further 20 names were added to the list.'[141]

The Royton Company was raised and allocated as the fifth Company. For the first three years the Royton Company carried out their drill practice in Royton at various places including Cooper Square, the village school and in a field near the White Hart, Edge Lane. The 1869 annual inspection for the *31st LRV* was held in Royton Park, when a large concourse of people turned out of the village and assembled on the hill overlooking the park.[142] Lieutenant Colonel Green Wilkinson, the inspecting officer praised them for being greatly improved from the previous year.

As part of the Cardwell reforms of the British Army, the Volunteers also underwent some changes. In July 1870, the capitation grant was raised to 35s per man, but to gain this new grant, new levels of proficiency were required. Officers and NCOs would have to gain a certificate of proficiency. The certificate was granted to the officer, after he had attended a month's course at a school of instruction in Manchester. He would increase his knowledge in drill, command, musketry supervision and general military duties. Once an officer had passed the exam, he would be rewarded with the letters 'PS' after his name in the *Army List*. The adjutant would be responsible for examining the proficiency of the NCOs. The Certificate of Efficiency was made compulsory for all officers within one year of being appointed to the Corps.
The decade of the 1870s was difficult, with numbers falling off and numerous public complaints in the local newspapers about the commitment of the officers. In early 1871, due to the lack of officer recruits, five non-commissioned officers were granted commissions as ensigns; namely Sergeant Major Humphrey Goodwin, Quarter Master

[141] Oldham Standard
[142] Oldham Standard

Sergeant James Lees Page, Colour Sergeant John Greaves, Colour Sergeant Hugh Shaw, Colour Sergeant George Hallsworth and Sergeant James Winterbottom. On reflection, this was a beneficial move for the corps, as these six men completed many years of service, and they must have been a steadying and constant influence on the Oldham volunteers. Hallsworth went on to be the longest serving Oldham volunteer finally retiring in 1904, after 44 years of service. John Greaves went on to be Honorary Lieutenant Colonel and was commandant of the corps for a short interim period.

1871 also saw the death of the founder of the Oldham Volunteer movement, Lieutenant Colonel Blackburne, after two days in a coma; he succumbed to cerebral disease on 30th September. Blackburne had been suffering with the condition for over 12 months and had kept it a secret from the Corps; it came as a shock to them all. Only a few days before his death, Blackburne had attended a battalion inspection carrying out his duties as normal. The whole battalion turned out for his funeral on 4th October. Major Thomas Evans Lees paid tribute to him at the prize presentation in December, mentioning his 'untiring zeal and energy which he had devoted' also 'He was not a volunteer for the sake of mere display of honour, but he had the cause warmly at heart.' With the death of Blackburne, Major Lees became the Lieutenant Colonel and commandant of the *31st LRV*.

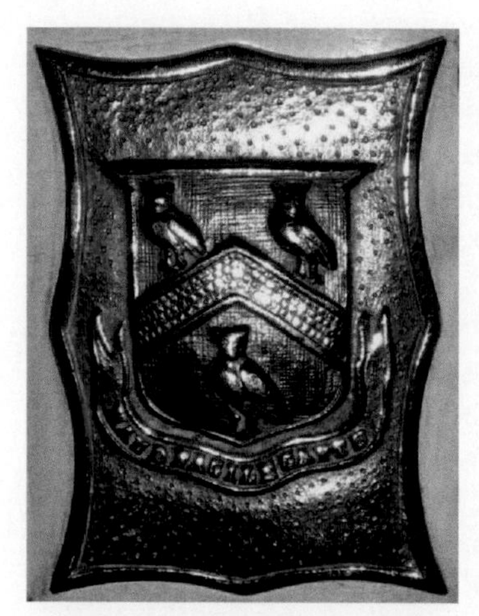

Officers Cross belt plate in use from 1870s onwards
(by permission of Simon Butterworth)

With the Corps now up to strength of six companies, the existing drill hall was proving too small; with not enough space to drill more than a dozen files at once therefore men looked on more often than not.[143] To overcome the space problem rooms were rented in an old mill at Rhodes Bank. Plans were also put in place to rectify the space situation at the Drill Hall. Work was started in 1872 to build a large drill shed and the existing drill hall was to be converted into offices and stores. This work was to cost the Corps £2,000 (about £125,000 at 2000 equivalent costs[144]). The building of the new drill shed was contracted to McTear & Co. Some people had expressed concerns about the safety of such a large roof, which was 160 feet long and had a span of 100 feet, without a central pillar. Mr Nicholls from McTear & Co, speaking at the prize presentation, assured them that it had been fully tested, 18 girders each capable of supporting five and half tons. On 19th October 1872, the new drill shed was used for the first time.

By the end of 1873 the debt on the new drill hall had

143 Oldham Chronicle

144 Based on calculations from House of Commons research paper 02/44 dated 11/7/2002

been nearly paid off, and to pay off the remainder and also boost the fund for the *31st LRV,* a bazaar was held in July 1874. This time the bazaar raised £1600 net. This was to be the last time the Oldham Volunteers would ask for any public monetary support for the next 20 years.

Even with the new drill shed, the Corps struggled in attracting the numbers and remained well below full strength, during most of the 1870s, and there was also discontent amongst some of the officers. In August 1874, three of the six company Captains resigned at the same time. Lt-Col Lees put the resignations down to change of circumstances for the officers concerned, but the Corps also lost a number of experienced volunteers.
In May 1878, after seven years in charge, Lt-Col Thomas Evans Lees had to retire due to ill health. Lees had been suffering with ill health for around 12 months and was diagnosed with cancer of the tongue; he eventually died at Scarborough in January 1879.
Lees' cousin, Edward Brown Lees took over command of the *31st LRV.* Edward B Lees had already moved away from Oldham, and live a gentleman's life but he was persuaded to return and take over the command of the Corps.
By the beginning of the 1880s, numbers had increased and the Corps was more or less at the full strength of 600.
In the early 1880s there was a rise in ant-Irish feeling in the country, Oldham was not so much affected as other parts of the country. By this time the Irish contingent in the *31st LRV* had dwindled to just a few, despite the large Oldham Irish population of around 10,000. At the beginning of January 1881, due to the anti-Irish (Fenianism) feeling in the north-west, all surplus ammunition was ordered to be returned to government stores at Chester.

After 20 years under the title of the *31st LRV,* the government introduced changes that merged the *31st LRV* with the *23rd LRV* and on 25th May 1880, they collectively were known as the *23rd LRV,* the title of the *31st LRV* was then consigned to the history books. This was not a popular change with the Oldham Volunteers, they still felt that they should be a separate corps, Lt-Col Edward B Lees made strong objections to the authorities to try and stop the merger. The only consolation was that Lees was appointed in overall command of the *23rd LRV.* The title of *23rd LRV* for the amalgamated corps was short lived and they were renumbered the *7th LRV* on 3rd September 1880. Companies A-F based at Ashton and companies G, H, J-M based at Oldham. The Ashton companies formed the right half of the battalion and the Oldham companies the left half. Despite being amalgamated with Ashton, for the day-to-day operations they effectively remained separate, only coming together four or fives times per year for battalion drills and the annual parade and inspection.

Independence

Oldham continued to push to become a separate Corps and in March 1882 an announcement was made by the Commander in Chief that he:

> *'desired to acquaint the general officer commanding the Northern district that in the army estimates for the ensuing financial that the necessary provision had been made for the cost of a second adjutant for the 7th LRV. The consentment of the 2nd adjutant is however conditional on the raising of two additional companies, which is hoped will be an easy task. Last night this intelligence was communicated to the men drilling at the armoury, and it was received with great satisfaction. Oldham will now have a separate establishment of its own.'*[145]

Within days, notices were placed calling for new recruits, to raise the required two companies, recruiting was brisk and by the beginning of May the *Oldham Chronicle* reported the following:

> *'Ever since the formation of the volunteer force in Oldham it has been joined to the Ashton volunteers, a town much inferior in importance and population. This has been rather galling to the Oldham volunteers and at various times expressions of regret have been uttered that the volunteer force should have to submit to this alliance. Representations were made to the War Office, Mr Hibbert MP has interested himself in the question and the consequence was that the War office authorities promised an independent adjutant on the condition that two companies were raised. The volunteer authorities set about this and the result is that two companies were raised and notification of this fact has been given. All that is now wanted is the appointment of an adjutant. It is the desire of the men that Major Pritchard, located at Ashton should be adjutant, and there is some prospect of the desire of the men being gratified by his appointment to Oldham.'*[146]

The Oldham Volunteers got their wish and Major Pritchard was appointed as adjutant, the Ashton Volunteers were appointed a new adjutant, Captain J.W.Lang from the *Lincolnshire Regiment*.

In June 1882 the Oldham and Ashton Volunteers had their last parade and inspection together as one unit and the following month a notice was placed in regimental orders:

> *'By order of the WO, dated 29 July 1882, the companies at Oldham who formed part of the 7th Lancashire Rifle Volunteers are now separated from the*

[145] Oldham Chronicle
[146] Oldham Chronicle

Ashton corps, are to be a new corps, and designated the 22nd Lancashire Rifle Volunteers. The companies of the corps to be lettered A to H.'[147]

The following year in March 1883, and under the leadership of Surgeon Fort, a small ambulance party was formed from members of the Corps. They received separate instruction from Surgeon Fort. At the same time the role of 'pioneer' was introduced, the Captains of each company had to select one man from their company to perform this role. Later in the year a signalling party was also introduced.

Officers of the 22nd (Oldham) Lancashire Rifles Volunteers date unknown
(by kind permission of Oldham Local Studies)

The annual inspection had, up until independence, always taken place at Ashton; now a suitable place had to be found to accommodate 750 men for battalion drill and inspection. The first annual inspection as a separate corps took place in July 1883 on a field in Clarksfield, this proved unsuitable, as it was rugged and uneven. The following year a field was used at Coalshaw Green, Hollinwood. 5000 spectators watched the volunteers go through their manoeuvres. This ground was also found not to be suitable and the *22nd LRV* actually had to return to Ashton for their annual inspections, as no

[147] Oldham Chronicle

suitable field could be found in Oldham. It was not until 1890 that they started to have the annual inspection in Chadderton Park.
The commanding officer appearances with the Corps was diminishing, living away in Westmorland was not conducive to commanding a Corps of 750 men. Quite often Major Ireland would stand in to carry out the duties of the Commanding Officer, and on 23rd May 1885, Lt-Col Edward B Lees resigned his commission and Major James Greaves Ireland was appointed as Lieutenant Colonel and commander of the *22nd LRV.*

In March 1888, it was announced that the Volunteer Corps were to become more closely associated with the regiments of the line. This association is seven years later than many other volunteer regiments in the country. The *Manchester Regiment* at the time consisted of two regiments of the line, two militia regiments and a loose connection with the six regiments of Volunteers around the Manchester area. The six Volunteer Regiments were to become Volunteer Battalions of the *Manchester Regiment.*

> *'The Oldham regiment has expressed its acquiescence in the arrangement, and in so doing has been the first of the six reserve regiments to do so.'*[148]

On 1st September 1888 the *22nd LRV* officially became know as the *6th Volunteer Battalion of the Manchester Regiment.*
The other volunteer corps included the *4th LRV (Wigan)* who became the *1st VB Manchester Regiment*, the *6th LRV (1st Manchester)* who became the *2nd VB*, the *7th LRV (Ashton U Lyne)* who became the *3rd VB*, the *16th LRV (3rd Manchester)* who became the *4th VB*, the *20th LRV (2nd Manchester or Ardwick)* who became the *5th VB.*

6th Volunteer Battalion Manchester Regiment

The change of title to *6th VB Manchester Regiment* made little difference to the running of the regiment, the officers remained the same and the Commanding Officer remained as Lieutenant Colonel James Greaves Ireland, though he was granted the honorary rank of Colonel. Perhaps Lt-Colonel Ireland thought this was an appropriate time to move on for in December of the same year he resigned his command and commission. It would seem that the Oldham Volunteers preferred to have a commanding officer of high social station for they invited John Crompton Lees to become the new commanding officer. John C Lees had retired as a Captain in the *31st LRV* some eleven years previously. He accepted the position and became the Lieutenant Commander of the *6th VB Manchester Regiment* in February 1889 and Major John Greaves who was the senior officer in the regiment was given the rank of Honorary Lieutenant Colonel.
By 1891 the drill hall and facilities, which were now nearly 20 years old, were starting to show their age, the drill hall was reported by Sergeant Major Slater in December 1891 as:

---

[148] Oldham Chronicle

> *'tumbling to pieces, and the accommodation at the place was altogether inadequate. They had only one small room for the use of 740 men. When there was a big muster, the men could not be accommodated in that room and they dared not go into the drill shed for fear of it falling on their heads. He thought some effort should be made to bring the matter before the public of Oldham, with a view of raising funds for erection of a new drill shed suitable to the requirements of the regiment. He was sure there were plenty of people ready and willing to give handsomely towards such an object.'*[149]

Shortly afterwards, a committee was formed to discuss how funds could be raised. The government gave no monetary support for drill halls, buildings or ranges therefore the money had to be raised locally. Matters worsened early in 1894, when the roof actually fell in and they had to stop using the hall and buildings. With the hall out of use drill was carried out at the Mutual School in Henshaw Street.

On 14th March 1894, a public meeting was held at the Town Hall to consider what steps could be taken, to defray the costs of building a drill hall and headquarters for the *6th VB*. The meeting was poorly attended and consisted mainly of the officers of the battalion along with the Mayor and a few others. Lt-Col Lees explained the lack of support from government and that it had been over 20 years since the Volunteers had appealed to the public for any money. He went on to explain, that any new hall must have the capability to drill 200 or 300 men, in all states of weather, as they could not always rely on a field. An architect had been employed to draw up some plans and it was calculated that the drill hall would cost £3,570 and the quarters would cost £2,400 and he appealed to the public of Oldham to assist them in raising the total sum of £5,970. There was a larger scheme costing £8,000, but this was not particularly discussed, as it was thought that it was too expensive, but as it turned out this option was the one that was taken and eventually the drill hall and buildings would cost around £9,000. (Around £655,000 in year 2000 costs)[150].

It was argued, that such a large covered area would be of great benefit for the whole of the town, over 5,000 people could be assembled in the hall, and the space could also be

[149] Oldham Chronicle

[150] Based on calculations from House of Commons research paper 02/44 dated 11/7/2002

used as a gymnasium. Mr T Taylor, the architect of Queen Street, explained the scheme to the meeting, it was to:

> *'comprise a drill hall 112 ft wide and 150 ft long, covering an area of 1,866 square yards. The hall would be roofed in such a manner that the whole area of the floor would have no obstruction from pillars etc, girders 6 ft deep in double section would span the hall and steel principals of 30 ft bearing would carry the roof, which would be covered in glazing and slating in equal proportions. The height of the hall would be 7 yards or 21 ft clear to the underside of the steel girders. The flooring would be of wooden blocks laid on a concrete bed. Adequate ventilation would be obtained by means of louvres in the roof and inlet ventilators to admit the fresh air. The hall would be about the largest drill hall in the north, and would be found admirable for large mass meetings, being capable of accommodating 5,500 standing persons, or comfortably seating 3,150 persons. A balcony runs the length of the hall, forming splendid accommodation for viewing the large hall... The armoury is placed so that the rifles can be delivered as the men finish drill and leave the hall. There is also a clothing store, in which all the accoutrements will find a numbered place. The officers and sergeants quarters would be on the first floor, and approached by a staircase common to both, each quarter will have a separate committee and recreation room with lavatory accommodation. The quarters for the men are also placed on the first floor in the left wing of the building; a separate staircase gives access to a large, well lighted recreation room, divided from the sergeant's mess by means of a moveable screen. When both these rooms are thrown into one a splendid dining room is made, or a room well adapted for smoking concerts etc. a bar is centrally placed. Each set of quarters will have access to the balcony from the various staircases. A dressing room is provided for the use of gymnasts, and a caretaker's house having every accommodation for cooking and attending upon mess dinners.'*[151]

A resolution was proposed by Mr J.W.Radcliffe, to open a public subscription, this was seconded and carried. Promises had already been made by prominent citizens, which were read out at the meeting, Mr Elliot Lees £250, Mr J.M.Cheetham £105, the Mayor Alderman Smith £100 and Mr James Collinge £100.

By the middle of July, the fund stood at just over £4,000 and by November a special general meeting was called, to discuss borrowing £3,000 on security of the new drill hall and quarters. In December an 'Assault at Arms' evening was organised at the Oldham Coliseum for raising funds, the event was well received with nearly a full house. 16 members of *6th VB* demonstrated bayonet exercise, Sergeant Haigh, clever feats of swordsmanship and Captain Wrigley, fencing. Exercise with cavalry sword and lance and boxing was also performed. The second part of the event was a concert given by the Oldham Rifles band with their conductor Mr Holloway.

[151] Oldham Chronicle

By the time of the next event the drill hall was nearly complete. On 11th May 1895, a Grand Military tournament was organised for raising more funds. This was held at Oldham Football club at Watersheddings with several thousand spectators present. The event included fencing, gymnastics, mounted sword combat, lemon cutting, sword against lance, boxing. There were band displays from *6th (Inniskilling) Dragoons, Welsh Royal Fusiliers* and *6th VB.*
The new drill hall and headquarters was finally finished in August 1895 and on 10th August a parade of 687 men used the new drill hall for the first time.
By 1904 the battalion still had an outstanding debt of £3,000 on the HQ and during this year they borrowed from the Public Works Loan Board to gain favourable terms and slowly pay off the debt over a period of 30 years.
In January 1896 the first formal event took place at the new headquarters when the annual gathering of the Sergeants of the six Manchester Volunteer Battalions took place. The *Manchester Guardian* described the event:

> *'A portion of the hall, screened off, made an excellent dining room. The company numbered 250. Effective decoration composed of trophies of flags, bayonets etc, relieved the monotony of bare walls; and the electric light, which furnished brilliant illumination, shining upon varied uniform and polished accoutrement, disclosed a exceedingly striking picture. Armourer Sergeant Taylor, of the Oldham battalion, presided, and the vice chair was taken by Quartermaster Sergeant Buckley.'*[152]

Senior officers from the other Manchester Volunteer Battalions were present as guests.
At the beginning of 1898, Lieutenant Colonel J.C.Lees retired and moved to Sligo in Ireland, although he still maintained a connection and was appointed as Honorary Colonel of the *6th VB*. Taking over the command of the Corps was James Robert Harries-Jones who was promoted to Lieutenant Colonel.
1898 also marked the retirement of one of the longest serving volunteers. Armourer Sergeant Joseph Taylor joined the Oldham Rifle Volunteers at its beginning in December 1859, and rose through the ranks to become a Sergeant in 1868, Colour Sergeant in 1871 and Armourer Sergeant in 1889.
With such a splendid drill hall and HQ, the Corps was able to start up a gymnastics class, or a school of arms, as it was also referred to. The class was under the direction of Colour Sergeant Mulcaster and on 1st August 1899, the first gymnastics competition took place.
The drill hall was not large enough to carry out full battalion drill; this normally took place in the nearby grounds of Blue Coat School.

[152] Manchester Guardian

Photograph of one of the 6th Volunteer Battalion companies c1900
(by kind permission of Ashton Local Studies)

Drill Hall of the Oldham Volunteers
(by kind permission of Oldham Local Studies)

South African War[153]

The South African War was the big opportunity for the volunteer corps to show their true worth. As the situation grew tense in South Africa, but before war had actually broken out, offers for service in South Africa were submitted by a number of volunteer corps during the summer of 1899, however the government rejected them. When war actually broke out on 11th October 1899, the offers were re-submitted and again they were rejected. What was known as 'Black Week', the week of 9th to 15th December, was to cause the government to change its mind. The British Army suffered defeats at Magersfontein, Stormberg and a major disaster at Colenso with over 1,000 British casualties.

In an interview with Colonel Harries-Jones by an *Oldham Chronicle* reporter on the 19th December 1899 Harries-Jones was still not clear what kind of duty the government would accept from the volunteers. At the time he thought that they might only be called upon to provide men for garrison duty at home. He had already received several requests from men volunteering for active service, and it was planned that at a parade a few days later, to ask those present, who would wish to volunteer for active service. Once he had this information and the call came from the War Office, he would be armed with the information of those who volunteered, and what their qualifications were.

Under growing public pressure, the government eventually agreed to accept the offers from the volunteers. On 16th December 1899, the offer to raise 1,000 volunteers in London, under the name of the City Imperial Volunteers was provisionally accepted.

When the government eventually decided to accept the offers made by the numerous rifle volunteers and Yeomanry corps to serve in South Africa, it issued a statement on 20th December 1899:

> *'Her Majesty's Government have decided to accept the offers of service in South Africa from the volunteers.*
> *A carefully selected company of 110 rank and file officered by one Captain and three subalterns will be raised (one for each British Line regiment serving in or about to proceed to South Africa) from the volunteer battalions of the territorial regiment.*
> *These volunteer companies will, as a general rule, take the place in the Line Battalion of its company serving as mounted infantry.*
> *The volunteer battalions from which a company is accepted will form and maintain a waiting company in reserve at home.*
> *The selection of men from the volunteer battalions for service with the Line Battalion in the field will devolve on the commanding officers of volunteer*

[153] also known as the Anglo-Boer War

> *battalions. The terms of enlistment for officers and men will be for one year, or for not less than the period of the war.'*[154]

Under the volunteer's existing 'terms of condition', volunteers could only be used in the event of invasion of Great Britain. Therefore, for them to be able to serve abroad, they would have to be temporarily enlisted in the Regular Army.
On 21st December, at short notice, the *6th VB* mustered in the drill hall, for the purpose of having their kit inspected, and to see who were prepared to volunteer for home and Foreign Service. The Colonel addressed the assembled men, saying how pleased he was that virtually the whole battalion had mustered and explained the reasons for the muster:

> *'First of all he wanted them to volunteer for something more than they had already volunteered for. They had already volunteered to serve their Queen and country in case of invasion or imminent national danger. Tonight he wanted them to go further than that. We were not in danger of invasion, nor were we, he hoped, in imminent national danger, but still the country was in great need of troops, and the War office had taken a new step, and now for the first time drawn upon an army of volunteers who were willing to go, and therefore, the first thing he wanted to ascertain was who were prepared to volunteer for active service at the front and secondly, what men were prepared to do garrison duty, either at home or abroad.*[155]

It was determined that 359 men of the battalion had volunteered for active Foreign Service and 169 for home garrison duty. Three officers volunteered for the front, namely, Captain John Jordan Shiers, Captain Percy Bamford and Lieutenant George Whittaker Hardman.
None of the ambulance corps, which numbered seventeen men, offered themselves as they had already offered their services to the St John Ambulance Association for service at the front, and were expecting to receive a summons to assemble in London.
The 110 men required to make up the active service company would be drawn from the six Manchester Volunteer Battalions, with a second company held in reserve. Harries-Jones felt that as the Manchester and Wigan battalions were bigger than the others, then those would probably provide the greater part of the active service Company.
The terms, for the men who volunteered, were:

1. They must be between the ages of twenty and thirty five.
2. Must be of good character.
3. Efficient with respect to battalion attendance.
4. Be first class shots.
5. Unmarried or widowed, with no dependant children.

---

[154] Oldham Chronicle
[155] Oldham Chronicle

6. Undergo a regular army medical to prove that they were fit.
7. They would be required to sign up for service of one year, or for as long as the war lasted.

The men accepted would be clothed in khaki and be temporarily signed up to the regular army.
With such strict terms for the volunteers to meet, it meant that the numbers of those eligible was greatly reduced from the original 359 Oldham men. The requirement of being a first class shot was the biggest restriction as Harries-Jones explains:

> *'it gives me a very small field of selection, because a good shot cannot be made in a year or two. Most of our 1st class shots and marksmen are men who are either over 35 years old or are married.'*[156]

The men selected were:

A Comp: Lance Sgt Wild (to rank as Cpl), Cpl Bowden, Pvts C.Garbutt, Buckley, Whitehead, Cleal, Chadwick, Ogden, French.
B Comp: Col Sgt R.Easthorpe, Pvts S.Pearson, J.J.Whitehead, P.L.Roberts, J.Rowland
C Comp: Sgt Barr, Lance Cpl Kershaw, Pvts Prescott, Stanfield, Gillam, Cowley, J.Scott, T.Schofield, Bugler Pinder.
D Comp: Pvts Belshaw, Sutcliffe
E Comp: Drummer Ashton Wild, Pvts Ashworth, Chadwick, Hollins, Hunter, A.Radcliffe, T.Mellor, F.Brooks, Garland, Rhodes, Cash, Elson
F Comp: Lance Cpl P.Taylor, Pvts A.Taylor, T.H.Wadsworth, E.M'Carthy
G Comp: Pvts W.Steeple, J.Stafford, J.Horsfall, J.W.Stainsfield, D.Hilton, J.T.Heron, T.Lawton, A.Bancroft, R.Carss, E.Holden, W.Dolphyn, J.Curran
H Comp: Col Sgt A.Easthorpe, Cpl Street, Pvts A.F.Kay, B.Thomas, J.J.Cheetham, S.Ferguson, N.M'Avady, W.Goodman, T.Eldon, W.B.Lord.

It was the intention of the Colonel to bring the battalion up to the full strength of 800. He saw no problem in doing this, as the recruits were coming on their own accord and the armoury had been besieged the previous night, with potential recruits. Over a two day period around 300 men applied to join the volunteers, a sign of the patriotism of the Oldhamers.
Harries-Jones was not entirely correct in his assumption about which volunteer battalions would be chosen, but he was correct in that the *6th VB* would not be included in the Volunteer Service Company. The men were selected from the *1st (Wigan), 2nd (Manchester), 3rd (Ashton)* and *4th (Manchester) Volunteer Battalion,* with a reserve of men from the *5th (Ardwick)* and *6th (Oldham) Volunteer Battalions*. The *5th and 6th Volunteer Battalions* were to provide 58 officers and men each, to form the reserve

[156] Oldham Chronicle

company, attached to the *2nd Battalion Manchester Regiment*, if that corps was ordered to the front.
A Volunteers Service Company was to be made up of one captain, two subalterns, one sergeant instructor, four sergeants, two buglers, two stretcher bearers, plus rank and file making a total of 116.
Those on the reserve list were required to be sworn in and placed on the regular list as Reservists. These men now started special drills, practising four nights per week; receiving 6d per day. Each man was measured for uniforms and they had an interview with a representative of the Prudential Assurance Company.
The women of Oldham were not to be left out, and arranged knitted socks, knitted Tam'o'shanters, balaclava helmets (Khaki), flannel shirts, vests, drawers, pocket handkerchiefs, writing material, pipes, tobacco, cigars and cigarettes to give to the volunteers before they left for active service.
As seemed to be now a tradition in Oldham, a song was penned and published in the *Oldham Chronicle,* as a tribute to the volunteers bound for the South African war.

'Tis wonderful and glorious,
The spirit of our land;
The love of Queen and country
That thrills from strand to strand –
That stirs men of all classes,
That moves our Knights and peers,
Our tradesmen and our artisans,
To join the volunteers.
Our volunteers, God speed them!
God guard them in the fight!
May he lead forth our armies:
He will defend the right.

Right nobly our reservists
Have answered duties call;
Right nobly have our colonists
Gone forth to fight or fall.
Well have our naval gunners
Deserved their countries cheers.
Now to the front Britannia calls
Her loyal volunteers
It needs not the conscription –
It needs not force nor law.

To raise true hearted Britons
To arm themselves for war.
One spirit, brave and noble,

That knows not, selfish fears –
The spirit of true loyalty
Inspires our volunteers.
From city, town and hamlet,
From hall and cottage home,
From north and south, from east and west,
With swift response they come.
"Ready!" Aye, each man ready
When he the summons hears,
To go where'er his country calls –
Her gallant volunteers.

And nobly have our women
With courage brave and high,
Sent forth their best and dearest
To conquer or to die.
Give them their meed of honour
As we raise the parting cheers,
And bid "God-speed" to everyone
Of our brave volunteers.

WATERHEAD M.L.A.

The first members of the *6th VB* to be sent to South Africa were those men of the bearer section accepted to serve with the *Royal Army Medical Corps* (*RAMC*). Orders were received on 19th February that the *6th VB* were to raise a bearer section consisting of one Non-commissioned officer and nine men. The ten men were selected, and on 27th February preceded to Ashton drill hall for medical examination. The medical was to prove a disappointment for three of the selected men, as they failed the examination, these were: W.Fallows of 92 Falcon St, A.Fallows of 8 Henthorn St and G.Armstrong of 16 Currie St. The remaining seven men were passed fit for duty. Armstrong got a second chance and later went out with the *2nd Volunteer Service Company.*
The send off from Oldham was a very special occasion, as it coincided with the relief of Ladysmith on 27th February 1900. The town was decorated with bunting and there was a great display of loyalty, it gave an additional éclat to the send-off arranged in honour of the seven members of the bearer brigade.[157]
A special assembly and dance was held for them at the drill hall, where a sovereign was presented to each man on behalf of Mr Platt. Afterwards there was a procession from the drill hall to the town hall in sleet and snow; however, even this could not dampen the ardour of the crowd. The whole event was heightened by the discharge of rockets. From the town hall the men then continued on the fire station tender, preceded by the volunteer band and members of the corps. The procession ended at Clegg Street

[157] Oldham Chronicle

railway station, where the seven volunteers took the train to Ashton, and assembled for further transport to their ultimate destination, South Africa.
Sergeant Howarth managed to get a letter back home before setting sail:

> *'I set sail on Saturday next on board the Glengyle from the Royal Albert docks, London. All our men set sail on Saturday last on board the Avoca and Aurania except myself and Pvt E Barber. We were rather low spirited when the Oldham lads left. They are divided into the various bearer companies and field hospitals that sailed last Saturday'*

A few days later, Howarth and Barber left for South Africa.
Sergeant Howarth was posted to the General Hospital at Kimberley. The hospital was a camp based on the fields of the De Beers Diamond mine, it was arranged in four sections; A,B,C and D. The A and B divisions were set apart for the worst of the medical cases with a few specials for surgical cases. C section was set aside principally for skin disease and surgical and all infectious cases, whilst D section was for the convalescent patients before they are sent to rejoin their regiments or to the rest camp. Howarth was appointed as a wardmaster in charge of around 270 beds spread over 35 marquee tents and two special surgical tents. He describes the camp in a letter to Lieutenant Colonel Fort:

> *'The sanitary arrangements are excellent and all the marquees are lit up with electricity which is supplied from the great De Beers Diamond mines plant. They have also laid a line of rails from the main line right through the centre of the camp, or the main street as we call it, which is of great benefit to the patients, as it saves all that rough and tumble ride in wagons from the station right out over the veldt to our camp. The worst thing about the place is the water. It is scarcely fit to drink unless it is boiled, and then it is very far from being clear. We are quite a long way here from the town or station. I should think that at least we are three miles out, but then if you want a good walk after you have had your day's work I think that you would have had quite enough without once going out... We have been issued each man with an extra blanket and they are very welcome, for with the sun's rays during the day being so very hot, I can tell you it is cruel at night, it is that cold. Just fancy us sweating during the day and being kept awake with cold during the night.'*[158]

The biggest complaint that Howarth had, was one of pay, as a member of the *RAMC* the pay was 1s.6d for Privates and 1s.9d for NCOs per day, compared with the 7s.6d per day that the *Cape Volunteers* were receiving. Even the St John's Ambulance men were receiving double the pay of the *RAMC* men, for effectively carrying out the same duties. Howarth also had strong opinions in the defence of his orderlies:

---

[158] Sgt Howarth Letter

> *'there was published in the Daily Graphic a letter from a nursing sister, in which she states that the orderlies are no use whatever only for lifting and carrying a patient. Now, which is the true nurse of the two – the orderly who has to attend to every want of the sick, no matter how objectionable it may be, or the nurse who goes round taking a few temperatures and giving out a few doses of medicine twice a day. Just fancy a man living from early morn till late at night amongst those terrible diseases – enteric fever and dysentery – and then to say he is no use only for lifting.'*[159]

Contracting diseases from the patients was a major problem for the orderlies and nurses. At the time of Howarth's letter around twenty of the hospital staff was sick with enteric fever.

Howarth had one other Oldham man with him at Kimberley, Private E.Barber. He did not know the whereabouts of the others, except for John.J.Nelson, who for a short period in May 1900, ended up as a patient with enteric at the hospital; however he recovered and returned to duties.

We shall learn more about the duties and conditions under which Sergeant Frank Howarth worked, later in the chapter on the *Duke of Lancaster's Own Yeomanry (DLOY)*, as by coincidence, he was stationed at the hospital where wounded of the *DLOY* were taken, after the action at Faber's Put.

6th VB Volunteers who served with Royal Army Medical Corps

Sgt Frank Howarth	12 Gartside St, Glodwick. Served as wardmaster at General Hospital – Kimberley.
Pvt James Booth	434 Manchester Rd, Shaw. Cotton Minder at Ash Spinning Company. On 19/11/1900 was mentioned in battalion orders for good service whilst serving in South Africa.[160]
Pvt E.Barber	1 Court, 2 Whitehead St
Pvt Thomas Lewis	21 Ripponden Rd
Pvt W.Lewis	17 Bertha Street
Pvt Joseph Nightingale	62 Eldon Street. Died of disease on 17 July 1901 at Harrismith.
Pvt John.J.Nelson	86 Chadderton Road. Brass finisher. Age 26.

All the men served for the duration of the war, returning individually around June/July 1902, except Joseph Nightingale who died whilst in South Africa.

Private R.Neilson of the *6th VB* also went out later with the *RAMC* in 1902 for a short period.

---

159 Sgt Howarth Letter

160 Oldham Chronicle

Private John James Shackleton is listed on the *6th VB* South Africa war memorial as serving with the *RAMC,* but he did not go out with the others, he left Oldham for South Africa in February 1900 as a St John Ambulance volunteer. Shackleton served with No.7 General Hospital in Pretoria. He was a cotton operative and lived at 11 Norbury Street, Oldham.

The 1st Volunteer Service Company ('I' Company of the 1st Battalion Manchester Regiment)

Served from 5 May 1900 to 22 May 1901

The *1st Volunteer Service Company* (*1st VSC*), without any of the Oldham volunteers, departed for South Africa onboard the freight ship *Greek,* sailing from Southampton on 14th February 1900.[161] They joined the *1st Battalion Manchester Regiment*, under the command of Lt-Col A.E.R.Curran on 15th March at Caesar's camp, Ladysmith. The *1st Battalion Manchester Regiment* had been in South Africa from 15th September 1899, being deployed there from Gibraltar.

They had just been involved in the defence of Ladysmith, which had been under siege by Boer forces from Mid October 1899, until the end of February 1900.

Kitted out for South Africa

At the beginning of April 1900, orders arrived in Oldham for a detachment of 20 men to be sent out to supplement the *1st VSC*, this was to consist of ten men each from the *5th* and *6th Volunteer Battalions.*

The men were selected from the 57 reserve men, and were quickly issued with the following kit:

Two pairs of boots, a field cap, a helmet cover, a frock jacket, two Khaki jackets, a puggaree, two pairs of puttees, a pair of trousers, two pairs of Khaki trousers, a pair of Khaki shoes, a greatcoat, a haversack, an insert helmet, a cap badge, a collar, a kit bag, a pair of braces, a cloth brush, a shaving brush, comb, two flannel shirts, two pairs of socks, a table knife, fork, comb, spoon, sponge, a clasp knife, two towels, razor and case, and other necessaries including straps, laces, grease tin, mess tin etc.[162]

To honour the volunteers going to South Africa, a supper was held for them, they were presented with many gifts including balaclava helmets, shirts, vests, drawers, socks, mufflers, handkerchiefs, £40 in money, tobacco, cigars which was divided among the men. On behalf of the officers, a carbine was presented to Captain Bamford.

In a speech Mr S.R. Platt said:

[161] WO108/88

[162] Oldham Chronicle

> *'that it was a unique experience, so far as he knew, in the history of Oldham – their townsmen being asked to volunteer in such a way to go and fight in a foreign country for their countries sake. That they had so volunteered and come forward showed clearly the grit of the Oldham people – they all knew that in a 'punsing match' no one could beat an Oldhamer. He hoped that the same spirit as that of the Oldham man who was in a square at Waterloo, and of whom a story was told, would animate the young men before him who had volunteered to go out to South Africa and join the great band of soldiers who were protecting the right and proper interests of our country.'*
>
> And Captain Bamford *'thought it was the first time they had sent any fighting men from Oldham volunteers, and he was proud to be at the head of them.'*[163]

The send off for the volunteers on 11th May was described as '*long to be remembered by all who saw the gathering.*' Nothing could be seen but a vast sea of faces covering High St, Yorkshire St and stretching right up the walls of the parish church. Just before 9 o'clock a rocket soared into the sky, a faint beat of drums was heard, gradually growing nearer and louder until the volunteer band marched into the square playing "Soldiers of the Queen". Then came the volunteers, who formed up near to the town hall steps. Following them, a roar from the crowd greeted the arrival of the men for the front. The noise of shouting and cheering was overpowering and the Mayor tried in vain for some time to obtain silence. After the speech, the Mayor called for three cheers for the Queen, for the men and for Lord Roberts. Slowly, the procession marched down to Mumps station with torches flaring and bands playing. The crush was tremendous.

Captain Percy Bamford

That night would also live long in the memory of Captain Bamford, writing on board the *SS Assaye*, '*Never as long as we live shall we forget that splendid sight, when thousands of our fellow citizens came to give us a send off which could not have been more heartily given in any other town in England. Each one of us thanks everybody in Oldham from the bottom of his heart for that reception, also for the kindness showed to us before we left. May we prove ourselves worthy of the position we hold. I have not the least doubt with respect to the men, that when an opportunity comes to them in the field of battle (if we arrive in time) that they will prove themselves worthy of their town and regiment, and the confidence put in them. I can say that out of the whole of the drafts on board, which includes over 60 different regiments, there is not a cleaner more well behaved and obedient draft than the 20 men I have under me.*'

The trip out to South Africa was a pleasant one for the volunteers. Captain Bamford appeared to be well respected by the men, as Private Emmott mentioned in a letter

[163] Capt Bamford Letter

from onboard ship; '*Captain Bamford is a first class officer and looks after us very well. He has given us 2 boxes of cigars today.*' The journey out to South Africa went without incident; the men took part in firing practice at sea by shooting at boxes and barrels floating in the sea.
In Captain Bamford's first letter from South Africa, they had joined the *1st VSC* and *1st Manchester Regiment* but had yet to see any real action. Writing from Tinta-Inyoni camp on 22nd June:
'*We arrived here quite safely after a very pleasant voyage on the 12th. We landed at Durban on the 11th, entrained at once and travelled straight to Ladysmith and came on to this place on Monday afternoon. It is about 8 miles North West of Ladysmith and 2 miles west of Modder Spruit station which consist of a tin shed and nothing more. Half of the battalion of the Manchester Regiment (1st) is in camp here and the remaining half 5 miles away. We are the only battalion of the 4th division who are not with the division. We are called the Drakensburg Defence Force. We can see Van Reenen's Pass in the distance. If anyone moves up we are the first to move, as the battalion have now got over the siege. Out of the volunteer company who went out with Captain Heywood, about 30 have been laid up. Captain Heywood has been down with enteric fever, but is better now. Lt Darlington of Wigan is laid up at Durban. There is very little to do here. There are 2 route marches a week and I am on outpost duty about 2 weeks. Half of the company go up one hill and another half up another one. It is a very stiff climb the hills being about 6000 ft high. The men make roads and sangers. It gets dark at 5.30 pm until 6.30 am. In the daytime the sun is very hot, but when it gets dark it is very cold. The camp is healthy being situated high up on the veldt. I am afraid that we won't see any fighting but we are living in hopes.*'[164]

The *1st Manchester Regiment* were part of the 7th Infantry Brigade under the command of Brigadier-General F.W.Kitchener. The other regiments in the 7th Infantry Brigade were the *2nd Battalion Rifle Brigade, 1st Devonshire Regiment,* and the *2nd Gordon Highlanders.* The 7th Infantry Brigade was part of the 4th Infantry Division under the command of Major-General N.G.Lyttleton. The 4th Infantry Division comprised of the 7th and 8th Infantry Brigades along with the *21st, 42nd, and 53rd Field Batteries*. This division and others made up the army know as the Natal Field Force under the overall command of General Sir Redvers Buller.

By the end of May 1900, most of the major battles of the war had been fought. British forces had captured Bloemfontein in March, and in May the Orange Free State had been annexed. On 31st May Lord Roberts, the Commander-in-Chief of the British forces in South Africa, occupied Johannesburg, a few days later on 5th June, Pretoria was also captured. The Boer army and the South Africa Republic government had left Pretoria at the end of May and set up government in Machadodorp, a small town situated on the ridge of the Eastern Transvaal Highveld.

---

[164] Capt Bamford Letter

It was hoped that the capture of Pretoria would bring the war to an end, but it was not the case and Lord Roberts had to pursue the Boers to try and draw them into a last conclusive battle to end the war.
General Bullers Natal Field Force was advancing through Natal, and by 12th June they had occupied Volksrust. Bullers force continued its march practically unopposed from Volksrust to Standerton. During this advance the 4th Division was left protecting the area from Laings Nek to Newcastle. Standerton became the base and supply point of the Natal Field Force for the next few months.

On 20th July, the *1st VSC* left Tinta Inyoni camp and marched to Elandslaagte station, where they entrained, along with stores, on two trains. All of the Oldham men went with the train, except for Private Ogden, who had been sent to hospital; Private Kershaw had also been sick a week in hospital and rejoined them at Zandspruit. The train was to take them to Zandspruit; it was not a comfortable journey, as they had to ride in coal wagons. Private Emmott was one of these: '*It was alright during the daytime whilst it was warm, but it was very uncomfortable during the night, as it was very cold, with a heavy dew falling. I was in the second train, which left at 3 o'clock. All along the line were to be seen signs of the war. Every bridge had been destroyed, both big and little, and most of them had been replaced – in some cases by temporary structures only.... I was in the truck next to the engine. The driver was very obliging. One of our men had some cocoa, and I had a piece of bacon and a small piece of bread. He cooked the bacon and gave us some hot water from the boiler to make cocoa and we quite enjoyed our breakfast... I can't say that I enjoyed the journey very much. Nineteen and a half-hours in a coal wagon is rather too long to be comfortable.*'

From Zandspruit they marched five miles to Mongrafspruit, to join the 7th and 8th Brigades under the command of Major-General Howard. They bivouacked for the night at Mongraftspruit. The following day Sunday 22nd July the *1st VSC* were to see their first action. They marched out at 8.30am with the *1st Manchester Regiment* and half a battalion of the *Leicesters* forming the third line, with the *Gordons* next line and the *1st Battalion King's Royal Rifles* leading. Private Emmott takes up the story:
'*We had breakfast about 8 am and along with several other regiments, including the Gordons and Leicester, went on the march, where to we did not know. After marching a few miles we formed up in fighting order. The volunteer company formed the supports. Soon afterwards we got alongside a hill on which our artillery had four guns shelling the enemy. This was our first view of the fighting. We advanced by short stages until within sight of the firing line, which was on the summit of a hill. We were at the foot of it. Shells kept coming over the top and bursting, we could hear them screaming through the air. However none of them reached us. The first shot was fired about 11am and about 2:30 our company was directed to picket two small hills which were supposed to be unoccupied by the enemy. We advanced with ten pace interval between each man. When about 200 yds from the foot we got a warm reception. The bullets fell about us like hail. Lieutenant Bamford seemed to be picked out for a mark. I was just*

behind him and bullets fell all around him. One struck the ground just between his feet. One man got a shot through his helmet, and another man had his rifle hit. We immediately rushed up the hills and drove them off. We did not fire a shot until we reached the top. They then mounted their horses and galloped away to the next ridge, and again opened fire on us, which we returned with interest. Our guns now put a few shells among them and caused them to retreat in haste, and so ended our first experience of being under fire. I felt decidedly uncomfortable the first few minutes, and had a strong inclination to duck my head when I heard the bullets whistling over me: I soon got used to it however. We were very fortunate in having no one hit. The adjutant complimented us on our behaviour. One of our companies lost one man killed and one wounded. We occupied the hill the whole of the night, and a miserable one it was. We had no blankets, and it was bitterly cold and raining heavily. We managed to get a drop of tea – about half a cupful each man, also some bully beef and biscuits. We were all very glad when it came daylight, I can assure you. I shall not forget Sunday July 22nd in a hurry.'[165]

The hill they had captured was called Gras Kop, the following day they retired from their position, to take up a rear guard for the rest of the troops. The next few days were spent at the rear, near Meerzicht, with very little action against the Boers taking place. On the 26th they found themselves on outpost duty at Vet Kop, one of the highest parts of the Transvaal, Emmott says '*It is, I have heard, about 6,000 feet above sea level. At night it is bitterly cold and a very heavy due falls. It is like a shower of rain.*'[166]

View from Zandspruit (now Sandspruit) with Gras Kop in the distance, scene of the Oldham volunteers first action

[165] Pvt Emmott Letter
[166] Pvt Emmott Letter

Private Emmott was skilled with slaughtering and dressing cattle, and was witnessed by one of the Quartermasters slaughtering some sheep and pigs. On 28th July, Emmott was taken out of the *1st VSC* and attached to the 5th Divisional Supply Column with the *Army Services Corps*. Emmott appears to have remained with the *Army Service Corps* until October. He was kept busy slaughtering and issuing meat for the regiments. He was killing on average six beasts and fifty sheep daily. During his stay with the *Army Service Corps* he had a near miss '*a shell which burst over a wagon on which two of us were sitting besides a goat. The smaller bullet just touched my companion on the tip of his nose and then buried itself in a bag of oats. The larger bullet killed the goat, striking it between the shoulders and passing through its heart.*'[167]

On 30th July, the *1st VSC* were out on reconnaissance, under the command of Major J.Watson, with three other companies of the *1St Manchester Regiment,* they came under shell fire and long range rifle fire for a couple of hours near Meerzicht. Two of the volunteers, Private R.Y.Fletcher (7095) and Private M.Whitehead (7118) were wounded. Whitehead was from the *5th VB* and had come over with Captain Bamford's detachment. Both men were invalided home.
Back at camp on the same day, there was a grass fire, which according to Emmott '*burned 5 out of 8 tents, along with blankets, overcoats etc. One of the men from Wigan who was left in camp in trying to put it out was very severely burned. Captain Bamford and the others lost their kit.*'[168] Private K.Ball (7006) from the *1st VB* died from his burns a few weeks later on 15th August. According to Capt Bamford, Ball '*by some means or other in trying to escape from his tent, he slipped and could not rise in time to save himself from the flames.*'[169]

Battle of Bergendal

The plan for Bullers Natal Field Force was to advance northwards and link up with the forces of Generals French, Hamilton and Pole-Carew who were advancing eastward from Pretoria towards Machadodorp.
In early August the 4th Infantry Division, along with the 2nd Cavalry Brigade, *61st Battery, Royal Horse Artillery* and a supply column of around 450 mule wagons and 300 ox wagons were concentrated around Meerzicht. On 7th August this column headed north easterly towards Amersfort, each regiment taking it in turns to act as advance, rear and flank guards. The Column was met by detachments of the Wakkerstoom, Piet Retief, Carolina and Swaziland commandos, under the command of Cmdt D.J.Joubert. The Boers were pushed along the Rooikopjes fighting a rear guard action all the way. By 8th August the *1st VSC* were at Amersfoort, then onwards to Ret Spruit on the 9th, 11th Vaal River, 12th Ermelo, 13th Klipfontein (Botha's Rust), and 14th

[167] Pvt Emmott letter
[168] Pvt Emmott Letter
[169] Newspaper interview with Capt Bamford

at Witbank. By the 15th the Column had reached Twyfelaar, nine miles north-west of Carolina. They remained here for 6 days, awaiting Lord Roberts orders.

During the march they had to endure strong, bitterly cold winds, over a veldt that had been burnt by the Boers. One of the reasons for the burning was that on the blacked surface of the burned veldt, khaki would show up plainly compared to the normal browned withered grass which was ideal camouflage for khaki. During the night, temperatures dropped to as low as minus 15 degrees, and it would have made it very uncomfortable for the men to get some sleep. Two men of the Rifle Brigade died from exposure during one of the nights. Captain Bamford mentions that the men's water bottles froze during the night. Besides the harsh weather conditions the food was also in short supply, Private Wallace Dolphyn writing on the 20th at Komati River; '*The food is the thing that troubles us most; 3 ½ biscuits, and not always that, and the bully beef. Well, when we have eaten it we feel hungry and the rest of the day we are without anything to eat. But what we get is supposed to keep a man for twenty-four hours.*'[170]

On 21st August the offensive against the Boers started with the column marching to Van Wyk's Vlei. On the 22nd some of the *Devon's, Gordon's* and *Manchester's* (not including *1st VSC*) went out on a sortie under the command of General F.W.Kitchener to drive the Boers of the hills to the east of the camp, unfortunately it was not a great success; '*and came back having nothing, but lost three killed and eight wounded. We escaped that day. The next day we went to Geluk. The next two days the outposts sniped from daybreak to sunset, the guns blazing away all day. Stray bullets and shells let into our camp. We were supporters to piquets on the 24th and 25th. A Long Tom shell let uncommonly near, but did us no harm.*'[171]
The following day Captain Bamford, accompanied by his servant Private G.H.Bowden, was in hospital sick with a fever, he remained there for the next two weeks missing the main action on the 26th and 27th at Bergendal.
On the 25th Lord Roberts arrived in Belfast to take overall command of the British forces. Lord Roberts with his Generals Buller, French and Pole-Carew gathered to discuss their strategy. The plan was for French and Pole-Carew's forces to concentrate their attack north of the railway and Bullers forces would advance towards Machadodorp, passing through Bergendal farm. The combined British forces were around 20,000 men, attacking a front of around 12 miles, against Botha's Boers of around 5,000 men.
On the morning of the 26th, Buller moved his force out of Geluk, there was heavy fighting with the Boers throughout the day, and the *1st VSC* came under fire from a Boer position on the high ground near Waaikraal. At about 1.30 pm. Private Dolphyn had been detailed to fetch and fill the water bottles for his section.

---

170 Pvt Dolphyn Letter
171 Capt Bamford letter

Going to the rear carrying 14 water bottles: '*I thought it was a grand opportunity to get a wash. It was the first wash I had had in four days, and it felt nice.*'[172] After filling the water bottles up, he returned to the position where he had left the section, but came across a company of the *Devonshire Regiment*. At this point they came under fire, two men were wounded, and shots were hitting the ground all around him. Eventually, Dolphyn found his company a mile to the west of the original position They were under hot fire: '*the shots from the enemy were coming like rain, and I had the 14 water bottles on me (each bottle holds over a quart), and they were beginning to get heavier. Guns were still going and bullets flying and it sounded like thunder. As night came on one of our section Lance-Corporal F. Munro, of Wigan, was shot through the head, and in another second two others fell, one shot in the arm and the other in the chest, both flesh wounds. The sight of these I shall never forget.*'[173]
During this engagement the *1st VSC* lost one killed, and two wounded. Lance Corporal F Munro (7019, *1st VB*) was killed and Private J F Holmes (7069, *3rd VB*) and Private A Wood (7053, *2nd VB*) were wounded but not seriously. During the night, at about 3 am they were awakened to Boer snipers, everyone '*had to rise and get a rifle and equipment, shivering with cold.*'[174] Captain Heywood, who was in command of the *1st VSC*, had a near miss when a bullet passed through his helmet.

Early on the morning of 27th August the British forces were deployed into their various positions ready to mount their attack. The 7th Infantry Brigade were positioned along a ridge towards Bergendal, the *1st Manchester Regiment*, including the *1st VSC* were detached to the right side of the line and were entrenched on the east side of the ridge, with a Field Battery.
The main thrust of the attack was towards a koppie at Bergendal, this was believed to be the key to the whole position, as it lay at the point where the Boer lines curved from a direction generally west and east to one north and south.
The morning was foggy and it was not until 11am before the artillery opened up and bombarded the koppie for around 3 hours. The koppie was held by around 70 men of the Johannesburg *Zuid-Afrikaansche Rijdende Politie (ZARP).* The *ZARP* endured the full force of the artillery and would not be moved.
The *1st VSC* were reserves for the firing line, the line extended at ten paces. They were laying down cutting out small trenches with their bayonets, all the time under fire, Dolphyn had just managed to get himself down behind the dirt and stones: '*when a bullet struck the top back part and knocked a lot of it down. Had it not have been for the stone I should have been hit in the shoulder. I have got the bullet in my pocket.*'
At around 2pm the order was given for the infantry to advance on the koppie, from the west this was led by the *2nd Battalion Rifle Brigade*, with support from the *1st Devonshire Regiment*. From the east the *Inniskilling Fusiliers* led the way supported by the *2nd Gordon Highlanders.* The *ZARP* continued to fire into the advancing British

[172] Pvt Dolphyn letter
[173] Pvt Dolphyn letter
[174] Pvt Dolphyn letter

Infantry but a final charge with bayonets fixed cleared the koppie, the *ZARP* putting up a hard desperate fight.
The moment that the koppie was won, the Boer line was breached and the whole Boer line broke and fled.

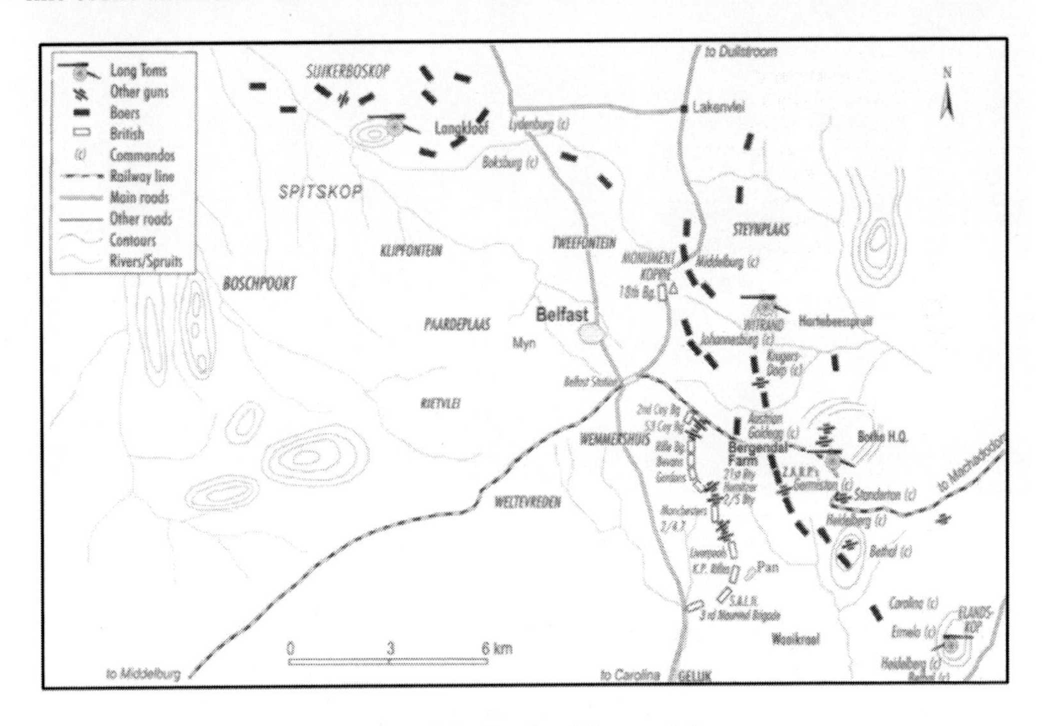

Plan of the Battle of Bergendal
(Source: South African Military History Society Journal, Vol 12 No.4, by Cecilia Jooste)

During this day Private J E Sterling (7139, *5th VB*) was wounded along with nine others of the *1st Manchester Regiment*.
The Battle of Bergendal was the last major pitched battle of the South African War; the British forces defeated the Boers in the battle, but Botha's main force remained intact. The commandos dispersed to Lydenburg and Barberton, and the guerrilla warfare stage of the war began. This second phase of the war lasted even longer than the first.
On 28th August the battalion marched to Dalmanutha, 12 miles east of Belfast where the *1st VSC* remained stationed acting as a garrison until 14th September. On 6th September the men tasted bread for the first time in over a month, when they were issued half a loaf instead of the biscuits.
It then moved to Schoemans Kloof, about 18 miles north of Machadodorp. Lieutenant Bamford rejoined his men here after recovering from his illness. During this period they were kept busy with digging trenches and outpost duty. The *1st Manchester Regiment* were tasked with guarding the road between Lydenburg and Schoemans Kloof.

Members of Volunteer service company at Schoemanskloof.
Private Dolphin of the Oldham volunteers is far right
(Source: 'Volunteer Infantry of Ashton under Lyne' by R Bonner)

During their period at Schoemanskloof the 1st VSC were employed in escorting convoys to and from Helvetia and Badfontein. On 7th October, a telegram arrived stating that the *1st VSC* was to proceed to Pretoria on the 11th en rout to England.
Colonel Curran the commanding office of the Manchester Regiment addressed the *1st VSC*;

> *'On the occasion of the departure of the volunteers en route to England the commanding officer feels that all the ranks of the 1st battalion Manchester regiment will share his regret at losing this company, of whose services he cannot speak to highly. Capt Heywood, his officers, NCOs and men have shown a knowledge of their work which has surprised him and they have all on all occasions proved themselves gallant in the field, while their conduct in camp has been exemplary. He is certain that Manchester will know how to appreciate the deeds of the men who have left home and employment to take up arms for their country and it must remain a source of gratification that a lasting band of union has been established between the volunteers and the regular battalions of the city.'*[175]

[175] Enclosure in Pvt Dolphyn letter

In the early hours of the 11th they marched to Machadodorp, acting as escort to a convoy with the Gordon's and Leicester volunteer companies.
They waited at Machadodorp there 6 days, bivouacked by the railway on a dirty bit of land before embarking for Pretoria. They then spent 2 nights in open trucks on the railway arriving safely in Pretoria without being blown off the line or being sniped at, both favourite past times of the Boers. The companies then went into a provincial volunteer camp.

The volunteer company crossing the river at Machadodorp
(Source: 'Volunteer Infantry of Ashton under Lyne' by R Bonner)

On the 25th a ceremony took place proclaiming the annexation of the Transvaal to the dominions of the Queen. A review was held in Church Square, Pretoria and the Royal Standard was raised to a salute of twenty-one guns. The Governor read the proclamation and the troops marched past Lord Roberts, the *1st VSC* were one of the companies that took part in the march past.

Review of the annexation in Church Square, Pretoria
(Source: After Pretoria: The Guerilla War Vol 1)

On 27th October all of the volunteer companies except four, *1st VSC* included, went down to Kroonstad and Bloemfontein. On the Sunday about 10 pm, an order came to go to the station and entrain for Germiston, Elandsfontein. They set out at about 3 am arriving about 6 am. Each of the volunteer companies was deployed to look after a goldmine. Bamford describes the conditions; '*We live in a house, the men live in a large room in the front. We have had electric light put in. There have been some very heavy storms lately. There is very little work to do. We have had 2 concerts here in the large room where the men live. Wadsworth and Dolphyn went to hospital when in Pretoria with dysentery, but were nearly all right, I believe, when we left. Ogden went to hospital here a few days ago, nothing serious, I think. Kershaw has joined the Imperial Military Railway as a fitter and so will stop out here. We left him in Pretoria, so I suppose they will get his discharge for him. Sgt Barr tried for a post as a clerk in the civil service and they told him word would be sent if he was chosen, but he has heard nothing yet. We have heard nothing about going home again, but you will know more about us at home, and what they intend doing with us, as we get no mails nor anything now being away from the regiment. I am still feeling fit and well. PS Emmott has also decided to stop here a short time.*'[176]

The *1st VSC* were employed in guarding the Simmer and Jack gold mine, Pvt Dolphyn describes his experiences at the mine, '*We have got plenty of duty here, one night in bed and the next on outpost, as we are guarding the mines we have got comfortable quarters as regards sleeping and dining, as we reside in what was formerly the miners*

[176] Capt Bamford letter

dining room. The room is lighted with electric light and it does feel a change from sleeping on the veldt.'[177]
At the beginning of April they left the mine and went to Natalspruit. They were stationed there for three weeks, during their time at Natalspruit an incident occurred one night; '*about 100 Boers came and tried to blow up the railway line, but they were seen and cleared off without doing any damage.*'[178] The *1st VSC* then travelled to Durban by way of Pietermaritzburg.
The *1st VSC* departed Durban on the 26th April 1901 on board the transport ship *Englishman*. They sailed via Cape Town and Las Palmas arriving in Southampton on the evening of 22nd May.[179]

The *1st VSC* departed Southampton the following morning, and the train carrying the men, arrived at Park Parade station in Ashton around 7 pm to a magnificent welcome from the Ashton people. The streets were decorated with many banners and a general holiday had been made. '*The train steamed slowly into the station, to the accompaniment of a salvo of fog signals, a hearty cheer was raised, and this was repeated, in increasing cadence, by the redcoats outside and the great crowds further away.*'[180] The volunteers left the station, and marched to Ashton Town Hall where the Mayor welcomed them home and the 'Old Hundredth' was sung with fervour. The Oldham volunteers then returned to the train station, and were on their way to Oldham by 8.30 pm. They arrived at Clegg Street station to a round of cheering and 400 of their fellow men from the *6th VB*. The returned volunteers, in a wagonette, proceeded through the town by way of Clegg Street, Union Street, Yorkshire Street to the Town Hall. All along the streets the pavements were packed with people who cheered the returning heroes to their hearts content. Outside the Town Hall crowds gathered, estimated at 30,000. The policemen struggled to keep a space clear in front of the Town Hall. At the Town Hall, waiting on a platform, was the Mayor (Councillor John Hood), along with others, including Mr Isaac Bamford, JP, Mrs Bamford and Mr W Emmott whose sons were part of the returning heroes. After a speech by the Mayor, praising and thanking the returning volunteers, they then proceeded to the drill hall. Col Harries-Jones welcomed them at the drill hall and praised them for their conduct in South Africa. Captain Bamford then said a few words '*He could assure them all that they were all glad to see Oldham again. He had set out with ten men and had brought eight back, and the other two were staying out in South Africa. Of the eight with him he need say nothing, they had only to look at them (hear, hear and laughter) but he would just say that they had been obedient and had done what they had to do without having been told twice.*'[181]

---

[177] Pvt Dolphyn letter
[178] Oldham Chronicle
[179] WO108/87
[180] Guardian
[181] Oldham Chronicle

The following day the *1st VSC* paraded in Manchester as honoured guests of the Mayor of Manchester.
On 9th October 1901 the Oldham volunteers of the *1st VSC* had the honour of being presented with their South Africa medals by Lord Roberts in Manchester.

1st Volunteer Service Company march into Albert Square, Manchester.
L to R: Lt H C Darlington, Capt B C P Heywood and Lt P Bamford
(Source: 'Volunteer Infantry of Ashton under Lyne' by R Bonner)

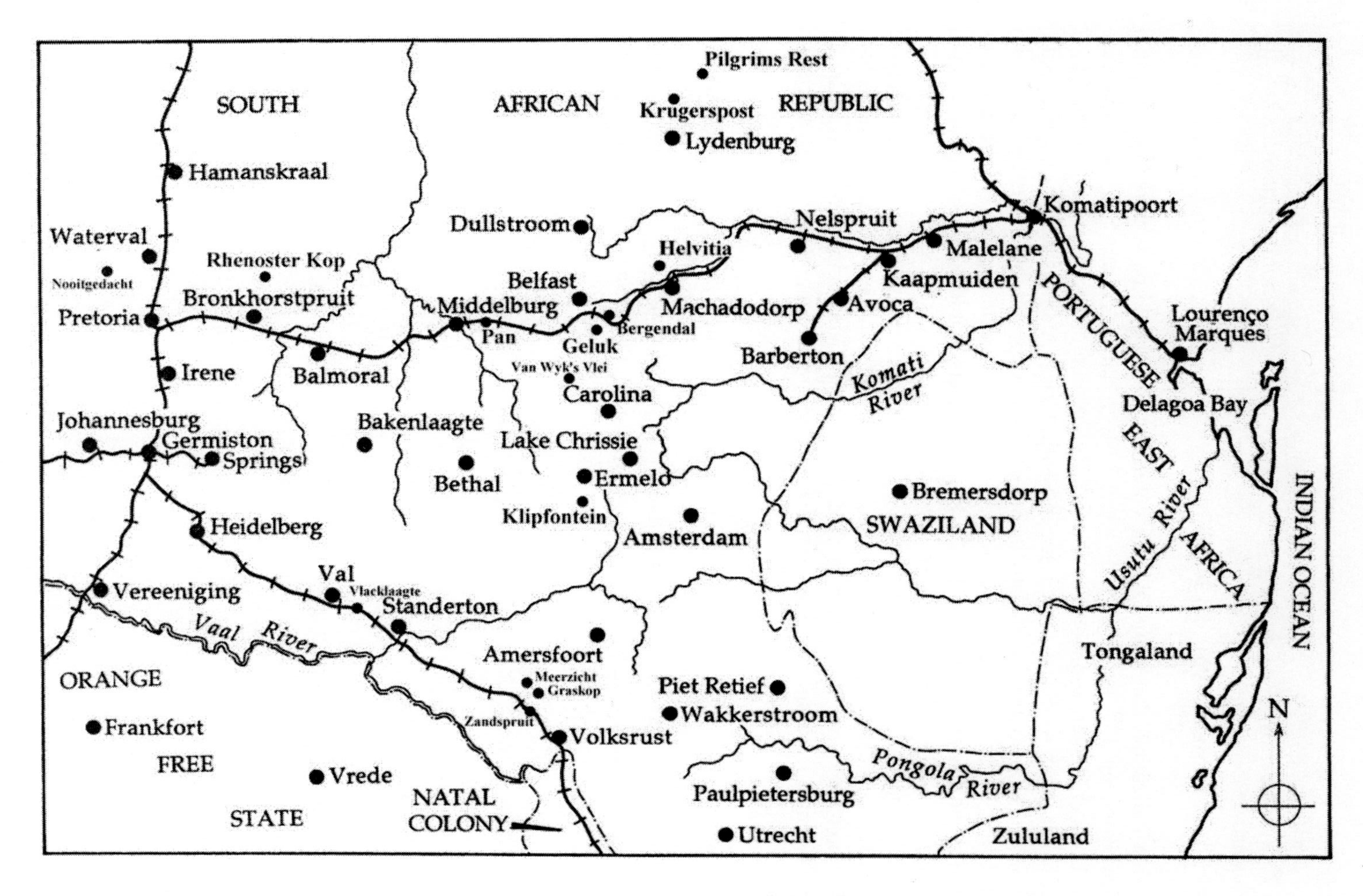

Main area of operations for the 1st, 2nd and 4th Volunteer Service Companies

The 2nd Volunteer Service Company (K Company of the 1st Battalion Manchester Regiment)

Served from 16 March 1901 to 5 June 1902

The first indication, that more Oldham volunteer men would be required out in South Africa, came on 15th January 1901, when Lt-Col Harries-Jones received a telegram from Colonel Gunter, commanding the 63rd Regimental district; stating that the *6th VB* must hold men in readiness for service in South Africa. A similar call was made to the *5th VB*. The 11 who went with Captain Bamford had depleted the original 57 men who were being held in the reserve company, which had been used for filling the gaps caused by bullets and disease in the *1st VSC*. Numbers would need making back up to the original number, plus one officer.

On 8th February, they had an enthusiastic send off to Ashton, to go for the fitting of their Khaki uniforms. The *2nd VSC* consisted of a half company of men from Oldham and a half company of men from Ardwick. The officers appointed were Captain G.Heyes and Lieutenant Stevens, from the Ardwick battalion and Lieutenant Hardman from the Oldham battalion.

On the 21st they awaited orders at the Ashton barracks, returning to Oldham on 1st March for a dinner organised by Lt-Col Harries-Jones in the Unity Hall, King Street. In addition to the 57 men due to go out with the *2nd VSC,* were the men due to go out later with the *3rd VSC*. At the dinner, Lieutenant Hardman was presented with a service revolver, whilst each of the men were presented with '*a handsome silver mounted briar pipe, tobacco, note paper, envelopes, a balaclava helmet, handkerchief and pair of socks.*'[182]

Colonel Harries-Jones, Major Hallsworth and Captain Thorpe travelled with the men, to see their departure; they sailed from Liverpool on the *SS Montrose* on 16th March arriving at Cape Town at 11:30 pm on 7th April.

Private Buckley describes his first sight of Cape Town, '*Cape Town is a beautiful place, and Table Mountain is a treat. It is flat at the top of it, and the mist hangs over it all day like a tablecloth, which is the reason why it is called Table Mountain*'[183] They could not land at Cape Town, as it was prevalent with the plague, but landed at Durban on the 11th. The following day, they made their way up to Pitermaritzburg, where they were issued with arms and ammunition, and then moved on to Pretoria arriving on the 15th April. Buckley describes the journey '*We crossed Tugela River about 2 am and on seeing the heights of Colenso did not wonder at Buller being driven back. We had breakfast at Ladysmith -three dog biscuits and coffee- and stayed there about three hours. We saw Bulvana Hill where the Boers had their long Tom, and traveled on*

[182] Oldham Chronicle

[183] Pvt J Buckley letter

through Dundee and Glencoe Hill, where General Symons was killed and up to Newcastle. Passing along the bridges you can see where they have been blown up, but they have all been rebuilt now. We saw Majuba Hill about dozen times. It kept coming and going out of sight. We stopped for the night at Volksrust. Going on, we had breakfast at Standerton, where there was some heavy fighting. They say that De Wet was round here, but that he cleared out when he heard that were coming up. We have seen no Boers up to now, but the country is swarming with our men and every station is guarded. We next got to Elandsfontein, where there was a big camp and a lot of diamond mines, and left for Pretoria the following morning, and just outside we saw a large camp of Boer refugees, women and children.'[184]

The *2nd VSC* left Sunnyside camp, at Pretoria, on 18th April travelling in open trucks guarding a cattle train until Belfast, arriving at Machadodorp on the 20th April. The same day they got their first taste of the Boers. '*The first night we got here the Boers attacked the camp. It was a great treat to see the star shells bursting and lighting up the sky so that the men in the trenches could see where the Boers were; but the enemy soon cleared off when they heard the big gun getting to work*'[185]

'*We turned out in great coats with rifles and bandoliers to see if we were ready, and we were told to sleep with all on ready for an attack, for the Boers are very thick around here.*'[186]

Things soon settled down and Buckley writes; '*There is not much fighting out here, it all seems to be sniping. This place is a big provision camp so the Boers may try hard to get in; and as the camp is not very strong (there are only 300 men here) we may have to stop instead of going to Lydenburg. We have started doing outpost duty, and it would be all right if it were not so very cold at night.*'[187]

The *2nd VSC* remained in Machadodorp for two weeks, carrying out railway convoy and picket duties, before receiving orders to join the *1st Manchester Regiment* at Lydenburg. Lieutenant Hardman was in command at this stage, as Captain Heyes and Lieutenant Stevens were sick with dysentery, along with Sergeant Jackson, Corporal Caley and seven privates from the Oldham volunteers and a similar amount of Ardwick volunteers. '*We started off with a convoy about three miles long on the 3rd of May. Our first days march was to Helvetia, the place where the Liverpool's were cut up and lost a 4.7 gun; second day to Schoeman's Kloof, third day to Badfontein, fourth day to Witklip, and fifth day to Lydenburg, where we joined our regiment. We are on guard at the entrance of the town. It runs one night in bed and one out; sometimes it runs two out of three on guard. We have been on three-quarter rations since we came to Lydenburg up to the 17th May, then we started on full rations.*'[188]

---

[184] Pvt J Buckley letter
[185] Pvt J Buckley letter
[186] Pvt Waugh letter
[187] Pvt J Buckley letter
[188] Pvt C Buckley letter

Armoured trains
(Source: After Pretoria: The Guerilla War, Vol 1)

The 2nd *VSC* was attached to the *1st Manchester Regiment* as K Company and was assigned to protect the eastern defences of the town.
On 13th May, Sgt Mulcaster describes a patrol out to Mission Camp, two miles from Lydenburg, where they were hoping to see some action against the Boers. They came across some natives who had been attacked by the Boers. '*They made one kaffir sit down, then shot him three places on the left side, then shot a young kaffir girl in the leg, and ran away amongst the hills. The 42nd Batt. R.F.A. (whose guns we were escort to) put a few shrapnels in their direction. What damage they did we could not say. It grieved our men very much that we had a walk for nothing, not even a pop at them. I think they must have known that there were some Oldhamers amongst the attackers.*'[189]

The following months were a continuous round of escorting convoys and garrison duty. Sentry duty was hard work, with the men carrying out fourteen nights on duty with only one night off. Private Rhodes describes the work; '..*it is very hard and dangerous work, climbing up kopjes, dongas and spruits and crossing the Crocodile and Buffalo rivers being up to the neck in it. Then we have to sleep in our wet clothes on the open veldt and wake up in the morning frozen to the ground.*'[190]

[189] Sgt Mulcaster letter
[190] Pvt Rhodes letter

Convoy duty took them as far as Machadodorp and Schoeman's Kloof. When not on convoy or sentry duty, they were employed sangar building and laying barbed wire.
There were a few incidents during this period to relieve the monotony of the daily round. On the night of 4th June, Boers attacked a farm just outside the town, but the pickets managed to drive them off. Some of the *1st VSC* spent time on outpost duty at Bridge Post, north of Lydenburg. On 25th August, the volunteers had their first close view of the fighting Boers, when General Ben Viljoen came into camp for a conference.
They remained at Lydenburg until 1st October, when they received orders to relieve the *Royal Irish Regiment,* who were on trek with Colonel Park's column.
The volunteers were soon to get a real baptism of fire when they came into contact with a large force of Boers at Krugerspost.

They started out on their trek at 7 pm on 1st October, '*to Krugerspost, arrived there about 3.30 am on the 2nd and with G Company we were sent to take up a position on the Boer's left.*'[191]
The Boers were driven '*further up country towards Pilgrim's Rest. Our company was told off to charge a kopje on the right. When we got to the top the Boers had skedaddled and left us in possession. Bullets were flying all round the show.*'[192] The column remained in the area for a further five days, destroying farms and bringing in the women and children, - who were subsequently sent to concentration camps. The column retired to Lydenburg with the Boers sniping at the rear guard for a few miles.
The column returned to Lydenburg by the 8th October, where they camped in the square of the town. For the next few weeks '*our time was chiefly occupied in route marching, escorting convoys, also escorting kaffir gangs to Spekboom Drift.*'[193]
The following month '*on the night of the 2nd November we left Lydenburg at 10.30 and marched all night to a place called Spitz Kop, a hill about 18 miles from here, and on the road we had to go through several spruits, some of which were over our knees, and here in a farmhouse we had a very fair haul. We took about twelve Boer prisoners, a lot of cattle and sheep, and a few horses, and then we returned arriving back about 8 pm. So you will see we marched about 35 miles in less than 24 hours, which I consider a good night's work. I can assure you it is very hard work doing night marches, as there are no proper roads, and we cannot see where we are walking.*'[194]
This had probably been one of the hardest marches the volunteers had undertaken (Sgt Mulcaster put the estimate at 50 miles for this trek). The Boers had been caught napping, and the British had timed the surprise for four o'clock in the morning, this being '*the psychological moment usually selected for the culmination of these enterprises.*'[195]

---

[191] Newspaper interview with Sgt Mulcaster
[192] Newspaper interview with unnamed Oldham volunteer
[193] Newspaper interview with Sgt Mulcaster
[194] Sgt C Dunkerley letter
[195] Newspaper interview with unnamed Oldham volunteer

A couple of weeks later, on November 18th, the volunteers were ordered out near to Hoffman's farm about five miles away to lay in wait there and attempt to surprise a Boer patrol carrying dispatches to Commandant Schoeman. '*The night was bitterly cold and we laid in wait for the Boers in a gully lying behind rocks. We had our bayonets fixed and were told to keep complete silence; when the Boers came we had to rush in and surround them. But nothing turned up, and we retired at twelve o'clock.*'[196] Some days later, another company of the *Manchester Regiment* went out on the same duty, and succeeded in coming in to contact with the Boers, killing four and wounding three.

On 19th November, the *2nd VSC* were then detailed to relieve G Company at Bridge Post. The *2nd VSC* were held in high respect. '*Just to show you what confidence Colonel Curran has in our Volunteer Company, he has dispatched us to Bridge Post, a most important position overlooking Krugerspost, and by far the most advanced post held by any British troops in the country, well away from the line, about eight miles out of Lydenburg, on a very high hill. The behaviour and discipline of the company is excellent, and the men have long settled down to work in a thorough, soldier like fashion.*'[197]
Sergeant Cyrus Dunkerley describes his time at Bridge Post '*a very high hill about eight miles from Lydenburg to the north-east. It is a post of observation, and a splendid position commanding the main road to Kruger's Post and Pilgrim's Rest... the only draw back being that we have to carry all our rations, water and wood to the top, as it is so steep that we cannot get the ration cart up. We now and then get a glimpse of the Boers who come on a ridge about three miles from us but they always keep out of range of our guns; it would not be wise for them to come within range. Our duty is to watch the enemy and report all their moves to the headquarters in Lydenburg.*'[198]
The *2nd VSC* remained at Bridge Post until 1st January 1902, where they were then ordered to join the battalion at Belfast. Whilst on their remote outpost duty, the *1st Manchester Regiment* had been involved in fighting at Elandspruit. The Boers attacked the column whilst they were bivouacked here, but they put up a gallant fight and '*defended their posts against heavy odds and inflicted great loss on the enemy.*'[199]
The *1st Manchester Regiment* suffered nine killed and seventeen wounded. An unnamed Oldham volunteer remarked on the action '*we had the bad luck to be out of it, though it was good luck in another way.*'[200]

The *2nd VSC* then re-joined the *1st Manchester Regiment*, attached to Colonel Park's column on the 6th January at Belfast. On January 16th they left Belfast, the column

[196] Newspaper interview with unnamed Oldham volunteer
[197] Sgt Mulcaster letter
[198] Sgt C Dunkerley letter
[199] Col Parks battalion orders
[200] Newspaper interview with unnamed Oldham volunteer

marched to Swartz Kopje, then Dullstroom, where they set up camp on the side of a hill. They were occasionally sniped at by Boers whilst here.
On the 21st they moved out of Dullstroom. Two companies of the *1st Manchester Regiment*, (one being the *2nd VSC,* the other being A company), two companies of the *Royal Scots*, two battalions of mounted infantry and two guns led the firing line marching by the Witpoort Road. They had marched about five miles when fighting commenced straight to the front. The companies were ordered to get behind cover. About an hour later, the Boers came swarming down the side of the hill in front, estimated at about 800 strong. The companies were told to get back to the top of the ridge, but as the retirement began, the enemy opened fire, and they had to get back under cover of the guns on the ridge. The companies that had been in the firing line, including the *2nd VSC,* went back towards camp, being relieved by E and H companies. Eventually the Boers were driven off after about four hours of fighting. Captain Menzies leading E and H companies was mortally wounded.
The following day the volunteers and 'A' company were sent to search some caves for Boers, taking a pom-pom gun with them. After searching for some time, no Boers were found, '*but when retiring they made their appearance from one of the many caves scattered about, and began firing at them. Some of the men had very narrow escapes, but fortunately none were hurt in the incident; they had to get away the best they could.*'[201]
On January 24th, at a place called Houtenbek, they again came in contact with the Boers. Here the Boers had rebuilt and were living on their farms, destroyed earlier in the war. For seven hours, in torrents of rain, the fight continued until the Boers were driven off. This was to be General Ben Viljoen's last fight, before the *Royal Irish* captured him the same night, whilst trying to escape.
The next morning the column continued on, fighting a rearguard action with the Boers, before making camp at Hoshof valley, where one of the mounted infantry, who had been mortally wounded a couple of days before, was buried. The next day the column left the valley but made little progress due to the very bad weather. The waggons stuck in the drifts as the oxen and the mules were unable to pull them through, so the weary men had to put their shoulders to the wheels, and standing waist deep in the water of the drifts, get the waggons through. For ten hours they were at this job, rain falling in torrents all the time.
The rain was a constant hindrance to the men. '*The rain comes down in sheets, and a man is wet in a minute, the rain had been increasing from the day the column left Belfast, there were wet blankets every night and everything soaking wet, but we got used to it.*'[202] Private Harry Whittaker writing home to his wife was getting fed up of the situation; '*I would like to see some of these big authorities out here sweltering their brains away under this red hot sun or else lying down at night in about 6 inches of*

[201] Newspaper interview with unnamed Oldham volunteer
[202] Newspaper interview with unnamed Oldham volunteer

water, with their blankets and clothes soaking, as we have done many a time after a 20 mile march.'[203]

The following day was a hard day's march, about 22 miles to Boehof, where they camped for the night. They had fine weather here and it was a chance for the men to dry out their blankets and clothes. The next day they marched to Lydenburg, however the volunteers only got a short rest here as they were detailed to take a convoy of supplies to Machadodorp on the 30th, taking General Viljoen with them as a prisoner. At Machadodorp they had a day's rest with the column and then started back again, reaching Lydenburg on 9th February. They left Lydenburg on the 11th and arrived at a station named Pan on 18th February. At Pan they rested through the day but then had a night march towards Klip Spruit against the Boer commandos of Scottish born, Captain Jack Hindon and Louis Trichardt. The *1st Manchester Regiment* lined the ridges above the farms of the Boers in the morning. The pickets of the Boers managed to get off a warning, enabling Hindon to escape in a mule cart. '*Result of operations; our losses nil, captured two families and practically the whole of Trichardt's and Muller's commandos, total 164, eight of whom were wounded. Two died of their wounds. Amongst the prisoners were four field cornets, Trichardt's son and nephew, 107 rifles, 100 horses, 1,200 rounds ammunition, 635 cattle, seven waggons, three cape carts, seven mules, 50 bags of meal, and one forge.*'[204]

Continuous Marching takes its toll on the uniforms
(Source: After Pretoria: The Guerilla War, Vol 1)

The following morning the men started their return journey to Pan. The *2nd VSC* were assigned the task of guarding the prisoners, escorting them from Pan to Middleburg and then on to Pretoria. In the meantime the rest of the *1st Manchester Regiment* had gone on to Belfast where the *2nd VSC* later caught up with them.

From there, on 2nd March, the column moved out to Bronkhurst Spruit and marched for several days in search of members of the Boer government in the hope of rounding them up, but with little success. They were at '*Wilge River on the 5th March, and on the 6th to Houvelfontein, 7th to Straffontein, 8th to Oogiesfontein, 9th to Brugspruit, 10th to*

---

[203] Pvt Whittaker letter

[204] Newspaper interview with Sgt Mulcaster

Balmoral, 11th to Wilge River.'[205] During one of the night marches they managed to capture 45 Boers at Rhenoster Kop. They then arrived at Rietfontein on the 12th and took the prisoners into Balmoral on the 13th. Whilst at Balmoral, Colonel Curran received a telegram from Lord Kitchener '*congratulating him on having such a good lot of men under him, and sending his heartiest praise for the hardships we have endured, and the good work we have done during the past few weeks. The Colonel also paraded our company and thanked us for the good work we had done since joining the regiment*'[206] The marches were gruelling for the men, each man was carrying up to 40 pound of kit on his back, marching straight through the veldts thick long grass, across rivers and rocks in the heat of the day.
From Balmoral they moved to Onvervacht, where they received orders that Colonel Park's column and two other columns were to take part in a 'drive'. Whilst on this march, Lieutenant Hardman became ill with enteric fever, but recovered after a weeks rest.
The column trekked and got into position on 23rd March for the first big drive, which took place on the 24th. The following order was issued at laager on the 25th; *The colonel commanding wishes to express to all ranks of the column his thanks for the excellent manner in which the orders for yesterday's drive were carried out, and his admiration for the splendid marching powers displayed by the Manchester Regiment, all of whom covered distances of more than 60 miles during the 48 hours. It has been a great pleasure to the O.C. Column to be able to bring this very fine performance to the notice of the General Commanding in Chief.*

The column rested at Vlacklaagte until 30th March (total distance covered by the Volunteer company from 1st January to 30th March approximately 900 miles). They then marched north through New Denmark, Spienkop, Tafelkop, Ermelo, Smithfield, Roodefort, and Nooitgedacht and arrived at Eikeborn on 10th April, ready to take part for the second drive. The drive was to head south and consisted of eight different columns, under the commands of Park, Williams, Wing, Mackenzie, Spens, Allenby, Stuart and Lawley and the overall command was that of General Bruce Hamilton. All the columns were formed up to create one long line, around 6 miles long. The line was constructed of picquets of 15 men each having its own wagon, the intervals between wagons was about 150 yards and each picquet had 75 yards in front of them a further five men with an intermediate post. All the wagons were linked together by a wire fence via the intermediate posts. Each night on the drive a continuous wire fence around 50 miles long was put up.[207]
'*Our column formed right of the line, and commenced the drive on the 12th finishing up at Val Station on the 14th. Results of the drive ; Boer losses, 1 killed, 1 wounded, 134*

[205] Newspaper interview with Sgt Mulcaster
[206] Pvt Whittaker letter
[207] History of Manchester Regiment by Wylly

prisoners, 2 cape carts, 85 rifles, 4000 rounds of ammunition, and a large quantity of horses'[208]

On the 15th April the *2nd VSC* were relieved by the *4th VSC*.
Lt-Col A.E.R. Curran wrote in battalion orders: "*After the battalion marches tomorrow K company will remain on their present camping ground, afterwards entraining for Elandsfontein, there to await orders for England. The commanding officer regrets to lose the services of this company. For nearly a year it has been with the battalion, and from the first was able to take share of all duties. It has marched many hundreds of miles, done much hard work, and gone through a considerable amount of hardship. It has maintained throughout the best traditions of the volunteer forces, and has reached a high state of efficiency, this happy result is largely due to the sense of duty and the untiring efforts of Captain Heyes, assisted by Lieutenants Stevens and Hardman.*'
The *2nd VSC* left the *1st Manchester Regiment* at Val on April 16th. The relieved volunteers proceeded to Elandsfontein, in readiness for returning home. They were given one last duty to perform before leaving for England. '*On the 20th the company was to escort Lord Milner to Cape Town arriving about 10:30 am on the 22nd. Proceeded to Point Camp and remained there until we were sent to Simonstown as guard over some prisoners, remaining there until the 14th May when we returned to Cape Town and embarked for England.*'[209]
On the way down to Cape Town they passed '*through the Orange River Colony, where we saw the 5th and 6th Manchester Militia.*'[210]
Shortly before leaving, both Captain Heyes and Lieutenant Hardman were both reported dangerously ill. Hardman was suffering from enteric fever, but was declared fit for duty on 3rd May, recovering in time to make the journey home but Captain Heyes remained behind to recover.
On 15th May 1902, the men of the *2nd VSC* departed from Cape Town on the transport ship *Dilwara,* arriving at Southampton, by way of Las Palmas on the 5th June. It was during this voyage that the war finally came to an end, with the surrender of the Boers being signed on 31st May. The men received the news of peace from the pilot navigating their ship into Southampton.
Not all of the men returned home on the *Dilwara,* Private Andrew went down with enteric fever in Pretoria and Private Ebdon with the same in Cape Town. Three of the Oldham men joined the *Mines Defence Force* and stayed in South Africa. These were Privates Armstrong, Schofield and Hibbert.
The *2nd VSC* stayed overnight in Ashton on the 6th June, only arriving back in Oldham on the evening of the 7th. Despite heavy rain some twenty thousand people turned out to welcome them home. '*Flags, streamers and bannerettes were on view in all directions.. .. a particular pleasing effect was produced by groups of bunting over the Brighton Hotel lamp with the motto behind on a purple ground in white lettering "A*

[208] Newspaper interview with Sgt Mulcaster
[209] Newspaper interview with Sgt Mulcaster
[210] Pvt Whittaker letter

hearty welcome to the boys of the 6th V.B." and by a similar adornment of the Fisherman's Home.'[211]
The men were met at the train station by crowds of people, and over 300 men from the *6th VB,* waiting to escort them to the Town Hall. After a ceremony outside the town hall, led by speeches from Alderman John Hood, they then proceeded to the drill hall.
At the drill hall, Colonel Harries-Jones addressed the men and praised their efforts in South Africa. They had received great praise from Colonel Curran whilst out in South Africa as the *2nd VSC* had done everything that the *1st Manchester Regiment* had done, and he had been sorry to see them go.
Lieutenant Hardman addressed the assembled men and said '*He was very much indebted to the whole company for the manner they had received them that night. They went out to South Africa, hoping to see a good deal and do a good deal. They had had plenty of hard work whilst they had been out and plenty of marching and other things, but no fighting, and he was sure they were all sorry they had none.*'[212]
Hardman was referring to the fact that the volunteers did not take part in any major engagements, but they certainly had their fair share of incidents.
In June 1902, the volunteers of the *2nd VSC* were presented with their South Africa war medals in Alexandra Park. The presentation was carried out by Alderman Hood, the Deputy Mayor. A searchlight was shone from the Oldham Church tower, and there were bonfires on Oldham Edge, Lowes, and the Coppice in celebration of the event.

---
[211] Oldham Chronicle
[212] Oldham Chronicle

The 3rd Volunteer Service Company (served with the 2nd Battalion Manchester Regiment)

Served from 23 March 1901 to 25 June 1902

The *3rd VSC* was to be made up of men from the *1st*, *2nd*, *3rd* and *4th VB* of the *Manchester Regiment*, but these battalions could not fill the requisite number of places, and the *6th VB* was asked if it could help make up the numbers. The Oldham men duly responded and supplied seven men.
The officers selected to command the *3rd VSC* were Captain G Lupton (*3rd VB*), Lieutenant Cronshaw (*1st VB*) and Lieutenant Routley (*2nd VB*). The men reported to the barracks at Ashton on 12th March 1901, and underwent a 10 day training program.
They sailed from Liverpool on 23rd March on the *SS Suevic*, landed at Cape Town on 15th April and then travelled to Worcester, about 120 miles north of Cape Town. The company remained at Worcester for a few days, then returned to Cape Town to go back on board ship for Durban. From Durban, they '*went through Natal to Van Reenen's Pass, on the border of Natal and the Orange River Colony, to garrison the pass. Here we stayed about three months, and had on the whole a fairly easy time garrisoning the various blockhouses in the neighbourhood of the place. We left on the 20th July for Harrismith to join the 2nd Battalion.*'[213] The *2nd Battalion Manchester Regiment* had arrived in South Africa on 6th April 1900, they joined the 17th Infantry Brigade under the command of Major-General J.E.Boyes, which was attached to Lt-General Sir Henry Macleod Leslie Rundle's 8th Infantry Division.
The 17th Infantry Brigade consisted of;

2nd Battalion Manchester Regiment
1st Battalion Worcester Regiment
2nd Battalion Royal West Kent Regiment
1st Battalion South Staffordshire Regiment
22nd Bearer Company
22nd Field Hospital

When the *3rd VSC* arrived at Harrismith, the *2nd Manchester Regiment* was out on patrol and did not return for two weeks. The 3rd *VSC* settled into the *2nd Manchester Regiment* camp, which was positioned on Basuto Hill, just outside Harrismith. When they eventually returned, the *3rd VSC* fully expected to be going out with them on trek, but orders had been received to say that the regiment had done such a good job in the Orange River Colony that it was time they had a rest. The *2nd Manchester Regiment* and the *3rd VSC* were to relieve the *Grenadier Guards* and *1st Leicester Regiment,* and take up garrison duty at Harrismith on 5th August. Sergeant Bailey, a veteran of the

[213] Sgt Bailey letter

previous campaign in South Africa remarks in a letter home about the food. '*The food we get is much superior to what I got in the campaign of 1880-81*'[214]

The 3rd *VSC* took over the part of the defences known as section C outpost, on Verde Hill, Reitz Road, Harrismith. Whilst in Harrismith, 49 men of the 3rd *VSC* joined a recently formed Mounted Infantry Company, Private Collins from Oldham was one of these men. The Mounted Infantry Company was created from men of the *2nd Manchester Regiment*, and was under the command of Captain Noble.

Their stay at Harrismith was not long, and on 1st September the *2nd Battalion Manchester Regiment,* along with the *3rd VSC,* were relieved by the *1st Battalion South Staffordshire Regiment*. On the 4th September, the battalion marched in a column, commanded by Lt-Col Reay, to Bethlehem in convoy with the *Royal Artillery* and *Imperial Light Horse* arriving back in Harrismith on 12th September with no incidents reported.

The battalion continued going out in convoys, Corporal W Davies describes one such trek and its hardships with General Broadwood's column on the 26th October; '*We made a forced march to Elands River Bridge, a distance of 18 miles, in 5 hours and 20 minutes – a record for this regiment... Just outside camp was an exceeding bad drift, and here the mules stuck. Then the order came for the infantry to take off their equipment and drag the wagons over the drift, and officers, sergeants, "Tommies", with their tunics off, were shouting, pulling, hauling, cursing and swearing like fiends. This was carried on for five hours, and at 2.15 am we were again on the move. Orders were issued that no one was to speak above a whisper, no smoking, and all dogs to be tied up. Like a huge snake the columns wound slowly along the road, with its mounted men thrown out as flankers.*'[215]

Sergeant William Bailey
(by kind permission of Kenneth Brown)

On 27th October, the volunteer company were camped on outpost duty at Eland's Kop. A few days later on 29th October Sgt Bailey wrote in his diary; '*About 60 Boers on an almost inaccessible kopje. Broadwood tried in the night to take it, but his men could not scale it. The columns returned to Eland's Kop and the volunteer company was fired*

[214] Sgt Bailey letter
[215] Cpl Davies letter

on when returning from their outposts. The mounted troops having all gone out they were the last to leave and my half company who were in the rear got it pretty hot until the flankers took up their position and covered our retirement.'[216]

Returning from Bethlehem on 5th November, the column was troubled by snipers, and the following day at Tiger Kloof spruit; '*Moving out early we seized a ridge just outside camp when the Boers opened fire on eight of H Company, who was cut off. After an hour heavy firing we drove the Boers into some rocks where we were firing for two hours longer till the big guns and the pom-poms came up and shifted them out. There was all the time the continuous flip flop of the Mauser followed by the whistle of the bullets, as they passed over us as we lay behind our heaps. One of the mounted men rode across the firing line for reinforcements and ammunition, the Boers firing all the time, and two sections of F Company rode and reinforced the party already there. Leaving them there we moved on fighting an advance guard action.*'[217]

The two sections of F Company under the command of 2nd Lieutenant Tylden-Wright acted as the rear guard for the battalion and were rushed by the Boers, three men were killed including Private R.Batey (8317 of *1st VB*) of the *3rd VSC*, three were wounded including 2nd Lieutenant Tylden-Wright and thirteen captured and taken prisoners. Ten of the captured were volunteers from the *3rd VSC*, Lance Corporals E.Hepworth & J.McCarthy, Privates J.Dawson, H.Duncalf, J.Durham, E.Green, E.Hepworth, S.Jackson, G.H.McCormack, J.O'Donnell, W.Taylor, A.Townsend, A.Turner and the Oldham volunteer Private C.Collins. The Boers took the prisoners over the Basutoland Border and set them all free without harm.

Later that day at Elands River Bridge, '*It was there we laid our poor comrades to rest. I being on guard over the Boer sick was unable to attend their funeral*'[218] Colour Sergeant Bailey was in charge of the funeral party.

Corporal Davies struck up a conversation with one of the wounded Boers who informed him that he was glad to be captured '*as he was heartily sick of the war*' and he believed many more Boers were of the same opinion.

[216] Newspaper interview with Sgt Bailey

[217] Cpl Davies letter

[218] Cpl Davies letter

Looking south down Tigers Kloof Spruit, the area where Oldham volunteer Collins was captured

The battalion now received orders to hold a line from Elands River Bridge to Bethlehem to stop the Boers from heading southwards. On 8th November, the *3rd VSC* were on duty on a ridge of this holding line, Corporal Davies takes up the story of the next few days; '*Our company were on outpost on a ridge when a terrible hailstorm broke on us. The stones were as large as pigeon eggs, and when they hit you it was like being fired at with a catapult at a very short range, and it made us dance and shout like maniacs, the pain being awful. After twenty minutes of this during which all the horses stampeded, it slackened and finally stopped. (Sgt Bailey remarked of the hailstorm;' We had never been caught in this sort of warfare before, and I don't want it again, indeed I would almost sooner face bullets.'[219]). The tents were washed out, and all our blankets were wet through. The next day we were troubled by snipers, on the right flank, who wounded one of H Company MI in the leg. The big gun coming into action killed 8 with one shell, and 8 were killed by rifle fire. That night we camped near Langberg. It was outpost again that night for the volunteers, and the next two days, whilst the mounted men were taking some ammunition into Bethlehem. All the*

[219] Newspaper interview with Sgt Bailey

day parties of Boers were moving about just out of rifle range to our extreme disgust. The mounted men brought out two companies of the East York's from Bethlehem to occupy a position on one end of Langberg.

We moved off early in the morning (12th November) and only marched four miles, fighting heavily all the way. We occupied ridge after ridge, fighting all the time, the big guns and pom-poms going like mad. When we reached the last ridge under a big strong kopje we lay for two hours, firing all the time. Captain Noble galloped through our line towards the next ridge, which the infantry had occupied once and retired from, being unable to see any of the enemy about. After about half an hour the sound of heavy firing came to our ears. Lieut. Holberton had a narrow shave, being struck with a bullet on the bandolier right over the heart. Two more men came in sight galloping like mad; one was a regular, who was hit in the shoulder, the other a volunteer called Rushton, hit in the elbow. They told us Capt. Noble[220] was mortally wounded. Just then the remainder of the party retired, the Boers being not 30 yards behind them. As the enemy appeared on the ridge we proceeded to get a little of our own back, and opened a heavy fire on them, driving them back in confusion. The ambulance and doctor went out to bring in Captain Noble and Private Connery. The Boers, strong in numbers, surrounded them, but did not hurt any of them.

Prinsloo[221], who was in command, sent word to the colonel by the doctor that we must surrender by 6 pm or he would give us 'socks'. Captain Noble died as soon as he reached the hospital and Private Connery was reported dangerously wounded. We pitched camp and settled down for the night. We were on outpost on one ridge, and on the kopje on which Captain Noble was killed we could see the Boers doing sentry-go just like ourselves. About 10 pm out of the darkness came a volley right into our midst, the bullets falling all round and amongst us. For a few minutes everything was confusion in the extreme; men running all over the place, dogs barking, horses dashing about. The Boers drove some horses over the ridge into midst of us to draw our fire but it did not come off. After the first few minutes excitement everybody recovered composure, and at the Captains word of command we extended and lay down, most of us without any cover. Every nerve was strained and quivering with excitement, and in every chamber was a round of ammunition waiting. What terrible suspense, and how long would it be to daylight! Flip, flop, going like mad on the right, they were firing into the column that was moving. When everything was quite we retired from our ridge and moved on to the one in rear.

It seemed as though we were lost and G Company with us. We could hear nothing but the whispering of the men and the occasional neighing of a horse in the distance. Captain Lupton was walking along the line as cool as a cucumber with a revolver in his hand encouraging his men. We went back to the ridge we had left and lined the ridge all night waiting for daybreak. When morning dawned Captain Lupton was

---

[220] Capt Charles Noble died 12 Nov 1901 of wounds received at Schalkie Farm, Nr Bethlehem, he commanded the Mounted Infantry of the 2nd Manchester Regiment. Buried at Harrismith military cemetery.

[221] Assumed to be Asst Chief Cmdt A.M.Prinsloo of the Bethlehem commando.

asleep on the ground with Captain King, both without a blanket, starved, and nearly frozen stiff. When it was properly light we found that the column had not gone more than 1½ mile. We retired safely and got away, the Boers fighting a rear guard action. For five hours they fired at us continually, the bullets splashing round our heels like hail and whistling round our heads. One of B Company was hit in the chest by a bullet that passed over our heads, they being in front of us as we were retiring. The mounted rearguard was driven in like a flock of sheep. We got away safely into camp. The next day we fought another rearguard action near to Elands River Bridge. That night we received a congratulatory message from General Rundle, and as a reward we were actually allowed to ride on waggons about six miles the next day. When we reached Harrismith we were paraded to go to Captain Noble's funeral – about 200 infantry, 300 mounted men, Generals Rundle and Dartnell, with their staffs – a perfect blaze of ribbons – and about 50 officers of all ranks, with two bands and the drums of our regiment. I was glad when it was over and we were marching back to camp. After giving us three days rest they took us out again, but we had very little fighting this time. We were out only five days this trek, and then we marched back to Harrismith. This time we were ordered down to Van Reenan's for garrison duty and I can assure you we all require a rest.'[222]

The 2nd *Manchester Regiment*, under the command of Lieutenant Colonel Reay, was now tasked with manning the blockhouse lines, Harrismith to Oliviers Hoek and Albertina to Van Reenen's Pass. On 13th December the *3rd VSC* were posted to Wilge River, eight miles from Van Reenen to build a blockhouse. '*This was commenced on the following day, and completed on the 18th, and was named "The Drift". They proceeded on to Nelson's Kop, and commenced another there on the 22nd.*'[223]

On a cold and wet Christmas day, work on the blockhouses stopped and the men were allowed to rest. '*On that festival each man received a Christmas pudding, a quarter of a pound of tobacco and a pint of beer.*'[224]

At Van Reenen's pass, there were nine blockhouses for the *3rd VSC* to garrison, each blockhouse requiring a 24-hour watchful eye, looking out for the Boers. On 23rd February 1902, a big drive was started from the North to Van Reenen's pass. The drive reached the volunteers line on the 5th of April. During the drive 860 Boers were captured.

On 13th April, the volunteers were relieved from blockhouse duty by the *East Yorkshire Regiment,* and they then marched to Van Reenen, where they entrained for Harrismith. After seeing snow on the Drakensburg Mountains on the 18th May, orders were received to move, and the train took them down to Durban.

---

[222] Cpl Davies letter

[223] Newspaper interview with Sgt Bailey

[224] Newspaper interview with Sgt Bailey

Nelson's Kop (large hill on right of photo) where Oldham volunteers built a blockhouse and spent Christmas day 1901

Volunteers manning a Blockhouse
(from 'Volunteer Infantry of Ashton under Lyne' by R Bonner)

The *3rd VSC* left Durban on 31st May 1902, the day conditions for surrender of the Boers was signed, and the war came to an end. They departed South Africa on board the *Syria* calling at Cape Town on 4th June, Las Palmas on the 19th and finally arriving in Southampton on the 25th June. They travelled by train the same day, to arrive in Ashton that evening, where a welcome reception was held for them at the Town hall by the Mayor and the officers, men and bands of the *3rd VB*. The Oldham men were discharged at Ashton barracks that night and returned to Oldham, after 15 months away from home.

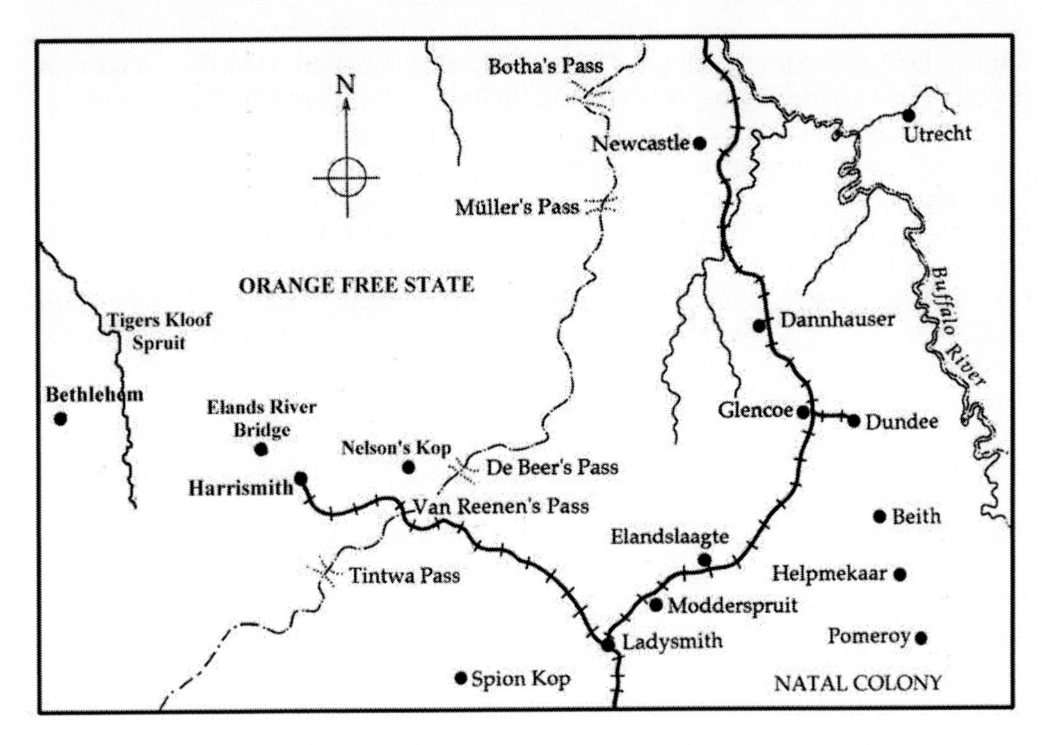

Main area of operations for the 3rd Volunteer Service Company

The 4th Volunteer Service Company (or M Company of 1st Battalion Manchester Regiment)

Served from 15 March 1902 to 1 August 1902

The fourth, and last call, for further volunteers came on 9th February 1902, when the *4th Volunteers Service Company* was requested to be formed.
On 13th March 1902, a dinner at the drill hall was held for the Oldham volunteers destined for South Africa with the *4th VSC*. Presentations were made to the men, of tobacco, socks, Balaclava helmets etc. The following day, they attended a muster at Ashton barracks joining the rest of the men destined for South Africa.
The *4th VSC* was commanded by Captain J.N.Eaton from the *3rd VB*, supported by Lieutenant G.K.Dury of the *1st VB* and Lieutenant J.H.Staveacre of the *4th VB*.
The men departed on 15th March, from Southampton, on the *SS Greek*. The *4th VSC* were messed in the bottom of the ship, and most of them suffered from seasickness. Private Gilham describes the sleeping experiences on board; '*You would laugh if you could see us at night sleeping in our hammocks, which are slung from two hooks in the roof. Some of the men tumble out of bed every night, and some of them are covered with bottles, lifebelts, buckets and other things which they don't know about.*'[225]
Other volunteer companies accompanied them on board, a number of these disembarked at Cape Town but the *4th VSC* remained on board until Durban, which they reached on April 12th. They entrained the same day, travelling through Pietermaritzburg and Colenso, Private Herbert Stott describes the scene at Colenso, '*Here along the railway line is literally strewn with the graves of our officers and men. The bridge that was blown up by the Boers still remains scattered on the ground. The place seems completely honeycombed with trenches and rifle pits.*'[226]
The train was heading for Val, so that the *4th VSC* could join up with the *1st Manchester Regiment*, however on reaching Standerton they were stopped due to Boer activity further up the line. The train crawled a bit further up the line and eventually stopped at Viakslaagte, where there was a fort and some blockhouses. '*The fort was made of sandbags and sheet iron. In we went, and stood in trenches. The officers told us to keep our eyes open as there was a big drive on, and the Boer was expected to come this way. We stayed in the trenches all night. It was very cold, but no Boers came, so off we set the next morning to a place called Greylingstad.*'[227]
They were heading for Val '*but owing to railway guard's mistake were taken to Greylingstadt, the armoured train depot, a beautiful place. We had to wait nine hours for a return train.*'[228]

---

[225] Pvt Gilham letter
[226] Pvt H Stott letter
[227] Pvt H Stott letter
[228] Capt Eaton letter

They reached Val late on the 14th April, where they slept by the side of the railway '*we rolled ourselves in our blankets, and had a ready made bed that night. In the morning I had a surprise, we came across several Oldham lads who came out twelve months ago, and bonny objects they looked. They had not been washed for four days. Their clothes looked like patchwork.*'[229]

At Val, they joined with Colonel Park's column, the *4th VSC* was attached to the *1st Manchester Regiment* as M company. They relieved the *2nd VSC,* who immediately departed for home.

On 14th April, they set off on a march towards Wildebeestfontein, according to Private Herbert Stott they travelled 19 miles that first day, 15 miles the following day, then 20 miles, each time they stopped they had to dig themselves a small trench. At the end of the fourth day (18th) they had their first encounter with the Boers. An exchange of gunfire lasted about one and half hours, but with little effect, however the Boers soon moved off. Herbert Stott recalls this first experience of gunfire; '*A few shots came uncomfortably close, but we returned them.*'[230] During this incident, the rain was coming down in torrents and Private S.E.Stott recounts his first experience in South Africa; '*I was in a trench 8½ hours and got a good soaking. We had only left the ship in which we sailed to South Africa a week when we got under fire. It is all work and no play here, marching in the day, digging trenches and laying barbed wires and being on guard at night.*'[231]

During the first few weeks many of the men were affected by all kinds of ailments, '*Most of our fellows have been bad one way or another, but I am in the pink of condition.*'[232] Private Harry Turner also wrote of the first few weeks marching '*treking is hard work, I have only had one wash in a week, and lucky to get that. I have not had my boots off since we got off the ship.*'[233]

Ernest Drinkwater – Served with 4th Volunteer Service Company

The column continued to cover the miles, arriving at Middleburg on April 26th. The men dug themselves trenches and fixed up barbed wire, before getting settled for the night. Private Herbert Stott describes what happened that night: '*After we had settled down everything was quite and pitch dark when suddenly jets of fire began to shoot through the darkness. The Boers had opened fire. Bullets came whistling over our heads and pattered on the breastwork in front of our trenches. The noise was simply deafening – the cracking of the rifles, the burr of the Maxims, the pom-poms and the nine pounder. It made me wonder if I should ever finish my apprenticeship at Platt Bros. However after an hour or so the fire began to slacken, and*

229 Pvt H Stott letter
230 Pvt H Stott letter
231 Pvt SE Stott letter
232 Pvt J Rhodes letter
233 Pvt H Turner letter

finally stopped altogether. Of course the Boers did not have it all to themselves. I am sorry to say we were not so fortunate this time as we were when they fired on us before, for a Sergeant in the next trench to me was shot through the stomach, and next morning we found three Hussars had been killed, two wounded and a kaffir shot through the head besides several horses and mules killed so we fared rather badly.'[234] The sergeant shot was Sergeant Chandler, the mess sergeant of the battalion, who died from his wounds a week later.

Taking cover in trenches

The column continued to patrol the area around Middleburg, Pan, Belfast and Wildebeetfontein. On 13th May the column was at Belfast, when a few days' later orders were received that the *Liverpool Regiment* would relieve the *1st Battalion Manchester Regiment,* in Colonel Park's column, and the battalion would take over the stations and blockhouses at Waterval Boven, Waterval Onder and Nooitgedacht. The *4th VSC* were posted to Nooitgedacht along with G Company.

The South African war came to an end on 31st May 1902, after two and half years of fighting, when conditions of surrender were signed by the Boer leaders.

The *4th VSC* departed from Cape Town on 9th July, on board the Union Castle liner *German,* calling at Las Palmas on 25th July, they arrived in Southampton on 31st July. When they arrived at Ashton on 1st August, they were escorted to the Town Hall by a large crowd and were heartily cheered along the line of the route. After partaking of a dinner, provided at the Town hall, they were marched to the barracks, and when later dismissed were driven in waggonettes to Oldham Road station, where they took a train for Oldham, Clegg Street station. As the time of their arrival in Oldham was not known beforehand, there was no organised reception, but the people in the vicinity gave them another cordial greeting.

[234] Pvt H Stott letter

Men of the 4th Volunteer Service Company and Imperial Yeomanry march to Manchester Town Hall for a civic reception
(from 'Volunteer Infantry of Ashton under Lyne' by R Bonner)

The members of the Volunteer Service companies were not the only Oldham men to go out to South Africa. Over 100 men went out from the Oldham St John Ambulance brigade, three of them were also members of the *6th VB*; Privates J.S.Lees, H.Hollins and T.Bennett.
Private Hollins served with No 4 General Hospital at Mooi River and later joined E Division of the South African Constabulary.
Five men went out to serve with the Baden-Powell police force, and members of the Oldham Troop of the *Duke of Lancaster's Own Yeomanry Cavalry* served with the Imperial Yeomanry out in South Africa.

With the Imperial Yeomanry in South Africa

A number of the Oldham Volunteers found alternative ways of taking part in the war in South Africa, as there were restrictions placed on volunteering for a Volunteer Service Company. Some men volunteered for the war with the Imperial Yeomanry as the Imperial Yeomanry were not as stringent in their requirements and married men could join.
The following *6th Volunteer Battalion* men joined the Imperial Yeomanry:

Corporal Arthur.H.Priestley, Sergeant G.Marsden, Sergeant William Chadderton, Privates G.Pownell, Frank Newton and F.Thompson.
Priestley, Marsden and Chadderton joined the *23rd Company Imperial Yeomanry* whose account is told in a later chapter.
Frank Newton (No 44985) attestation papers show that his occupation was a farrier, he was 22 years old and unmarried. His parents, James and Sarah were living at 301 Lees Road, Oldham. He joined the Imperial Yeomanry in May 1902 and served out in South Africa with the *35th Battalion Imperial Yeomanry* from 26th May 1902 to 8th Nov 1902.
G.Pownell (No 28819) joined *42nd Company, 12th Battalion Imperial Yeomanry.*

In celebration of the recently announced peace in South Africa, and to commemorate the fact that the Oldham volunteers would be returning home, a poem, composed by a young Oldham lady, was published in the Oldham Standard on 9 June 1902:

Oh! list ye all who long to hear of our gallant volunteers,
They are coming back to Oldham; let us give three hearty cheers
For the heroes of the battlefield, who have faced its horrors grim,
Determined never to allow England's glory to grow dim.

And have they not succeeded, and fought a gallant fight?
Undaunted by the battle and the glare of its ruddy light;
When the cannon roared and thundered loud, and bullets fell like rain,
They still spurred on courageously, and cheered 'gain and 'gain.

Welcome home, ye Lancashire boys! We admire and love ye still;
How we glory in your splendid pluck, it makes our hearts' blood thrill
With pride we can boast such lads, such Britons brave and true,
Who've sacrificed their precious lives to fight for me and you.

Welcome! thrice welcome back to your native home
Happy we feel to behold you, as we watch you steadily come.
How proud we are to honour you, how heartfelt are our cheers,
How fervent is the welcome for our gallant volunteers.

(Composed by Florence H Butterfield , 30 Radcliffe Street, Oldham, Age 16)

South African War Memorials

In October 1902, a thanksgiving service was held at St Stephens church for the active service companies, during this service came the first call for some kind of public memorial to the Oldham men who served in South Africa.

Reverend Jabez Orton told the assembled:

> *'I well remember how when Colonel Harries-Jones asked the men who were lined up before him who among them were willing to go out to the seat of war, every man as one, I believe, stepped forward and thus expressed his willingness. All survived but Joseph Nightingale. I should like to suggest to my fellow townsmen present and absent that our pride in and our appreciation of these men who have for their countries sake, risked their lives, under whatever condition, should take a more tangible form by the erection of some public memorial in a church or other public building in the town, with the names inscribed of all who went forth, that our children in the coming generations may know who were their brave forefathers who fought so unselfishly for Queen, King and country by which they have brought undying credit to the town to which they belong.'*[235]

A few weeks later a subscription fund was opened for purposes of erecting a memorial. The memorial to the *6VB* men who took part in the South African war was finally unveiled at the annual prize distribution on 2nd December 1905. The memorial was a large brass tablet, which was let into the wall of the interior of the drill hall. Sir Elliot Lees, the only son of former commanding officer Thomas Evans Lees, had the honour of unveiling the memorial.

> *'Elliott Lees who addressing the men of the active service contingent as 'comrades of the SA field force' said that he almost smelt the dead horse and heard the oaths at 1 am reveille, almost heard the ice broken in his pail to wash when he thought of those days, but besides the hardships there were also joys in the experience there. Three cheers were given on unveiling and three more cheers for Elliott Lees.'*[236]

Elliot Lees had served in the South African war as an officer in the Dorset Yeomanry. It had been hoped that Elliot Lees would join the Oldham volunteers but his path took another direction into politics and he became a conservative MP for Oldham in 1886. Elliot Lees became the 1st Baronet Lees, of Lytchet Manor, Dorset.

Manchester Regiment Memorial, St Ann's Square, Manchester

The memorial in St Ann's Square, Manchester was raised by public subscription and is erected 'To the memory of the following officers non-commissioned officers and men who fell in the war in South Africa 1899-1902 gallantly serving their sovereign and country' There are three bronze plaques which record the names of eight officers and 309 men who gave their lives during the war. The memorial was to the men of the

---

[235] Oldham Chronicle
[236] Oldham Chronicle

Manchester Regiment, both regular soldiers and those who served in the Volunteers battalions. The only Oldham volunteer casualty, Private Nightingale, is named on one of the plaques.
The memorial was unveiled on 26th October 1908 by General Sir Ian Hamilton. (He was Lord Kitcheners Chief of Staff during the South African war.)

St James Conservative club, Ripponden Road
Unveiled in June 1902 in honour of its members who had served out in South Africa, the following names were listed.

Sgt Cyrus Dunkerley – 6VB
Pvt Fred Dunkerley – 6VB
Pvt Handel Ogden – 6VB
Pvt Arthur Prescot – 6VB
Pvt Thomas Lewis – RAMC
Pvt John Needham – ROSB
Pvt James W Whitaker – LF
Pvt Charles Hunt – 1st RB
Pvt Wm Halliwell – KRR
Pvt Thos Piggott – MR
Pvt John Halkyard – RORLR
Pvt Daniel Beswick - SJA

Social composition of the Oldham Rifle Volunteers

A study of the 1863 Corps returns was carried out, to try and determine the social composition of the *31st LRV* in the early years of its formation. In the 1863 Corps returns, all volunteers who had joined in the years of 1859, 1860 and 1861 were counted and then checked against the 1861 census to determine their occupation. There were 200 men listed who had joined in these years but only 90 of these could be identified positively in the census. This gives us a sample of 45%, which is not high but gives an idea of the type of occupations of the volunteers.
From the table below, it can be seen that the majority of the volunteers were skilled workers or professionals, those who had sufficient means to pay for the fees. This is confirmed by Captain Blackburne's statement to the 1862 Royal commission that:

> '*the great bulk of them are artizans.*'[237]

Occupations of some of the *31st LRV* in 1860

Occupation	Number
Engineer or mechanic	22
Skilled worker	20
Manufacturer with own business	9
Clerk	8
Cotton Mill operative	8
Tailors & Drapers	6
Publican or Beer seller	3
Solicitor	3
Surveyor	2
Warehouse man	2
Sales/trader	2
Carter	1
Coke Burner	1
Office Boy	1
Student	1
Surgeon	1

With the introduction of the subsidies from government in 1863, this provided opportunities to those that could not previously afford to join the volunteers, to now apply, this did not mean that anybody could join; each potential volunteer still had to be recommended by at least two current volunteers. As long as the man put in the required amount of drill practice then the cost of being a volunteer was minimal as the uniform was also provided free from the Corps funds.

---

[237] 1862 (3053) Royal comm. to inquire into condition of Volunteer Force

This introduction of subsidies changed the social composition of the corps, from a predominately middle class, to an increasingly working class composition.
From the 1867 returns, 260 volunteers can be identified as having joined in the period 1864 to 1867 (there would have been others that joined and left during this period). From a study of the 1871 census, only 69 of these can be identified positively and their occupations determined.

Occupations of some of the *31st LRV* in 1867

Cotton Mill operative	24
Skilled worker	15
Labourer	10
Shop/sales	8
Mechanic	7
Clerical	3
Others	2

Again this is not a high percentage sample of the occupations of the volunteers, but what it does show is a marked increase in the working class workers from the cotton mills and follows the trend of the rest of the country, that the volunteers were becoming predominately working class.

Commanding Officers

Lieutenant Colonel John George Blackburne - Commandant 1860 to 1871

John George Blackburne, was born in London on 4th June 1815. From an early age he showed an interest and skill in drawing and reproduction of buildings. At the age of 13 he was articled to William Dunn of Oldham, a surveyor who had a good reputation for training apprentices. Blackburne obviously impressed his employer, as he was made a partner of the practice in 1835, and remained so until Dunn's death in 1840. Blackburne then started his own Civil Engineering practice, and became recognised as one of the leading civil engineering surveyors in the area. Blackburne was involved in many of the surveying and planning works for significant projects around Oldham, such as railway construction, laying out of new streets, larger houses and of course new mills. In addition to the surveying business, John also had business interests in the Lowside Colliery.

(By kind permission of Oldham Local Studies)

His practice flourished and he brought into the business his son, John William and also formed a partnership with James Lee Page, with the practice being known as *Blackburne, son and Page*. Both John William and James Lee Page were also members of the *31st LRV*. John George Blackburne was respected within his profession and was a member of the Institute of Civil Engineers, he was a fellow of the Geological Society and he was for a period the president of the Manchester District Society of Surveyors and Valuers.[238]

John married Sarah Clegg, daughter of the Hatter, James Clegg, in 1837. They lived in Union Street, Oldham for many

[238] Oldham Evening Chronicle

years before moving to Dryclough. Sarah died on 6th November 1858, as a tribute to her memory John had a window placed in the Oldham parish church dedicated to her memory, No.4 South side – 'Parable of the Talents'.
John died from cerebral disease on 30th September 1871, aged 56. According to his death certificate he had been suffering with the disease for 15 months and for the last two days of his life he was paralysed.

Lieutenant Colonel Thomas Evans Lees - Commandant 1872 to 1878

(By kind permission of Oldham Local Studies)

Thomas Evans Lees was born at Greenbank on 2nd July 1829, and was the only son of James Lees, Esq., who was a very successful businessman in the Oldham cotton spinning industry. James Lees was also the Mayor of Oldham during the municipal year 1853-54. The Greenbank Lees family were recognised as one of the oldest established families in Oldham, involved in the cotton industry. It is interesting to note, that Lieutenant Colonel John Lees, the original founder of the Oldham Volunteers, was a distant relation of Thomas Evans Lees.
When his father, James Lees died, in 1871, he left the business and the bulk of his estate, estimated at over half a million, to Thomas. Soon afterward Thomas went into partnership with his cousin Edward W Wrigley, who had for some time acted as the company manager and cashier. The company then traded under the name of *T.E. Lees & Wrigley*. The new company continued to prosper and by the time of his death, the company was one of the largest in the Oldham borough, with around 15,000 spindles in its mills. Thomas was a wealthy man and did not need to work, and for the last three years of his life he left the running of the company to his cousin Edward Wrigley.

In politics Thomas was a conservative, he was a strong supporter of the party and was chairman of the Conservative election committee in 1865 and 1868, then in 1872 he supported John Morgan Cobbett in gaining success in the general election for the Conservative Party. In 1877 Thomas was himself chosen by the party to contest the election but lost to John Tomlinson Hibbert.
His other civil duties included that of a county magistrate, and also being appointed as Deputy Lieutenant of the County on 7th February 1873. He took a keen interest in the Blue Coat School, of which he was a trustee. He will also be remembered as a liberal giver, he gave to the Church of England and particularly St Mark's church, Glodwick.
Thomas joined the *31st LRV* in the first 12 months of its existence and was responsible for raising the second company, of which he became the Captain. Thomas was a keen and enthusiastic supporter of the Volunteer cause. When John George Blackburne was raised to the Lieutenant Colonelcy, Thomas was gazetted Major and then when Blackburne died he succeeded him as Lieutenant Colonel. In 1878, he gave up his commission, and was succeeded by his cousin Edward Brown Lees. Thomas left the Corps as he was suffering from cancer of the tongue. The cancer appeared soon after the election contest in March 1877, when he appeared as the Conservative candidate. The disease caused him a lot of pain, and he eventually succumbed, at Scarborough, on the 13th January 1879. His body was returned to Oldham and he was buried at Chadderton cemetery
Thomas was married to Miss Turnbull, a lady born in Mexico, of English parentage. He had one son and five daughters, two other sons died early in life. Their family residence was Woodfield, Werneth Park. His surviving son, Elliot Lees was later to become the 1st Baronet Lees, of Lytchet Manor, Dorset, and he was conservative MP for Oldham in 1886.

Lieutenant Colonel Edward Brown Lees - Commandant 1878 to 1885

Edward Brown Lees assumed command of the *31st LRV* in 1878. At this stage Edward had already moved away from Oldham, and by 1881, could be found living at Kelbarrow near Grasmere in Westmoreland.
He was an extensive landowner and proprietor of several collieries, these business concerns meant he was a regular visitor back to Oldham, but still not the ideal commanding officer when he was living outside of the Oldham borough.
He formerly resided at Clarksfield, and was part of the Clarksfield Lees family dynasty, a prominent family in Oldham with business concerns in coal and extensive land owners. Edward Brown Lees was the son of John Lees and Mary Ann (nee Brown) and also the cousin of Joseph Crompton Lees. His grandfather James Lees, the founder of the Clarksfield Lees dynasty, had been a Major in the *Oldham Loyal Volunteers* for a short period.
He was appointed Justice of the Peace for the county in 1867, and regularly attended court in Royton before he moved. He had a reputation as an efficient and painstaking

officer, always ready to advance the movement. In politics he was a Conservative and was a strong adherent of the church.
Lees resigned his commission in May 1885 and two months later bought Thurland Castle, Longsdale near Lancaster.
On 27th August 1896, he died unexpectedly at Hollinwood station. He was:

> *'awaiting arrival of a train to Manchester. On arrival at the platform he entered the lavatory, and directly afterwards a porter hearing a peculiar noise, proceed there and found the gentleman lying on his back. A doctor was called but he was pronounced dead due to sudden failure of heart. On the same morning Lees had presided over a meeting of the directors of the Chamber Colliery company, Col Lees was 53 and leaves a wife and family.'*[239]

Lieutenant Colonel James Greaves Ireland - Commandant 1885 to 1889

James Greaves Ireland was born in Oldham, in 1850, to Thomas Ireland and Sarah (nee Greaves). The Reverend Thomas Ireland was the vicar at St Thomas Church, Werneth. James was married in his father's church, on 8th September 1875, to Eleanor Ascroft.
He was involved in the cotton manufacturing trade, and by 1881 his occupation was listed as a cotton broker.
It is not clear what happened in James life, but in 1889 he had resigned from the volunteers, and by 1891 he appears to have left his family and is a lodger at a house in Southport described as living on his own means. By 1901 he is again a lodger, this time at a house in Stretford and described as a commercial traveller.
James died in 1908 only 58 years old.

Lieutenant Colonel Joseph Crompton Lees - Commandant 1889 to 1898

Joseph Crompton Lees was born in 1844, the son of Joseph Lees and Sarah Ann (nee Milne), he was also the cousin of Edward Brown Lees, a previous Lieutenant Colonel of the corps. His grandfather, like Edward Brown Lees, was James Lees, the founder of the Clarksfield Lees dynasty.
He resigned his position of commanding officer on 20th April 1898 and became the battalions Honorary Colonel. Shortly afterwards he moved from Oldham to set up home at Newtown Manor, Leitrim, Sligo, Ireland where he died on the 1st March 1907.

Lieutenant Colonel James Robert Harries-Jones – Commandant 1898 to 1903

James was born in Bolton in 1852, to Robert Harries Jones and Mary Ann (nee Newton). Robert was a curate and the family moved around with his vocation, Mary was originally from Hollinwood, Oldham. It appears that James, along with his brother

---

[239] Oldham Standard

Ivan, came to Oldham in their teens and stayed with their mother's side of the family in Oldham, and in 1871 they were both living at Lime House.
James became a solicitor and he established a partnership in 1879 with his brother, Llewellyn, on Clegg Street, they also had a practice in Hollinwood.
Harries-Jones was granted the honorary rank of colonel on 20th April 1898.
During the period 1889-1892, he sat on the town council as Conservative member for Hollinwood. During his period of command he was extremely popular amongst the men, being most considerate to the whole of them. For his long connection with the volunteers he was awarded the Volunteer Decoration (VD). He was a Freemason in the Friendship lodge, president of Oldham law association and also very fond of music.
In August 1902, he was married in the Parish church of Weeton, near Leeds. His bride was Florence Irving, 2nd daughter of Mr John Widnall of Huby Park.
James died on 8th May 1920 leaving a widow and daughter.

Lieutenant Colonel George Henry Hollingworth – Commandant 1903 to 1907

George Henry Hollingworth was born in Oldham in 1853, to Harry Lees Hollingworth and Sarah (nee Dunkerley). He joined the Oldham Rifle Volunteers as a 2nd Lieutenant in 1877 and worked his way up until being appointed Lieutenant Colonel in October 1903.
George's career took him into the mining industry, becoming a manager at Chamber Colliery Co, then specialising as a mining engineer he jointly set up the firm, *Messrs Booth & Hollingworth.*
George married Frances Rosa Cooper in 1885, and very soon afterwards they set up home in Bredbury, Cheshire. George continued to support the Oldham Volunteers whilst living in Bredbury, as his work also took him to Oldham.
George died on 27th March 1915, at Brinnington Lodge, Stockport where he had lived for several years.

Lieutenant Colonel Charles Hodgkinson - Commandant 1907

Charles Hodgkinson was born in 1859, to Charles Hodgkinson and Ann Bolton (nee Phillips) in Fenny Stratford, Buckinghamshire. Charles Senior was a career policeman, and came to Oldham with his wife around 1867 when he was appointed the Chief Constable of Oldham.
Charles did not follow his father's career path, instead he became a solicitor, living with his parents in Werneth Old Road, Oldham. Charles joined the Oldham Volunteers in June 1881 as a 2nd Lieutenant. In the 1890s he moved away from Oldham to live in Penistone, Yorkshire but continued his connection with the Volunteers whilst living there. On the 24th June 1891, he married Lillian Wild of Oldham.
Charles became the Lieutenant Colonel of corps at a difficult time, just when it was changing to the new territorial force.

Training Camps

The first ever camp, was organised by Captain Armitage for the 3rd company. He arranged and paid for a small camp at Standedge, during the Oldham wakes in August 1861. The tents, being pitched not far from the Great Western Inn, on the Marsden side of the hill. Each day they practised drill for four hours per day.
From 1872, the government started paying allowances to Volunteer Corps, for attendance at camps. Travelling expenses were paid and 10s per head paid to a Corps, for each volunteer in camp for six days. This was later increased in 1890, to an allowance of 16s. Despite this allowance, it would not have been enough to fully fund a camp and money would have been used from the Corps own funds to subsidise the camps.
The camp was one of the big inducements for young men to join the Volunteers, in a period when holidays were very seldom and paid holidays were unknown, going on a Volunteer camp was effectively a paid holiday. Combine this with a trip away from your hometown, with your friends; this must have been quite attractive to a lot of young men. The routine of the camp life would have been far less arduous then the jobs they were leaving behind in the cotton mills.
Camp was an important part of the training, it was one of the few times that all companies of the corps could train together, normally drill and training would have been on a company basis, with each company drilling on separate evenings.
Camp was intended as an opportunity to drill and practice as a whole, but it was also a major social event with entertainment provided, and all types of sports and activities organised. In the earlier years, it would be quite normal for family and friends to come and visit the camp for a day or two, and the men would be granted half a day off to spend with their family. Of course camp was also a time to experience some of the hardships that a soldier would suffer whilst out in the field, such as the experience of the first major camp for the Oldham Volunteers.
The first full camp for the Oldham Rifle Volunteers was in August 1879, where they experienced a rough week encamped at Lytham, one of the most inclement wakes seasons ever:

> *'The tents were pitched in lines with the utmost exactness and regularity, about which the most fastidious martinet would fail to find a fault. 20 men under the command of Captain Page set up the camp prior to the rest arriving.' 'Little drill could be carried out due to the continuous rain. The rain penetrated the canvas and fell on the volunteers as they lay at rest. In addition a stiff wind prevailed through the night and almost overturned the tents. In some cases the pegs were loosened, and, we were told by some of the volunteers, with a rather rueful countenance, that it was not very pleasant to have to get up at 3 o'clock in the morning and secure their tents, for fear they might be carried away with the gale. At night they had to lie down on a hammock stretched upon a*

covering of straw. The report was that the camp was thoroughly enjoyed by all. The men had been supplied with government rations. The conduct of the volunteers had been exemplary. Whilst in camp each private receives from the government 6d per day, a Corporal 9d, Sergeant 1s. Recruits appeared in the new uniform, spiked helmets and scarlet coats, whilst the older volunteers wore the old green uniforms. All the men will however ultimately wear the new uniform.
Athletic sport competitions we held, 19 events including tug of war, tent pitching, tent striking, mile race, ½ mile race, high jump, long jump, race in heavy marching order, three legged race. The camp lasted 1 week, Saturday to Saturday.'[240]

About 500 men went on camp. Normal routine was reveille at 6am, breakfast at 8 am, dinner at 1 and tea at 5. Every man had to be in camp by 9:30 pm unless he had special permission with lights out at 10:15 pm.

The camp in 1883 at Doncaster, was the first camp since gaining independence from Ashton, over 600 men camped on the common surrounded by the famous St Ledger racecourse. The people of Doncaster gave the men of Oldham a warm welcome, and over 2,000 turned out to greet them at the railway station when they arrived. The camp was a great success; cricket matches and shooting matches were arranged against the Doncaster Volunteers.
The organising of camp was a major affair, with the Quarter Master and a number of volunteers travelling a few days before to set up. The 1884 Blackpool camp at Raikes Hall, consisted of 92 bell tents, three large store tents, officers mess tent, officers retiring room, sergeants mess, recreation tent and canteen. For the men's sleeping comforts each tent was supplied with 18 Ibs of straw.
The camp at Cleethorpes in 1887 would be remembered only for the torrents of rain for the first part of the week and the dismissal of a number of the men. Privates Jon Clegg and W.Priddy of H Company who were:

'dismissed with ignominy for using filthy and obscene language and refusing to obey orders of their superior officer whilst on camp at Cleethorpes, ordered to pay the capitation grant of 30s.' In addition the bugle band declined to play, 'a court of inquiry has been held, with the result that Drummer Joseph Taite has been dismissed for refusing to play, and Private Joseph Knight for disgraceful conduct in having fired pebbles from his rifle with a blank cartridge'[241]

[240] Oldham Chronicle
[241] Oldham Chronicle

The camp at Southport in 1888 was marked by an incident with Corporal Wilding. Whilst on duty in camp, during a heavy rainstorm, his bayonet was struck by lightening; he was struck dumb with shock for a while, but escaped serious injury.

The following year's camp at Harrogate was noted for an incident with one of the locals:

> *'John Joseph Ibbotson a cab proprietor in Harrogate was charged with being drunk and being drunk whilst in possession of loaded firearms. The prisoner got drunk and obtained possession of a double-barrelled gun, went into the camp field and fired at random. The cartridges fired were blank and several were found upon him. Lt Jones and several volunteers brought the prisoner to the police station. It was a miracle the guard did not bayonet him, going about the field in the manner that he did. The guard sounded the assemble and made a cordon around the camp. Fined £1 11s or go to prison for 1 month.'*[242]

Harrogate Camp 1899
(By kind permission of Oldham Local Studies)

[242] Oldham Chronicle

The 1890 camp at Conway, took place shortly after a local boating tragedy. The Oldham Rifles Band organised a musical evening within the walls of the Castle, in aid of the men who devoted their time to search for the bodies of the victims.
The vocalists were Colour Sergeant H.Neild, Colour Sergeant Spencer, Sergeant Birdsall, Lance Sergeant Chadderton and other members of the battalion. The concert realised £15, and after expenses were paid, the sum of £10.10s.7d was handed over to the searchers. The *Oldham Chronicle* reported the send off, which the volunteers received on their day of departure.

> *'On Saturday morning the men were up in good time, in order to prepare themselves for their departure home. The time for leaving camp was fixed at 1.15, having to march to Llandudno Junction, a distance of about two miles. On arriving at Conway Gate the battalion was met by the search party in the late disaster, and led by them to the station, eight of whom carried their boat, named the volunteer, which was gaily decorated with flags. On arriving at the station the coxswain presented the battalion with a newly painted stern board of the boat, as a mark of their appreciation of the manner in which the corps had treated them. The stern board will be hung in the mess room at headquarters.'*

The stern board was placed in the Sergeants mess, and the men of the mess commissioned Bandmaster Robinson to get a similar board made, which would in its turn be presented to the coxswain at Conway.

1890 - The 6th Volunteer Battalion march to the station with the search party and an appreciative Conway crowd following them

The 1892 camp at Ripon saw the *6th VB* pitted against the *1st VB (Ripon) West Yorkshire Regiment* in a shooting competition and also at Rugby Football. Ripon were narrow winners in the shooting match, beating *6th VB* by 495 to 493 points. Ripon also won the Rugby Football match.
During the 1893 Conway camp, the bandmaster Randle Taylor wrote and performed a piece called 'Conway Camp'.
The 1897 camp at Conway was a disaster, with the most wretched weather all week. The tents, issued by the War Office, had canvas that was so thin that they let in rain and ropes so frayed that the tents blew away.
The Blackpool camp in 1898 was a joint affair, with the *1st, 3rd, 4th and 6th Volunteer Battalions* of the *Manchester Regiment* all camped midway between the South shore and St Annes.

6th Volunteer Battalion on camp
(By kind permission of Oldham Local Studies)

The onset of the South African war changed camp arrangements, this year it would no longer be a regimental camp, but a brigade camp on a large scale with up to 10,000 men on Salisbury Plain. In March 1900, a letter was sent to 250 employers to see if they would agree to two weeks leave for the men. Unfortunately it would not be in the traditional wakes week when the *6th VB* normally took their camp. To comply with

government regulations, they needed at least 50% of the battalion to go on camp. 488 men indicated willingness to go to camp, and not a single employer refused to grant leave to their employees. The Salisbury Plain camp took place from 2-16th June. Around 540 men from the *6th VB* went to camp along with the *1st, 4th and 5th VB Manchester Regiments, 1st, 2nd, 3rd and 5th VB Cheshire Regiments, London Volunteer Rifles* and the *Honourable Artillery Company.*
The camp was poorly organised, with respect to the provision of food, which was supposed to have been organised by the regular army. Men were going without breakfast, supply of bread was poor, and in consequence some drill exercises were cancelled. Apart from this the *6th VB* acquitted themselves well and they:

> *'earned the encomiums of the commanding officers, and were at the same time undoubtedly the most popular regiment on the camping ground. One fact may be mentioned in support of this. The Munster Fusiliers accorded them a send off and played them down from camp to the railway station, a distance of 1 ½ miles with their fife and drum band, an honour not conferred to any other regiment.'*[243]

This camp was an exception for the volunteers from Oldham and Ashton. The time for these brigade camps was Whitsuntide, but for both Oldham and Ashton this was not the traditional holiday time, normal time for holiday or wakes was at the beginning of September, and this was when they normally took their camp. Therefore, the following year in 1901, the camp was back to its traditional Oldham holiday time with one week at Fleetwood.
In December 1901, the government announced that the Volunteers would have to commit themselves to more training in battalion and tactical operations, this could only be achieved by taking part in brigade camps, for a pre-requisite amount of days training, so that a suitable standard of military training could be achieved. It also stated, that it realised that the civilian occupations of some volunteers will not admit of their complying with the minimum conditions necessary, and that consequently it would loose the services of such men, but it was preferable to have a somewhat smaller number of highly trained officers and men, sufficient to meet all the demands for home defence.
The employers of Oldham refused to let the Volunteers in their employ go for more than one week to camp, and that the camp could only be organised during the traditional Oldham wakes at the beginning of September. The *6th VB* went to camp at Salisbury Plain in 1902, but without the other Manchester Volunteer Battalions. The *6th VB* carried out some mock battles, with the assistance of the *Royal Horse Artillery.* Towards the end of the week a number of men became very ill from picking and eating fungi, all of the six men of the *6th VB* recovered, but one man from the *Royal Horse Artillery* died from the poisoning.

---

[243] Oldham Chronicle

6th VB Training at Salisbury Plain in 1906
By kind permission of Bill Mitchenson

The 1903 camp at Towyn, in North Wales, gained the distinction as the worst camp ever, it was a very wet and the cyclist's tents were washed away with Sgt Faber of the cyclists company, also loosing his photographic equipment. An unnamed volunteer tells a tale about this particular camp:

> *'It appears that a fatigue party had been ordered to erect a hospital tent under the direction of Harry W--. Suddenly a gale sprang up, and the hospital tent went up in the air just like a balloon and carried way ten of our boys, who had become entangled in the ropes. The cries of the men as they sailed away to the moon were heart rendering. Jack S—just before entering the first bank of clouds could be heard distinctly to say he would do it no more. What he meant I do not know, but their sins are all forgiven. I borrowed a field glass to take a last parting look at them, and to my dismay I could distinctly see Bill H—try to push Don M—off the tent pole just before they were lost to sight. We are informed that a round nosed clogg fell from the clouds and struck the Chief Constable of Llandudno with such terrific force that he is not expected to recover. The clogg has been sent up to London to be analysed and we find that it belonged to Jack F--. Roger W—is the only pioneer left, and we shall not have him long, as since this terrible accident he has tried to commit suicide on average 5 times per day by flinging himself in Cardigan Bay. I hear a new planet has been discovered going in a northerly direction, it passed over*

> *Chester this morning. It might be the hospital tent and the boys going home on furlough.'*[244]

The Towyn camp cost the Battalion £300, plus damaged equipment, if they had been on a government brigade camp, then this cost would have been be covered by government. A renewed appeal was made to the employers, to let the men go to brigade camp at Whitsuntide.
The 1904 brigade camp was at Milntown at the foot of Glen Auldyn, 1.5 miles from Ramsey, lasting for two weeks from the 22nd May. All of the six Volunteer Battalions and the *Manchester Royal Army Medical Corps* were on camp. The *1st, 2nd, 4th and 5th VB* remained on camp for two weeks, but the Oldham and Ashton Corps only one week. It would seem that the commanding officer had got agreement from the employers for the men to camp outside the traditional wakes holiday, but unfortunately could not get agreement for the full two-week camp. It was obvious that not all employers agreed to this new arrangement, as only 630 out of a total of 856 volunteers managed to go to camp.

6th VB Training at Salisbury Plain in 1906
By kind permission of Bill Mitchenson

A renewed appeal was made by Lt-Col Hollingsworth to the employers, but he still could not get them to agree to the two weeks, and yet again for the 1905 camp they had to go to brigade camp for one week whilst the rest of the Volunteer Battalions, except

[244] Oldham Chronicle

Ashton, were there for two weeks. It was not until the 1908 camp, in the Isle of Man, before the Oldham and Ashton Volunteers got permission for two weeks camp. By this time they were no longer the *6th VB* but, had by then, become the *10th Battalion Manchester Regiment*.

Oldham Rifle Volunteers Camps

1879 – Lytham

1880 – Southport (camping ground at the top of Portland Street)

1881 – Buxton (Fairfield Common)

1882 – No camp

1883 – Doncaster (Camped on St Ledger race course)

1884 – Blackpool (Raikes Hall)

1885 – No camp

1886 – Harrogate

1887 – Cleethorpes

1888 – Southport (Camped on ground near the New Inn)

1889 – Harrogate

1890 – Conway (Camped on Conway Marsh)

1891 – Conway

1892 – Ripon (Camped on the race course ground)

1893 – Conway (Morfa)

1894 – Conway

1895 – Blackpool

1896 – No camp

1897 – Conway

1898 – Blackpool

1899 – Scarborough (Camped on ground near Burniston Road)

1900 - Salisbury Plain (Perham Down)

1901 – Fleetwood (Camped next to Government rifle range)

1902 – Salisbury Plain (Bulford Camp)

1903 – Towyn, North Wales

1904 – Milntown, Isle of Man

1905 – Salisbury Plain (Park House Camp)

1906 – Salisbury Plain (Windmill Hill camp)

1907 – Salisbury Plain (Windmill Hill camp)

1908 – Ramsey, Isle of Man

Training, Drill and Field Exercises

The War office circular of 1859, outlined what the planned role of the volunteer was envisaged to be:

'*The nature of our country, with its numerous inclosures, and other impediments to the operations of troops in line, give particular importance to the service of volunteer riflemen, in which bodies each man, deriving confidence from his own skill in the use of his arm and from his reliance on the support of his comrades – men whom he has known, and with whom he has lived from his youth up – intimately acquainted, besides with the country in which he would be called upon to act, would hang with the most telling effect upon the flanks and communications of a hostile army.*'[245]

Order Arms.

The main emphasis was on the use and handling of the rifle. Shortly afterwards a manual was produced called '*The Drill and Rifle instruction for Corps of Rifle Volunteers*', soon afterwards it was know as '*The Green Book*' due to the colour of its cover.
This manual covered areas of drill, field movements, skirmishing and skill at arms. It only covered the basics of military training, and the War Office felt that this would be sufficient for the volunteers, as outlined in the war office circular:

> '*It should not be attempted, therefore, as regards Rifle Volunteers, to drill or organise them as soldiers expected to take their place in the line, which would require time for instruction that could ill be spared; but it should be rather sought to give each individual Volunteer a thorough knowledge of the use of his weapon, and so to qualify the force to act efficiently as an auxiliary to the Regular Army and Militia, the only character to which it should aspire.*'[246]

Present Arms.

In February 1860, the government authorised that each Corps could obtain the services of a regular drill instructor. To carry out this drill instruction and training the *31st LRV* appointed Sergeant Major Holt, late of the *6th Dragoon Guards*. Payment for this full time instructor came from the Corps funds and not the government, costing the Corps 2s.6d per day with lodgings provided for by the Corps. This type of employment in the Volunteers must have been

[245] War Office circular 13 July 1859
[246] War Office circular 13 July 1859

a source of useful employment for many retired regular army NCOs around the country and they were effectively the only source of military experience for most Corps including Oldham.
The standards of the Corps were obviously improved over the years, with the help of these ex-regulars. In 1863, the War Office introduced regulations requiring the Volunteers to meet a minimum standard, and introduced an annual Certificate of Efficiency. This required that the volunteer had to attend a minimum of six company drills, three battalion drills, and be proficient in drill, musketry and field exercises. In addition he was required to attend the annual inspection of the Corps. For recruits, they had to attend a minimum of 30 drills in their first 18 months, but this was increased in 1881, to 60 drills in their first two years. If the volunteer met all this criteria he was entered as an 'effective' and the Corps could claim the capitation grant for that man.
The officers and NCOs were also required to become proficient in drill and musketry, a certificate was granted to the officer after he had attended a month's course at a school of instruction in Manchester. In 1882, an examination in tactics was introduced for officers of the rank of Captain and above, this was a voluntary examination, but if passed it would earn that officer an extra 10s grant and the letter 't' after his name in the *Army List.* Captain Charles Hodgkinson was the first to pass this examination.

The first known major field exercise that the Oldham Volunteers took part in, was in April 1884, when a mock battle was arranged with the Saddleworth Volunteers, who had only recently had a title change from *34th WYRV* to *2nd VB Duke of Wellington's Regiment*. There was some red tape in obtaining permission for the Oldham Volunteers to go into a neighbouring county, but eventually permission was given and what became known as the 'Battle of Lydgate' went ahead.

Battle of Lydgate

The 'idea' was that the Saddleworth Volunteers should take up a position in some stone quarries lying on the left of Platting Road, from the Star Inn to Lydgate and that the Oldham Volunteers would attempt to dislodge them. At 3.30 pm the Oldham Volunteers left the armoury and marched by Huddersfield Road to Scouthead. At 4.45pm a flanking party under Captain Goodwin left, and proceeded by way of Leesbrook and Springhead. When the former arrived at Scouthead, scouts were sent over the adjoining fields to feel for the enemy, whose scouts were discovered near the Star Inn, and the Oldham men advanced cautiously and steadily, taking advantage of stone walls or

Charge Swords.

Port Arms.

anything that afforded them cover. As the enemies scouts retired along Platting Road Sergeant 'Sam' and a detachment were ordered to double through a farmyard and cut off their retreat, a feat which 'Sam' said he could have accomplished if he could have 'getten a bit nearer um' but the enemy was too long of leg and too light in weight for 'Sam' who declared he would go in training for the next 'do'. When the High Moor cricket field was reached, Captain Hallsworth deployed his men, whilst Captain Thomas kept his men in reserve. A few dropping shots told that the skirmishers were in range, but at this point the bugle sounded 'cease fire' and the Saddleworth commander asked that a few moments grace might be granted as his men were not yet in position. The interval passed and the action commenced in earnest. Captain Hallsworth's men advanced in capital order, gallantly led by their lengthy Lieutenant under a raking fire from the Saddleworth men from their elevated position, which would have laid many a good man low had it been for real. They rushed on, however, from stone wall to stone wall, keeping as well under cover as to the nature of the ground would admit until their ammunition was done, when Captain Greaves ordered Captain Thomas to reinforce them, which the latter did most efficiently, the enemy gradually withdrawing (disputing every yard of ground) to their stronghold, the quarries, from which it would be impossible to dislodge them except by the flanking party coming up in time to cut off their retreat, and the directing officer is said to have exclaimed, like Wellington of old, 'oh, that night, or Goodwin, would come!', when he appeared in sight, on the enemies left flank, with half of his company and Lt Jones, he inquired anxiously for the other half company, which had been entrusted to Lt Hollingworth, and rated him soundly for disobeying orders. But 'George' was all right, as the sequel will show. When Captain Goodwin arrived at Grotton he divided his company, and gave one half to Lt Hollingworth, instructing him to feel for the enemy higher up the hillside and to join him at the top, whilst he took his men up a bridle path, supposed to be known only to himself, to enable him to take the enemy in the rear of their left flank, which he did, as we have stated before. The half company under Lt Jones was ordered to dislodge a few men who had taken up a good position inside a corner of the quarries, and were annoying our men by a galling fire. They had scarcely advanced 20 yards when the directing officer discovered a company of the enemy crossing a field in their rear, evidently with the intention of getting our men between two fires. He at once ordered Lt Jones and his men to return and get procession of a stonewall over which the enemy intended coming. The order was promptly obeyed and they opened a rapid fire upon them. Just then the missing Lieutenant and his half company appeared and took the enemy in the rear. Being hemmed in on two sides by stone walls at least 6 feet high, and between two fires, the directing officer asked Captain Roberts who was in charge of the detachment to surrender, which he did, though some of his men seemed disinclined and one exclaimed 'I knew we should be 'copt' as soon as ever we came into this feilt'. The bugle then sounded 'cease fire' and the battle was over resulting in a victory for Oldham, one Captain and his company having surrendered, eight men taken prisoners by Captain Goodwin's company and two scouts captured on the right of the quarries. The Oldham men marched off the ground to the cricket field, where the Saddleworth men, four companies strong and their band met them. They were formed up in column of companies and marched past, after which they said goodbye, and went their separate ways, well satisfied with the day's proceedings. About a mile nearer home, and in a field kindly lent by a farmer, the Oldham men found their old and well tried friend, who never fails, Quarter Master Page, and his satellites, Quarter Master Sergeant Thorpe and Armourer Sergeant Threlfall, assisted by the Pioneers, in charge of a load of Rubie's XX and several baskets of bread and cheese. Arms were piled and officers and men fell to with a will that plainly indicated that the exercise had not taken away their appetites. After the frugal meal, which was witnessed, by hundreds of spectators the men started on their homeward march of 3 ½ miles which was enlivened by songs etc, materially assisted by the bugles. They arrived back at barracks at 8 pm and were dismissed after being complimented by Major and adjutant Pritchard, who had supervision of the day's proceedings, for the very efficient way in which they had done their work. A sensation was caused at Bottom O'th Moor as the baggage wagon passed through with its load of empty barrels and boxes, on top of which were seated the pioneers and the driver.[247]

Later that year, in October, a repeat mock battle was organised this time it ended in disarray, the *Oldham Chronicle* reported on this affair:

> *'Plenty of spectators on the hills and road around the scene of action, Lydgate Hill. Oldham force was four companies numbering with privates, officers, etc about 150 men, commanded by Major Goodwin, Capt Hallsworth, Lt Hodgkinson and Lt Harries-Jones. Major Goodwin led the three companies on horseback from the armoury to Austerlands. The 4th company under Lt Hodgkinson took the Lees road in order to take the enemy on the flank. The main body got to Austerlands about 4:30 and at once threw out their advance guard to search the surrounding country. The scouts posted by the Saddleworth corps, which numbering about 130 and commanded by Major Hirst, had long before taken up their position of defence around Lydgate Hill – gradually fell back, and no shots were fired until Newhouses was reached, when the G Company, from Lees, which formed the advanced guard, and was now stationed behind the wall of the High Moor cricket field, opened the ball, and temporally stopped the advance. The defenders were further strengthened by several files of men from the main body on the hill, and the fire being returned, some quick work commenced ending in the withdrawal to the field behind of the Saddleworth men. The crowd became entangled with the combatants, so much so that all orders were impracticable. A number of rough*

[247] Oldham Chronicle

> *scuffles took place between Oldham and Saddleworth volunteers. The principle danger lay in these scrimmages, as the men in order to increase the reality of the fight, fixed their bayonets, contrary to orders, and the wonder is that no serious casualty occurred. The umpires ordered cease-fire, with no conclusive victory for either side.'*[248]

When the Oldham Volunteers became a Volunteer battalion of the *Manchester Regiment*, quite often field exercises would be conducted with the other Manchester Volunteer Battalions, one such exercise took place on Crompton Moor in July 1903, with the *3rd, 4th & 5th VB* and around 300 men from *6th VB*. They mustered at the Market Place, and were taken by tram to Moorside. The idea of the exercise was that an army marching via Rochdale and the junction to Huddersfield had halted at Newhey and placed an outpost line running north and south from Ogden reservoir to Grains Bar. The *6th VB* were to furnish troops for the portion of outpost line from Grains bar across Crompton Moor to the Moorcock Inn and the road leading from junction to Rochdale. Cyclists were used to reconnoitre the road, from junction via Delph, to the crossroads at Diggle station; other cyclist's sections reconnoitre the road from Grains Bar to Delph. After a successful exercise refreshments were served to the men at Brunn Farm.

Reviews

The initial large growth of the Rifle Volunteers, throughout the country, and their increasing popularity, led to a national review of the Rifle Volunteers in Hyde Park with over 20,000 volunteers from around the country marching past Queen Victoria and the Prince Consort. A number of Corps from Lancashire including the three Manchester Corps attended, the Oldham Corps were not present.
These reviews were a means of popularising the volunteer movement, and an inducement to encouraging new recruits.
The first review that the Oldham Rifle Volunteers attended, was a review for over 8,000 Lancashire and Cheshire Volunteers, at Newton-Le-Willows, on 11th August 1860. The *31st LRV* took their place as the eighth company of the first battalion of the second brigade. The *Manchester, Sheffield and Lincolnshire Railway Company* offered their services for free, to take the Corps to the Newton Review.
The review was a mass of shades of grey, relieved by the scarlet coats of the *Lancashire Hussars, Duke of Lancaster's Own Yeomanry* and two companies of the *84th Regiment* who lined the ground. The review was remembered by those taking part, for the delays in the trains transporting them to Newton, and the wet weather.

---

[248] Oldham Chronicle

31ST LANCASHIRE RIFLE VOLUNTEERS.

REVIEW AT NEWTON-LE-WILLOWS,
On SATURDAY, August 11, 1860.
Volunteers intending to take part in the Review must give in their names THIS AFTERNOON, to the Sergeant on duty.
*** The Public can obtain Tickets for the Stands, on application to Sergeant Woollacott; or to Mr. John Hirst and Mr. John Coops, Booksellers.
JOHN G. BLACKBURNE,
Captain Comm

Newspaper advert for the Newton review

A more spectacular and grander review at Knowsley followed, where the Earl of Derby reviewed around 12,000 volunteers. The whole affair was carried out on a grand scale, with military precision, not only in the organisation of the volunteers but also the spectators. It was estimated that there were over 150,000 spectators. Catering for the event was equally as grand; pies distributed to the Volunteers weighed between 5 and 6 tons, and were conveyed from Liverpool in 10 carts. The ale brewed at Knowsley was contained in 25 hogsheads. In making the pies for the volunteers, around 8,000 Ibs of flour, 6,000 Ibs of veal and ham, 500 Ibs of butter and 2,000 eggs were used. Alcohol for the general public consisted of unlimited supply of champagne, burgundy, brandy, whisky etc. plus 1,000s of bottled ale and porter. Also a large quantity of Soda water, lemonade and soft drinks were supplied. Mr Morrish (caterer for the event) had on the ground 60 barrels of mild ale and 50 barrels of Allsopp's superior bitter.
Sandwiches used 30 hams, 15 rounds of beef, 50 tongues, 1,000 Ibs of roast beef, 2,000 Ibs of bread and 300 Ibs of butter. There was also consumed about 3,000 Melton Mowbray pies from Leicester, 1,000 dozen of large veal and ham pies, 500 dozen of small pies and 500 Ibs of Cheshire cheese. The Liverpool health committee supplied 20 water carts.
The *Lancashire Hussars* led the march past with 200 troopers. Next in procession was the artillery with 4 battalions numbering upwards of 2,000 men. Then followed the Rifle Volunteers, with the *31st LRV* being part of the third battalion of the fourth brigade.

In contrast to this splendid show of wealth and pomp, after the volunteers had finished target shooting, poor people would visit the practice targets and pick up something towards a living, by collecting the remains of the balls, which were fired against the targets. They used a cane to follow the hole made by the bullet in the ground and then dig it out. They would make a few pennies selling the scrap lead.

A second review was held at Newton-Le-Willows in August 1861, the *31st LRV* were able to take three companies, and a 22 strong Drum and Fife Band to the review, which again was a large affair with around 7,700 volunteers attending.

In 1862, there was a review at Preston, which the *31st LRV* took part in, which was marked by heavy rain and one of the spectator stands collapsing, luckily there were no serious injuries. The following year the *31st LRV* received praises for their march past, at the October review in Heaton Park, Manchester.
In September 1864, a Grand Volunteer review was held at the Manchester racecourse, Higher Broughton, with over 3,000 volunteers from Manchester and surrounding towns taking part, including the *31st LRV*. The review was held before Colonel McMurdo C.B., Inspector-General of Volunteers. The following year, a similar review at the same venue was held before the new Inspector-General of Volunteers, Colonel Erskine. At the end of this review the volunteers were regaled with pies and ale.
In August 1866, a grand review was held in York, in front of the Prince and Princes of Wales, over 20,000 volunteers attended this review. The *31st LRV* funds were low and for those that went to the York review, they had to pay half of their own railway fare.
In September 1868, around 350 men of the *31st LRV* attended a review and sham fight at Heaton Park, Manchester. This was a great success and the sham fight that took place was well received by the assembled crowd. This event was again held in September 1870, with around 6000 volunteers attending, with the *31st LRV* sending 300 men. It was considered after this event, that the park was too small for any further events, but the review and sham fight was revived at Heaton Park again in 1874 with around 5000 volunteers on review, which was watched by 40,000 spectators. Oldham and Ashton formed part of the 1st Brigade.
The coronation of King Edward VII, in August 1902, was a great occasion and celebrations were held in Oldham, the *6th VB* marched through the town to Alexander Park, and then fired a *feu de joie,* and three lusty cheers for his majesty. Two lucky men attended the actual coronation in London; they were Captain Bamford and Sergeant Fallows, who both received Coronation Medals for their attendance.

Incidents, Discipline and scandal

Those men who failed to attend the minimum number of drills, and make themselves efficient, were liable to pay the full amount of subscriptions, because the Corps could not claim the money for that man from government. On a number of occasions volunteers were taken before court, forced to pay the subs and then discharged from the Corps.
On one occasion in 1871, three men were brought before Royton petty sessions for breach of the Volunteer Act.

> *'Pierce Bradbury Cook, Amos Collier Ashworth and Charles Howarth of the 31st LRV were all summoned for one year's subscription of £1. As they had not made themselves efficient then they were due to pay the subs. Cook agreed to pay the amount and then discharged. Ashworth said he had no money to pay it and was vulgar in his manner. Blackburne stated that Ashworth's manner on parade was similar to that shown in court. He was sentenced to 1 months imprisonment with hard labour, and was removed from the dock whistling 'ri*

> *fol de lol &c. Providing the arms and accoutrements were returned uninjured then no further proceedings would take place and they would cease to be members of the 31st.'*[249]

Another incident left the commanding officer with no choice, it was proved that in 1877 Sergeant Eugene Schulze, of D Company, borrowed money from a pawnbroker and deposited with him one of the regimental challenge cups, as security for the loan, in direct violation of the agreement under which all challenge cups are held, and for which he was dismissed with disgrace. In the expulsion of Sergeant Schulze, the Corps lost a good shot, he had represented them at many prize competitions including Wimbledon and it was a matter of great regret to many of his friends, as generally he was considered to be a good character.

In the camp at Southport in 1880:

> *'an extraordinary and regrettable affair, which has caused a good deal of talk, occurred at the camp on Tuesday. It appears that early in the morning Private Alexander M'Dowell of H company (Captain Shaw's) had misconducted himself and was put into the guard tent. The men on duty however had great difficulty in keeping him there and when the orderly officer for the night, Capt Greaves was going his rounds he saw M'Dowell lying outside and smoking. He was told M'Dowell would not stay in the tent. Capt Greaves repeatedly ordered M'Dowell to get up but he refused. He at last rose and pulling off his tunic challenged the Capt to fight and when the guard was ordered to put him in the tent he struck at the orderly officer saying that he 'would do for him' before the week was out. M'Dowell was at once secured and subsequently tried by court martial. His sentence was read up to him on parade, and it was that he should be drummed out of the regiment. This was done, but prior to doing so the buttons and facings of his regimentals were cut off, just in the same ignominious manner as the sours of an offending knight were taken in olden times. The band played the 'Rouges March' and in this degrading manner M'Dowell was escorted out of camp in the presence of a number of spectators. No sympathy was evinced for him. His mother and sister who were at Southport provided him with other clothing and he returned to Oldham.'*[250]

Over the 49 years of their existence, the Oldham Rifle Volunteers were fortunate not to have any fatal accidents involving firearms, some of the other Volunteer Corps were not so lucky. In October 1877, a Private Henry Mason, of the *96th Regiment*, was shot at Ashton Rifle range butts during the prize shooting competition (Ladies Challenge Cup). Mason was acting as a marker. The coroner's verdict was death by misadventure. The coroner blamed the Ashton Volunteers for:

---

249 Oldham Standard
250 Oldham Chronicle

> *'great laxity both in class and prize firing, and that the public are greatly in danger by the inattention to the rules laid down in their book of instructions, especially as regards to look-out men'.*[251]

In 1866, a member of the *40th LRV* (3rd Manchester), Private Holt of No.9 Company, was shot and killed from behind, by a careless volunteer loading his rifle whilst fully cocked.
Oldham did have some near misses. On 4th May 1875:

> *'a sad accident happened to drill Sergeant John Kinder, who has been attached to the 31st LRV for 9 or 10 years. About 6 o'clock he left his house in Ludworth St, near the armoury and proceeded to the shooting range at Chadderton for the purpose of marking the scores of Colour Sergeant Taylor, Sergeant Trelfall and Sergeant Davenport, who had decided to have a private practice. It appears that the men began firing at the 500 yard distance and Trelfall and Davenport having fired their compliment retired to the 600 yard range, leaving Taylor behind. Kinder supposing that all the three had finished their rounds at 500 yards went up to the target to rub off the shot marks and just as he took hold of the target with his right hand, he received the ball from Taylor's rifle in the front of his wrist. After the bullet had penetrated the flesh in a zig zag course it had passed out at the back of the elbow, near the joint. The wound bled copiously and Kinder was obliged to lie in the grass until a cab arrived. He was then conveyed home and was promptly seen by Dr Prestwich, who said no bones were broken. The sufferer is progressing favourably. He does not cast any blame on Taylor and is satisfied that the wound was the result of pure accident. It cannot for a moment be presumed that Taylor (who is regarded as a steady shot) when he fired saw Kinder approaching the target. On the other hand we understand that Kinder is very venturesome when engaged in marking.'*[252]

The incident with Kinder was obviously an accident, but the following incident was a reminder of the dangers of weapons in the hands of ill-effected men.
What was described in the Oldham press as a *Sensational affair at Oldham Rifle Barracks – Staff Sergeant runs amuck* took place on 3rd April 1902.
At just after ten o'clock at the drill hall:

> *'Sergeant Major Findlater, Sergeant Instructor Mitchell and Sergeant Instructor Hennessey, engaged apparently in their daily routine work. Outside the gates Sergeant H Davies, the caretaker and Sergeant Wild were engaged in conversation, when they heard the sound of quick firing, five or six shots following each other in rapid succession. Turning towards the orderly room*

[251] Oldham Standard
[252] Oldham Standard

door under the porch, Wild saw Findlater rushing out covered over the upper part of the body with blood and heard him shouting "Murder". Hennessey followed with a revolver in his hand, which he pointed at Wild. The latter shouted out "Don't fire at me" and Hennessey dropped the weapon and said he would give himself up, as he had had enough. He then went quietly to the police station with Wild and gave himself up. It was soon found out that Findlater had been shot in the right jaw, the bullet passing out at the cheek, and there was a splattering of blood on the wall near where he had stood. Mitchell was shot in the neck. A more minute examination of the orderly room led to the discovery of four bullet holes. The injured were taken to the Infirmary. The surgeons probed for the bullet in Mitchell's wound, which was at the back of the neck, and succeeded in finding and extracting it. Findlater's wound was examined, and the surgeons could not satisfy themselves whether or not there was any foreign matter in it. The injuries were dressed, and the men sent home, neither of the wounds being likely (unless complications such as blood poisoning set in) to be very serious. Findlater went back to the infirmary in the evening, and a Rontgen rays photograph was taken, which made positive the first supposition that the bullet which stuck him had altogether passed out.'[253]

Both George M'Leod Mitchell and Maurice Hennessey had not been with the Oldham volunteers more than three months, both had seen considerable service in the regulars, Mitchell was with the *2nd Battalion Manchester Regiment* in South Africa, where he had been wounded three times. Hennessey had served in the *Royal Welsh Fusiliers* and had many years service in India, Crete and Egypt, his last foreign service being in the expedition of the allied forces for the relief of Peking. James Henry Findlater had been in Oldham a number of years, joining as a Sergeant Instructor and subsequently being promoted to Sergeant Major.

Hennessey was sent to trial at Liverpool Assizes on the 2nd May. It transpired that Hennessey had joined the Oldham Volunteers in January and been subsequently appointed as recruiting sergeant, this meant an increased pay of 7s.10d per day, plus 1s.6d for every recruit accepted. Initially he performed his duties satisfactory, but then he started drinking heavily and was reprimanded for using insubordinate language to Sergeant Major Findlater. On March 25th he was absent for duty, and was found drunk, unfit for duty and the adjutant, Major Strickland, made a report to HQ with a strong recommendation that Hennessey should be immediately removed, and Sergeant Mitchell be given the post of recruiting Sergeant.

Hennessey's wife was called as a witness; she explained that her husband had suffered with severe malaria during his time abroad. He had been invalided home from China and she had seen a great change in him over the past 18 months due to the illness. He had been very peculiar and he got very depressed at times. Not long ago they had lost their youngest child, and this had affected him very much.

---

[253] Oldham Chronicle

Hennessey was charged with attempted murder, the jury found him guilty of the charge, but insane at the time so as not to be responsible for his actions. He was sent to jail until His Majesty's pleasure be known. His army pension was unaffected.

On the ranges

The most important part of training for the volunteers, after drill training, was rifle practice; members were encouraged to practice as often as they could. The first range for the *31st LRV* was established at Chadderton Park, where a small 300-yard range was constructed. In the early days the men were encouraged to practice every Wednesday and Saturday. Shooting was carried out according to the Hythe regulations, by these regulations the men were divided into first, second and third classes. To gain advancement into each class the volunteer had to attain a specified number of points at various lengths on the range. To advance from a third class shot into second class shot 15 points have to be gained out of 20 rounds at the following ranges. Five rounds at each distance of 150 yards, 200 yards, 250 yards and 300 yards. Once second-class status has been achieved, then advancement to first class is achieved by scoring 12 points at ranges of 400, 450, 500 and 600 yards. To achieve the status of marksman seven points must be scored at ranges of 650, 700, 800 and 900 yards; a marksman was entitled to the privilege of wearing the distinctive badge of a silver rifle and two arrows on his sleeve. When Sergeant Potter of the 2nd Company went to the Hythe School of Musketry in 1861, for a two-week instruction in musketry, he came out top of the 54 members of his class, bringing great credit and honour not only to himself but also the *31st LRV*.

For the better shots in the regiment, there were opportunities to compete in competitions organised around the country. One of the first competitions that the *31st LRV* took part, was that of the Hightown Rifle Contest at Liverpool, in October 1860. Private Humphrey Goodwin (later to gain a commission and rise to rank of Major) competed in the Lord Lieutenants prize of 100 guineas, he gained a creditable equal second, tying with another eight competitors. Sergeant King Mowbray also entered this competition. The following year, in August 1861, some of the *31st LRV* men again went to Hightown, this time the competition was know as the Altcar Rifle Contest and was organised by the recently formed *Lancashire Rifle Association*. This time four men went from Oldham; Sergeant Wollacott, Privates Winterbottom, Goodwin and Greaves. Private Goodwin used the 'Edge' rifle in the Association Prize. In the 1862 meeting, Winterbottom (now a corporal) gained 2nd prize in the Mayor of Liverpool's prize cup.

The Oldham men were at a disadvantage in some of the competitions, as the shooting was up to 600 yards, and they only had a practice range capable of shooting up to 300 yards. This disadvantage was soon to be rectified, plans were put forward in early 1862, and work started in August 1862 for a new range to be constructed. The new range would allow for shooting at distances up to 1000 yards. The new site was at the bottom of Burnley Lane and extended to the Nordens, which is near to the wall surrounding Chadderton Park.[254] A mound was constructed at the end of the range, which was 20 feet high, 60 feet wide at the bottom and tapered to four feet at the top. Mr John Spencer, of Prince Albert Street, was contracted to carry out the works. The new range opened on 18th October 1862. It was claimed to be one of the finest in the country and the range was christened by a three-way competition between the *31st LRV*, the 9th Company (Fallowfield) of the *1st Manchester Rifles* and the *34th (Saddleworth) West Riding Rifles*. Unfortunately the *31st LRV* lost both matches. This was the first inter Corps contest they had lost, previous competitions had them winning against the *23rd LRV (Ashton)* and *1st Manchester Rifles*. Throughout the years, many such events were organised, not only did they serve the purpose of encouraging better shooting but they were also great social occasions. After the competition it would be quite normal for the Oldham men to entertain their visitors in the local public house or hotel. After the inaugural competition at Chadderton, the Manchester and Saddleworth men were entertained at the Kings Arms Inn. Similarly when inter company matches were arranged these again were social occasions, ending with dinner and entertainment in one of the local public houses or hotels. Details of the Oldham Volunteer Corps known competitions against other corps can be found in *Appendix 9*.

In order to promote, and encourage, the men to keep up their rifle practice, annual shooting competitions were introduced. The inaugural annual competitions were held in November 1861, with the top prize being:

> *'an exceedingly elegant and massive silver cup has been presented for competition by Thomas Melodew. Cup decorated with the Oldham arms together with the motto 'Defence; not defiance'. Plus inscription ' Mellodew Challenge Cup'*[255].

The officers and local tradesmen offered other prizes. The Mellodew Cup was competed for, at distances of 200 and 300 yards, with five shots at each distance. The winners of the various competitions in this inaugural year were; James Winterbottom, Sergeant Wollacott, Ince Grime, Humphrey Goodwin and the Mellowdew Challenge Cup was won by W Bennett.

The following year, the Worthington Cup was introduced by Deputy Lieutenant Nathan Worthington. This cup was competed for many years, and was still being competed for up to the end of the Volunteers in 1908. The cup was introduced when the new range at Chadderton opened and therefore was competed for at longer ranges, the competitor had five shots at 400, 500 and 600 yards.

Over the years various competitions were introduced, local businessmen or gentlemen normally presented the individual prize competitions and the team competition trophies were subscribed for, by the officers of the Corps.

---

[254] Oldham Chronicle

[255] Oldham Chronicle

To further the interests of the Oldham volunteers at national 'prize meetings' it was decided to form the *Oldham Rifle Club*. On 28th April 1866:

> *'a numerous attended meeting of 31st LRV held at Kings Arms hotel to take into consideration the formation of a rifle club in connection with the corps. Chaired by volunteer William Henry Potter. Unanimously resolved that a rifle club should be forthwith formed. One of the objects of the club is to enable those volunteers who are members of it to contest at 'prize meetings' including Wimbledon and Altcar, in order that the 31st might be represented on those occasions. Hitherto the expense has fallen upon the members themselves and as a majority of the corps are working men it may perhaps have been that the best shots have not taken part in the contests, and the credit of the corps may have suffered. The rifle club will be the means of bringing out such members who may have a taste for rifle shooting, and it is believed the club will be a useful auxiliary to the corps. It will be open to the public to subscribe, it is intended in aid of the funds to have a concert in the workingmen's hall next month'*[256].

To join the *Oldham Rifle Club*, members had to pay a small weekly fee; this fee was used for prizes, for the competitions that were held every month. The idea was that lots of small prizes were offered at each of the monthly competitions, so that those less skilled at shooting would become members, and take part in the contests and have a better chance of winning something. An example of a prize list from one of the monthly competitions was;
1st- metal tea pot, 2nd- 6 electro-plated forks, 3rd- butter cooler, 4th- carvers, 5th- hot water plate, 6th- pocket knife.

The average working man would not have been able to spare money, nor probably spare the time to be active members of the rifle club, it was normally down to those members of the artisan classes who were involved in the club, and also the ones who could afford to attend the national shooting competitions.

In the Altcar competition of 1870, the Oldham men gained some creditable scores with Sergeant Major Goodwin coming 10th out of 390, in the Cotton Brokers prize and Colour Sergeant Corbitt coming 10th out of 441, in the Lord Lieutenants Prize.
The big national competition was the annual *National Rifle Association* competition at Wimbledon, in 1871 the *31st LRV* sent down a team of volunteers to compete.
Col Sgts Corbitt, Connard & Kershaw, Sgts Sugden, Tetlow, Slater and J Green, Cpl Robinson and Private Yale were the competitors. They entered for the Alexandra Prize, Windmill Prize and the Queens Prize. An amusing tale is told of this trip:

[256] Oldham Standard

> *'Lance Cpl Original carried a package, which he was told not to show anyone until Wimbledon. A fair lady at Guide Bridge station persuaded him to open it to let her have a look. A reporter suddenly appeared and saw it as well. The package contained the sign for the tent at Wimbledon. A piece of artistically carved wood, almost shaped like a lozenge, about 2 feet 6 inches in length, and containing the following mystic emblems and inscriptions marked in inverted commas: - At the top there was the handle of a 'door bell' to which no door bell or wire was attached, and underneath was the word 'Don't' meaning not to pull it. Below this was the numeral '8', signifying the number of the tent in the alphabetical division of the encampment, immediately following which was the announcement 'Oldham Roughyeds Crib' and below these words were 'four photographs' and the names of the persons photographed viz; 'Colour Sergeants Corbitt, Connard and Kersham and Sergeant Sugden'. Underneath these names appeared the words '31st Lancashire' followed by the significant intimation over a door knocker of 'up to the'.'*[257]

No prizes were won by the *31st LRV* at Wimbledon the best scores were.

Alexandra Prize – Sgt Tetlow, 39 points
Windmill Prize – Col Sgt Corbitt, 32 points
Queens Prize – Sgt Tetlow, 39 points

In the 1878 Wimbledon competition, the Oldham volunteers faired a little better, Colour Sergeant Slater shooting for the Alfred prize at 200 yards scored 30. Colour Sergeant Sugden in the Windmill prize scored 31. Colour Sergeant Corbett in the Windmill prize scored 27. Corporal Tindall and Colour Sergeant Slater were successful in gaining positions in the 'sixty' who have to shoot for the Queens prize. They each won £12. Colour Sergeant Slater gained a total number of points in all comps of 281 giving him 15th prize of £10. He won 1st prize in the Wills Prize and won £10. In the Queens prize he won the NRA badge and £12.

In 1877, the *31st LRV* were at Altcar, for the 17th annual prize meeting of the *Lancashire Rifle Association* and accredited themselves well. In the Leigh Challenge Cup, Colour Sergeant Corbitt won 2nd prize, in the military breechloaders competition, Colour Sergeant Slater won 4th prize of £4.

The Battalion Challenge Cup, value of 100 guineas, was competed for by 10 men from each battalion, the Oldham team shot very well. At the close of firing at 500 yards, Oldham were leading by 13 points but they fell off at the 600 yard range and finished 4th. Results were as follows for the top four teams.

1st - *6th LRV (1st Manchester)* – 761 points
2nd - *1st LRV (1st Liverpool)* –747 points
3rd - *5th LRV (2nd Liverpool)* – 746 points
4th - *31st LRV* – 740 points

---

[257] Oldham Standard

The range at Chadderton was closed down in July 1876 and a new range opened at Peacote. This new range was a backwards step for the Oldham, as it was now further away in distance from the HQ, and the range only had a maximum range of 600 yards. The Peacote range was situated just south west of Sholver.

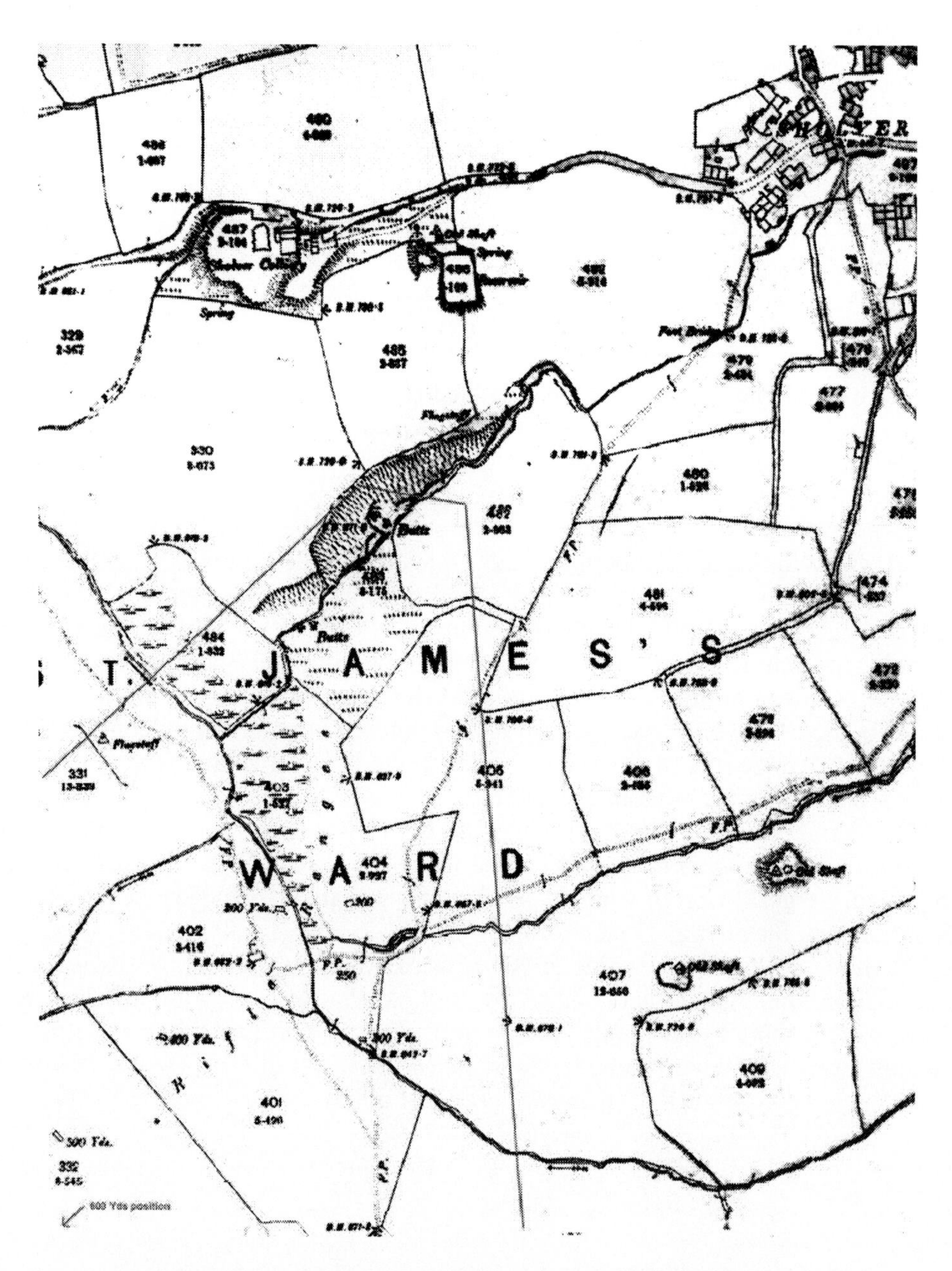

1891 map showing Peacote Firing range , South West of Sholver

With the Peacote range so far from the HQ, it meant that teaching the new recruits in the basics of shooting, involved a long walk and consequently a waste of valuable training time. Eventually, early in 1888, the corps gained permission to open a small, two-section, 100 yard range, in a disused quarry on Oldham Edge, it was being used for the first time by the end of March 1888.
With the arrival of the Lee-Metford rifle, which had a maximum range of 1,800 yards, the range at Peacote was deemed too dangerous and a new shooting range had to be found. The government, in 1882, had introduced a Military Lands Act and in 1897 it was amended, and a new Military Works Act was passed, which enabled the Volunteer Corps to acquire land for the construction of ranges, these ranges would have been built, with the aid of a loan, from the Public Works Loan Commissioners. In conjunction with the *5th VB Manchester Regiment* at Ardwick, a new range was constructed in 1898 at Diggle, Saddleworth, for use by both battalions. This new range was quickly given the nickname of 'Klondike'. Rail services to this new range were poor in the early days, and a trip to the range in the afternoon, would mean the men not getting back until nine or ten at night.
The South African war brought into question not only the marksmanship of the regulars, but also the Volunteers, and the lack of rifle practice and rifle clubs to encourage this practice. The *Oldham Rifle Club* had demised around 1895, probably due to the cost of shooting, and the cost of taking part in competitions was too expensive for most men. The majority were young working class men, mill operatives, iron workers etc, who could not afford the expense, which was necessary to enable them to become good shots. It was estimated that he must spend at least a sovereign upon the accessories over and above those supplied by the government. The government paid for only sixty rounds of ammunition for every volunteer's practice during a year. Amongst the necessary items required to become a good shot would be binoculars, scoring book, white pencil and black paint for the sights, the match slide, a shooting bag for his ammunition and paraphernalia, special rifle oil and a rifle case. In addition to this, he had to pay a five pence fare to get to the range and six pence for someone to carry out the marking on the range. So in April 1901, it was decided to revive the *Oldham Rifle Club* and appeal to the Oldham public for donations of money and prizes, to try and encourage the young men to take part and improve their marksmanship.

Regimental Prize shooting competitions

Over the years, a number of prize shooting competitions were shot for, by the Oldham Rifle Volunteers. The various competitions were held throughout the year, culminating with a prize presentation at the end of the year.
Prize presentations were a public event, normally held in the Town Hall. These could be quite grand affairs, with special guests invited from other Corps and it was quite common for the Mayor of Oldham to be the honoured guest distributing the prizes.

The last public prize presentation in the town hall was held in 1893, for the next five years, the prize presentation was a more subdued affair, held in the drill hall with no public invited. The public were allowed back to watch the presentations in 1899.

One of the earliest and longest lasting competitions was the 'Worthington Challenge Cup' – also known as the 'Deputy Lieutenants Challenge Cup'. The competition was introduced in 1862 by Nathan Worthington Esq., JP, Deputy Lieutenant of the county. Worthington was an early supporter of the Oldham Volunteers, he presided over the initial formation meetings, he also organised the Volunteers Balls in the first few years. He died in November 1872 at his residence, Colliery Hill House, Hollinwood. The competition carried on after his death, as it continued to be sponsored by his children.
The competition was open only to those efficient volunteers, who have passed out of third class and been in the Corps for at least 12 months, it was shot over distances of 400, 500 and 600 yards. The cup was subject to a competition until won by the same man at two consecutive contests, or three different times at intervals. The cup was to be considered the property of the commanding officer until won as above mentioned.
The winners of the Worthington Challenge Cup, are listed in *Appendix 11* along with some of the other known competitions.

Oldham Rifles Band

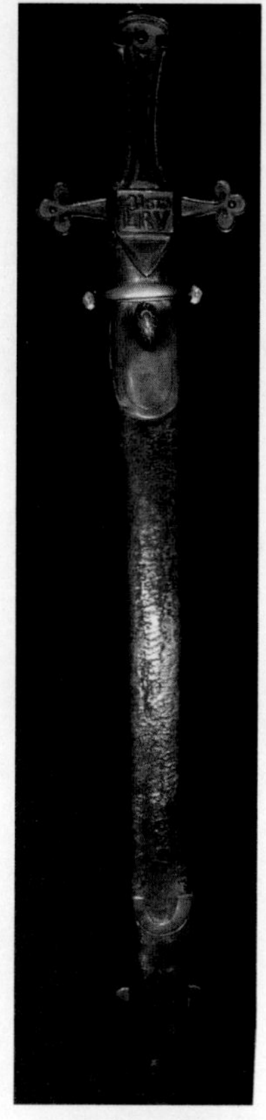

31st LRV 1856 Pattern Drummers sword

By kind permission of the 10th Bt Manchester Regiment & 40/41st RTR Trustees

No respectable Corps, Volunteer or otherwise, can be without its own marching band. They added an extra dimension to the Volunteers, giving them a more colourful appearance at public ceremonies. The government provided no grants for bands, as they were not considered a necessity, so funding of the band had to come from either public subscription, or funded from the Corps own subscriptions. Each Company would have to contribute to the cost and upkeep of the Corps band. In addition to the contribution from the Corps, the band was also able to raise funds on its own accord, by organising its own private or public performances.
On 17th February 1860 a notice was posted:

> *'that a band is intended to be established and organised in connection with the corps, and the committee are open to receive offers from leaders of Bands in Oldham and its districts for Honorary services. The band selected will be fully equipped by the corps.'*[258]

A month later, the Millbottom Band was selected as the first Oldham Rifles Brass Band. In celebration, the volunteers marched through town preceded by the band, as they had no uniforms; they all wore their caps recently supplied by Mr Gillham. A large crowd gathered to watch them.
Twelve months later, a Drum and Fife Band was formed to compliment the brass band and it was established in time for both bands to be present, at the presentation of the *31st LRV* colours in Chadderton Park on 6th April 1861.
One of the originators, and tutors of the band, was Benjamin Needham, known as 'Old Benny', he was formerly a member of the *Oldham Local Militia* band, and was renowned for being adept on the shrill fife.
In 1871, a new *Oldham Rifles Band* was formed, from the existing Oldham Church Sunday Schools band, which was a well established band that had been around since 1863.
In 1872, the Drum and Fife Band was dismissed for insubordination. From the mid 1870s, the *Oldham Rifles Band* entered many competitions, travelling to places such as the Isle of Man and Newcastle. The band won many prizes over the years and had a reputation for being a good contesting band.

[258] Oldham Chronicle

In 1876, Oldham decided to hold their own competition on the drill field at Nook. Over a dozen bands, from Lancashire and Yorkshire entered, and on 5th August, the first ever Brass Band Contest took place in the Oldham borough; it was deemed a great success.
The following year, in the practice room behind the White Hart Inn, a meeting was held to discuss the possibility of a 2nd Oldham Band Contest, as last years was such a success, the plan was to make it an annual event. For the 2nd contest, fourteen bands entered including Blackdyke Mills, Boarshurst, *7th LRV*, *34th YRV* and Darwen. The contest held on the drill ground, Nook again. This time at dusk the ground was illuminated by powerful Lime lights.[259]
According to the 1881 Volunteer Regulations, bands were allowed to recruit boys of ages between twelve and sixteen, two boys were allowed per company, to be used as drummers and buglers, and up to twelve boys in the band in addition to the adult members.

abt 1886 - 22nd Lancashire Rifle Volunteers Band
(By kind permission of Oldham Local Studies)

From around the beginning of 1880, the band conductor was Mr A Owen, and they enjoyed a successful period under his leadership. In the three years up to the end of 1883, the 1st year they took £24.11s in prize money, 2nd year £57 and in the 3rd year £133.13s. In 13 competitions over this period, the *Oldham Rifles Band* won seven 1st prizes.
In 1885, the band were presented with a number of bugles and side drums, a drum major staff, and one bass drum, which were given by the gentry of the town. Side

---

[259] Oldham Standard

drums were presented to the corps by Mr Hilton Greaves. The two daughters of the late Mr John George Blackburne gave the Drum-Majors staff.
In March 1886, the Bugle Band made an appearance in their recently received new uniforms. In September 1888, Lieutenant Colonel Greaves on behalf of Mrs T.S.Buckley made a presentation to the Bugle Band. The gift was a leopard skin, from a leopard shot in Africa by Mr T.S.Buckley, consul for Denmark in Sierra Leone, and formerly a Colour Sergeant in A Company of the *31st LRV*.
Under Mr Owens leadership, in the period from 1880 to 1899, the Oldham Rifles band entered 179 contests and was successful in obtaining 160 prizes, consisting of 50 first prizes, 44 second prizes, 33 third prizes, 18 fourth prizes, nine fifth prizes and six sixth prizes.
In 1899, a bazaar was held at the drill hall, in order to raise funds for buying new instruments, to replace the existing ageing instruments and also help to pay for tuition.

6th Volunteer Battalion Manchester Regiment Band
(By kind permission of Oldham Local Studies)

Known Bandmasters of the Oldham Rifle Volunteers

1865 – Bandmaster James Mellor
1867 – Bandmaster Mr Dawson
1868 – Bandmaster Mr W Hilton
1873 – Bandmaster Joseph M Robinson
1886-90 – Bandmaster James E Robinson
1892 – Bandmaster Holloway
1893 – Bandmaster Randle Taylor
1898/99 – Bandmaster Mr S Shaw
1902 – Bandmaster George Blackwell

Cyclists Volunteers

Cycling had made a huge social impact in the Victorian age and many cycling clubs were formed in the Oldham area. The use of the cycle had not gone unnoticed by the military, it became more developed in the Volunteer Corps, probably due to the nature of the work they would have been employed to do, in working on the flanks of line regiments, and where mobility and reconnaissance work was necessary.
The other great attraction that probably did not go unnoticed by the government is that a cycle did not require to be hired, or fed, and was therefore a cheap form of transport.
The first experiments by Rifle Volunteers using cycles were during an exercise at Easter in 1885.
In June 1887, the first notice was posted requesting Oldham cyclists to join the Corps. The cyclists would be employed in duties such as scouting and carrying dispatches. For a number of years these cyclists amounted to no more then three or four men in the Corps, in 1893 the War Office sanctioned the formation of a cyclist's section in each Volunteer Battalion. It was not until January 1896, that Oldham called for an official cyclist's section to be formed, and by the end of February they had enough men to make up the new cyclist section of the *6th VB*.
This newly formed 15-man section, complete with their cycles equipped with rifles and accoutrements, led a parade through Oldham in July 1896.
During the annual camps, whilst carrying out field exercises, the cyclists were able to practice their skills in reconnoitring, making surveys and protecting a retreating force.
In an interview, Colonel Harries-Jones considered that the cycle would prove of immense benefit to the volunteers.

> *'On the roads of this country, such an improbable contingency as an invasion ever arise, cyclists would be able to do work of the utmost importance. The cycle is a means of mobility which cannot be regarded too highly; and a great deal might be done to make the man on wheels such a formidable element as no army at present possesses.'*[260]

The cyclists remained just a small section, until the onset of the South African war. During this period, the *6th VB* was increased by two new companies and one of these new companies, it was hoped, would be a Cyclists Company of over 60 men. By early August 1900, a promising start had been made to adding a company of cyclists to the authorised establishment, recently raised from 804 to 1004. At first, it was thought there would be enough room for the cyclists, in the extra 200 places recently made, but as there were already 970 names down, such an idea was out of the question. The decision to come under the War Office order, which makes a special allowance for a full Cyclists Company was taken, rather than just adding another company with cyclists in it. By mid August, 40 cyclist volunteers had come forward. Captain

[260] Oldham Standard

Patterson and Captain Shires were responsible for raising the Cyclists Company, and a great interest was being shown from members of the existing Oldham Cycling clubs.
Members of the Cyclists Company had to provide their own cycles, but in addition to the ordinary grant, were entitled to a grant of £2 per head, for the use of their machines for military purposes and incidental expenses.
In the end, it aspired that K Company became the Cyclists Company, any members of the original K Company who were not cyclists, transferred to one of the other companies in May 1901. Second Lieutenant Norman Kershaw Leach assumed command of the Cyclists Company, in December 1901.
Corporal Whittaker and Private Feber were appointed as the first instructors for the Cyclists Company.
In August 1901, they were issued with khaki uniforms.
The Cyclists Company took part in all the field exercises that the rest of the companies of the battalion were involved in, and they also took part in cyclists only exercises. Over the Easter holidays in 1904, they were part of a 500 strong cyclists only exercise at Chester. This included cyclists from a large number of the Lancashire and Cheshire Volunteers. They were split into two forces, the red force defending Chester and the white force as the attackers. Oldham cyclists were part of the red force.
The Oldham Cyclists Company disbanded when the *6th VB* was converted to the *10th Battalion Manchester Regiment* in 1908.
In other regiments, the cyclist's sections remained part of the military thinking and used by the volunteers for many years and were only ended with the trenches of the First World War.

Uniforms

The question of uniform was normally left to the individual corps, but the War Office did issue guidelines and advice. The War Office had organised a committee to come up with recommendations, and draw up some patterns regarding colour and shape for Rifle Volunteers. The patterns were not compulsory and it was down to the Lord Lieutenant of each county, to approve the uniforms proposed by each Corps. The sealed pattern produced by the War Office consisted of tunic, trousers, gaiters, cap, and greatcoat together with waist belt, sling and pouch. The colour of the uniform was a light brownish grey, the material serge or tweed.
The War Office pattern was seen by a lot of Corps as looking poor and almost poverty stricken in appearance. Most adopted their own style of uniform with a more military looking appearance.

UNIFORM AS RECOMMENDED BY THE WAR OFFICE.

The choice for the first uniform of the *31st LRV,* was carried out by committee. On 12th December 1859, the committee put before the volunteers two examples of uniforms, the first being a uniform selected by the committee (this uniform was on display in volunteer John Greaves tailors shop on Yorkshire Street, so it can be assumed he made it) and the second, a uniform similar to that of the Manchester Rifle Corps. The first uniform was selected with some slight modifications. This was a grey uniform with scarlet facings. It was decided that the fittings for the accoutrements, should be silvered and not bronzed. A few days later another meeting was convened to discuss the uniform and at this meeting it was decided that the belt and other accoutrements should be of brown leather and that a felt cap of the pattern, a semi-shako, submitted by Mr Gillham, should be adopted. It should be noted that Mr Gillham had offered a room adjacent to his hat factory in Henshaw Street for the use of the Corps for drilling, so this probably influenced the decision of choice of hat supplier. Within a week of the decision for the style of accoutrements being made, a change was made, and it was finally decided that the:

> *'belt was to be of plain patent leather, with breastplate and buckle of bronze, the centre of each containing a device in silver gilt. The small ornament on the cartouche box is also to be in silver, as well as a small trumpet in front of the cap.'*[261]

Mr James Haworth of Lever Street, Manchester, supplied the accoutrements.
There was some controversy over the new uniforms for the 2nd Company. It appears that Captain T.E.Lees had received estimates from the various tailors and clothiers in Oldham, as to the price they would undertake to supply each uniform, once he had obtained these estimates he went to Manchester, where he found a firm that offered to make them for 1s less than the Oldham tailors, and gave the order to the Manchester tailor without making enquiries as to whether the Oldham tradesmen would undertake to supply them at the same price. This created anger among the Oldham tradesmen (some were also volunteers) and the volunteers were of the opinion that the money should be spent among the workmen of Oldham. The Oldham tradesmen got their way for the next order, as they supplied the uniforms for the 3rd Company at the Manchester price; Mr Greaves, Mr Holme, Mr Speek and Mr Wild were selected as the suppliers. The uniforms for all three companies were the same.
There is not sufficient information to determine exactly how the first uniform of the *31st LRV,* or for that matter, latter uniforms, would have looked but an artists impression has been included in these pages to give the reader a general idea of how they may have looked based on the available information.

A large amount of the volunteers training consisted of practising firing positions and also of practising firing on the ranges. To protect the uniforms from wear and tear they were issued with 'knee caps'. These knee caps were sometimes worn with full dress when assembling for reviews or inspection.

In 1861, new regulations were published by the War Office, which tried to clarify the uniform situation for the volunteers. Generally the volunteers were to use the current

---

[261] Oldham Standard

British army dress regulations as their guide. The regulations also set down guidelines on the accoutrements and a model set was placed at the Military stores for inspection. It also laid down the regulations for proficiency badges. The following badges were permitted to be worn by the volunteers:

- Range of 300 yards: best marksmen, a rifle embroidered horizontally
- Range 350 to 600 yards: best marksman, a rifle embroidered horizontally with a star immediately above it.
- Range of 900 yards: every volunteer obtaining seven points and upwards in the 1st class, a rifle embroidered horizontally with two stars immediately above it.
- Range between 650 and 900 yards: the volunteer obtaining the greatest number of points above seven in the 1st class, a rifle embroidered horizontally with three stars immediately above it.

For those volunteers who obtained a certificate of 'Instructing in Musketry' they could wear crossed muskets and crown. None of the badges were allowed to be worked in gold.

With the formation of the *7th Administrative Battalion* in 1863, there was now a requirement that both corps should be clothed alike. There appeared to be much deliberation, as it was not until August 1865 that both Corps were finally clothed the same. The new uniform remained grey with scarlet facings, the headdress being a shako with a red and black bob.
By 1868, there were men who were entitled to be awarded 7 year service badges. The badge was silver, in the centre was the numeral 'VII' with the word years, surrounding which in a scroll, are the words '*31st Lancashire Rifle Volunteers*' surmounted by a crown. The badge was worn on the right arm.
In 1871, there was a major change to the uniform, when it was changed from the drab grey to dark green with scarlet facings, the headgear remained as a shako, this change was also effected by the *23rd LRV*, as both units were battalioned together. In September 1871, both the *31st LRV & 23rd LRV* mustered for their annual inspection in their new uniforms, after the inspection they celebrated with a march through the town, finishing at the drill hall, where the men were regaled with substantial meat pies and ale.
In 1875 a slight change was made to the shakos, when they were fitted with chains.
In 1877, the volunteers were re-clothed again and some slight changes were made to the uniform, the scarlet facings were changed to light green and the headgear was changed from a shako, to a Busby with tuft. Only two years later, it was decided that the Corps would adopt the scarlet uniform, as worn by most regiments of the line, and was the only colour the government would allow volunteers to change their uniform too. The first scarlet uniforms with green facings, arrived in June 1879, and were issued to all new recruits.
For the next two years, the Oldham Volunteers paraded and drilled in a mix of the two different types of uniforms. It was not until the battalion parade in June 1881 that all

six companies of the Oldham Volunteers were completely changed over to the scarlet uniform. The main reason for this extended period was cost; it had been an expensive exercise for the Corps costing over £3,000.
In July 1880, all busbies were exchanged for the new blue cloth Home Service helmets.
In December 1882, shoulder straps and badges for caps were issued, reflecting the recent change of regiment number to 22.
In March 1888, it was announced that the Volunteer Corps were to become more closely associated with the regiments of the line, and the *22nd LRV* were to be re-titled the *6th Volunteer Battalion Manchester Regiment*. This prompted a further change to the uniform, all tunics were returned to stores over April, May and June of 1888, and by July the facings on all tunics had been changed from green to white. The *Oldham Chronicle* described the change:

> *'The change is decidedly an improvement giving a neater and cleaner appearance in the uniform, but in addition to the change which is expected will take place shortly, a further improvement will be altered in the tunic by the addition of 'The Sphinx' with the word 'Egypt' immediately under the little brass ornament. These details to civilians may appear trifling matters but to those who wear the scarlet they have an attraction not easily understood by others.'*[262]

In August 1891, each man was issued with equipment under the army regulation orders which included water bottle, mess tins and a greatcoat fastened on the back by a number of straps from the shoulders and waist band.[263]
In 1897, Glengarries where exchanged for new Field Service caps. The Glengarry cap had been introduced for the rank and file of Infantry Regiments in 1874, it is not known if the Oldham Corps adopted it from this date, but we can assume it would have been adopted sometime after 1874.

In 1892, the 'Volunteer Decoration' was granted to officers and a 'Long Service Medal' for other ranks, in 1893. To qualify for either of these decorations, 20 years service had to be achieved. These decorations were introduced, at a time when the Volunteer Corps was suffering from poor recruitment and retention, and were probably introduced as an incentive to the longer serving members, to stop them from leaving the Corps.

In 1905, the men were issued with their new khaki uniform and wore it for the first time in June, at Brigade camp on Salisbury Plain. The khaki uniform was the 2nd dress for the battalion.

---

[262] Oldham Chronicle
[263] Oldham Chronicle

6th Volunteer Battalion Waist belt clasp

By kind permission of Simon Butterworth

6th Volunteer Battalion Cap Badge

6th Volunteer Battalion Forage Cap

By kind permission of the Museum of the Manchester Regiment

6th Volunteer Battalion Officers helmet

By kind permission of the 10th Bt Manchester Regiment & 40/41st RTR Trustees

6th Volunteer Battalion Officers helmet plate

31st LRV c1865
31st LRV c 1875
31st LRVc1878
22nd LRV c1885
6th VB MR c1890
Cyclist 6VB MR c1900

Colours

Under the regulations laid down by government, the Rifle Volunteers were not allowed to carry colours, a more common practice was to present corps with suitably inscribed silver bugles, but a lot of the Volunteer Corps ignored this regulation for carrying colours, including the *31st LRV*.

In November 1860, a subscription fund was set up by the ladies of Oldham, for the purpose of raising enough money to present the *31st LRV* with bugles, cymbals and marching colours. Mrs Hallsworth, of High Street, and wife of one of the volunteers, acted as the treasurer for the fund. The money was very quickly raised and within a few weeks they had enough in the fund to place an order to a flag maker in London.

On 6th April 1861, the volunteers mustered on their shooting ground in Chadderton Park for the presentation of their colours. A large crowd turned out to watch the presentation, entrance to the presentation was at a cost of one shilling, to go towards the Volunteers Fund, and the charge did not deter many of the working classes who gathered in any advantageous ground they could find including the top of the walls surrounding the park and trees. It was estimated that around 5,000 spectators watched the ceremony. The *31st LRV* colours were presented by Mrs Lees of Greenbank, three cymbals were presented by Mrs Litler of Frankhill and three silver bugles were presented by Mrs Lees of Clarksfield. During the presentation of the cymbals, the crowd outside of the park managed to gain entry, with some of them running onto the ground hotly pursued by constables, much to the amusement of the crowd. After the presentation, a song written by Mrs Lees of Greenbank (nee Miss M.A. Stoddart), was sung by the Blue Coat Schoolboys, with music composed by Sidney Pratten.

A sound was heard on England's shores-
A murmur from afar,
The roll of drums, the roar of guns,
From nations met in war,
Then deep, not loud, throughout the land
One note pealed in our ears;
And in response, as England's guard,
Up rose her volunteers.

For Queen and State, for hearth and home,
For God and fatherland,
For rights ancestral blood hath bought,
In serried ranks we stand.
Who says the days of chivalry
Are gone with bygone years?
We bid them look along the lines
Of England's volunteers.

We know who stills the roaring seas
The people's rage and guile;
While stand our youth, a wall if tire,
Around our much loved isle
Defence, and not defiance, rings
Amid a nations cheers;
And with one heart and voice all cry,
God bless our volunteers.

31st (Oldham) Lancashire Rifle Volunteers regimental colours
By kind permission of the 10th Bt Manchester Regiment & 40/41st RTR Trustees

31st (Oldham) Lancashire Rifle Volunteers Queens colours
By kind permission of the 10th Bt Manchester Regiment & $40/41^{st}$ RTR Trustees

Weapons

The first weapon used by the Rifle Volunteers was much changed from that used by their volunteer predecessors. During the Napoleonic wars, the rifle was a specialised weapon used by only a few regiments, such as the famed 95th Rifles, most British soldiers were using the smooth bored, flintlock *Brown Bess* musket. By the middle of the nineteenth century, the British army had changed to rifles with a percussion cap hit by a hammer. Loading was still predominantly muzzle loading.
When the government first allowed the Rifle Volunteers to be formed, it was of course on the condition that the Volunteers would be funding themselves, but due to a change in government, the new more Volunteer friendly government, announced on 1st July 1859 that the volunteers would be issued, at government expense, muzzle loading Long Enfield (1853 pattern) rifles and bayonets, at a rate of one per every four men enrolled. It considered this amount sufficient for instruction purposes, and if Volunteers were ever to be called out for service, rifles would be supplied for every man. In exchange for this, then the Volunteers had to agree to provide a safe firing range of at least 200 yards, a secure place of storage for the arms, a set of approved rules and also make themselves subject to an annual military inspection. The issue of arms increased in October 1859 to 50% of the men enrolled, and within 2 months the government agreed to supply 100% of all rifles for all effective men.
The government allowed the Volunteers to use rifles other than Enfield's, including breechloaders, on the understanding that if these rifles were not the regulation gauge in barrel and nipple, then no practice ammunition could be supplied by the government for these arms. Even though other types of rifles were allowed, the government expected that all the volunteers should be proficient in the use of the rifle common to all regular forces of Her Majesty, i.e. the Enfield.
It is known that some of Oldham's volunteers bought their own rifles, and used them in competitions. Humphrey Goodwin used a rifle known as the 'Edge' at the Altcar Competition. Small-bore rifles were also used, the *Oldham Rifle Club* held a competition for this class of rifle.
The Enfield rifle was mass produced, at the purpose built government factory at Enfield, which reputedly could produce 1,200 per week.
The rifle itself, consisted of 63 different parts including screws and small parts. The barrel was 3 feet 3 inches long, and the length of the complete rifle, without bayonet, was four feet seven inches, with bayonet, six feet one inch, its total weight being 9 Ibs 3 oz. The barrel was rifled with three grooves with a turn of one in seventy eight inches. The long Enfield rifle was considered a good rifle for infantry of the line but too long, heavy and unwieldy for rifle corps. The government started to replace the Volunteers long Enfield rifle in 1860, with the more modern, and the much preferred short Enfield rifle. The short Enfield had a barrel length of 2 feet six inches and a total weight of 8 Ibs 7 ¾ oz. The government was issuing short Enfield's to the Volunteers in 1861, replacing any Long Enfield's that had already been issued. The short Enfield was issued with a sword bayonet.

Enfield Rifle, short pattern, calibre 0.577", range 1,000 yards, muzzle loading

In response to other European armies adopting breech loading rifles, leaving the British army behind, in 1867 a transitional breech loading rifle was produced, this was done by converting existing Enfield rifles and fitting them with a Snider breech block. This conversion consisted of a hinged trap being inserted in the breech of the Enfield rifle. A fixed charge 'boxer' cartridge was used with this rifle.
In September 1870, the government authorised the issue of the Snider-Enfield to the volunteers. A few months later in November the *31st LRV* was issued with the Snider-Enfield rifle. The first occasion of the men using this rifle, was in February 1871, when 20 men with Col Sgt Taylor, and 20 men with Col Sgt Corbitt arranged a shooting match. Shooting was below average, as they were not used to the feel of the new rifle. They afterwards retired to the Coach and Horses Inn.
The Snider-Enfield was slightly heavier than the short Enfield weighing in at 8 Ibs 9 oz and its length was 49.25 inches. Its big advantage was of course the higher rate of fire, which was around ten rounds per minute, compared with an average of three rounds per minute, over the muzzle loading short Enfield.

Snider-Enfield Rifle, calibre 0.577", range 1,000 yds, breech loading

The Snider-Enfield was a stopgap for the army, whilst a new breech-loading rifle was being developed. The newly developed rifle for the British Army was the Martini-Henry rifle, which was introduced in 1871; some of the volunteers managed to try them out when they were first introduced. A small number of the Volunteer Corps were receiving the Martini-Henry by 1879, but it was not until October 1881, that the Oldham Volunteers were issued with it. To try it out, the Sergeants mess once again,

organised a friendly shooting competition where, Colour Sergeant Corbitt's team beat Colour Sergeant Slater's team. The Martini-Henry had a range of 1,000 yards.
The Martini-Henry was the British Army's first designed from scratch breech loading rifle and served the British Army and colonies for many years and was used in the Zulu wars.

Martini-Henry Rifle, calibre 0.45", range 1,000 yds, breech loading

By 1888, the Martini-Henry was being replaced in the British Army by the Magazine Lee-Metford (MLM) rifle, but the volunteers had a long wait before they were to have the pleasure of using the Lee-Metford. Besides the volunteers being probably last on the list to receive any new weapons, there was also the problem that due to the increased range of the Lee-Metford, up to 1,800 yards, meant that their existing firing range was not deemed safe enough. This rifle was a rear-locking bolt system and had an eight (later ten) round magazine with a seven groove rifled barrel, designed by William Ellis Metford. The Lee-Metford rifle was the last of the rifles to use black powder cartridges. The firing rate was considerable better at 20 rounds per minute over the Martini-Henry's ten rounds per minute.
The government authorised the issue of the Lee-Metford to Rifle Volunteers in 1895, and it was in November 1897, that the Oldham Sergeants were receiving instruction in its use, ready for use on the new firing range at Diggle, which opened in 1898. By this time, the Lee-Metford was being replaced in the British Army by the Lee-Enfield, so the Volunteers were probably receiving the old stock of Lee-Metfords from the British Army.

Lee-Metford Rifle, calibre 0.303", range 1,800 yds, magazine loading

Lee Metford Bayonet stamped to 6th VB Manchester Regiment

The Lee-Metford had a short life in the British army, and was replaced by the Magazine Lee-Enfield (MLE) from 1895 onwards. The Lee-Enfield rifle was a modification of the Lee-Metford, combing Lee's bolt action with RSAF Enfield's new rifling system, the reason for the change of rifles was due the innovation of smokeless cordite powder. The Lee-Metford turned out to be prone to rifling pattern wear-out when using cordite rounds, which led to a loss of accuracy fairly quickly. The Lee-Enfield with its deeper and square profiled pattern coped with the cordite ammunition much better. There is no information as to when the Oldham Volunteers started using the MLE but its is highly likely that those volunteers who took part in the South Africa war would have been issued with the MLE, though the Lee-Metford was still being used by some units during the war.

The Lee-Metford bayonet pictured above is stamped on the handle end with '6 MAN' showing that it belonged to the *6th VB* Manchester Regiment.

The Short Magazine Lee Enfield (SMLE), was introduced into the regular army in 1904, and from this period onwards, the ex regular army MLE rifles were inherited by the volunteers, and were continued to be used by the volunteers and subsequent territorial regiments up to 1914.

Besides the use of rifles, some of the men were also trained in the use of Machine Guns. On 18th January 1890, Lt-Col J.C.Lees obtained a Certificate of Efficiency in the practice and theory of musketry from Hythe and also qualified to instruct in the drill and mechanism of the Maxim-Nordenfelt and Gardner machine guns. Machine guns had been authorised for use by the volunteers as early as 1883, but the government did not fund the issue of any machine guns. If a Volunteer Corps wanted a machine gun, then it had to be privately purchased, at an average cost of £300, or they would have to raise funds from a public appeal. It is not until June 1902, that the Oldham Volunteers acquire a Maxim machine gun, when it arrived at the barracks with blank ammunition and a carriage. Sgt T.G.Robinson attended the Royal Small Arms factory in Birmingham, for instruction in machine gun drill.

The Maxim machine gun was first adopted by the British Army in 1891. Designed by the American-born inventor, Sir Hiram Maxim, it was the first machine gun to operate entirely by mechanical means. With gas generated by the propellant, channelled into operating the moving mechanisms, it could fire 650 rounds, of .303 calibre, a minute, from a continuously fed belt of ammunition. Water circulating within a surrounding brass enclosure kept the barrel cool.

6 VB with Maxim Machine Gun

The Final Years

After the South African war, there was a growing urgency amongst politicians and military leaders to reform the army. Immediately after the South African War, there was a large loss of men from the *6th VB*, which was mirrored in other Corps around the country. This was a predictable loss, as the crisis of South Africa was now over, but in addition the proposed reforms for the Volunteers that were being discussed, not only had an effect on the morale of the volunteers, but also had a detrimental effect on recruiting. By the end of 1902, the Volunteer Force as a whole, had lost around 20,000 men during the year.

The lessons of South Africa needed to be implemented, and there was also the growing force and threat of Germany. It was felt that the British army did not have the necessary training or experience to fight a war in Europe.

By 1903, the British Army was being re-equipped and new training methods were being introduced. The Norfolk commission, in 1904, examined the role of the Volunteers, and it reported that the levels of efficiency were not good enough for home defence, and urged for better training facilities and the organisation of the Volunteers into brigades and divisions.

The shortage of officers was a continual problem for the Volunteer Corps, and in September 1903 the *6th VB* were short of 12 officers, but they were slightly better off than the other Manchester Volunteer battalions *1st VB* were 17 short, *2nd VB* – 16, *3rd VB* – 10, *4th VB* – 19 and the *5th VB* – 21.

The changes for the regular Army and the Volunteers were finalised by Richard Haldane, the Secretary of State for War, in the 1906 Liberal government. The regular Army were to be organised into a highly trained British Expeditionary Force of seven divisions, which were to be available at short notice to go anywhere in the world. For the Volunteers, Haldane's answer was to bring in the Territorial and Reserve Forces Bill. The aim was to replace the existing Volunteer units with a Territorial Force that was to be organised into fourteen divisions, fourteen cavalry brigades, Army Troops and Coast Defence Units. All of these units were to form part of the home defence in time of war.

From August 1906 until early 1908, Haldane campaigned around the country dining with Commanding Officers and visiting the Volunteers to explain his new scheme. In December 1907, Mr RB Haldane came to Oldham, to the annual prize presentation and also to promote the TA scheme. At the meeting:

> *'Mr Haldane told them that they, who were to form part of the territorial army, would have greater facilities and opportunities given to them to become more efficient soldiers of the crown, but on the other hand he told them plainly that they would be required to give more energy and effort towards making themselves fit to be entrusted, as he proposed to entrust them, with the defence of the hearths and homes of England.'*[264]

At the meeting Lt-Col Hodgkinson explained that Oldham, like other battalions was suffering from a shortage of officers. The battalion strength was now at about 800 men; under the TA scheme they must have 1000 men. He hoped that Mr Haldanes visit would inspire men of the town to join, and meet the numbers by 31st March next.

In the end, H and I Companies were disbanded and the establishment of the battalion was reduced. The NCOs and men of these two companies had to give their names to the Sergeant Major stating which of the other companies they would be preferred to transfer too.

All the officers and NCOs attended an attestation ceremony at the drill hall on 1st April 1908, to transfer their services to the new Territorial Force and the new regimental name of the *10th Battalion Manchester Regiment*. The following day the privates of the battalion were formed for a similar ceremony.

[264] Oldham Chronicle

Duke of Lancaster's Own Yeomanry – Oldham Troop 1873 - 1908

There had been an absence of 45 years of Yeomanry in Oldham, before another troop was to be raised. On the demise of the *Oldham Troop of Yeomanry Cavalry* in 1828, three of the existing Yeomanry troops in Lancashire, decided to continue by amalgamation into one corps to meet the requirements of the letter from Lord Lansdowne (the Secretary of State for the Home Department) in December 1827 to Lord Derby. Lord Lansdowne stated that any Yeomanry corps retained in the future should be at least three troops strong, and each troop was to consist of not less than 50 men. On 18th April 1828, the amalgamation of the Bolton, Wigan and Furness Troops was approved and the *Lancashire Corps of Yeomanry Cavalry* was formed. It consisted of 14 officers, 193 other ranks and was commanded by Captain (now Major) Braddyll from the Furness corps. At the initial formation of the new corps the officers had petitioned for the distinction of a 'Royal' prefix, but it was not approved.[265] It was not long before this was rectified, and in September 1834, His Majesty King William IV, informed Major Braddyll that from henceforth the corps should be known as the *Duke of Lancaster's Own Yeomanry Cavalry.*

It is not intended to write the history of the *Duke of Lancaster's Own Yeomanry (DLOY)* in this chapter, as this has already been ably done in 'Chain Mail – The History of the Duke of Lancaster's Own Yeomanry 1798-1991' by John Brereton. The purpose of this chapter is to write only about some of the details of the *Oldham Troop* within the *DLOY*, where known, and their part in the South Africa war through the letters of members of the *Oldham Troop* supplemented by other sources. Details of the uniforms of the *DLOY* can be found in the publication 'The Uniforms of the British Yeomanry Force 1794-1914, 6: The Duke of Lancaster's Own Yeomanry' by L. Barlow and R.J. Smith.

During the early history of the *DLOY*, other localised troops were formed, in 1844 a troop was raised at Rochdale and in 1846 one at Worsley.

From around 1850, the headquarters for the *DLOY* was at Worsley, this was also the seat of the Egerton family, who as successive Earls of Ellesmere served as the regiments Colonels and commanding officers, up until the early part of the 20th Century.

The *Furness Troop* was disbanded in December 1872, and under a War Office notice it was transferred to the newly formed *Oldham Troop.*

It was in 1873 that a troop was formed at Oldham, commanded by Captain Howarth Ashton. Ashton, who was born in Middleton, he had been an officer in the *DLOY* since November 1863, and had previously been a Lieutenant in the *Worsley Troop.* He brought his experience to the newly formed troop. It appears Ashton quickly got the

[265] 'Chain Mail' page 15

troop into shape, by the time their first inspection was conducted on 22nd May 1873, the Inspector of Yeomanry, Colonel Seager, commented:

> *'There is one troop which I particularly wish to remark upon, I mean the Oldham troop, a troop which has, I believe, been formed since last January. It reflects great credit upon the officers and men that this troop is sufficiently acquainted with its work to be present upon permanent duty. The officers and men must have worked very hard indeed.'*[266]

At the formation of the *Oldham Troop*, two local Oldham gentlemen were commissioned as officers, Fred Platt as Lieutenant and Robert Whitehead Buckley as Cornet. The *Oldham Troop* recruited its members not only from the Oldham area, but also from Ashton, Stalybridge, Middleton, North Manchester and even in later years had members from Halifax. Lieutenant Platt gained his promotion to Captain in 1878 and left the *Oldham Troop* to take command of his own troop, his vacancy being filled by James Edward Platt.

An additional *DLOY* troop was raised in 1877 at Broughton, in November 1880 a troop at Blackburn was raised, the same year the troop at Wigan, which had been established since the formation of the *DLOY*, was struck off the rolls.

Captain Howarth Ashton remained the *Oldham Troop* commanding officer until October 1880, when the command was passed to newly promoted Captain Robert Buckley. Three years later in 1883, the command of troop was in the hands of Captain James Edward Platt. Whilst Platt was commanding officer of the troop, he spent a considerable amount of his own money on making improvements, buying new saddles, new helmets and plumes and new cloaks. Each new recruit that joined the troop got a new uniform and not the cast off from a previous trooper whilst Platt was in charge.

By 1895 the *DLOY* was formed into squadrons, each squadron consisting of two troops, their arrangement was:

A Squadron – Oldham and Rochdale Troops
B Squadron – Broughton and Worsley Troops
C Squadron – Bolton and Blackburn Troops

Around the beginning of 1896, it appears that Platt had a disagreement with his superior officers over the appointment of officers, there is no information as to the exact circumstances but the disagreement was serious enough for him to resign from the *DLOY*, and in support of their commanding officer around 30 men also followed his lead and resigned from the *Oldham Troop*. The dispute may have been about the appointment of Edward Johnson-Ferguson as 2nd Lieutenant to the troop, Johnson-Ferguson was not a local, he lived in Ecclefechan, Dumfriesshire, Scotland and perhaps Platt felt that an officer so far away could not be beneficial to the troop. At a

[266] Oldham Standard

meeting later in the year between him and the men who had also resigned, the local newspaper reported Platt as saying:

> *'He only hoped it had got a better officer and who would have the regiment as much at heart as he did.'*[267]

Each troop had on permanent staff a Regimental Sergeant Major; this post had been held by James Starns from the *Oldham Troop*s beginning in 1873. Some time in the late 1880s, Zephariah Jennings, formerly of the *2nd Regiment Life Guards*, took on the post. Jennings retired a few months prior to the resignation of Major Platt, and in his place William Henry Griffiths was appointed to the post of Regimental Sergeant Major. Griffiths was appointed in September 1897, he joined from the *Princess Royal Dragoons*. He was to later take the troop out to South Africa. When Griffiths left for South Africa, Sgt Major Chittleborough of the *3rd Hussars* replaced him.

Just prior to the South Africa war in 1899, a further two troops of the *DLOY* were raised, one at Liverpool and the other at Blackpool.

Oldham Troop of DLOY at Queen Victoria's Jubilee celebrations
By kind permission of Oldham Local Studies.

[267] Oldham Standard

Training

The *Oldham Troop's* first training took place at Lancaster in June 1874. 50 men set off from Werneth Park at 6 am, it took two days to get to Lancaster, with an overnight stop in Chorley, arriving at Lancaster by noon the following day. The *Oldham Troop* had some success at this training camp, with Sergeant Taylor winning the troopers race. Lancaster seems to be the venue of choice for the annual training camp, until 1892, when it changed to Southport, where the great expanse of sands were put to great use in exercising the horses and practicing regimental manoeuvres. The annual training camp remained at Southport until 1899, with the exception of 1896, when a joint training with the *Cumberland & Westmoreland Yeomanry* was carried out at Carlisle.
For the camp in 1900 they moved slightly along the coast to Hightown, and this was the venue for the next four years. The following years were:

1905	Lowther Park, near Penrith, Cumberland
1906	Brackenber Moor, Near Appleby
1907	Caerwys, Montgomeryshire
1908	Rhyl, North Wales

'A' Squadron on camp, Hightown 1900, Lt Wrigley is seated centre left.
(By kind permission of the Duke of Lancaster's Own Yeomanry Museum)

Local training was conducted once a week, this was normally dismounted training carrying out sword exercises. The drill hall of the *Oldham Rifle Volunteers* was used for this activity. In later years mounted training was conducted weekly at the Skating

Rink, Union Street. They also carried out mounted squadron drill training with their fellow 'A' squadron members, the *Rochdale Troop*. One such squadron drill exercise in May 1898 saw them at Chadderton Park, the exact same place where the *Oldham Troop of Yeomanry Cavalry* had exercised some seventy years previously. The *Oldham Troop* paraded at the Town Hall at 2.15pm, under the command of Captain Lees and Lieutenant Johnson-Ferguson, whilst the *Rochdale Troop* paraded about the same time in Rochdale under Lieutenant Royds, both troops marched to Chadderton and met at 3.45pm, and performed evolutions before a good sized crowd. At 5pm they marched back to their respective towns.

Victorian era Duke of Lancaster's Own Yeomanry Helmet Badge

South Africa War with the 'Fighting Dukes' (23rd Company Imperial Yeomanry)

The South African War was the big opportunity for the Yeomanry to show their true worth. As the situation grew tense offers for service in South Africa were submitted by a number of the yeomanry corps during the summer of 1899, but the government rejected them. The offers were re-submitted, when war actually broke out on 11th October 1899, again the offers were rejected. What was known as 'Black Week', was to cause the government to change its mind. During the week of 9th – 15th December, the British Army suffered defeats at Magersfontein, Stormberg and a major disaster at Colenso with over 1,000 British casualties. The government now realised that they were going to need more troops then they had at their disposal with the regular army. The methods the Boers were using to fight the war were not suited to the tactics of the British Army, whose infantry were marching slowly around the country and heavily reliant on their supply lines. The Boers were mounted, expert shots and could move around the country much faster than the British infantry. A situation realised by General Sir Redvers Buller, who the day after Colenso sent a telegram to the War Office:

Imperial Yeomanry
Slouch hat badge

> *'Would it be possible for you to raise eight thousand irregulars in England, they should be equipped as mounted infantry, be able to shoot as well as possible and ride decently.'*

A recognition that the versatility of the Boer forces, needed to be matched with the same style of troops.
On 24th December 1899, a Royal Warrant was issued creating the *Imperial Yeomanry*. The warrant asked of the existing Yeomanry regiments to provide companies of approximately 115 men each. The *Imperial Yeomanry* were not to be used as cavalry, but were to be mounted infantry.
Details of the Royal Warrant:

1. Her Majesty's Government have decided to raise for active service in South Africa a mounted infantry force, to be named "The Imperial Yeomanry".

2. The force will be recruited from the Yeomanry, but Volunteers and civilians who possess the requisite qualifications will be specially enlisted in the Yeomanry for this purpose.

3. The force will be organized in companies of 115 rank and file, one captain and four subalterns to each company, preferably Yeomanry officers.

4. The term of enlistment for officers and men will be for one year, or not less than the period of the war.

5. Officers and men will bring their own horses, clothing, saddlery and accoutrements. Arms, ammunition, camp equipment and transport will be provided by the government.

6. The men to be dressed in Norfolk jackets, of woollen material of neutral colour, breeches and gaiters, lace boots, and felt hats. Strict uniformity of pattern will not be insisted on.

7. Pay to be at Cavalry rates, with a capitation grant for horses, clothing, etc.

8. Applications for enrolment should be addressed to colonels commanding Yeomanry regiments, or to general officers commanding districts, to whom instructions will be issued.

9. Qualifications are: Candidates to be from 20 to 35 years of age, and of good character. Volunteers or civilian candidates must satisfy the Colonel of the regiment through which they enlist that they are good riders and marksmen, according to the Yeomanry standard.

The clause of having to provide their own horse would have precluded a lot of the men who were willing to volunteer. This clause was very quickly relaxed, and the government allowed £40 per man to find his own mount. By 25th December, offers from 35 men from the *Oldham Troop* had been put forward for active service. At this time, the *Oldham Troop* consisted of 56 men; however this included young and new men, who were not deemed suitable for active service. Captain Lees also put forward his name for active service; Lees had previously seen service in Africa at Bulawayo.

A number of generous Oldham citizens donated horses to the troop for free, but the main bulk had to be bought with the government allowance. On 2nd January, there was a parade of horses at the Fire Station with a view to purchases, over 100 horses were paraded, but only eight were selected. Horses had to be between 14-1 and 15-3 hands and no grey horses were allowed. A further parade of horses was carried out on the 8th, this time 90 were viewed with a better success rate of 16 horses being selected.

By 5th January, the Oldham volunteers had been whittled down to 22 men; these men paraded at Victoria Station, Manchester, and then marched to Chorlton Town Hall for a medical examination. Five men failed the medical, leaving just 17 men from Oldham enrolled for active service. On 8th January, the following men were sworn in: J.B.Wild, G.W.Haslam, T.W.Ormrod, F.Brierley, T.Gibbs, R.Miller, F.A.Makin, J.H.Kershaw, W.Ashworth, C.L.Travis, A.H.Priestley, H.Waterfield, A.Brooksbank, J.W.Dransfield, E.Jones, G.Rodgers and J.W.Hartland.

The *Oldham Troop*, along with the *Rochdale Troop* was required to muster at Blackpool on 15th January, to begin training and preparation, before departing for

South Africa. Before departing Oldham, a number of the men were treated to farewell dinners, such as Trooper Gervase Rodgers. Around 200 people gathered at Coldhurst Church School, where he was presented with a purse of gold, a bible, a prayer book, and a pipe. Rodgers worked at the Prudential Insurance Company, and his boss informed him that his position would remain open until he returned. A similar dinner was held for Trooper James Dransfield at the Star Inn, Springhead where his work colleagues from Messrs R.Chadwick & Co, coal merchants and carriage proprietors presented him with silver cigar holder and case and a box of cigars. Dransfield worked as a bus driver between Oldham and Springhead, and was known by locals as *'Jammy Chadwick'*.

The men had a warm welcome in Blackpool, the Mayor of Blackpool taking it upon himself to ensure that the Yeomanry volunteers were made to feel at home, the Officers were quartered at the Clifton Hotel, the Sergeants at the New Inn and the rest of the men at other hotels, all free of any cost. In addition to the free accommodation the men had free access to the Alhambra, Grand Theatre, Winter Gardens, and free rides on the Corporation and Fleetwood tramways. The following day the men were issued with the standard infantry rifle the Lee-Enfield. This would have felt a lot heavier and more cumbersome than their normal fire arm; the Lee Metford Carbine.

The Oldham men trained with men from the other troops of the *Duke of Lancaster's Own Yeomanry*. The new company was to be known as the *23rd Company Imperial Yeomanry* and they would be part of the *8th Battalion*. Captain George Kemp of the *Rochdale Troop* was placed in command. Kemp was also the Member of Parliament for Heywood. The *8th Battalion* was made up of the *23rd (Lancashire) Company IY*, the *24th (Westmoreland & Cumberland) Company IY* and the *77th (Manchester) Company IY*. The commanding officer for the *8th Battalion* was a Reserve Officer, Colonel A.P.Crawley, who had seen previous service in South Africa in 1879 during the Zulu campaign, and was involved in the Sudan Expedition in 1885.

Captain George Kemp MP

The new *23rd Company IY* was to be split into four troop sections and a gun section, each with its own officer. No 1 section was made up of men mainly from the Oldham and Rochdale troops. No 2 section was made up of men mainly from the Bolton and Worsley troops. No 3 section was made up of men mainly from the Broughton troop and No 4 section, with men mainly from the Blackburn troop. Whilst out in South Africa the sections were renamed into A, B, C and D troops.

During training the two Colt machine guns arrived, and 16 men were allocated to them and trained in their use. The Colt machine guns were mounted on the patented galloping carriage invented by Lord Dundonald.

Each day the men were put through their paces, a typical day consisted of:

- 6 am muster at the stables to feed and groom their horses.
- 8.30 am, exercise horses.
- 12.30 pm proceed to range to practice target shooting.
- 2.30 pm bayonet exercise at Raikes Hall.
- 6 pm to 6.30 pm attend horses at stables.

In the first few days Trooper Richard Miller was raised to the rank of Farrier-Sergeant of the company.
The training took its toll on some of the men, Trooper Haslam of the *Oldham Troop* badly injured his ankle whilst attempting to vault on his horse, the injury was so bad that he had to be discharged and sent home, he was replaced by another Oldham man; Trooper Lofthouse.
A strong qualification for the company was marksmanship, unfortunately one of the Oldham troopers failed on this account, Trooper Hartland (living at Manchester Street) could not gain improvements in his musketry and was sent home.

By the end of January orders had been received announcing their departure, initially it was to be from a South coast port, but Captain Kemp protested and this was changed to Liverpool, departing on 10th February. With the date of departure now known, preparations were made to ensure that the men could return home, to put their affairs in order and say their goodbyes. The Mayor of Blackpool arranged for a magnificent banquet for all the men at the Alhambra, on the evening of 1st February. The final event of their training was an inspection by Colonel Sheringham, of the *22nd Regimental District,* who was pleased with what he saw after putting the men through their paces for over three hours. The Oldham men returned to their hometown after the inspection, and they were given just over a day to put their affairs in order. What the men did not know, was that the Mayor and the town had arranged a magnificent 'send off' for them.

> *It 'was one of the most remarkable scenes ever witnessed in the town. The departure of the ten Oldham ambulance men for the seat of war was a huge affair, but the "men in khaki ordered South" came in for even greater attention at the hands of the public. At the height of the demonstration it was estimated that not less than 40,000 persons were packed into the space in front of the Town Hall and along the streets branching off.'*[268]

In the town hall, the Mayor and Mayoress, and many of the dignitaries of the town greeted the men. They were each presented with a chest protector, a pound of tobacco,

---

[268] Oldham Chronicle

a pound of chocolate, a pound of writing paper and a sovereign presented by Alfred Butterworth JP who said:

> *'He felt that they were fighting a just cause, and he trusted that they would never be ashamed of saying that they came from Oldham. There was a good deal of pluck in the Oldham people and he believed that the men before him would do credit to the town.'*[269]

On leaving the Town Hall, the Mayor said a few words to the gathered crowd and hearty cheers were given for the men in Khaki. The crowd broke out into a rendition of 'Auld Lang Syne' accompanied by the band of the *6th VB Manchester Regiment*. A brake transported the men down to Mumps station where they caught the train to Manchester and onwards. All along the railway line to Central station, scores of fog signals were exploded, and in the words of the reporter of the *Oldham Chronicle;* the scene was truly a memorable one.
The *23rd Company IY* were to leave from Liverpool on the White Star Australian liner *Afric,* on the evening of Sunday 11th February, however, they were delayed in getting to Liverpool, as the area was suffering Siberian conditions, with up to a foot of snow on the ground, this caused some delays with the trains.
The Yeomanry were very lucky in gaining passage on the *Afric*, in that:

> *'the troopers are not required to live on a mess deck of the regulation transport type, with slung hammocks for sleeping berths, but will occupy the third class cabins of the vessel, which are such a splendid feature in the steamers running in the White Star Australian Line. No doubt the troopers will duly appreciate the special comfort, not to say luxury,... The food to be supplied by the White Star Line to the Yeomen is of the usual high class character provided for the ordinary cabin passengers. So that both on the score of sleeping arrangements, as well as in the, perhaps, more important regard of diet, the Imperial Yeomanry going out by the Afric have much to be grateful for.'*[270]

After a day of embarkation, the ship finally sailed late on the Sunday evening, watched by a large cheering crowd.
The voyage was pretty uneventful, but pleasant, during the voyage Trooper Wild was promoted to Corporal. There was some excitement, when a stowaway was discovered hiding in one of the lifeboats, his name was Smallwood and was a member of the *DLOY*. He had been rejected for service due to his age, but managed to stay with the regiment and was not shipped back to England. Corporal Wild tells of his fate;

---

[269] Oldham Chronicle
[270] Oldham Standard

> *'The man Smallwood that I told you about is now servant to our adjutant Captain Leslie, so that he has got a good position after all the trouble of coming out as a stowaway.'*[271]

During the voyage another Oldham man received promotion, Trooper Dransfield was appointed to be orderly for Captain Kemp.

The troops disembarked from the *Afric* on 5th March 1900 at Table Bay, Cape Town, from there they had a 12 mile march to the base camp at Maitland.

The men spent around ten days at Maitland camp, before being moved northwards up to Picquetberg Road camp. The camp took its name from being situated on a road that leads to the village of Picquetberg, some 40 miles away. The camp was about a mile and half from the Picquetberg Road railway station where the *23rd Company IY* were stationed along *24th Company IY, 7th Company IY (Leicestershire), Compton's Horse, 4th Middlesex Militia* and a half battery of *CIV Artillery*, altogether about 1200 men.[272]

Shortly after arriving in the camp, Colonel Bebbington inspected the *23rd Company IY*, and they were passed fit for work at the front.[273]

From this base, the Imperial Yeomanry was responsible for patrolling the area and protecting the railway line, which led up to Kimberley. Corporal Wild describes the typical duties they carried out whilst based at this camp:

'We send strong patrols out in the country, but do not see much of the rebels. They shift when we are coming. Each man carries 100 cartridges. All our men are very well, not one having fallen sick since our arrival here……. Last Monday our company and the Cumberland had a march of 27 miles to a small village or town called Ceres. It took us three days to go there and back. My horse fell lame coming back, so I had to walk ten miles in the broiling sun ,which was very hard work, I can assure you. The sun actually burns all the skin of your face. Ceres is the most beautiful place that I have ever seen. It lies in a valley, and there are mountains all around it so it never is really cold, as they form a shelter for the town. It seems there are some rebels living there, so that is the reason we went, and they had a meeting the same morning we got there, but soon dispersed on our approach. ... We had to go through a pass six miles in length – all up hill, nearly – called Mitchell's Pass, at the foot of which lies the town. On our arrival the English residents cheered us and sang 'God save the Queen' and 'Rule Britannia' and gave us cakes, grapes, apples, figs, hot tea etc, which were very acceptable after our long march. On the Tuesday we marched to Speinfontein, another ten miles, so you see we had plenty to do. On the Wednesday we returned to our camp.'[274]

The men did get opportunities for some recreation whilst at Picquetberg Road camp, they travelled to Talbot Road, about five miles away, where the *2nd Volunteer Battalion Lincolns* were stationed and a football match was arranged.

---

[271] Cpl Wild letter
[272] Cpl Wild letter
[273] Trooper Dransfield letter
[274] Cpl Wild letter

'It ended as a draw of one goal each. It was the association game, and we think we should have beaten them easily at Rugby. They gave us a splendid tea – tea with real milk in it, tinned salmon, butter, sardines, jam and cakes, and the men paid for it themselves.'[275]

23rd Company IY Trooper
(from Trooper Johnson's book, by kind permission of the Duke of Lancaster's Own Yeomanry Museum)

The men had to be ready for action at all times:
'We sleep by our arms every night, ready to turn out at a moments notice. Although we have had no fighting we are doing good work guarding Lord Roberts lines of communication. We are under 12 hours notice to proceed to the front, and expect the order any day; the sooner the better, as I am itching to get at them, and my bayonet is in good condition. I am enjoying myself immense. We have hardships to undergo, but we make the best of them.'[276]

[275] Cpl Wild letter
[276] Trooper Rodgers letter

The Oldham men appeared to be doing well for themselves, whilst here Troopers Ormrod and Making were promoted to Lance Corporal and Trooper Rodgers was appointed orderly to Lieutenant Heap. The prolonged stay of the *23rd and 24th Companies IY* at the Picquetberg Road camp was galling with many of the men, they were frustrated at not being sent up to the front when so many other Yeomanry regiments had been sent there. Trooper Arthur Priestley complained that; *'the 42nd Company of the Imperial Yeomanry arrived, and were next sent by train to Bloemfontein. He did not know of any other company which has had the knocking about which his company received, and it certainly put a damper on men who had given up everything to fight for Queen and country.'*[277] Within a few days, Priestley and the rest of the company were to get their wish. On 9th May, the companies marched via Ceres and Gondini to Worcester, arriving on 12th May.

By 16th May, the troops entrained and moved up country to Belmont, close to the Orange Free State border. Belmont, - 50 miles South-West of Kimberley - had been the scene of heavy fighting in November, and the scenes of half covered dead bodies of men and horses would have been a grisly reminder that the men were now in the front line of the war. '*We saw numbers of dead bodies their rotting amongst the rocks, where they had been hurriedly and inadequately buried. It was an awful sight, and the stench was awful.*'[278]

A camp was set up at Belmont: '*We have our tents pitched on the battlefield of Belmont, and it is a grand sight to go and visit the ruined Boer laager. I and twelve others have been left behind to look after the sick horses and stores. The others have gone up country with Sir Charles Warrens column, so you will see the news in the papers of what our boys are doing probably before I shall.*'[279]

The company had joined the force, being commanded by Lieutenant-General Sir Charles Warren. This force was tasked with the suppression of the Boers in the Griqualand West district. A considerable portion of Griqualand was in the hands of the Boers, who were joined by others, expelled from the districts south of the Orange River. Within a few days of the Yeomanry arriving at Belmont, the column was out tracking down the Boers. Before setting out with the column, Captain Kemp had a few words for the men: '*we were now entering the enemy's country and he hoped each one would not forget the seriousness of the undertaking, the lives of their fellow troopers depending on each one doing his duty.*'[280]

The Column left Rooipan for Douglas, on the night of 20th May, with a force consisting of the *Munster Fusiliers, 23rd and 24th Companies Imperial Yeomanry, Cape Police,*

---

[277] Trooper Priestley letter

[278] Trooper C Whittaker interview

[279] Cpl Wild letter

[280] Cpl Whitehead letter

Duke of Edinburgh's Own Volunteer Rifles, *Warrens Scouts* and two guns of the *Canadian Field Artillery*.
This force, marched in two columns, one being under the command of Colonel Hughes, and the other under Colonel Spence.

Imperial Yeomanry Camp and hospital for sick horses at Belmont
(Source: With the flag to Pretoria, Vol II)

Colonel Hughes column took the direct route through the veldt and waited about seven miles from Douglas for the other column. Here they dismounted and took up a position on a koppie facing a road, where Boers had been seen earlier in the day. '*We waited with our rifles loaded, sitting behind the rocks, with a keen frost biting our finger ends, until 6am, and then daylight began to show.* '[281] Nothing was seen of the enemy so they moved on towards Douglas. About three miles out they stopped, waiting for the column to catch them up. The Boers had been observed in a laager on the banks of the Vaal River about 2,500 yards from the road.
The order came at 8.20am for the artillery, and in a few minutes the first shell was fired, the excitement amongst the troops being intense, though they appeared very cool as they dismounted ready to proceed to help the *Duke of Edinburgh's Own Volunteer Rifles*. One of the shells burst in a cooking kitchen where the Boers had just had breakfast. It scattered them and after a few more shells they retired, firing shots as they fled.

---

[281] Cpl Whitehead letter

The *Cape Police* and *Warren's Scouts*, under Colonel Hughes, had led the advance in skirmishing order towards Douglas. The Boers had left behind their wagons and food, which was taken back into Douglas.
On the afternoon of the 22nd, the Boers, about 300 strong, opened fire on a detachment of 25 Imperial Yeomanry and Scouts, and wounded Captain Parkin (*24th Company IY*) slightly in the thigh. The *Canadian Field Artillery* again came into action, as also did the Maxim of the *Duke of Edinburgh's Own Volunteer Rifles* (*DEOVR*), at dusk the Boers retired. The Imperial Yeomanry behaved excellently throughout the encounter, with Colonel Hughes and his scouts bringing in a large quantity of sheep and goats captured from the Boers.[282]

Surprise attack at Faber's Put

Whilst at Douglas, Warren received intelligence reports that there were between 700 and 2,000 Boers occupying large sections of the country west of the Vaal River. Warren's plan was to mount an attack on the townships of Campbell and Griquatown, and the only place where he felt he could mount his attack, without serious loss of life, was from Tweefontein. But first he had to capture Tweefontein. The column left Douglas on 24th May. Warren selected a farmstead called Faber's Put (also known as Faber's Spruit), ten miles east of Tweefontein, as the base to mount the attack on Tweefontein. Warren's force surrounded the farm at Faber's Put on 26th May and captured the farmer who was a Boer leader, but they could not mount their attack on Tweefontein until the supply waggons caught up with them. Here the column set up camp and sent out patrols each day to test the Boers. On 27th May, *A Troop* (Oldham and Rochdale men), under the command of Lieutenant Heap, was sent from Faber's Put to escort some wagons back to Douglas.
Faber's Put consisted of: '*two farm houses about 800 yards apart at north –east and north-west, and the Infantry picquets occupied the whole of this front, the Infantry being bivouacked near the north-east farm house, where were also my headquarters; the men of the Intelligence Branch and Warren's Scouts and some Infantry were at the north-west farm house, while the Yeomanry and Artillery were in the hollow occupying the kraals around the water and northern portion of the garden, providing the picquets on the ridges south-east and south-west.*'[283] The two kraals (low stone wall cattle enclosures) were used to stable the horses.
On the 29th, some of the Yeomanry were fired upon and the camp was stood too, but nothing further happened and they were back in camp after an hour. The following morning was a different story.
The Boer attack came from three directions, from the east, led by Forster, they attacked the camp lines of the *DEOVR*, and the farm house where General Warren and his staff

[282] Press Association Report
[283] General Warrens dispatch dated 29/6/00

were based. From the South, led by Commandant-General De Villiers, they crept to within 50 yards of the Yeomanry positions. The third, came from the west side led by Cmdt Ventner, their objective was to take the kraal with the horses and aim down careful rifle fire onto the camp from their high position.
De Villiers force, was reputed to consist of around 56 Boers, with many of them his best shots. Warren suggested that many of these Boers knew the farm well, and hence why they were able to get so close to the camp.

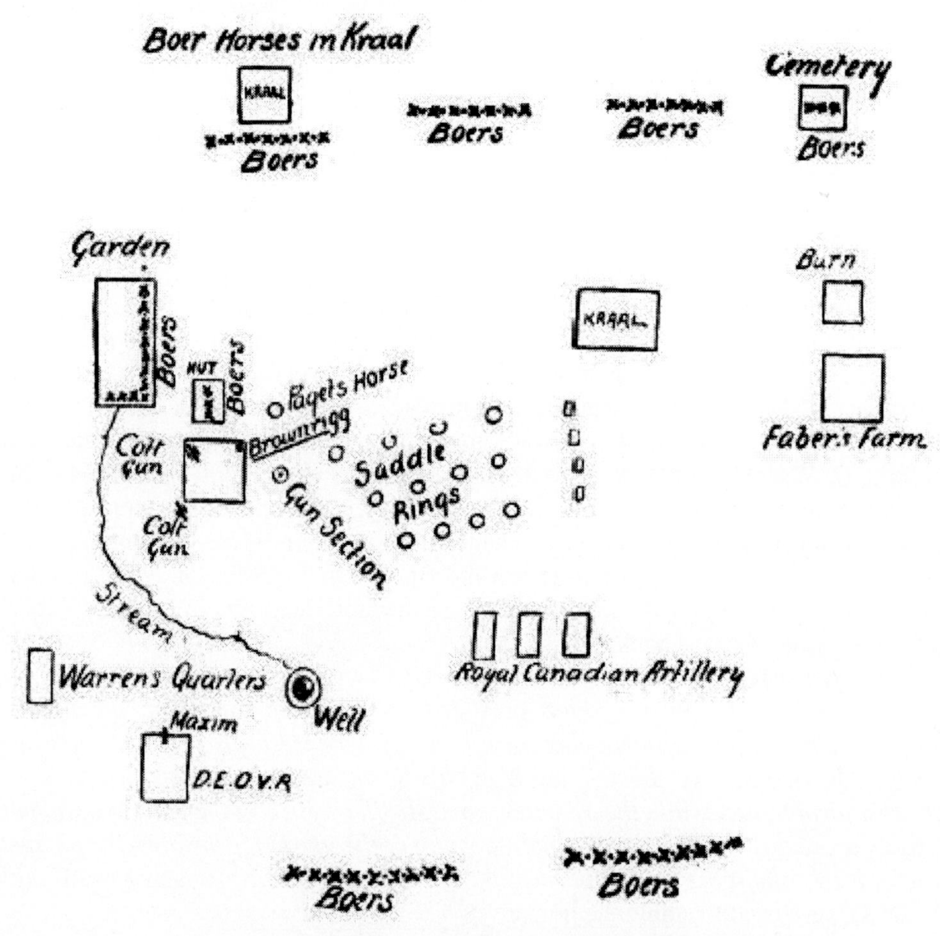

Sketch of Faber's Put battlefield by Trooper Brownrigg

The *23rd Company IY* were positioned between the two kraals, the troop sections made tight circles, each circle being surrounded by their saddles to form some sort of protection, their rifles stacked in the centre of the circles. The Gun section of the *23rd Company IY*, with their two colt guns, was positioned about 30 yards from a small ruined stone stable and closest to De Villers' Boers. A section of *Paget's Horse* was also camped close to the stable. The *24th Company IY,* were some yards to the east, and the four guns of the *Canadian Field Artillery* was behind them.

Trooper Whittaker was on stable guard and describes the lay of the land: *' we had our horses near the main guard. Then behind us was a garden full of apple and other fruit trees, and all around was thickly covered with cactus bush. The outlying pickets were all round, but the mistake was that they must have been too far apart.*'[284]

It was a cold night with the temperatures dropping below freezing, (on previous nights they had ½ inch of ice in the water buckets in the morning). Whittaker had decided to go and wake up his fellow troopers, so they could start preparing a sheep they had commandeered for breakfast. '*I walked rather fast across the skyline, and the Boers must have seen me and have thought that I had seen them, and was going to warn my mates. At any rate I heard three shots and heard the bullets whiz past me*'[285], so as the camp was just beginning to stir, they were suddenly under heavy small arms fire. The men threw off their blankets, grabbed their guns and took shelter behind their saddles the best they could, some being shot as they rose from their beds.

A heavy fire was directed by the Boers upon the space between the two farmhouses, which meant that communication between the infantry and the mounted troops was cut off. The Yeomanry horses took fright at the firing, broke through the kraal walls and stampeded, the Cape horses remained quiet.

Very heavy fire was being taken at the kraal, where *Paget's Horse* and the Colt Machine guns were positioned. Trooper Brownrigg, of the Gun section graphically describes the action against De Villers Boers: '*At first alarm the Colt gunners grabbed their revolvers (had no rifles then, but have now) and rushed to their guns. God knows why we were not all killed who crossed the few yards of open ground from our ring to the guns. Inside 10 minutes both Colts were pumping bullets into the garden at a rate of 400 a minute, but not for long. Bang, bang crash on the shields came the heavy Martini bullets and smash into pieces went No. 2 gun shield, and immediately after No. 1 shield was knocked off unbroken, and Gunner David Rew killed stone dead by a bullet through the temple...*

One gun was inside the kraal at the corner angle, and the other outside at the other corner. I thought, now if I get a rifle and go to the far corner, I may be able to draw the fire .. and give 'em a chance to start, and by jingo! I got what I wanted. I lay flat on the ground and opened fire. My first man was kneeling in the act of firing, partly covered by a large cactus. Bang! Up went his arms, and he rolled over. Then I was spotted, and don't forget it Dad, that things did get lively round me. It was a good job I lay flat as a fluke, for by jove! The bullets splashed the wall just a few inches above my head.. Both guns were momentarily out of action. However, Mr. Brocklebank, our officer, got down to us from the other extreme end of the camp (the officers quarters at least 250 yards off), and scathless too, which was a marvel... I shall never forget

---

[284] Interview with Trooper C Whittaker

[285] Interview with Trooper C Whittaker

seeing him come up to his own little Colt section (14 of us). He simply rushed into us at a wild run ... and as he came he shouted 'Colt section, Gun section, stand to your guns! I replied, 'We are at then now Sir, with Sergeant Storey.' He smiled and said, 'Good, I thought you would be.'.... Away I went to my corner and rapidly emptied my magazine, when suddenly I saw a crowd of men stand up and begin to run down the garden. It was the enemy retreating. I gave a holy yell and .. shouted to the gun boys to get the guns (firing) again as the rebels were on the run. Then I commenced firing as quickly as I could till the rebels reached the scrub. Then I went into the garden and took three Martini rifles and six bandoliers off three wounded Boers.'[286]

Trooper Johnson's sketch of the Attack at Faber's Put
(From Trooper Johnson's book, by kind permission of the Duke of Lancaster's Own Yeomanry Museum)

During this action the *Canadian Field Artillery* managed to bring their guns into play, and fire some shells into the retreating Boers', the Canadians lost one man killed and two men wounded.
On the west side of the camp, where Ventner's Boers were positioned, Captain Kemp describes the action: '*I was awakened by a deafening crash of rifle fire at 5.30 am. – it was like the twanging of countless fiddle strings, and a perfect hail of bullets swept across every side. One went through my panniers, and another in the wallets by my head. I got up at once, seized my carbine, and on the Colonel (Hughes) calling out we dashed out in the direction of where we thought the heaviest fire came from. There was not the slightest hesitation, no panic, every man getting his rifle and bandolier before going. After going about 100 yards we lay down and fired where we thought the enemy were, the bullets whizzing by all the time. In the first rush Capt. Huntington was hit,*

[286] Trooper Brownrigg letter

and five men killed – Orrell, Derbyshire, Coulston, Hackforth and Barry. We then advanced again, and I shouted "Come on, lads", and they came just as on parade (During this advance Sergeant Major Griffiths roared with laughter as the bullets flew about them). We lay down and fired at the sky line, as we could see no one. We were without any cover whatever. A 24th company man, Todd, who was on my right a yard off, said, "this is a nice breakfast for us" and the next minute was shot dead through the head. It soon got light, and we again advanced up to the trenches the rebels had dug in the night, only to find two Boers, one dead and the other dying; all the rest had fled, leaving bandoliers, cartridges and cloaks. Before the last advance I shouted "fix bayonets," though we had none to fix, and I think it is very likely that made them run as soon as they did.. We then formed up again, and awaited orders. Ten men and an officer (Lieutenant Lethbridge), of Paget's Horse had come in the afternoon before; every single man was hit, five killed, and Lieutenant Lethbridge was shot with an explosive bullet, and he had to have his arm off – this was within 60 yards of my bed. It was truly the most marvellous escape for me.'[287]

Most of the horses had stampeded, with only 12 left of the 128 that were in the Kraal. Captain Kemp's pony, 'Ceres', was one of the 12 left, and he and some others, galloped after two men in the scrub and brought them in.

During the early action, Sir Charles Warren and his staff rode on horseback from his farm, to the other farm, they came under heavy fire, Major Kelly, A.D.C., was severely wounded, Lieutenant Paton was shot in the knee and Major Heath had his horse shot under him.

The attack lasted just over an hour, and the British casualties amounted to twenty killed and thirty wounded. The *23rd Company IY* had suffered the worst out of all the units at Faber's Put, with six killed and twelve wounded, their fellow Yeoman in the *24th Company IY* also suffered, with five killed and six wounded. The wounded were taken to the farmhouse, which had been made into a hospital. The cattle kraal was used to lay out the dead, where they were placed side by side wrapped in their blankets, they were buried later in the afternoon: '*It was a very sorrowful service, and there were not many dry eyes. General Sir Charles Warren, who was very much affected, read the service, and the trumpet sounded the last post.*'[288]

---

[287] Captain Kemp letter

[288] Trooper R Whittaker letter

Trooper Johnson's sketch of the Cemetery at Faber's Put
(From Trooper Johnson's book, by kind permission of the Duke of Lancaster's Own Yeomanry Museum)

Captain Kemp describes some of his wounded men: '*Looker of Norden, was wounded in the groin, in the first five minutes, but under the heaviest fire, cried out, "I'm a'reet," and went on firing till his rifle was shattered with a bullet. Carter and he both refused water when brought, so that others might have it. Sergeant Mason was wounded in the back of his head; Agnew in the foot, badly; Brunner slightly in the back; Gibbs dangerously in the chest – but he is better today and we hope he may pull through – Storey slightly in the face; Turner (Captain Huntington's servant) in the arm; and Poole in the arm.*'[289]

The use of explosive bullets by the Boers was a discovery that did not go down to well amongst the men: '*It makes one very bitter against the rebels to find their cartridges cut round the head so as to be explosive.*'[290]

The Oldham men who were at Faber's Putt during the action were; Colour Sergeant Griffiths, Farrier Sergeant Miller, Troopers Dransfield, Jones, Waterfield, Clegg, Culeen and Charles Whittaker.

Trooper Rodgers who was not at Faber's Put, along with *A Troop* and most of the other Oldham men, expressed his feelings in a letter home: '*We were all sorry to miss it, and yet we cannot help but feel thankful for the narrow escape*'.[291]

---

[289] Captain Kemp letter
[290] Captain Kemp letter

Warren's dispatch to Head Quarters describing the attack glossed over the mistakes that he had made. According to Warren, Faber's Put was a good position; it had '*plenty of water, was in a hollow surrounded by hills where horses could be kept more or less secure from musketry at long ranges.*' Warren also goes on to state that '*It was fortunate that our troops were not taken by surprise in this attack as otherwise the loss would have been greater.*'[292]

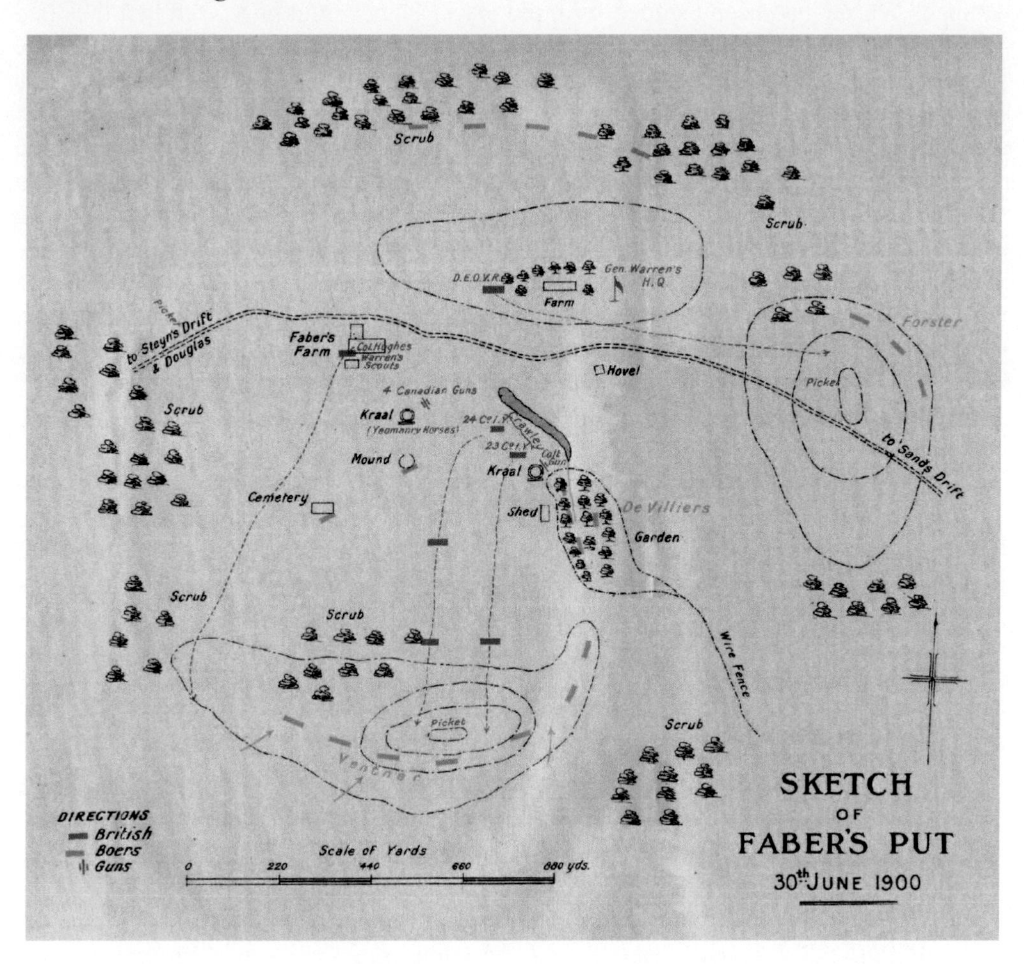

Sketch of Faber's Put from 'Times History of the war in South Africa'

One of the Boers, Martinus Lotter, was with Venter's group during the attack, he was later captured and from jail in Cape Town he wrote a poem about the action at Faber's

[291] Trooper Rodgers letter
[292] General Warrens dispatch dated 29/6/00

Put, which was later published.[293] The poem mentions that Warren had received two warnings of the imminent attack, by three deserters from the Boers, yet he still did not prepare the camp defensively. Warren had estimated that there had been between 500 and 600 Boers involved in the attack, Lotter puts the number at 170 with Venter, 60 with Forster and 56 in the garden with De Villiers, around half of Warrens estimate.
In reality Faber's Put was not the best choice for a camp, it simply invited an attack by the Boers. The Boers knew the area well, and would have been able to reconnoitre the camp, as Warren had been camped for a few days. They would have seen that they had done little to establish defences in the camp, and they would also have known that the force consisted mainly of volunteers and not regulars. The Boers could more or less surround the camp, with the advantage of the high ground, and due to the thickness of the bush and spacing of the pickets, were able to get within 50 yards of the heart of the camp without being detected. As Trooper Whittaker explains: the '*Boers crawled in between the pickets and into the garden, and to within fifty yards of where we were with the horses. Three or four of them got into a building and filled the window space up with rock, only leaving space enough to shoot through. These men were only 25 yards away from us.*'[294] It had been a perfect surprise by the Boers; most of the men were not even up or dressed, before the bullets started flying into the camp. Trooper Clegg from Oldham, in *D Troop*, was certainly of a different opinion to Warren:
'*I think that had General Warren given the order for us to entrench ourselves before lying down that most of the lives lost would have been saved. As it was we had no cover at all. He decided to remedy this when it was too late. Another mistake was made in stacking our rifles in the centre of the ring. When the firing commenced we rushed for them and they fell to the ground, and I don't think any of us got our own, I remember being told by some that they were at a great disadvantage through the breeches having sand in, and the bolts consequently would not work for a few minutes. I never slept without my rifle being at my side after that*'[295]
A leaked memorandum from Lieutenant Colonel Hughes criticised Warren's dispatch, and this criticism appeared in the Cape newspapers within a few weeks.[296]
Warren went on to '*consider that this attack was a very fortunate occurrence, as with the very splendid shooting of so many of the rebels in this part of the country it would have been impossible to have attacked and taken the position about Campbell and Girquatown without a far greater loss than was sustained at Faber's Put, and with our small force we could not have hoped to have killed so many of the enemy in any attack we could make, as their mobility is so immeasurably superior to ours.*' And '*Since the action of Faber's Put, the rebels in all directions have continued to surrender in increasing numbers, and with one consent the whole of the rebels say that the repulse*

[293] Translation of Poem is held in Duke of Lancaster's Own Yeomanry Museum
[294] Interview with Trooper Whittaker
[295] Interview with Trooper Clegg.
[296] Sam Hughes biography by Ronald G Haycock

at Faber's Put and great loss they sustained there caused a sudden collapse of the rebellion.'[297]

On this Warren was correct, the Boers had hoped that the largely untested volunteer infantry and Imperial Yeomanry would fold under fire, but due to the bravery of the *23rd Company IY* and the other units, the Boers were repulsed and what could have been a complete disaster was prevented.

Trooper Brownrigg was also of the opinion that they were poorly prepared to defend the camp and explained the changed situation in the camp after the fight.

'Guards were doubled, and stone walls built round the saddle rings. The hut was pulled down, and one of our Colt guns entrenched there, and the gun boys slept with it. Another Colt gun was placed on the highest point on the right, and its crews of men and a full picket were on guard duty all night. Also, the guns of the Royal Canadian Field Artillery were employed and put in a good position. Now, had they come a second time, they would have been unable to get within 1,000 yards of the camp, and would have had a warm reception. Also, after the fight, every morning every man was wakened up, and lay with his arms under cover till daylight, but, of course, all this should have been done before.

I don't know who is responsible. The men are very bitter about it. I enclose two plans of the battlefield – one of the battle, and one of our positions afterwards.'[298]

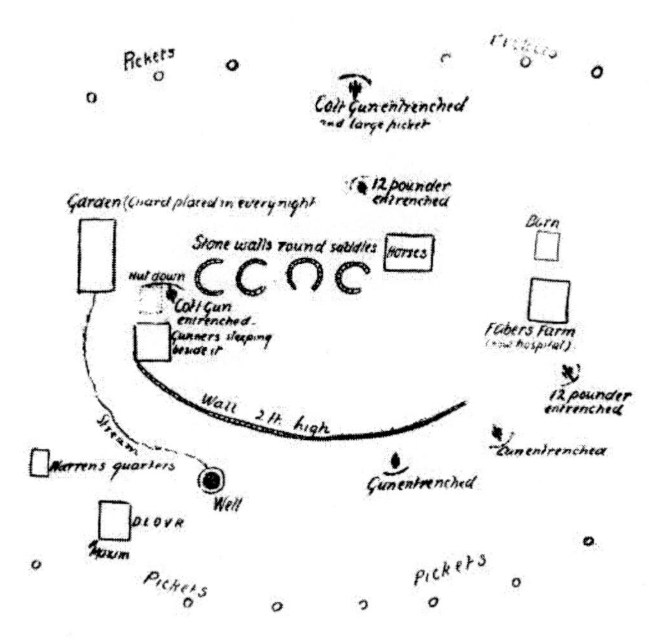

Sketch of Faber's Put defences after the battle, by Trooper Brownrigg

---

297 General Warrens dispatch dated 29/6/00

298 Trooper Brownrigg letter

1902 photograph of Faber's Put looking out over the spring to the farm
By kind permission of Western Cape Archives and Records Service

The incident of Captain Kemp ordering his men to fix bayonets, was the subject of a poem by a noted poet of the time, the Reverend Hardwicke Drummond Rawnsley, and published in his book in 1901.

To Captain George Kemp, M.P.
FROM Lancashire, thanks

We had no bayonets there to fix,
And we were in a snare.
But Kemp had learned the Boerish tricks.
And Kemp could do and dare;
The night was still, his voice was large,
"Fix bayonets, men!" he cried, "and charge!"

Just now the darkness hummed and chirred.
Just now it spat with fire;
Flame ceased, and thro' the mist we heard
Boer voices shout, "Retire!"
Their sheathes our phantom bayonets found.
And soon the "boys" were sleeping sound.[299]

[299] 'Ballads of the War' by H.D. Rawnsley

The wounded men were transported to the General hospital at Kimberley, where Oldham man, Sergeant Howarth of the *6th Volunteer Battalion Manchester Regiment,* was stationed with the *RAMC* as the wardmaster of A section. The wounded arrived at the hospital on 11th June, on the train from Vryburg. Getting the wounded to Vryburg would have been a terrible journey in ambulance wagons, as ambulance wagons had no springs, and on the rough dirt roads the wounded men would have had a very uncomfortable journey.
Sergeant Howarth, to his great dismay, discovered that the wounded he received were from the '*23rd and 24th Companies of the Imperial yeomanry, of which detachment the Oldham troop form a portion. They are all wounded men, and to see their limbs when they are being dressed is enough to turn sick a tender hearted man, and to hear their groans as the medical officers are probing in the wounds for bullets or broken bones is most pitiable. With them came two of the Royal Canadian Field Artillery, one of whom had a Boer bullet in his hip. He was operated upon, and the bullet extracted. He bore up wonderfully, and was as cheerful after it was over as he was before they took it out. There is also Trooper Gibbs, of Rochdale, amongst the number. He was shot through the breast, and it came out at the lower part of the shoulder blade. There is a Manchester man here also, with one of his arms shot clean through the bone – this is his left arm. His right arm is shot through, just above his wrist, and one of his feet is off. You see they had a pretty rough time of it. One of the Cape Volunteer Medical Staff Corps, who was with the Yeomanry with ambulance wagons, was talking to another NCO when a shot was fired, and the bullet went through the other NCOs fleshy part of the neck and hit the other NCO in the right ear, lodging in the internal part of the ear. They also took that out this afternoon without chloroform, and I can tell you they did put him through it, and no mistake.*'[300] In a later letter, Howarth explains that Trooper Gibbs[301] '*was shot through the left lung, but it was also a treat to see the manner in which he bore his pain and never murmured.*'[302]

A Troop, rejoined Warren's force on 2nd June, and the following day they were advancing on the Boers, towards Campbell. '*They however retired. We advanced again on the Monday morning (the next day), and about 10 am our cannon fired the first shot. We all felt ready to get at them, and avenge the deaths of the lads who fell fighting for their Queen and country the Wednesday morning previous. The enemy however did not give us a chance. They retired, and later in the day (4th June) we occupied Campbell without opposition and news was brought in that the rebels were disbanding and returning home.*'[303]

---

[300] Sgt Howarth letter
[301] Trooper Gibbs was a member of the Rochdale troop and was home by Nov 1900, he was toasted at a dinner by the Oldham Troop in December 1900. His wound caused him to lose the use of the upper portion of his left arm.
[302] Sgt Howarth letter
[303] Trooper Rodgers letter

At Campbell, the *Troops* of the *23rd and 24th Companies IY* were split up and sent to different places, one *Troop* went back to man Faber's Put, whilst *A Troop* was sent back to Douglas for garrison duty.
Corporal Wild joined them at Campbell, along with six others who had brought up 12 remounts. He was expecting to rejoin *A Troop*, but discovered that they were back at Douglas, and most had not taken part in the action at Faber's Put. On 7th June, due to the Boers unsuccessful attack at Faber's Put, Griquatown had been captured without a fight.

Trooper Johnson's sketch of the camp at Campbell
(From Trooper Johnson's book, by kind permission of the Duke of Lancaster's Own Yeomanry Museum)

The *23rd Company IY* was reinforced by a draft of twelve men in June, eight of these men were from the DLOY, the rest civilian volunteers, none of them from Oldham.
For the most of June, the *23rd Company IY* and Warren's column, continued to hunt out the Boers: '*We have been on the march for the greater part of the last two weeks, and as far as our column is concerned we have been successful in driving out and capturing all the Boers and rebel commandees out of Bechuanaland and West Griqualand. We had all sorts of hardships to contend with, such as insufficient food, night marches in all sorts of weather, and night guards three or four nights together.*'[304]

[304] Trooper Rodgers letter

During this two week period a large number of Boers were brought in, Trooper Rodgers was on duty at Blikfontein, when 175 Boers were brought in by *Warrens Scouts*. '*They were a dirty, filthy lot of scoundrels, and I was on sentry duty at the time, and as they passed by me I felt as though I could have sent my bayonet through them. It turned out that they were the same commando who made the night attack upon us about three weeks ago, when we lost a few of our brave comrades.*'[305] These were Commandant General De Villers and his men.

In July, whilst stationed at Blikfontein, about 90 miles north-west of Kimberley, they received word that Boers were marching towards them to mount an attack. The camp was put into a state of readiness, one of the Colt guns was mounted on a high wall, so that they could shoot all round the camp over the heads of the Yeomanry. The Boers did not make an appearance and the scare was soon over.

Effectively by the end of July, the British had secured the Northern Cape area, and had secured the important railway line from Mafeking and Kimberley, to the south.

Respite at Kuruman

They left Blikfontein in July, and after a three day march arrived in Kuruman. Kuruman is about 125 miles North-West of Kimberley, on the edge of the Khalahari desert. It had been in the hands of the Boers for over six months, until being relieved by British forces on 24th June. Sir Charles Warren then left his column at Kuruman and returned home. *B Troop* did not go to Kuruman with the rest of the *23rd Company IY*, instead they were detailed to join Brigadier General Henry Hamilton Settle's column, with whom they stayed for around four months, distinguishing themselves at an engagement with the Boers at Hoopstad on 20th October.

From Kuruman, fifteen of *A Troop*, including Corporal Wild, departed on a long patrol searching the farms in the area for Boers. Trooper Rodgers describes the patrol: '*I've just returned from a 200 mile patrol in the direction of the Longburg mountains, and I have been within 150 miles of the German West African border. I was away on the patrol eight days, and out of that had two days rest, and I think 200 miles in six days is fairly good travelling. We crossed part of the Kalahari desert and in consequence suffered from the scarity of water. We had to go 35 and 40 miles at a stretch before coming to any water. The poor horses felt it, I can tell you; I felt sorry for them. The patrol numbered 15 officers and men all told. The idea of the patrol was on account of a body of Boers having taken up their quarters in the Longburg mountains. Our duty was to capture them, but as usual they retired. They were between 50 and 60 strong, but they couldn't face a small force like ours. They have since been surrounded. We managed to get one prominent Boer leader, whom we brought to camp; he is now in jail. As I write this I am on sentry duty in one of the numerous forts which surround Kuruman.*'[306]

[305] Trooper Rodgers letter

[306] Trooper Rodgers letter

Whilst at Kuruman the *Pretoria Police* were recruiting and offering attractive rates of pay; '*The pay is 10s a day for privates, 12s 6d for Corporals, and 15s for sergeants. Griffiths has put his name down to join. I expect he will join as a sergeant. Service is for three months or longer, as the men may desire.*'[307] In fact, 33 men from the *23rd Company IY* put their names down to join, and were all passed by the doctor as fit, but the forms were never sent on by Colonel Crawley. Many of the men were not happy with this situation, as they had been given promises in England; '*before we left England we were told we would be given a chance to join the police if we wished to stay out.*'[308]

Whilst at Kuruman, Trooper Dransfield and Captain Kemp both had a bout of enteric fever, Kemp recovered fairly quickly and Dransfield was sent to Vryburg, where he recovered and went on to join the station staff.

The *23rd Company IY* remained at Kuruman until mid October, with little further incidents, in fact they had time to organise some sporting activities. A sporting day organised on the 3rd October involved the *23rd Company IY, Cape Mounted Rifles, Cape Police, Royal Field Artillery* and the *Duke of Edinburgh's Own Volunteer Rifles.* It was watched by the officers of these regiments, including Captain and Lady Beatrice Kemp, who distributed the prizes. Events such as lemon cutting; jumping over eight hurdles (won by Corporal Waterfield's team); Heads and Posts; Tent pegging; and the Victoria Cross race which consisted of jumping over two hurdles, dismounting and picking up a dummy man, - which weighs about 8 stones -, and then over two more hurdles, and running home, altogether about 500 yards.

The *23rd Company IY* had a fairly easy time of it based here, and even started to get settled, Whittaker describes his time at Kuruman; '*We stayed there several months and began to think that the war would be over before we left. There were a lot of us there – Yeomanry, Regular soldiers, Cape Police, Cape Mounted Rifles and others. We spent most of the time buck shooting, and the natives eventually came down from the hills and built us huts of reeds and rushes. They would build you a nice hut for 10s... Some of our fellows had not only a hut, but had it fenced all round with a reed fence. We had plenty of enjoyment there.*[309]

The *23rd Company IY* eventually departed Kuruman, and arrived in Kimberley on 17th October after a five day march of around 150 miles, travelling via Blikfontein, Boltsap and Barkley West. Trooper Dransfield re-joined the company at Kimberley, but unfortunately he was struck down with enteric fever for a second time, and died on 27th November at Kimberley. Whilst there, Trooper John Clegg was promoted to Corporal.

Whilst at Kimberley, the *23rd Company IY* continued to carry out patrols of the local area including sorties out to Boshof (where they escorted a convoy drawn by traction engines), Alexandersfontein and Spitzfontein searching for Boers without any real success. At Kimberley, *B Troop* rejoined the *23rd Company IY* and the Gun section was

---

[307] Cpl Wild letter

[308] Interview with Trooper Clegg

[309] Interview with Trooper C Whittaker

disbanded with the members of the section being spread across the other troops. Lieutenant Brocklebank, who commanded the gun section, gained a regular commission and joined the *1st (King's) Dragoon Guards*. The two Colt guns were removed from their unserviceable carriages and mounted on an armoured train.[310]

With Brigadier General Settle's Column

At the end of October, they left Kimberley with General Settle's Column and headed southward, passing through Koffiefontein. By November 4th they were at Honey Nest Kloof, where Colonel Sir Charles Parsons joined them with 1,500 men. During this march Captain Kemp, along with Sergeant Major Griffiths, Trumpeter Bullough, Troopers M.Smith, W.Halliwell, W.Handley and E.A.Heap had been detailed to search a farm for some Boer rebels, they were expected to be gone no more than an hour, however when they did not arrive back, men were sent out to the farm to find them but they were not there, the worst was assumed, that they had been ambushed and captured by the Boers, causing concern and anxiety among the *23rd Company IY*. They had gone missing early in the morning, and it was not until it was getting dark in the evening that Captain Kemp and his men rode into the camp at Honey Nest Kloof: '*When they arrived they had a lively tale to tell about Captain Denison, of the Scouts, bringing orders from the commander, Colonel Parsons, to go and search farms. As he had only four men, it proved a much longer undertaking than all expected. Of course Colonel Crawley new nothing of this. The men had a lively time, and covered a great area of country, returning to camp none the worst except in being as hungry as hunters.*'[311]
The column continued on its relentless march with their main occupation being that of setting fire to all farms disloyal to the British. All was quiet, until they were on the road to a small town called Luckhoff on 27th November. A commando of around 700 Boers led by Judge Hertzog, had positioned themselves on a line of koppies, with the intention of surprising the rearguard of General Settle's column. The fight lasted five hours, with only two men killed and ten wounded. One of the wounded men was Sergeant Fairclough of *B Troop*. It was an action that the *23rd Company IY* were able to show their mettle again. The *23rd Company IY*; '*was protecting the right flank. We took possession of a large kopje that made the flank secure.*'[312] Corporal Wild was in the leading file going up the koppie: '*the Boers just missed shooting me; but we soon had them spotted, and then we gave it them hot.*'[313] After a short fight the Boers were driven away, leaving a few dead and wounded behind on top of the koppies. After the action and later in camp on the same day, just before the picquets were being posted, the *23rd Company IY* were paraded and addressed by Colonel Crawley: '"*The Generals (Settle and Parsons) have wished me to express their very highest admiration of the*

[310] Chain Mail by Brereton, P54
[311] Trooper Rigg letter
[312] Cpl Wild letter
[313] Cpl Wild letter

work done by the Imperial Yeomanry on the right flank this morning. The position which they took under a hot fire the generals thought to be impregnable; and they couldn't believe their eyes when they were told the Imperial Yeomanry occupied and were holding the high Kopjes on the extreme right flank; in fact they wanted to shell these positions, thinking they were still occupied by the Boer's, and it was only on Captain White and myself assuring them that it was the Imperial Yeomanry who were in possession that they desisted from firing. Personally, all I can say is that the finest infantry in the world couldn't have behaved better but, you would do all that was asked of you, while the hotter the fire the more did you prove that you were true Yeoman. This is the highest compliment I can pay you" Colonel Crawley added that as a soldier he would like to see the fire that would make DOL's flinch.'[314]

Somewhere around this time, the exact dates are unclear, 'A' troop lost its commander, Lieutenant Heap, who had been sent home sick, was back in Rochdale by the beginning of January 1901.

The *23rd Company IY* continued with Settle's column, which was tasked with hunting down General De Wet, and the commando leader Judge Hertzog. On the march, the column would burn down the farms of any known Boer commandos at any opportunity. The column must have been a sight to behold, as it slowly snaked its way across the country, Trooper Rigg describes the column: ' *Throughout the march we had been commandeering horses, cattle, sheep, goats, Cape carts, wagons etc, and we had brought all the loyal English, Dutch, and Kaffirs as refugees with their portable belongings. In our column were the mounted and dismounted soldiers, and the artillery, the wagons, Cape carts, and small two wheeled carts of the convoy (some of which have as many as 20 oxen or mules attached) all driven by blacks. The noise they make has to be heard to be believed, while they use their tremendously long whips with cruel effect upon their charges. Then there were the prisoners with their necessary guards and the hundreds of commandeered horse and cattle, and thousands of sheep with their black drovers. All these made up a procession the like of which you have never seen in England.'*[315]

Conditions on the march would be awful for the men; the rain came down in torrents for days at a time. On the morning of December 5th they woke up in camp ankle deep in mud, the rain had soaked their blankets, which had still been wet from the previous nights. There was no way to gain shelter from the relentless rain, and it proved too much for some. A Lancashire Fusilier, who had been on picquet was found in the morning he '*had died in a stooping position under a big boulder, while on sentry-go, with rifle in hand.*'[316] Trooper Rodgers considered the rain to be worse than the Boers: ' *the one thing we dreaded the most was the rain. We are not afraid of the Boers, but I think we are afraid of the rain.'*[317]

---

[314] Trooper Rigg letter
[315] Trooper Rigg letter
[316] Trooper Rigg letter
[317] Trooper Rodgers letter

Duke of Lancaster's Own Yeomanry – Oldham Troop

With General Parsons column

By 6th December, the column found itself in Edenburg, where they stayed for a few days. Whilst here General Parsons took over the command of the column and General Settle returned home. Colonel Crawley, the commander of the *8th Battalion*, was promoted to second in command of the column, which in turn meant that Captain Kemp was appointed the commander of the *8th Battalion* in his place. Lieutenant Huntington then took over from Kemp as commander of the *23rd Company IY*.

The column then continued on up to Bloemfontein, camping just outside the town on 20th December. The men were hopeful that they could spend Christmas in some kind of comfort. Two days later they received orders to entrain, and after an uneventful journey arrived at Victoria West station, were they stayed for Christmas. The officers treated the men to whiskey and '*many of us not being used to intoxicating drink got "over the line".*[318] The *23rd and 24th Companies IY* were then dispatched, ahead of the main body, to Carnarvon about 50 miles away to protect the town from the Boers. The Boers under the command of Hertzog, were reported to be 1,600 strong and heading for the town. The companies were tasked with holding the town until the rest of the column could catch up. They arrived in Carnarvon one and half days ahead of the Boers. Trooper Rodgers was on duty: '*I was on sentry duty that morning about 5.30 am when I observed a cloud of dust rising from the veldt, two miles away from my post. We raised the alarm, and everybody got ready to face the worst. We really expected, if it came to fighting, to be swept off the face of the map, for it was a poor place to hold as regards fortifications. Time went on, and we were expecting to hear the first shot fired any moment, when we observed another cloud of dust. At first we thought this was our column, but it turned out to be Colonel De Lisle's flying column in pursuit of the enemy, so we were saved. How thankful we felt!'*[319] It was a close shave for the *23rd Company IY*, if the 1,600 strong Boers had been given the opportunity to attack, there would have been many casualties, with no hope of keeping them out of Carnarvon.

Once the column, under General Parsons, had caught up with the *23rd Company IY* at Carnarvon they continued on their sweep of the veldt looking for the Boers.

By the end of January 1901, the *23rd Company IY* had been posted to Lange Kloof, they had, had a two and half day march, and when they arrived found that the Boers we all around the area in strong numbers. Trooper Rodgers explains the position they were in: '*We were hemmed in, and isolated from any of our columns. There was no denying that we were in a tight fix, but we had been chosen for this special work, and we mean to stick. Our Captain said he knew he could rely on every man doing his duty. We had only been here a day when we had a skirmish in the pass, and drove the enemy off, mortally wounding two, capturing another, also three horses, and killing two. They got more than they bargained for. We were expecting an attack on all sides any moment,*

---

[318] Interview with Trooper C Whittaker

[319] Trooper Rodgers letter

and horses were kept saddled up, ready for any emergency. I wish you could see the position we hold, it's a natural fortress in the pass, and six men could hold any number at bay.'[320]

They left their station at Lange Kloof, and by the middle of March they had moved to Cookhouse. During this period there was a promotion for Captain Kemp to that of Major, dated 2nd March 1901. From Cookhouse, they entrained on 18th March, travelling overnight to arrive at Rosmead Junction the following morning, where they were met by a draft of new recruits, who had just recently arrived from England, to reinforce the company. The relief contingent had left Southampton on 15th February, on board the Cunard transporter *Aurania.*
Immediately on arrival, '*Major Kemp and Sergeant Major Griffiths took the recruits for a little drill, as they had only just got their mounts from the re-mount officer at Rosmead Junction. Fine fun we had watching them attempt to mount their new steeds.*'[321]
The following morning, reveille was at 4 am, ready for parade at 5 am. In order to try and get the new recruits ready in time, Sergeant Major Griffiths went around waking the new recruits at 2 am, even pulling some of them out of their beds. Despite this very early start for the new recruits, a lot of them were confused in the dark; they could not find their horses, saddles or kit, a lot of them did not make the parade at 5 am and some even had to be left behind as the column marched off. They eventually caught up when the column came to their first halt.
During the first days march the new recruits were told off into their sections, with the old hands put in charge of the recruits as subsection leaders. All the old hands were keen to help the new recruits settle in quickly. On the morning of 21st March they arrived in Oorlogspoort, a pass through the Zurberg, it was being held by a detachment of the *5th Lancers* and a company of the *Wiltshire Regiment*. The following morning, after an overnight stay, they were on the march towards Steynsburg, to join Colonel Henniker's column. Around this time Sergeant Major Griffiths was rewarded for his hard work, with a commission as Lieutenant in the *23rd Company IY.*

Relief contingent and Colonel Henniker's column

It soon became apparent the new drafts were not up to an acceptable standard. Some of them had joined straight from civilian life, and had received very little training prior to being dispatched to South Africa: '*only a very poor percentage of them could even mount, and none of them knew how to put a saddle on a horse.*'[322] Lieutenant Huntingdon, and the newly commissioned Griffiths, was tasked with getting the new men up to a suitable standard. They spent a number of weeks at Graaff-Reinet drilling them day and night. It took nearly three months before they were deemed fit for active

[320] Trooper Rodgers letter
[321] Trooper Rigg letter
[322] Interview with Cpl Wild

service. As a consequence of the training required by the relief contingent, the original volunteers could not yet return home.
In the middle of April the *23rd Company IY* along with the *24th, 65th* and *71st Companies IY*, left the column under the command of Colonel Crawley heading through the mountain to Graaff-Reinet. However due to Boers being reported in the area of Kendrew, they were diverted back to the column and spent some time patrolling around the area of Fish River eventually ending at Bethesda Road station where they rested for a few days. From here they entrained and travelled to Aberdeen Road. Major Kemp then left the company for Johannesburg and to make arrangements for the men of the original *23rd Company IY* to be sent home, as by now they had served well over the 12 months they had originally signed up for.

Action near Pearston

In the latter half of April, they were stationed at Sundays River, near Pearston, patrolling the area for Boers. They caught up with them on 22nd April, Corporal Wild describes the encounter: '*They had a splendid position on a range of kopjes overlooked on each side of the road, which was only wide enough to go four abreast. So they had an excellent chance of killing a lot of us. The advanced guard did not see them on account of the thickness of the bush. The Colonel and staff had gone on in front to mark a place to camp for the night, having marched 30 miles in the heat of the day, when suddenly a terrible fire came right among us from both sides. It was so sudden as to somewhat surprise us, as our information was that the Boers had fled. Our Colonel had charge of all the Yeomanry and Bushmen, VIR (Australian Bushmen). The two guns at once got in position, and after sending a few shells on the kopjes to cover our advance the Yeomanry and Bushmen charged kopje after kopje at the point of the bayonet, but found that the Boers had gone away at seeing them coming with cold steel. It was now getting dark, so we had to give up the chase as the way the Boers had gone was very narrow and thickly lined with bush on each side for miles, some had to relinquish the chase, some of our men being out till 9pm. I don't think we killed any Boers. They wounded seven of our men, but I am glad to say, only slightly. One was Graham Brooks, who was in my troop, but lately has been acting as messenger to Colonel Henniker. He was shot through the neck, but will soon be alright.*'[323] The Boers were under the command of Malan who a few days later joined up with Commandant G.J.Scheepers commando.
The day after the action, the *23rd* and *24th Companies IY* (about 80 men), went up the valley towards Water Clough, chasing the Boers and forcing them up one of the slopes of the Coetzee mountains, where they held their position. The Yeoman returned to camp, as they had gone as far as was advisable with their small force.
On April 26th they reached Sundays River, by this time Corporal Wild describes that the old *23rd Company IY* had now dwindled down to only 40 men, and two new

[323] Cpl Wild letter

officers had come to take the place of those who had gone home. The two new officers were Lieutenant Palka, who quickly ended up in hospital with fever, and Lieutenant Chapman, a former trooper in the Manchester Yeomanry.

On the 27th, the *23rd Company IY* were up in the mountains positioned on two koppies overlooking the road. A detachment of *Bushmen* were out on patrol, and twelve of the *Bushmen* were escorting a signaller to heliograph news to Colonel Henniker, when a heavy mist suddenly came down. As they were no longer able to signal, they headed back to camp. A party of Boers ambushed them, two men were killed and one wounded. The ambush took place a couple of miles from where the *23rd Company IY* were positioned, they could hear the shooting, but could not tell in which direction it was coming from. Once the mist had cleared, they recovered and buried the dead.

They remained in the mountains until May 2nd, when they received orders to rejoin the column at Pearston. Whilst in the mountains, they endured freezing conditions with nothing more than one blanket and an overcoat each. As the wagons could not get up the hills, they also suffered with lack of food.

After a few days in Pearston, they marched to Somerset East where they lost another of the new officers due to sickness, Lieutenant Chapman who had suffered with the cold in the mountains. Another new officer joined them, Lieutenant Spratt, formerly a corporal in the CIV's. From here they travelled to Thorngrove station, near Cookhouse, whilst here on 9th May, they were informed by Colonel Henniker that the original members of the *23rd Company IY* had received orders to mobilise at Worcester for home. Only 40 answered the muster roll out of the original 136 who went out. They immediately gave up their horses and saddles for re-distribution to others.

Whilst at Worcester, a farewell message written by Lt-Colonel A.P.Crawley, commanding the *8th Battalion Imperial Yeomanry*, was read out to the departing men. Extracts from this address: '*It is with great regret that I am not able personally to wish you, my comrades of the last fifteen months, good-bye, God speed, and a safe voyage home, as I am engaged in organising those who are to fill your places. ... I can conscientiously state that throughout your fifteen months of active service you have won the admiration and respect of all whom under you served. It was evident, from the outset, the determination displayed by all ranks to do their duty under whatever circumstances they found themselves, and if any further proof was necessary it was forthcoming at Faber's Put when you were surprised under the most trying circumstances that troops could be placed, and later again and again on each and every occasion. ... This war is the first one in which Yeomanry have been employed, and with no previous experience of warfare and superficial training it was your high moral sense of duty and determination which has produced the brilliant record you can take away with you.*'[324]

[324] Address by Lt-Col Crawley dated 7th May 1901

Return Home for the original 23rd Company IY

What was left of the *23rd Company IY*, sailed on the transporter *Avondale Castle* from Cape Town, arriving in Southampton three weeks later on 9th June. From Southampton, they travelled straight to Fulwood barracks at Preston, where they were discharged. A grand reception was held for the returning Rochdale men and Major Kemp, but the return of the Oldham men went virtually unnoticed in the town, with only Trooper Rodgers receiving a welcome by his fiancé and friends as he got off the train at Hollinwood.

With Colonel Doran's Flying Column

Lieutenant Griffiths volunteered to stay on in South Africa and was appointed commandant of the *23rd Company IY.* Shortly afterwards he was promoted to Captain. Colonel Henniker's column was taken over by Lt-Colonel W.R.B.Doran in June 1901. As of 8th July 1901, Colonel Doran's Flying column consisted of the *23rd Company IY* (141), *Warren's Mounted Infantry* (181), *11th Company IY* (134), *24th Company IY* (125), *"M" Battery R.H.A.*, 2 guns and *Cape Colony Cyclists* (4)[325]

On 14th July, General French ordered four columns under Sir Charles P Crewe, G Wyndham, Col Beauchamp Doran and Scobell into the Camdeboo Mountains to try to trap Cmdt Gideon Scheepers commando. Scheepers was, however, able to escape with the bulk of his commando. Only 28 of his men were captured of whom eight were later executed.

On 1st August the column attacked a laager at Waterkranz, surprising seven of Smit's men asleep in a farm and capturing a number of Smit's horses, and a cart with the Commandant's papers.
For the rest of the year, Doran's column spent most of their efforts trying to track down the Boers. On 2nd September, they caught up with Lotters commando at Garstland Kloof, near Cradock. Doran's flying column attacked the commando and drove them into the mountains, killing one and capturing 30 horses. A few days later, Lotters commandos were caught in their laager, at Groenkloof near Petersburg, by Colonel Scobell's column. After a hard fight they surrendered, with 19 Boers and ten British soldiers killed. Lotter was one of the prisoners, and was later tried and executed.
Later in the month Doran's column was on the trail of Smut's commando.
From November 1901 onwards the main Boer commando activity was concentrated in the North West Cape under Generals Smuts, Malan and Manie Maritz. November and December found Doran's column and the *23rd Company IY* in the area around Sutherland and Matjesfontein.

---

[325] London Gazette 20 Aug 1901

Colonel Doran's Flying column drying out blankets after a downpour
(Source: After Pretoria: The Guerilla War, Vol II)

On 9th of December, when the column was heading towards Tontelboschkolk, they were successful in surprising the Sutherland Boers, under Nesser near Brandwagt, - 30 miles east-north-east of Calvinia -, where one Boer was killed and eight captured. On the approach of the column, the Boers in the neighbourhood of Tontelboschkolk broke up into a number of small parties, and moved south into the Clanwilliam District.
On 16th December the Boer leader, Asst Chief-Cmdt Kritzinger, with 100 men came into contact with the *Grenadier Guards* at Blockhouses near Hanover. The exchange was sharp and short, Kritzinger and twelve of his men were wounded and captured, the rest escaped to the south, and were pursued into the Aberdeen district by Doran's flying column and troops under Major Lord Cavendish Bentinck.
For the rest of December and January 1902, the *23rd Company IY* and Doran's column were employed mainly in covering the blockhouse line, and in escorting convoys to supply depots.

Defence of Middlepost farm

In the early days of February 1902, Smuts, Malan, and several other Boer leaders were active in the country round Calvinia.
On the morning of 5th February, Colonel Doran and around 350 men left camp with the purpose of locating the Boers. Doran took about 100 men to a distant farm in search of Geldenhuis, one of the Boer leaders, whilst the remainder, with the guns and the wagons, moved slowly along the main road to a farm at Middlepost, (50 miles south-

west of Calvinia) were they camped at noon. This small force of 250 men consisted of the *11th, 23rd and 24th Companies IY*, and a troop of *Cape Police*. Captain Saunders of the *24th Company IY* was in command in the absence of Colonel Doran.
A force of about 100 Boers, led by Veg-Gen J.L.Van Deventer, occupied a high koppie 1,500 yards from the farm, and other Boers in smaller parties were on the broken ground encircling the camp. In the afternoon the Boers attacked the camp, they concentrated a withering fusillade on the wagons. Captain Saunders had to abandon the wagons and concentrate his defence upon his guns and the farm. When night fell, the Boers rushed in and commenced looting the wagons, which they afterwards set on fire. The scene ensuing was described by a reporter as being "infernally picturesque." Having gutted the wagons the Boers soon made it apparent to take the guns as well. A fusillade, more furious then ever, was directed on to the spot where the guns had been during the afternoon. It was however, to no avail – the guns having been secretly shifted when darkness descended. After about two hours fighting the Boers gave up their attack for the night, and the defenders were untroubled save for a few stray shots.
At daylight the fight recommenced, with the British alert and eager, despite the fact that their hunger had been growing during the night, they had not eaten since noon the previous day. The enemy now made an onslaught on to the small koppie at the back of the farmhouse. Under cover of a well-directed fire many of the Boers crept up behind rocks to within a few yards of the rifles of the British. The marksmanship of the Boers at this point was so good that to lift one's head above the schanzes meant sure and instant death. A remarkable thing now occurred, the Boers nearest the schanzes, keeping their heads and bodies under cover, actually started throwing stones at the schanzes to knock them down. However by this time, the guns, having got the range of the Boers firing supports, began to pepper them to such effect that their fire died away, and the storming party had to beat a hasty retreat. At this juncture the Boers hoisted a white flag, and on the cessation of firing began to collect their wounded in a wagon, this operation last about an hour.
The Boers then made a further attack, firing from a longer range, however the appearance of Colonel Doran, on their flank, relieved the tension, allowing the whole column shortly afterwards to retire about six miles and camp for the night. The men fought with admirable spirit, and though several small parties were isolated during the whole of the fighting, not a man surrendered, even when during the latter part of the fight the Boers outnumbered them by at least four to one, and the troops were without food and almost without water'[326]
The fight was a costly one with 11 killed, 30 wounded and all the wagons lost; the *23rd Company IY* suffered two killed; Private R.Isherwood (20511) and Private James Hume (25579). Severely Wounded –Private Z.Bentley (28802) and Private D.Seddon (25601); Dangerously wounded –Cpl R.Lancaster (20516); Slightly wounded – Privates J.M.Harness (23768), E.Butterworth (23754), W.A.Jessop (21372),

[326] Press Association report

J.Martindale (23780) and Cpl A.Rawston (23788) slightly wounded in the leg. Lieutenant John Anderson Bingham was dangerously wounded in the head and died five days later. He had been a Lieutenant in the *8th VB Liverpool Regiment* before volunteering for the *23rd Company IY.*
The South African war came to an end on 31st May 1902, after two and half years of fighting when conditions of surrender were signed by the Boer leaders.
Unfortunately this was not the last incident for the *23rd Company IY*, Lieutenant H Devereux Spratt was with a party of 20 men of the *23rd Company IY,* near to Mortimer in the Cape Colony on the 2nd June, when a Boer commandant, not being aware that peace had been declared, opened fire, and Lieutenant Spratt, Privates William Samuel Hales (25504) and Frank Hanley (25573) were killed. Cpl Frank Boardman (20495) was slightly wounded in the shoulder.

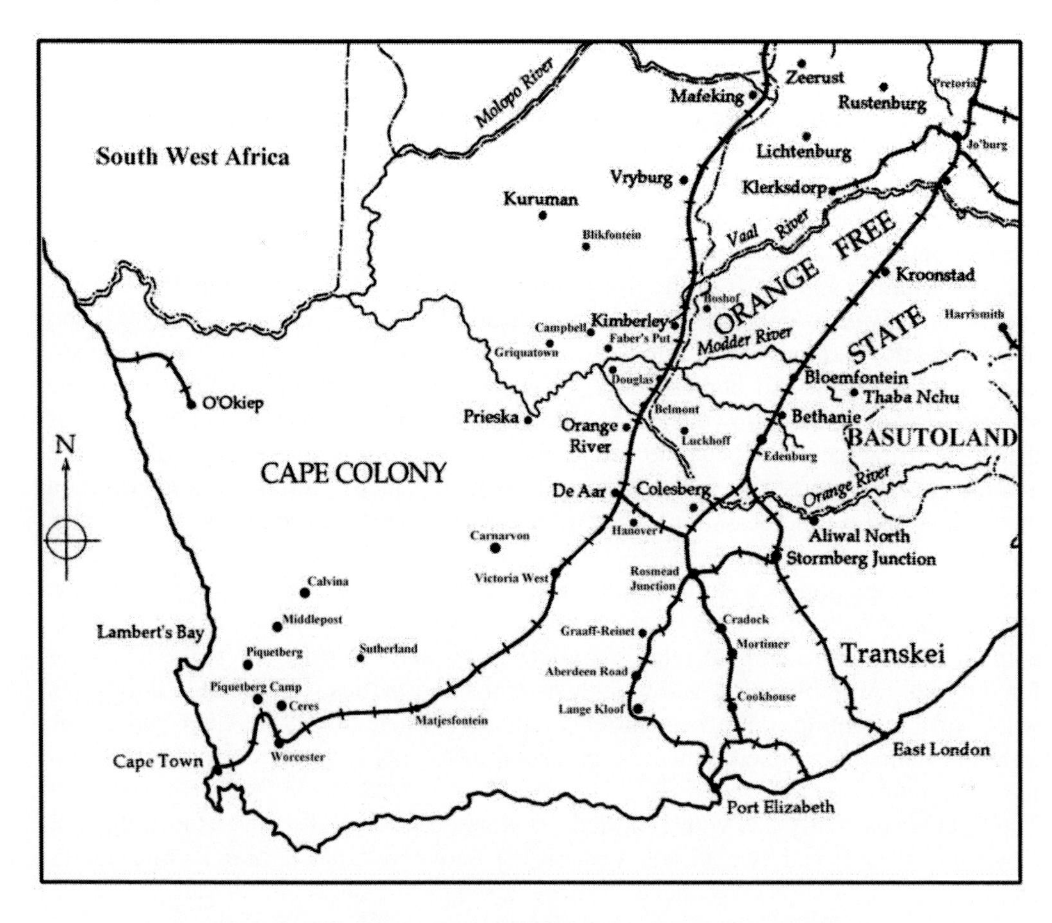

Area of operations for the 23rd Company Imperial Yeomanry

Duke of Lancaster's Own Yeomanry – Oldham Troop

A study of the Queens South Africa medal rolls and the Public Records Office *WO128* series of attestation papers for the *23rd Company IY* reveal some interesting statistics. Of the 148 NCOs and men who went out with the first draft in February and April 1900, 75 of them were members of the *DLOY*, 17 where from local infantry volunteer battalions or ex-military, 47 where civilians and 9 were unknown. This meant that the first draft was just over 50% *DLOY* men.

It is quite a different story for the relief drafts that followed in 1901 and onwards. Of the 212 NCOs and men in these relief drafts only 23 can be identified as being members of the *DLOY*, 36 were from local infantry battalions or ex-military, 67 were civilians and 86 could not be determined as their information is missing.

The effect of George Kemp being chosen as the commanding officer of the *23rd Company IY,* appears to have been quite marked in Rochdale, as they provided the highest proportion of volunteers from all of the towns in the north-west. 53 men can be identified as being from Rochdale who served with the *23rd company IY*, which relates to nearly 15% of the total contingent.

Sergeant Flitcroft with Kitcheners Horse

Whilst the *DLOY* were recruiting and making preparations to go to South Africa, one of the ex *Oldham Troop* members, Sergeant John Flitcroft (born about 1864), was also preparing to go to fight in the war. There would have been nothing to stop Flitcroft joining the rest of the *DLOY* members in the *23rd Company IY*, but perhaps he considered that the manner, in which he left the troop, would not be helpful to troop relations if he was to rejoin. Instead, he decided to try his luck by enlisting in a regiment that was being formed out in South Africa. Flitcroft left Oldham and travelled to South Africa in early January 1900.

Regiments were being formed in the Cape, which consisted of men who had made their way to South Africa from various parts of the world. Two such regiments were *Roberts Horse* and *Kitcheners Horse*. These regiments were initially to be called 'The second and third regiments of the *South African Light Horse*, but the names were changed, mainly at the request of the men, as a compliment to the new Commander-in-Chief and his chief of the staff.

Flitcroft joined *Kitcheners Horse* as a Private on 1st February, but his potential and pedigree was soon recognised, and he was quickly promoted to Sergeant.

Both *Kitcheners Horse* and *Roberts Horse* were employed in the operations undertaken by Lord Roberts in February 1900, for the relief of Kimberley, and in his advance to Bloemfontein. *Kitcheners Horse* along with Flitcroft was to see action very quickly.

On 9th February the Mounted Infantry Division, under Colonel Hannay, left Orange River station. On 11th February, they came in contact with Boers at Rymer Springs and after some fighting, the Division on the 12th reached Ramdam, where Lord Roberts was concentrating his army; but the bulk of Kitcheners Horse had preceded the rest of the Mounted Infantry, joining General French before midnight on the 11th. At 2 am on the

12th, they set out with French for Dekiel's Drift, on the Riet. The division then advanced to the Modder River, on February 16th they reached Klipsdorp, Flitcroft takes up the story: '*we found the enemy on a kopje at 6.30 am. We drove them from there in about three hour's time with our artillery. The enemy's artillery fire was very good, and if their shells had burst properly I and a lot more would have been killed as three shells came within a few yards of us all round. After that we found them on another kopje a few miles to our right, then the fight started. Our squadron was ordered to take up another position about a mile and half across the enemy's front, and immediately we got on the gallop the bullets came like a hailstorm for about a mile and a quarter. It is a surprise to us all yet how we got through alive, but we did with a few wounded, thank God. Our Captain was grazed in the neck and he lost his horse. As I was passing him he shouted, "Go on, boys, never mind me," and the bullets were all around him. However we got to the riverbank, got our horses down, dismounted, went back a little way, and advanced in skirmishing order. When we got to the top to fire there was our Captain laid down right across our firing line; he shouted out, " Don't fire, men, I am here." Lieutenant Beuchanan, myself, and a trooper ran out to carry him in, but when we got to him he could run back with us. Then we advanced and got a very warm reception. The battle lasted until 8.30 pm. My troop of 21 officers and non-commissioned officers and men shot over 600 rounds, and we were now without food. We were on the march early next day without breakfast, and towards 7.30 pm we found the Boer laager. We were without water, both men and horses, and the river not two miles off, where the enemy was on February the 18th. The battle started at 5.55am. At 6.30 we dismounted and advanced in extended order to within about 600 yards of the enemy's position, and laid there firing till 1.45 under a scorching sun, without water. We then got the order to rally; our men were dropping right and left; the bullets came as thick as rain. We ran as far as we could, and then dropped completely exhausted, and what was worse, our Lieutenant, who was left in charge of the horses, had taken them away, and we could not find him or the horses. However, I and a few others made our way to the ambulance wagon, and got a drink of water; then I started to look for the horses. I heard that they were at a farm about three miles away, where I found them and all our officers having a good feed. That was at five minutes to four. I went to our Lieut. And asked him where my horse was, and told him that he should not have left us without horses. He said that he had been ordered by a staff officer, and before he could show me where my horse was the Boers had the place surrounded. They had been hidden behind a large kopje. However, we made a very stubborn fight before Captain Arnold surrendered. We lost two Lieutenants – Karson and Beuchanan – and four men and a few wounded. I must say the Boers treated us kindly, and did all they possibly could for our comfort.*'[327] Flitcroft and the rest were taken prisoner and taken to Pretoria.

Flitcroft somehow managed to escape and get back to his regiment, but came down with enteric fever for a time, after this he was doing various jobs in the regiment such as Transport Sergeant and then Quarter-Master Sergeant. He was later posted to

[327] Sgt Flitcroft letter

Kronstadt in sole charge of a troop. The last information that is known about Flitcroft is that whilst on a scouting mission, a Boer sniper shot him in the back, and writing from hospital in Pretoria, in September 1900, he was expecting to be shortly sent down to Cape Town, where on 19th December he was discharged from *Kitcheners Horse.*

South African War Memorials

Memorial erected on 15th August 1903, in Lees Cemetery, Thomas Street, Lees, Oldham.

TO THE MEMORY OF
TROOPER
JAMES Wm. DRANSFIELD
OF THE 23RD COMPANY
IMPERIAL YEOMANRY
WHO DIED AT
KIMBERLEY, SOUTH AFRICA
NOVEMBER 27th 1900
ALSO OF
PRIVATE JAMES BRENNAN
OF THE 5TH BATTALION
MANCHESTER REGIMENT
WHO DIED AT
NETLEY HOSPITAL
JANUARY 10th 1902
AFTER BEING INVALIDED HOME
FROM SOUTH AFRICA.

Weapons

When the *Oldham Troop* was formed in 1873, the troopers were issued with the 0.45 inch calibre Westley-Richards Carbine. At the inaugural meeting of the troops shooting club in October 1873, at the Chadderton firing range, they were using this weapon. A competition was held with shooting at 150, 200 and 250 yards, 5 rounds at each distance. 1st prize was won by Private France, 2nd Private Seville, 3rd Sgt Dolphin, 4th Private Armitage and 5th Corporal Kershaw. The Westley-Richards was a capping percussion lock breechloader. It was originally developed in 1858 and was known as the 'Monkey-tail', from the long curved lever at the top of the breech block, which, when lifted up, opened the breech.
This single fire rifle used a paper cartridge with a 0,45 inch lead bullet at the tip and a felt wad behind. One of its problems was that the black powder fouled the barrel and the breechblock lever, which hindered rapid fire.
By 1880 the troop, along with the rest of the regiment, were using the breech loading, rifled Martini-Henry carbine.
Some time around 1897, the troop were re-armed with the lighter Martini-Metford carbine. This carbine had a .303 calibre and weighed around 6Ib 11 oz. Its range was 2000 yards, and when the trooper was mounted, was carried in a leather boot on the rear offside of the saddle.
All ranks within the *DLOY*, from Sergeant to Private were issued with a carbine, the officers, Sergeant-Majors, Quartermasters and Trumpeters carried only pistols, besides their swords. The pistols issued by the government, up to the end of the 1880s, were very antiquated, they were only a single shot muzzle loader. Most officers would have purchased their own pistol, a revolving chamber type, such as the Adams, Colt, and Smith & Wesson.[328]
For those going to the war in South Africa, they were issued with the standard Lee-Enfield rifle (MLE) the same as the infantry. They were not issued with a carbine, as their duties in South Africa were not that of a cavalry regiment but of a mounted infantryman.

Lee-Enfield Rifle, calibre 0.303", range 2,000 yards, magazine loading

[328] 'Chain Mail' Page 32

After the South African war, the Lee-Enfield Rifle became the standard issue rifle for the new styled *Duke of Lancaster's Own Imperial Yeomanry*.

During the South African war, the *23rd Company IY* created a gun section and took with them, two quick firing Colt Gun's (0.45 inch calibre), mounted on a Dundonald galloping carriage. Prior to the gun being received, a demonstration of its capabilities was demonstrated to Yeomanry officers at Runnymede Ranges, in Surrey.
The officers got a chance to fire the gun at 500 yards range, and its great accuracy was demonstrated. The Dundonald galloping carriages were then brought out, the gun limbered up and after galloping down the range, brought into action at an unknown range. After two or three sighting shots the gun was soon ready for full action. After a rapid-fire demonstration the gun was taken off the carriage immediately, by one man, who carried it away on his shoulder, showing, however quick the fire was the gun never got too hot to be handled.
A third demonstration was arranged when the Dundonald carriage was galloped up in front of the targets, unlimbered and the horse taken away, then another gun opened fire on it at between 500 and 600 yards. The result was that little or no damage was done to the carriage, though there were plenty of shots put on the shield and wheels. As proved at *Faber's Put,* the shields were not so effective when fired upon at closer range.
The Colt gun was simply constructed, the whole of the weapon could be stripped and the parts reassembled in one minute and twenty nine seconds.

Colt mounted on Dundonald Carriage
(Source: After Pretoria: The Guerilla War Vol 1)

Into the 20th century with the Duke of Lancaster's own Imperial Yeomanry

As a result of the South African war the role of the Yeomanry was changed, no longer were they considered to be cavalry but their role was now that of a mounted infantryman, their carbines and swords were returned to stores and in its place the men were issued with the Lee-Enfield Rifle. The name of the regiment also changed to the '*Duke of Lancaster's Own Imperial Yeomanry*' (*DLOIY*).
The new 1901 regulations, required that the regiment should have a strength of 596, all ranks, organised into four squadrons and a machine gun section. A horse allowance of £5 per man was also introduced, which encouraged the recruitment of non-horse owners, as they were now able to hire their horse when required.
The new regulations also extended their liability of service; they could now be called out in times of emergency not only in Great Britain, but also any British possessions in Europe. In line with their new role as mounted infantrymen, the War Office insisted on the Yeomanry using smaller and sturdier horses, 'cobs' rather than the traditional chargers. These 'cobs' were more suitable for long campaigning and rapid dismounting in action.
When Queen Victoria died, two officers and 60 men of the *DLOIY* paraded at the funeral in February 1901. Quarter Master Sykes, Troopers Frank Pickford, Bradshaw, Dickenson, Lofthouse, Hindley and also Captain Lees represented the *Oldham Troop*.
In May 1902, the *Oldham Troop* vacated their old HQ and stores in Regent Street to a new HQ in Bow Street. The troop continued to grow, and by September 1902 they were at they're highest ever on the roll with 76 men.
After some ten years in charge of the *Oldham Troop*, Major Lees retired in April 1906 and the men presented him with a silver mounted horn inkstand. Captain Bibby took over the command of the troop.
As with the Rifle Volunteers, the Yeomanry were also to be part of the Haldane reforms, with the introduction of the Territorial and Reserve Forces Bill. The Yeomanry regiments were to be organised into fourteen cavalry brigades. The *DLOIY* were to become a divisional cavalry regiment in the *42nd East Lancashire (Territorial) Division.*

APPENDIX

Appendix 1 – Members of the Oldham Association in 1799

Ashton, William; Markfield, age 27, 1 child, 1 woman
Barlow, Edward; Oldham, age 18
Barlow, Robert; Oldham, age 26, 3 children, 1 woman
Barnett, Peter; Oldham, age 36, 7 children, 1 woman
Bentley, Robert; Holebottom, age 16
Brierley, Benjamin; Chapel Street, age 35, 1 child, 1 woman
Brown, James; Oldham, age 24
Buckley, John; Holebottom, age 36, 6 children, 2 women
Burrow, John, Jun; Markfield, age 18
Burrow, John; Markfield, age 24, 2 children, 1 person infirm, 1 women
Cheetham, James; Oldham, age 29, 2 children, 1 woman
Clegg, James; Oldham, age 25
Cocks, James Dr; Oldham, age 28, 1 woman
Farrand, John; Oldham, age 21
Fawcett, Richard; Oldham, age 18 (Oldham Yeomanry)
Fletcher, Henry; Markfield, age 28
Fletcher, James; Oldham, age 29, 1 child , 2 women
Fletcher, William; Markfield, age 30, 2 children, 2 women
Furnivall, Benjamin; Oldham, age 31, 3 children, 1 woman
Hodson, Issac; Markfield, age 20
Lawson, William; Chapel Street, age 42, 1 child, 1 woman (Oldham Yeomanry)
Lees, Edward; Oldham, age 25
Lees, John; Oldham, age 52, 5 women
Marshall, James; Oldham, age 22, 3 children, 1 woman
Mills, John; Markfield, age 27, 1 child, 1 woman
Mills, Thomas; Markfield, age 28, 1 child, 1 woman
Nield, William; Chapel Street, age 22, 2 children, 1 woman
Ridgehouse, William; Holebottom, age 17
Rowland, James; Oldham, age 19
Taylor, James; Markfield, age 19
Taylor, John, Jun; Chapel Croft, age 22; 1 child, 2 women
Taylor, Robert; Chapel Street, age 37, 1 child, 1 woman
Taylor, Thomas, Oldham, age 36, 4 children, 1 woman
Travis, John; Markfield, age 27, 3 children, 1 woman
Travis, Joseph; Oldham, age 22
Whittaker, Edward; Oldham, age 38, 2 children, 2 women
Whittaker, James; Oldham, age 46, 2 children, 3 women
Wilde, James, Jun; Oldham, age 18
Williamson, George; Holebottom, age 23, 2 children, 1 woman
Wood, John; Oldham, age 36. 4 children, 3 women
Wrigley, John; Goldburn, age 20

Appendix 2 – Officers in the Oldham Loyal Volunteers 1800-1802

Name	Commissions
Booth, John	Capt 1/3/00
Chippendale, William	Ensign & Adjut 1/3/00,
Clegg, James	Ensign 1/3/00
Cocks, James	Lt & Surg 1/3/00
Fletcher, Henry	Lt 1/3/00
Fletcher, James	Ensign 1/3/00
Lees, Edward	Capt 1/3/00
Lees, John	Maj 1/3/00
Wright, John	Lt 1/3/00

APPENDIX

Appendix 3 – Officers in the Oldham Loyal Volunteers 1803-1808

Name	Commissions	Notes
Barker, Thomas	Capt 6/9/03, resigns 28/1/04	Hat Manufacturer on Henshaw Street.
Barlow, Henry	Lt 6/9/03, Capt 28/1/04	Rhodes House. Later Clerk to the magistrates.
Booth, George	Lt 28/1/04	Coal proprietor and cotton spinning. Living at Church Lane.
Booth, John	Capt 6/9/03, resigns 28/1/04	Coal proprietor, Greenacres.
Chippendale, William	Capt Lt & Adjut 6/9/03, Capt 28/1/04	Married Catherine Lees, Lt-Col Lees daughter on 2 Sept 1802, died 10 March 1822 aged 50. Manager and part owner of Alkrington collieries. Living on Church Lane.
Clegg, Arthur	QM 6/9/03, Lt 28/1/04	
Clegg, James	Ensign 6/9/03, Capt 28/1/04	Born about 1753, Died Nov 1818
Cocks, James	Lt & Surgeon 6/9/03, Capt 28/1/04	Born about 1771
Duncuft, James	Ensign 28/1/04, Lt pre 1808	Coal proprietor
Fletcher, Henry	Lt 6/9/03, Capt 28/1/04	Born about 1771
Fletcher, James	Lt 6/9/03	Born about 1770. Later into Cotton Spinning, Shore Mill , Greenacres Moor.
Jones, Joseph	Lt 28/1/04	Son of William Jones, first Mayor of Oldham. Owner of a number of coal collieries.
Lees, James	Major 6/9/03, resigns 28/1/04	Founder of the Clarksfield Lees. Married the daughter of Joseph Jones. Coal proprietor and land owner.
Lees, John		
Lees, John	Lt-Col 6/9/03	Born about 1747, Died April 1823
Less, Edward	Capt 6/9/03, Maj 28/1/04	Born about 1774, son of Lt-Col Lees. Later of Werneth Lodge.
Mayall, Samuel	Lt 28/1/04	
Mellor, James	Ensign 6/9/03	
Travis, Joseph	Ensign 6/9/03, Lt 28/1/04	Born about 1777
Whittaker, Thomas	Ensign & QM 28/1/04	Cotton Manufacturer, West Street.
Winter, William	Chaplin 6/9/03	Minister at St Peters church from 1796 to 1838. He was also a master at the grammar school.
Winterbottom, John	Ensign 6/9/03, Lt 28/1/04	
Wnett, Thomas Wilkes	Ensign 6/9/03	
Wright, John (1)	Capt 6/9/03, resigns 28/1/04	
Wright, John (2)	Ensign May 04	

Appendix 4 – Officers in the Oldham Local Militia 1808-1816

Name	Commissions	Notes
Ball, Thomas	Lt 24/2/09	
Barlow, Henry	Maj 15/2/09	Living at Rhodes House
Beswicke, John	Capt 15/2/09, Maj 8/6/10	
Billott, Abraham	Lt & Surgeon 15/2/09	
Chippendale, William	Capt & Adjut 24/9/08	
Clegg, Arthur	Capt 15/2/09	Grenadier Company captain
Clegg, Edward	Ensign 24/2/09, Lt 30/4/10, resign April 1813.	
Crompton, Abraham	Ensign 4/6/10, Lt 11/4/12	
Crompton, John	Capt 15/2/09	
Crossley, John	Capt 15/2/09	born at Scaitcliffe 23/5/1778. In 1803 appointed a guide to the army in case of invasion. 1807 an ensign in the West Halifax Volunteers. Died 11/12/1830.
Duncuft, James	Capt 15/2/09	
Eastwood, John	Lt 22/4/09	
Gartside, John	Lt 11/1/14	
Hardman, Robert	Lt 15/2/09, resign April 1813	
Harris, John	Lt 26/4/10	
Harrison, James	Ensign 24/5/09, Lt 30/4/10, resign Dec 1813	Resigned due to moving away from Oldham.
Higginbottom, Joseph	Lt 2/3/14	
Hollinworth, Thomas	Lt 15/2/09	
Horsefall, Luke	Ensign 22/4/09, resign April 1810	Transferred to Bradford LM Regiment
Jones, Joseph	Capt 15/2/09	Brother of William Jones, first Mayor of Oldham. Owner of coal collieries.
Lees, Edward	Lt-Col 15/2/09	
Lees, James	Lt 3/1/14, resigns Dec 15	
Lees, John	Lt-Col 24/9/08	Died April 1823 age 76.
Lees, John	Capt 15/2/09, resigns Dec 1813	Resigned due to death of his brother and increased business responsibilities.
Mashiter, James Moor	Lt 3/1/14	
Mayall, Samuel	Capt 15/2/09, died April 09	
Milne, Abraham	Lt 24/2/09	
Robinson, Joshua Kay	Lt 15/2/09, Capt 26/7/11, resigns April 1813.	
Sutcliffe, William	Capt 31/5/09	
Taylor, John	Lt 15/2/09, Surgeon 9/2/11	
Tetlow, Thomas	Lt 3/1/14	
Travis, John	Lt 15/2/09	
Travis, John	Ensign 24/2/09, Lt 30/4/10	
Travis, Joseph	Capt 24/9/08	
Whittaker, Thomas	QM 24/9/08	
Wilcock, John	Ensign 24/4/10, Lt 26/7/11	
Winterbottom, John	Capt 24/9/08	Light company Captain
Winterbottom, Joshua	Lt 15/2/09	Cotton Manufacturer, Greenacres Moor. Died April 1810
Wright, John	Lt 24/9/08	

APPENDIX

Appendix 5 – Officers & Men of the Oldham Troop of Yeomanry Cavalry

Name	Rank or Commission	Notes
Ashton, James	Pvt 1823	
Ashton, Robert	Pvt 1824	
Bates, William	Pvt 1823, resigned May 1826	
Bamford, Edward	Pvt, Cpl 1823	
Bamford, William	Pvt, Cpl 1824	
Bamford, Thomas	Pvt 1824, resigned April 1826	
Bamford, Richard	Pvt 1827	
Barlow, Robert	Pvt	
Booth, George	Pvt	
Bridges, George	Pvt 1824, resigned by 1826	
Buckley, Joseph R	Pvt 1823	Discharged for reasons unknown after 1826 riots
Buckley, Robert	Pvt 1823, resigned by 1826	
Campbell, James	Pvt, resigned May 1826	
Clarke, John	Pvt, resigned by 1823	
Clegg, James	QM	
Clegg, James	Pvt 1824	
Clegg, John	Joined 1826	
Clegg, Richard	Lt 24/6/17	Son of James Clegg, Hat Manufacturer.
Coupe, John	Pvt, resigned by 1826	
Crompton, Abraham	Pvt, resigned by 1827	
Crompton, John	Pvt 1823	
Crowther, John	Pvt, resigned by 1824	
Daltry, Thomas	Pvt	
Daltry, William	Pvt	
Dunn, William	Pvt 1823	
Dyson, John	Pvt, resigned by 1823	
Evans, George	Pvt 1826	
Fallows, John	Pvt, resigned by 1826	
Gleadhill, James	Pvt 1823	Discharged for reasons unknown after 1826 riots
Gray, William	Pvt, resigned by 1827	
Griffith, Thomas	Pvt 1823, resigned May 1826	
Halkyard, Harry	Joined before 1826	
Hallsworth, James R	Joined 31 March 1826.	
Haigh, Johnathan	Pvt	
Hilton, John	Pvt 1823	Absent without leave for 1827 training
Hindle, James	Pvt, resigned by 1826	
Iveson, John	Joined before 1826	
Jones, William	Sgt	First Mayor of Oldham
Knott, William	Pvt	
Lees, John	Pvt Joined by 1826	
Lees, William	Pvt, Cpl 1819, resigned before 1826	

Name	Rank or Commission	Notes
Lowe, Thomas	Pvt 1823, resigned before 1826	
Marsland, James	Pvt, resigned by 1823	
Mellor, Charles	Joined 22 March 1826	
Mellor, Joseph	Trumpeter	Also leader of Oldham Coronation Brass Band for 20 years. Died 12 Nov 1857, at the age of 56.
Milne, Abraham	Pvt, resigned by 1823	
Milne, James 1	Pvt, Sgt 1819, Pvt	Absent without leave for 1827 training
Milne, James 2	Pvt 1826	Joined during the 1826 riots. Absent without leave for 1827 training.
Milne, John, Junr	Pvt	Discharged for being absent without leave during 1826 riots.
Milne, John, Snr	Pvt	
Moss, Samuel	Pvt	Troop Farrier
Nelson, Joseph R	Pvt	
Newton, James	Pvt Dec 1819, resigned by 1826	
Platt, Thomas S	Pvt, joined by 1827	
Pollit, Michael	Pvt, resigned by 1826	
Radcliffe, John	Pvt , Joined by 1826	
Radley, James	Pvt	
Rowland, Edward	Cpl, Resigns 1819	
Rowland, James	Sgt	
Schofield, Andrew	Pvt 1823, resigned by 1826	
Schofield, James	Pvt, joined by 1826	
Seddon, Joseph R	Pvt, resigned by 1826	
Shaw, Abraham	Pvt, resign 1823	
Simpson, William	Pvt	
Smethurst, John	Pvt	Son of James Smethurst Innkeeper and Auctioneer of Shude Hill. Died July 1818 of consumption, age 36 years.
Taylor, James	Pvt, resigned by 1826	
Taylor, James Mayer	Cornet 24/6/17	Brother of John Taylor
Taylor, John	Capt 24/6/17	
Taylor, Joseph	Pvt, joined by 1826	
Taylor, Thomas	Cpl, resigned by 1826	
Tower, William	Pvt, resign 1823	
Travis, George	Joined 21 March 1826	
Watson, Thomas	Pvt Dec 1819	Discharged for disobedience of order during 1826 riots.
Wilde, John	Pvt	
Wilde, Jonathan	Pvt, resigned by 1823	
Wood, Radcliffe	Pvt, resigned by 1826	
Wrigley, Miles	Joined by 1826	
Wrigley, Samuel	Pvt	

APPENDIX

Appendix 6 - A list of special constables

sworn before the Rev John Holme clerk, 28 April 1826

Name	Address	Occupation
Henry Barlow	High Street	Tin plate worker
John Schofield	High Street	Druggist
Josiah Fithow	High Street	Shoe maker
John Dodge	High Street	Printer
William Scott	High Street	Rope Maker
Joseph Ogden	High Street	Confectioner
Joseph Bailey	High Street	Tin plate worker
William Oakes	Yorkshire Street	Clock Maker
Thomas Cussons	Yorkshire Street	Cotton Manufacturer
David Child	Yorkshire Street	Butcher
Thos Cussons Junr	Yorkshire Street	Cotton Manufacturer
John Chapman	Yorkshire Street	Joiner
Peter Corns	Yorkshire Street	Shop Keeper
Jonathan Marsland	King Street	Timber Merchant
James Ramsden	King Street	Coal Miner
Joseph Renshaw	King Street	Hatter
Thomas Ogden	King Street	Hatter
John Ogden	King Street	Hatter
William Whitehead	King Street	Weaver
Thomas Clegg	King Street	Hatter
Jos Winterbottom	King Street	Coal Master
Jn Radley Junr	King Street	Engineer
Jas Wolfenden	Duke Street	Librarian
John Holt	Manchester Street	Cotton Spinner
John Wrigley	Manchester Street	Hatter
Charles Bradbury	Manchester Street	Cotton Spinner
John Mills	Manchester Street	Cotton Spinner
Thos Dorman	Manchester Street	Coach man
Jn Bamford	Market Place	Grocer
Jam T Clegg	Market Place	Gentleman
Jn Jones	Market Place	Shopman
Wm Waddington	Market Place	Grocer
James Heap	Lord Street	Book Keeper
Jas Jackson	Lord Street	Saxton
Adam Fletcher	Lord Street	Carder
Richard Bamford	Lord Street	
Joseph Moseley	Lord Street	Machine Maker
William Bradley	George Street	Hatter
Thomas Jones	George Street	Book Keeper
Oliver Lawson	Union Street	Timber Merchant
Jeremiah Bouskill	Union Street	Maker up
Mathew Sedgwick	Priors	Manager
George Toulston	Priors	Throstle Major
Wm Winterbottom	Priors	Carder
Joseph Marsland	Priors	Engineer

Name	Address	Occupation
James Cocker	Priors	Overlooker
James Parkins	School Croft	Coach proprietor
Josh Jones Junr	Mumps	Cotton Manufacturer
George Steeple	Mumps	Butcher
James Wilde	Mumps	Shopkeeper
Jn Milne	Mumps	Cotton Manufacturer
Abraham Clegg	Mumps	Cotton Manufacturer
Radcliffe Chadwick	Mumps	Machine Maker
Peter Newton	Soho	Butcher
Josh Wharton	Soho	Engineer
Wm Wilde	Bottom of moor	Cotton Spinner
Danl Hilton	Bottom of moor	Cotton Manufacturer
Danl Mellor	Bottom of moor	Cotton Manufacturer
Adam Fletcher	Bottom of moor	Cotton Spinner
Thos Conbin	Bottom of moor	Carder
Josh Dunkerley	Bottom of moor	Shoe Maker
James Schofield	Bottom of moor	Roller coverer
Joseph Greenhalgh	Bottom of moor	Tin plate worker
Jonathan Garside	Bottom of moor	Overlooker
John Slater	Bottom of moor	Cotton Spinner
William Coxon	Holebottom	Butcher
John Winterbottom	Holebottom	Carpenter
Isaiah Moss	Holebottom	Blacksmith
John Chadwick	Holebottom	Hatter
Richard Livesey	Holebottom	Engineer
John Wolfenden	Horsedge	Weaver
James Mellor	Greaves St	Cotton Spinner
Moore Benjamin	Greaves St	Painter
Joseph Child	Cock House Fold	Mechanic
John Chadwick	Henshaw St	Shopkeeper
Josh Rowland Junr	Orleans Mill	Cotton Manufacturer
Brierley Rowland	Orleans Mill	Cotton Manufacturer
Jn Buck	Busk	Weaver
Jn Hague	Acre Mill	Cotton Manufacturer
Saml Radcliffe	Lower House	Cotton Manufacturer
Robert Tweedale	Lower House	Cotton Spinner
John Lees	Lower House	Cotton Spinner
James Greaves	Ditcan	Cotton Manufacturer
John Taylor	Stamp Stone	Cotton Spinner
Robert Greaves	Hill	Cotton Spinner
James Fletcher	Green Gate	Overlooker
James Saunderson	Green Gate	Overlooker
Richard Marsh	Green Gate	Overlooker
Joel Wrigley	Green Gate	Overlooker
James Taylor	Green Gate	Engineer
Jn Taylor	Furtherfield	Overlooker
Jn Dunkerley	Watersheadings	Cotton Spinner
Joseph Cooper	Fowleach	Cotton Spinner
Jn Seville	Fowleach	Cotton Spinner
Assheton Booth	Pit Bank	Coal Master
James Lees	Green Bank	Cotton Manufacturer
Robert Lees	Mount Pleasant	Cotton Manufacturer

APPENDIX

Name	Address	Occupation
Josh Newton	Mount Pleasant	Spinner
John Taylor	Side of Moor	Cotton Spinner
James Wilde	Side of Moor	Painter
Joshua Hibbert	Side of Moor	Cotton Carder
James Collinge	Commercial Mills	Cotton Manufacturer
John Lancashire	Commercial Mills	Cotton Manufacturer
James Cheetham	Clock Street	Warehouse Man
John Whitehead	Hollinwood	Book keeper
Josh Simpson	Hollinwood	Book keeper
Jas Winterbottom	Hollinwood	Shopkeeper
William Bradbury	Werneth	Cotton Spinner
Cornelius Backhouse	Werneth	Coal Miner
Isaac Hall	Cowhill	Maker up of twist
Joseph Jagger	Copster Hill	Weaver
Thomas Livesey	Chamber Hall	Manager
Thomas Ogden	Chamber Hall	Farmer

Appendix 7 - Officers of the Oldham Rifle Volunteers 1859-1908

Regimental Number in brackets

Name	Commissions	Notes
Alexander, David Mitchell, Rev	Hon Chaplain 1861, retired 1864	M.A. (Brasenose College, Oxford). Vicar of Oldham Parish Church from 1861 to 1864. Incumbent of Hanover Chapel, 1864 to 1870. Died 1921
Andrew, George Parry	2nd Lt 12/2/96, Lt 18/12/97, Capt 28/10/98, resigns 13/12/02	
Apthomas, Griffith	2nd Lt 2/5/00, Capt 21/3/03, resigns 26/3/04	Eye surgeon living at 5 Union Street in 1895.
Armitage, Samuel Harris Dr	Capt 20/11/60, retired 5/12/63	Originally assistant surgeon of the corps but resigned this post to become Captain of 3rd company. retired due to ill health and moving away
Bagshaw, William	2nd Lt 28/1/93, Lt 28/12/93, Capt 3/7/97. Resigns 11/4/06	Living at 35 Queens Road in 1895.
Bamford, John (477)	Ensign 11/12/63, Lt 3/5/65	
Bamford, Percy	2nd Lt 25/5/98, Capt 30/8/99	Son of Isaac Bamford JP. Transferred to 10th Manchester Reg. First Oldham Volunteer officer to see active service.
Baumont, Albert Edward	2nd Lt 14/5/81, resigns 14/4/83, rejoins as Lt 9/12/85, Capt 25/7/91	Solicitor in the practice of Baumont and Mills at 27 Queen Street.
Blackburne, Charles Edward (271)	Ensign 17/2/66, Lt 16/5/68, Capt 22/12/70, resigns 31/3/75	Solicitor and agent for Pelican life office, 20 Clegg street, residence Homeleigh. Born about 1846. Son of J G Blackburne.
Blackburne, John George (1)	Capt 1/2/60, Maj 13/12/62, Lt-Col 17/3/70	Resides at Dryclough, Civil Engineer of Blackburne, Son & Page. Also coal proprietor at Lowside Colliery. Born about 1816 in London. Died Oct 1871.
Blackburne, John William (6)	Ensign 13/12/62, Lt 11/12/63, Capt 16/5/68, Hon QM 2/8/71, Resigns 8/11/73	Was Col Sgt. Dryclough, Civil Engineer of Blackburne, Son & Page. Born about 1840. Son of J G Blackburne.
Blackburne, William	Ensign 1/2/60, Lt 13/12/62, resigns 18/12/63	Born about 1835. Mining Engineer and surveyor.
Bodden, George	Lt 11/4/85	Spindle & Flyer Manufacturer. Born about 1850.
Booth, Arthur Clifford	2nd Lt 13/1/06, Lt 7/2/07, Capt 13/2/07	Transferred to 10th Manchester Reg. Wounded 18 June 1915.

APPENDIX

Name	Commissions	Notes
Cacharnaille, Alfred Julius James , Rev (1734)	Acting Chaplain 14/2/77, resigns 29/11/92	M.A. (Gonville and Caius College, Cambridge) Vicar at St Mary's from 1876-1892, Rector of Cheriton, Hants, 1892 to 1894; vicar of All Saints', Forest Gate, 1894, Died 18/5/95
Clegg, Alfred	Ensign 29/11/61, Lt 13/12/62, Capt 11/12/63	Son of Kay Clegg , brother of Harry Clegg. Born about 1840, died Oct 65.
Clegg, Charles Edward	Ensign 12/6/69, Lt 17/9/70, Capt 22/8/74, Maj 9/9/82	Solicitor, born about 1840, died 1884
Clegg, Harry (711)	Ensign 17/2/66, Lt 22/11/68, Capt 21/3/70, resigns 1/8/74	Solicitor, Hartford Cottage, Werneth (Kay, Clegg & Son) Born 17/1/1842. Son of Kay Clegg. Moved to Anglesey. Died 26/1/1909.
Clegg, Joseph Eric	2nd Lt 16/5/00, Lt 30/8/02, Capt 30/4/04	Living in Crompton, born about 1880. Transferred to 10th Manchester Reg.
Crompton, Abraham (249)	Lt 27/3/61, Capt 13/12/62 resigns 1/8/74	Cotton Spinning, High Crompton. Living at The Firs, High Crompton in 1902.
Edwards, Ernest Booth	2nd Lt 30/11/01, Lt 13/6/03, Capt 9/9/04, resigns 22/11/06	Chartered accountant, born about 1876. Resigned as he moved away from Oldham. Residence 158 Chamber Rd in 1901.
Farquhar, James	1907 2nd Lt	Transferred to 10th Manchester Reg
Fort, Thomas (1879)	Assist Surgeon 6/7/78, Surg 20/8/79, Surg-Maj 5/4/93, Surg-Lt-Col 15/6/98, Hon Col 24/12/04	Born in Preston about 1853. Died 13/3/1921. Came to Oldham as young man. Factory Surgeon and also Police Surgeon. Residence 105 King St in 1901.
Fort, Henry Mellor	2nd Lt 7/12/07	Son of Thomas Fort, born about 1881. Transferred to 10th Manchester Reg
Goodwin, Humphrey (9)	Ensign 22/12/70, Lt 12/3/72, Capt 10/4/75, Maj 28/5/84, resigns 8/10/87	Original volunteer joining in 1859 as a volunteer rose to rank of Sgt Maj before gaining commission. Roller leather merchant, coronation street, Mumps. Born in Buxton, Derbyshire about 1833.
Greaves, Arthur Hilton	2nd Lt 8/10/87, resigns 29/2/91	Son of Hilton Greaves, born about 1867.
Greaves, Daniel	Lt 21/9/60, resigns 13/9/62	Of Derker, Cotton Manufacturer, born about 1830.

Name	Commissions	Notes
Greaves, Hilton	Lt 1/2/60, resigns 2/3/61	Leading cotton spinner in Lancashire, owner of Derker, Oxford, Waverley and Moss mills. County magistrate. Living at Derker Hall. Retired to Hankelow, Cheshire where he died. Born 22/9/22, died 11/2/95
Greaves, John (10)	Ensign 22/12/70, Lt 7/12/72, Capt 24/11/77, Maj 30/12/85, Hon Lt-Col 16/2/89 retired 9/11/1892	Original 1859 volunteer rose to rank of Col Sgt before gaining commission. Tailor and gentleman's outfitter in Yorkshire Street. Retired at age 65. Died June 1898 aged 71.
Halkyard, Henry, Dr (250)	Assist Surgeon 27/3/61, Surg 13/12/62	Surgeon, born about 1817 in Oldham.
Hallsworth, George Henry (21)	Ensign 22/12/70, Lt 1/6/73, Capt 25/6/79, resigns 9/7/04	Longest serving volunteer, joined as a private in 1859 and worked through ranks to a Colour Sergeant before gaining a commission. Was a Plumber & decorator in the firm of Buckley, Son & Hallsworth. Died 3/1/1910 aged 74. Also Warden of Parish church and 'Overseer of the Poor'. Residence 144 Greengate St in 1901.
Hardman, George Whittaker	2nd Lt 25/10/99, Lt 12/12/00, Capt 25/6/02	of Waterhead, son of Mr Joseph Hardman, Cotton spinner, Bangor mill. Transferred to 10th Manchester Reg. In autumn of 1914 went with the 10th Manchesters to Egypt, but was called home the following year and as the doctors would not let him go back he was associated with the 3rd Batt 10th of which he had command for some time until his discharge in 1917. Died 26/9/40 at the age of 68.
Harries-Jones Ivan (2652)	Lt 14/10/82, Capt 8/1/90, resigns 6/5/93	Brother of James R Harries-Jones, cotton broker, born about 1858.
Harries-Jones, James Robert (1788)	2nd Lt 22/8/77, Lt 8/1/79, Capt 9/9/82, Maj 18/4/91, Lt-Col 18/3/98, resigns 15/8/03	Solicitor of JR & LG Harries-Jones, 20 Clegg Street. Living at Lime House, Montgomery St, Hollinwood.
Hart, William	Ensign 11/12/63, resigns 65	
Heywood, George William	2nd Lt 25/5/89, Lt 6/9/90, Capt 21/11/94, resigns 3/7/97	Barrister. Born about 1861.

APPENDIX

Name	Commissions	Notes
Hodgkinson, Charles (2298)	2nd Lt 18/6/81, Lt 1/7/81, Capt 6/3/86, Maj 4/5/98, Lt-Col 1/11/07	Solicitor. Transferred to 10th Manchester Reg. Son of Charles Hodgkinson, Snr who was Chief Constable of Oldham.
Hollingworth, George Henry (1794)	2nd Lt 22/8/77, Lt 8/1/79, Capt 28/5/84, Maj 7/1/93, Lt-Col 31/10/03, retires 31/10/07	Civil Engineer of Booth & Hollingsworth, 19 Queen St.
Hutchinson, Edward William Roberts	Acting Chaplain 25/3/93, resigns 11/7/03	St Johns vicarage, Werneth.
Ireland, James Greaves (853)	Ensign 22/11/68, Lt 12/6/69, Capt 12/3/72, Maj 16/1/78, Lt-Col 23/5/85, resigns 21/12/88	Son of Rev Thomas Ireland living at Werneth vicarage. Cotton Broker. Born about 1850.
Ireland, John Hilton	2nd Lt 3/7/78, resigns 24/7/80	Brother of JG Ireland. Born about 1857.
Jackson, William Jun	2nd Lt 6/11/97, Lt 28/10/98, resigns 15/4/99	
Kershaw, Frank	Lt 24/2/86	Solicitor in Clegg Street, born about 1863.
Kershaw, Hugh	2nd Lt 17/7/95, Capt 16/7/97	
Kilner, William	Ensign 12/6/69, Lt 16/9/71, resigns 28/4/75	Accountant, estate agent, registrar of marriages for Oldham in Clegg St, living King St
Leach, Albert	2nd Lt 24/2/06	Born about 1876, medical student. Transferred to 10th Manchester Reg Captain in 1/10th Manchester Regiment. Wounded 4 Aug 1915. Died 20/1/1950
Leach, John Bernard	2nd Lt 9/5/03, Lt 23/7/04, Capt 26/5/06	Born about 1879, accountant's clerk. Transferred to 10th Manchester Reg
Leach, Norman Kershaw	2nd Lt 27/7/01, resigns 6/5/03	Born about 1882. Dec 01 in charge of Cyclists company
Lees, Edward Brown (831)	Ensign 6/5/67, Lt 16/5/68, Capt 15/10/70, Maj 12/3/72, resigns 8/8/77, Lt-Col 17/7/78, resigns 22/5/85	Clarksfield
Lees, John Crompton (832)	Ensign 6/5/67, Lt 8/5/69, Capt 2/8/71, resigns 24/11/77, rejoins as Lt-Col 9/3/89, resigns 20/4/98	Coal proprietor, Clarksfield. Living at Park House, Shaw. Magistrate.
Lees, Thomas Evans (136)	Capt 29/10/60, Maj 17/3/70, Lt-Col 12/3/72, resigns 15/6/78	Of Hathershaw house then Woodfield
Mattinson, Beraulph Clegg	Lt 1/7/81, resigns 17/10/85	Solicitor of Supreme courts, born about 1858.
Mayall, Edward Arthur	2nd Lt 2/5/00, Lt 30/8/02, Capt 10/10/03, resigns 26/3/04	Cotton Spinning business. Firm of Mayall & Massey at Waterhead. Born Manchester about 1873.
Mellor, John William	Lt 20/11/60, resigns 6/12/61	

Name	Commissions	Notes
Midgley John James (1415)	Ensign 15/6/72, Lt 1/6/73, Capt 8/5/80, Maj 7/1/88, resigns 4/2/91	Born about 1840. In his early life was with the Cape Mounted Rifles and saw active service with them. Chairman of Higginshaw Spinning Company. Retired and moved Lymm, died Jan 1896
Neild, John	Ensign 15/6/72, Lt 1/6/73, resigns 24/6/76	
Newton, Geoffrey Robson	2nd Lt 11/4/06, Capt 14/6/07	Born about 1885. Transferred to 10th Manchester Reg. Wounded 27 June 1915.
Nicholson Abraham (2651)	Lt 23/9/82, Capt 3/3/88, resigns 25/5/97	Town clerk of Oldham, born in Salford. Lived at 107 Windsor Road. Died 1904 aged 56.
Nicholson, Roger Brighouse	2nd Lt 2/5/00, Lt 30/8/02, Capt 16/1/04, resigns 12/2/07	Instructor of Musketry 5/11/04, resigned as he moved away from Oldham. Son of Abraham Nicholson, born 1880.
Orton, Jabez William (2655)	Acting Chaplain 6/12/82, Colonel in TF 1/4/08	Vicar at St Stephen's, Lower Moor. Born about 1844, died March 1926.
Page, James Lee (71 & 2211)	Ensign 22/12/70, Lt 12/3/72, Capt 7/8/75, retires 28/2/80. Rejoins as QM 19/5/80, resigns 16/11/89	Original 1859 volunteer rose through ranks to QM Sgt before gaining a commission. Surveyor (Blackburne, son & Page), later Blackburne, Page & West, civil engineers. Resided Cliff cottage, Werneth Hall Rd. So popular that when he resigned was pressed to accept QM of regiment. Died Oct 1899 aged 69.
Patterson, William	Lt 20/3/86, Capt 30/1/92, Maj 19/12/03, Hon Lt-Col 13/11/06.	Transferred to 10th Manchester Reg. And went on to become Lt-Col of 10th Battalion. Lived at 157 Huddersfield Road.
Prestwich, Joseph MD	Assist Surgeon 22/12/70, Surg 1/10/77	Born in Prestwich about 1833.
Redfern, John	Ensign 31/1/63, Lt 11/12/63, Capt 12/6/69, Resigns 15/10/70	Solicitor, lived at Retiro House, born in Oldham about 1840.
Rowland, Joseph Jun	Ensign 21/9/60, Lt 2/10/62, retired before 1866	Of Rushbank
Rubie, John Edwin (2199)	2nd Lt 15/5/80, Lt 1/7/81, Capt 30/12/85 , resigns 27/1/88	
Rye, John Buckley	Lt 29/12/86, Capt 7/1/93, Maj 1/11/07	Son of William Rye who was Mayor of Oldham in 1868/9. Set up the firm of 'Taylor & Rye' Yarn Merchants, Manchester in 1891. Transferred to 10th Manchester Reg and went on to become Lt-Col of 10th Battalion in 1913. Died a bachelor in 1934 aged 76.

APPENDIX

Name	Commissions	Notes
Saville, John	Lt 6/2/86, Capt 9/1/92, resigns 19/6/97	
Shaw, Hugh (144)	Ensign 22/12/70, Lt 1/6/73, Capt 17/4/78, resigns 14/12/89	Joined 3/10/1860 as a private rose through the ranks to Col Sgt. Owner of cotton spinning firm. Born about 1834. Died July 1919.
Shaw, John Mellodew (2342)	Lt 16/11/81, Capt 7/1/88, resigns 9/1/92	Solicitor, born in Oldham about 1858.
Shires, John Jordan	2nd Lt 4/4/94, Lt 10/9/95, Capt 14/7/97	Medlock Mills, local magistrate. Transferred to 10th Manchester Reg
Smyth, Thomas Henry (1673)	Lt 8/3/76, Capt 9/9/82, resigns 23/12/91	Solicitor in practice of Blackburne & Smyth, Clegg Street. Originally from Lincolnshire came to Oldham in 1874. Lived at 12 Edward St, Werneth. Born 1848 died Nov 1913.
Sparrow, Robert Lancelot (2654)	Acting Surgeon 6/12/82, Surg-Lt 6/12/82, Surg-Capt 4/11/93, Surg-Maj 22/1/98, Surg-Lt-Col 7/1/03, Hon Col 24/12/04	Irishman by birth, came to Oldham from Cornwall when a young man. Lived at 316 Manchester Road, Hollinwood. Died age 60 Nov 1910.
Taylor, William Jun	2nd Lt 25/8/97, Capt 28/10/98	Transferred to 10th Manchester Reg
Thomas, Henry (1612)	Lt 31/3/75, Capt 9/9/82, resigns 7/1/85	
Thorp, Samuel Alfred (2133)	QM 21/12/89, Hon Capt 20/2/95	Previously QM Sgt for 15 years before gaining commission. Educated at Blue Coat school. Worked at Messrs Bradbury & Co, Wellington works. Transferred to 10th Manchester Reg. Died Feb 1921 aged 74.
Turnball, Charles	Ensign 12/6/69, Lt 17/9/70, Capt 22/8/74	
Tweedale, James Frederick (4)	Ensign 20/11/60, Lt 29/11/61, Capt 11/12/63, resigns 7/12/72	Original volunteer joining in 1859 as a private and was the corps Honorary secretary, gained a commission when 3rd company was formed. Solicitor and commissioner in all courts. Summerscales & Tweedale, Edward St, Werneth. Born about 1826 in Uppermill.
Wakelam, Edgar, Dr	2nd Lt 25/10/99. Capt 12/12/00, resigns 8/8/03	Physician and Surgeon, originally from Staffordshire. Lived at 566 Huddersfield Road. Born about 1858, died July 1909.

Name	Commissions	Notes
Walters, William, Rev (653)	Hon Chaplain 3/5/65	Born in Barnwood, Gloucestershire in 1833. M.A. (Christ Church, Oxford) Vicar at St Mary's 1864-1873, vicar of Pershore, 1873 to 1894; Archdeacon of Worcester, 1889; rector of Alvechurch
White, William	Capt 12/12/00, resigns 25/6/02	
Whittaker, Henry	Ensign 23/4/68, Lt 21/3/70, Capt 7/12/72, resigns 1/8/74	Wellfield, New Mill, Rochdale
Wilde, Leonard Clay	2nd Lt 10/10/00, Lt 30/8/02, Capt 30/4/04	Commercial Clerk. Capt of cyclists company 7/5/04. Living at Edward Street, Werneth in 1900. Had been a captain in the Church Lads brigade. Transferred to 10th Manchester Reg . Born about 1881, died 3/11/1964 in Norwich.
Willberforce, William Francis, Rev	Acting Chaplain 23/5/74, resigns 14/6/76	Vicar at St Mary's 1873-1876. M.A. (University College, Oxford)
Winterbottom, James	Ensign 15/6/72, Lt 1/6/73, resigns 2/12/76	Original 1859 volunteer rose through ranks to Sgt before gaining a commission.
Wrigley, Arthur Edward	2nd Lt 17/4/89, Lt 10/5/90, Capt 20/5/93, resigns 9/3/98	Lived at Thorneycroft, Werneth.
Wrigley, Henry (139)	Ensign 2/10/62, Lt 11/12/63, Capt 17/2/66, resigns 12/70	Joined 3/10/1860 as private rose through the ranks to Col Sgt before gaining a commission. Solicitor at Murray & Wrigley, 32 Yorkshire Street. Born about 1835.

Robert Lancelot Sparrow

John Buckley Rye

Thomas Fort

APPENDIX

Rev Jabez Orton

George W Hardman

Abraham Nicholson

Appendix 8 – Adjutants Oldham Rifle Volunteers

On 29th February 1860 the government authorised the appointment of adjutants from ex-officers of four or more year's experience. It was not until the creation of the 7th Administration battalion before an adjutant was appointed and then only one was appointed to cover both the Oldham and Ashton corps.
In May 1872 the government introduced serving Regular officers to be appointed as adjutants of volunteer corps with 5 year attachments, but it was not until the appointment of Captain Henry McLeod Young that a serving regular officer was appointed exclusively to the Oldham volunteers.

1863-67	Captain P O'Gorman (7th Admin Battalion adjutant) Served in the Crimea. In an after dinner speech Major Blackburne described him as 'an old soldier who had been reared in a different school to that of the present day, and who was not over partial to modern innovations. He was a strict disciplinarian and a thorough gentleman.'[329]
1867	Captain Wilford
1868- Aug 1885	Major Edmund Charles Prichard (Regimental No: 2650) Retired as a Lt from the 18th Regiment of Foot on 1/2/68. Retired as adjutant 17 August 1885
Oct 1885 – Nov 1889	Captain Henry McLeod Young Joined from the 1st Battalion Royal Inniskilling Fusiliers. Resigned on being appointed a District Inspector of Musketry in the North West District.
Nov 1889 – Jan 1892	Captain G P Hatch Joined from 2nd West India Regiment. Resigned on receiving an appointment under the Sultan of Zanzibar.
Jan 1892 – Feb 1897	Captain Anthony Lumb (Promoted Major 30/1/94) Joined from 1st Battalion, Somerset Light Infantry (Prince Albert's). Shortly after rejoining his parent regiment he was severely wounded with a bullet to the neck fighting at Peshawar in August 1897.
Feb 1897 – May 1903	Captain Edward Silver Strickland. Joined from Royal Dublin Fusiliers. Formerly East Kent Militia and 64th Foot.
Nov 1903 – Oct 1905	Captain Leslie Blundell Bristow Noyes. Passed from Royal Military College Sandhurst to Duke of Wellington's West Riding regiment in March 1896. Served with the 76th Regiment in South Africa, Burma and Madras. Born about 1876.
Oct 1905 -	Lieutenant James Alexander Armstrong Joined from Royal Inniskilling Fusiliers

[329] Oldham Chronicle

APPENDIX

Appendix 9 - Rifle competitions against other units.

Date	Opposition	Venue	Result
Nov 1861	23rd LRV (Ashton)	Ashton	Won
July 1862	1st Manchester Rifle Volunteers (9th Company)	Fallowfield	Won
Aug 1862	34th WYRV (Saddleworth)	Rocher Brow, Diggle	Won
Oct 1862	1st Manchester Rifle Volunteers (9th Company)	Burnley Lane	Lost
Oct 1862	34th WYRV (Saddleworth)	Burnley Lane	Lost
July 1863	1st Manchester Rifle Volunteers (9th Company)	Fallowfield	Lost
Aug 1863	1st Manchester Rifle Volunteers (9th Company)	Burnley Lane	Lost
Aug 1864	1st Manchester Rifle Volunteers (9th Company)	Barton Moss	Lost
Nov 1864	1st Manchester Rifle Volunteers (9th Company)	Burnley Lane	Lost
Oct 1865	1st Manchester Rifle Volunteers (9th Company)	Burnley Lane	Lost
Dec1865	1st Manchester Rifle Volunteers (9th Company) & 8th LRV (Heywood Company)	Astley, Manchester	Lost
Aug 1867	24th LRV (Rochdale)	Rochdale	Lost
Oct 1867	Stockport	Tiviotdale, Stockport	Lost
Nov 1867	23rd LRV (Ashton)	Burnley Lane	Won
Jan 1868	72nd Highlanders	Burnley Lane	Lost
March 1868	24th LRV (Rochdale)	Burnley Lane	Won
May 1868	6th WYRV (Huddersfield)	Longley Hall, Huddersfield	Won
Aug 1868	6th WYRV (Huddersfield)	Burnley Lane	Lost
Sept 1868	6th WYRV (Huddersfield)	Longley Hall, Huddersfield	Lost
May 1869	24th LRV (Rochdale)	Rochdale	Lost
June 1869	8th Kings Regiment of Foot	Burnley Lane	Won
Sept 1869	6th WYRV (Huddersfield)	Longley Hall, Huddersfield	Lost
Oct 1869	6th WYRV (Huddersfield)	Burnley Lane	Won
Dec 1869	1st Manchester Rifle Volunteers (9th Company)	Astley Range	Draw
June 1870	8th Kings Regiment of Foot	Burnley Lane	Won
July 1870	6th WYRV (Huddersfield)	Longley Hall, Huddersfield	Lost
Dec 1871	101st Royal Bengal Fusiliers	Burnley Lane	Won

Date	Opposition	Venue	Result
Jan 1872	101st Royal Bengal Fusiliers	Bushes, Ashton	Lost
Mar 1872	24th LRV (Rochdale)	Burnley Lane	Won
Oct 1872	8th LRV (Heywood Company)	Burnley Lane	Lost
Oct 1872	6th WYRV (Huddersfield)	Burnley Lane	Lost
Nov 1872	6th WYRV (Huddersfield)	Crossland Moor, Huddersfield	Draw
Feb 1873	101st Royal Bengal Fusiliers	Burnley Lane	Won
May 1873	8th LRV (Heywood Company)	Broadoake, Bury	Lost
May 1873	8th LRV (Bury Company)	Broadoake, Bury	Won
June 1873	19th LAV, Manchester Artillery	Astley Range	Won
Sept 1873	19th LAV, Manchester Artillery	Burnley Lane	Won
Sept 1873	8th LRV (Heywood Company)	Broadoake, Bury	Won
June 1874	8th LRV (Heywood Company)	Broadoake, Bury	Won
Nov 1874	1st Manchester Rifle Volunteers (11th Company)	Burnley Lane	Lost
April 1875	1st Manchester Rifle Volunteers	Burnley Lane	Won
March 1877	23rd DRV (Glossop)	Pea Cote	Won
May 1877	1st Manchester Rifle Volunteers (8th Company)	Pea Cote	Won
May 1877	23rd LRV (Ashton)	Brushes, Ashton	Won
July 1877	23rd DRV (Glossop)	Glossop	Won
Aug 1877	8th LRV (Heywood Company)	Broadoake, Bury	Lost
Sept 1877	8th LRV (Heywood Company)	Pea Cote	Won
April 1878	23rd DRV (Glossop)	Pea Cote	Won
Sept 1878	23rd DRV (Glossop)	Glossop	Won
Nov 1878	23rd LRV (Ashton)	Pea Cote	Won
July 1879	34th WYRV (Saddleworth)	Diggle	Won
Aug 1879	34th WYRV (Saddleworth)	Pea Cote	Won
Sept 1879	23rd DRV (Glossop)	Glossop	Lost
Oct 1880	23rd DRV (Glossop)	Glossop	Won
Oct 1881	2nd DRV (Bakewell)	Peacote	Won
Dec 1881	7th LRV (Ashton)	Peacote	Won
March 1882	1st Manchester Rifle Volunteers (9th Company)	Peacote	Won
March 1884	1st Manchester Rifle Volunteers (9th Company)	Peacote	Won
May 1886	2nd VB West Riding (Huddersfield)	Huddersfield	Lost
April 1887	2nd VB West Riding (Huddersfield) and 1st VB Lancs Fusiliers (Heywood)	Peacote	Won
June 1887	1st VB Loyal North Lancashire Regiment (Preston)	Peacote	Lost
Sept 1888	4th VB Cheshire Regiment (Hyde)	Peacote	Lost
June 1889	5th VB (Ardwick) Manchester Regiment	Peacote	Won

APPENDIX

Date	Opposition	Venue	Result
Aug 1889	3rd VB (Southport) Liverpool Regiment	Altcar	Lost
March 1890	3rd VB (Ashton) Manchester Regiment	Peacote	Lost
Aug 1890	2nd VB Manchester Regiment	Facit	Won
April 1891	Sgts rifle match between all VB of Manchester Regiment	Astley	Won
April 1891	2nd VB (Burnley) East Lancashire Regiment	Peacote	Won
May 1891	2nd VB (Burnley) East Lancashire Regiment	Burnley	Won
1891	3rd VB (Ashton) Manchester Regiment		Won
1891	Southport	Southport	Won
Sept 1892	1st VB West Yorkshire Reg (Ripon company)	Ripon	Lost
April 1902	Duke of Lancaster's Own Yeomanry (Oldham troop)	Diggle	Won
April 1903	2nd VB Manchester Reg	Diggle	Lost
May 1906	4th VB Manchester Reg	Diggle	Lost

Appendix 10 - The Lancashire Rifle Volunteer Corps 1859 – 1908

1st (Liverpool)	Formed 9 June 1859, 1st Admin Bn 1863, part of 1st Corp 1880, 1st VB The King's (Liverpool) Reg 1888
2nd (Blackburn)	Formed 4 Oct 1959, 8th Admin Bn 1864, consolidated 2nd Corps 1880, 1st VB The East Lancashire Reg 1889
3rd (Blackburn)	Merged with 2nd 1860
4th (Rossendale)	Formed 4 July 1859, 3rd Admin Bn 1861, consolidated 3rd corps 1880, 2nd VB The East Lancashire Reg 1889
5th (Liverpool)	Formed 19 Aug 1859, 2nd Admin Bn 1861, part of 5th Lancashire (The Liverpool Rifle Volunteer Brigade) 1862, 2nd VB King's (Liverpool) Reg 1888
6th (Manchester)	Also known as 1st Manchester, formed 25 Aug 1859, formed 6th corps 1880, 2nd VB Manchester Reg 1888
7th (Accrington)	Formed 20 Sept 1859, 3rd Admin Bn 1861, consolidated 3rd corps 1880, 2nd VB The East Lancashire Reg 1889
8th (Bury)	Formed 22 Sept 1859, consolidated 8th Corps 1880, 1st VB The Lancashire Fusiliers 1883
9th (Warrington)	Formed 16 Sep 1859, 9th Admin Bn 1865, consolidated 9th corps 1880, 1st VB South Lancashire Reg 1886
10th (Lancaster)	Formed 20 Sept 1859, 5th Admin Bn 1862, consolidated 10th corps 1876, 1st VB The King's Own (Royal Lancaster) Reg 1883
11th (Preston)	Formed 4 Oct 1859, 6th Admin Bn 1861, consolidated 11th corps 1880, 1st VB The Loyal North Lancashire Reg 1883
12th (Preston)	Formed 7 Oct 1859, merged with 11th 1860.
13th (Southport)	Formed 6 Dec 1859, 13th corps 1880, 3rd VB King's (Liverpool) Reg 1888
14th (Edge Hill)	Formed 10 Nov 1859, merged with 13th 1862
15th (Liverpool)	Formed 10 Jan 1860, 15th corps 1880, 4th The King's (Liverpool) Reg 1888
16th	Not formed
17th (Burnley)	Formed 16 Jan 1860, 3rd Admin Bn 1860, consolidated 3rd corps 1880, 2nd VB The East Lancashire Reg 1889
18th	Not formed
19th (Liverpool Lowland Scottish)	Formed 18 Jan 1860, 2nd Admin Bn 1860, part of 5th Lancashire (The Liverpool Rifle Volunteer Brigade) from 1862, 2nd VB King's (Liverpool) Reg
20th	Not formed
21st (Wigan)	Formed 20 Jan 1860, 4th Admin Bn 1860, consolidated 4th corps 1880, 1st VB Manchester Reg 1888
22nd (Liverpool Exchange)	Formed 30 Jan 1860, 1st Admin Bn 1860, merged with 1st 1863
23rd (Ashton-under-Lyne)	Formed 7 Feb 1860, 7th Admin Bn 1863, 7th corps 1880, 3rd VB Manchester Reg 1888
24th (Rochdale)	Formed 24 Feb 1860, 12th corps 1880, 2nd VB Lancashire Fusiliers 1883

APPENDIX

25th (Liverpool)	Formed 9 Jan 1860, absorbed into 8th Lancashire Artillery volunteers in 1864
26th (Haigh)	Formed 9 Feb 1860, disbanded 1864
27th (Bolton)	Formed 2 Dec 1859, amalgamated with 82nd 1876, 14th corps 1880, 2nd VB The Loyal North Lancashire Reg 1887
28th (Manchester)	Also known as 2nd Manchester. Formed 21 Feb 1860, absorbed 70th 1860, and was itself absorbed by 33rd 1864.
29th (Lytham)	Formed 28 Jan 1860, 3rd Admin Bn 1860, consolidated 3rd corps 1880, 2nd VB The East Lancashire Reg 1889
30th (Fishwick)	Formed 16 Jan 1860, absorbed into 11th 1860
31st (Oldham)	Formed 1 Feb 1860, 7th Admin Bn 1863, consolidated 7th corps 1880, formed 22nd corps 1882, 6th VB Manchester Reg 1888
32nd (Liverpool)	Formed 28 Jan 1860, also known as Victoria Rifles, 2nd Admin Bn 1860, absorbed by 5th in 1862
33rd (Ardwick)	Formed 28 Jan 1860, absorbed the 28th 1863, became 20th corps 1880, 5th VB Manchester Reg 1888.
34th & 35th	Not formed
36th (Accrington)	Formed 7 Feb 1860, absorbed by 7th 1861.
37th (Ulverston)	Formed 29 Jan 1860, also known as North Lonsdale, 1860 subdivided into five parts: 37A (Ulverston); 37B (Barrow); 37C (Hawkshead); 52nd (Dalton), with 53rd (Cartmel) and 75th (Broughton) subdivisions making the 5th company, all 5th Admin Bn 1861, consolidated 10th corps 1876, 1st VB The King's Own (Royal Lancaster) Reg 1883
38th (Fairfield)	Formed 20 Jan 1860, 1st Admin Bn May 1860, merged with 1st 1862.
39th (Liverpool)	Formed 2 Feb 1860, also known as Liverpool Welsh, 2nd Admin Bn May 1860, part of 5th Lancashire (The Liverpool Rifle Volunteer Brigade) from 1862, 2nd VB King's (Liverpool) Reg 1888.
40th (Manchester)	Formed 16 Feb 1860, known as 3rd Manchester, formed 16th corps 1880, 4th VB Manchester Reg 1888
41st (Liverpool)	Formed 16 Feb 1860, disbanded 1864.
42nd (Childwall)	Formed 3 Feb 1860, disbanded 1870
43rd (Fallowfield)	Formed 11 Feb 1860, merged with 6th 1861
44th (Longton)	Formed 2 March 1860, absorbed into 11th 1866
45th (Liverpool)	Formed 27 Feb 1860, 1st Admin Bn 1860, part of 1st Corp 1880, 1st VB The King's (Liverpool) Reg 1888
46th (Swinton)	Formed 24 Feb 1860, 4th Admin Bn 1860, 4th corps 1880, 1st VB Manchester Reg 1888.
47th (St Helens)	Formed 29 Feb 1860, amalgamated with 48th in 1880 to form the 21st corps, 2nd VB The South Lancashire Reg 1886
48th (Prescott)	Formed 15 March 1860, attached to 1st Admin Bn 1863, amalgamated with 47th 1880 to form the 21st corps, 2nd VB The South Lancashire Reg 1886.
49th (Newton-Le-Willows)	Formed 3 March 1860, attached to 9th 1862, 9th Admin Bn 1865, consolidated 9th corps 1880, 1st VB The South Lancashire Reg 1886
50th	Not formed

51st (Liverpool)	Formed 3 March 1860, disbanded 1866
52nd (Dalton)	Formed from the 37th on 9 April 1861, absorbed into 37B (Barrow) 1870, Dalton personnel transferred to 37A in 1875, part of 5th Admin Bn
53rd (Cartmel)	Formed from the 37th on 9 April 1861, part of 5th Admin Bn
54th (Ormskirk)	Formed 15 March 1860, 13th corps 1880, 3rd VB King's (Liverpool) Reg 1888.
55th (Leigh)	Formed 3 March 1860, 4th Admin Bn 1860, consolidated 4th corps 1880, 1st VB Manchester Reg 1888
56th (Salford)	Formed 5 March 1860, 17th corps 1880, 3rd VB The Lancashire Fusiliers 1886
57th (Ramsbottom)	Formed 26 March 1860, 3rd Admin Bn 1861, consolidated 3rd corps 1880, 2nd VB East Lancashire Reg 1889
58th	Not formed
59th (Leyland)	Formed 29 Feb 1860, 6th Admin Bn 1861, consolidated 11th corps 1880, 1st VB The Loyal North Lancashire Reg 1883
60th (Atherton)	Formed 6 March 1860, 4th Admin Bn 1860, consolidated 4th corps 1880, 1st VB Manchester Reg 1888
61st (Chorley)	Formed 6 March 1860, 6th Admin Bn 1861, absorbed into 11th 1868.
62nd (Clitheroe)	Formed 27 March 1860, 8th Admin Bn 1864, consolidated 2nd corps 1880, 1st VB East Lancashire Reg 1889
63rd (Toxteth)	Formed 9 April 1860, 2nd Admin Bn 1860, part of 5th Lancashire (The Liverpool Rifle Volunteer Brigade) from 1862, 2nd VB King's (Liverpool) Reg 1888.
64th (Liverpool)	Formed 25 April 1860, also known as Liverpool Irish, 2nd Admin Bn 1861, 18th corps 1880, became 5th (Irish) VB The King's (Liverpool) Reg 1888
65th (Rossall)	Formed Feb 1860, most members were masters and senior boys of Rossall school, 5th Admin Bn 1863, junior boy's cadet corps formed 1873, converted to Engineer cadets 1890
66th (Liverpool)	Formed 25 April 1860, 1st Admin Bn 1860, part of 1st Corp, 1st VB The King's (Liverpool) Reg 1888
67th (Worsley)	Formed 7 May 1860, 4th Admin Bn 1860, consolidated 4th corps 1880, 1st VB Manchester Reg 1888
68th (Liverpool)	Formed 31 May 1860, also known as Lyceum corps, 2nd Admin Bn 1860, part of 5th Lancashire (The Liverpool Rifle Volunteer Brigade) from 1862, 2nd VB King's (Liverpool) Reg 1888.
69th (Liverpool)	Formed 31 May 1860, 1st Admin Bn 1860, part of 1st Corp, 1st VB The King's (Liverpool) Reg 1888
70th (Droylesden)	Formed 5 May 1860, absorbed by the 28th in 1862
71st (Liverpool)	Also known as Liverpool Highland, 2nd Admin Bn 1860, part of 5th Lancashire (The Liverpool Rifle Volunteer Brigade) from 1862, 2nd VB King's (Liverpool) Reg 1888.
72nd (Liverpool Old Swan)	Formed 8 June 1860, absorbed into 51st in 1862
73rd (Newton)	Formed 8 June 1860, absorbed by the 80th 1863

APPENDIX

74th (Liverpool St Annes)	Formed 2 July 1860, absorbed by the 1st in 1862
75th (Broughton-in-Furness)	Formed 28 Aug 1860, 5th Admin Bn 1861, disbanded 1863
76th (Farnworth)	Formed 3 July 1860, 4th Admin Bn 1860, consolidated 4th corps 1880, 1st VB Manchester Reg 1888
77th (Widnes)	Formed 1 Oct 1860, disbanded 1863
78th (Manchester)	Formed 2 Nov 1860, absorbed by 33rd 1862
79th (Liverpool)	Formed 16 Feb 1860, part of 5th Lancashire (The Liverpool Rifle Volunteer Brigade) from 1862, 2nd VB King's (Liverpool) Reg 1888.
80th (Liverpool)	Formed 8 Jan 1861, also known as the 'Press Guard'. Became 19th corps 1880, 6th VB The King's (Liverpool) Reg 1888
81st (Withnell)	Formed 20 Feb 1861, 2nd Admin Bn 1861, then attached to 2nd corps, moved to Wheelton 1865, disbanded 1876
82nd (Hindley)	Formed 14 June 1861, joined with 27th in 1876
83rd (Knowsley)	Formed 11 Feb 1861, 1st Admin Bn 1863, disbanded 1872
84th ((Padiham)	Formed 18 Feb 1861, 3rd Admin Bn 1861, consolidated 3rd corps 1880, 2nd VB The East Lancashire Reg 1889
85th	Not formed
86th (Liverpool)	Formed 18 May 1861, also known as Custom's House corps, 2nd Admin Bn 1861, part of 5th Lancashire (The Liverpool Rifle Volunteer Brigade) from 1862, 2nd VB King's (Liverpool) Reg 1888.
87th (Nelson)	Formed 7 Feb 1862, 3rd Admin Bn 1862, disbanded 1865
88th (Haslingdon)	Formed 27 Feb 1863, 3rd Admin Bn 1863, consolidated 3rd corps 1880, 2nd VB The East Lancashire Reg 1889
89th	Not formed
90th (Fleetwood)	Formed 3 June 1868, 3rd Admin Bn 1868, absorbed 1870
91st (Flixton)	Formed 14 Aug 1872, 4th Admin Bn 1872, consolidated 4th corps 1880, 1st VB Manchester Reg 1888

Appendix 11 – Oldham Rifle Volunteers, Regimental Prize Shooting Competitions

The Mellodew Challenge Cup –
An exceedingly elegant and massive silver cup presented for competition by Thomas Mellodew Esq. Cup decorated with the Oldham arms together with the motto 'Defence; not defiance'. Plus inscription ' Mellodew Challenge Cup'. Money prizes are added by the officers. Competition is open to all efficient volunteers. Must be won by the same volunteer at two consecutive contests or at intervals before becoming his property. The cup to be considered the property of the commanding officer until won as above mentioned. Distances 200 and 300 yards.

1861	Pvt Bennett	1872	Pvt Haslam
1862	Sgt Horsley	1873	QM Sgt Corbitt
1864	Cpl Hallsworth	1875	Sgt Eugene Schulze
1866	Colour Sgt H Goodwin	1876	Sgt Tetlow
1867	Sgt Sugden	1877	Col Sgt Sugden
1868	Sgt James Whittaker	1878	Col Sgt Sugden
1869	Sgt Threlfall	1879	Sgt Randle
1870	Cpl Green	1880	Sgt Randle
1871	Ensign Page		

Worthington Challenge Cup – Deputy Lieutenants Challenge Cup.
Competition open only to those efficient volunteers who have passed out of third class and been in the corps for at least 12 months. Distances 400, 500 and 600 yards.

1862	Cpl Winterbottom	1884	Sgt Clegg
1864	Sgt Goodwin	1885	Sgt H Bailey
1866	Sgt Greaves	1887	Sgt Ellis
1868	QM Sgt Page	1888	Capt Young (new cup)
1869	QM Sgt Page	1889	Sgt Ellis
1870	Col Sgt Threlfall	1890	Bandmaster Robinson
1871	QM Sgt Corbitt	1891	Col Sgt Arnold
1872	Pvt Wolsencroft	1892	Pvt Charles Ellis
1874	Col Sgt Sugden	1893	Sgt H Davis
1875	Col Sgt Sugden	1896	Col Sgt J Arnold
1876	Sgt Buckley	1898	Armourer Sgt Taylor
1877	Band Cpl Robinson	1899	Captain W Patterson
1878	Col Sgt Slater	1900	Col Sgt Davis
1879	Sgt Robinson	1901	Captain W Patterson
1880	Sgt Rendle	1902	Sgt P Taylor
1881	Lance Cpl Driver	1903	Pvt H Cockcroft
1882	Sgt Whiteley	1904	Sgt John Wild
1883	Armoury Sgt Threlfall	1905	Sgt John Wild

APPENDIX

Radcliffe Challenge Cup –
Presented by Samuel Radcliffe Esq. JP, money prizes being added by the officers. It is open to all efficient volunteers and must be won by the same volunteer at two consecutive contests or at intervals before becoming his property. The cup to be considered the property of the commanding officer until won as above mentioned. The final winner of the cup will not be entitled to the money prize attached. Distances 200 and 500 yards.

1872	Sgt Major Batchelor
1873	Sgt Eugene Schulze
1874	Sgt Eugene Schulze
1875	Lance Cpl Wolstencroft
1876	Col Sgt Slater
1877	Col Sgt Taylor
1878	Col Sgt Slater
1881	Lance Cpl Driver
1882	Sgt Arnold
1883	Band Sgt Robinson
1884	Bugle Major John Tindall
1885	Bugle Major John Tindall
1886	Col Sgt R Slater
1887	Bugle Major John Tindall
1888	Sgt Wild
1889	Cpl Coupe
1890	Pvt Wm Smith
1891	Sgt Ellis
1892	Sgt Wild
1893	Pvt H Davis
1898	Pvt Charles Ellis

Good attendance Prize –
Presented by Fred Platt Esq., DLOYC to be won by the same volunteer twice in succession or at 3 different intervals, together with 2 guineas given by George Wainwright Esq. with money prize added by the officers of the corps. Open only to volunteers who have during the volunteer year attended at least 4 battalion parades and 26 other drills. In order further to encourage good attendance at drills each volunteer is allowed to add one mark to his score for every 10 drills in excess of the necessary 30 drills. In counting for the drills in excess the battalion parades in uniform from June 11 to July 2nd inclusive will count as 2 drills. Distance 200, 500 and 600 yards.

1866	Colour Sgt Page
1868	Sgt Taylor
1869	QM Sgt Page
1870	Sgt Sugden
1871	QM Sgt Corbitt
1872	Sgt Sugden
1873	Col Sgt Taylor
1875	Sgt J Taylor
1876	Sgt Eugene Schulze
1877	Col Sgt Slater
1878	Cpl Standing
1879	Col Sgt Slater
1880	Bugle Major Tindall
1881	Lance Cpl Driver
1882	Armoury Sgt Threlfall

Clegg Challenge Cup –

Presented by Joseph Clegg, open to those members efficient for five years. Only won by two successive wins or three different times. Distance 500 and 600 yards. Five rounds at each. In 1886 changed to being efficient for two years and ranges 200, 500 and 600 yards, seven rounds at each, kneeling at 200 prone at 500 & 600. 1886 was first time Sgt Instructors could compete in prize comps

1875	Col Sgt Taylor	1887	Capt Young
1876	Col Sgt Corbitt	1888	Bugle Major Tindall
1877	Col Sgt Taylor	1890	Sgt Maj Slater
1878	Col Sgt Slater	1892	Pvt Charles Ellis
1879	Col Sgt Corbitt	1893	Col Sgt J Arnold
1880	Col Sgt Corbitt	1897	Sgt R Coupe
1881	Sgt Cocker	1898	Capt Patterson
1882	Band Sgt Robinson	1899	Col Sgt Davis
1883	Col Sgt Taylor	1900	Sgt Inst Bailey
1884	Col Sgt Slater	1901	Col Sgt Easthorpe
1885	Sgt John Jackson	1902	Armourer Sgt John Taylor
1886	Sgt Inst T Liles		

Lees Challenge Cup -

Presented by John Lees Esq. of Clarksfield.

1879	Sgt Standing	1886	Sgt C Ellis
1880	QM Sgt Thorp	1887	Sgt Adam Jackson
1881	Sgt Standing	1889	Sgt Jackson
1882	Lance Sgt Wiberton	1890	Sgt Batkin
1883	Sgt John Arnold	1892	Sgt Wild
1884	Sgt James	1893	Sgt W Swallow
1885	Sgt John Arnold	1898	Pvt Charles Ellis
1886	Sgt C Ellis		

Hamilton Challenge cup –

Presented by George Hamilton Esq., open to those who have been efficient for 5 year. 200, 500 and 600 yards, 5 rounds each.

1880	Pvt S Farrar.	1886	Col Sgt John Taylor
1881	Lance Cpl Marlor	1887	Sgt Maj Slater
1882	Cpl John Wild	1888	Capt Young
1883	Lance Cpl Ashcroft	1889	Sgt Wild
1884	Col Sgt Healey	1890	Bugle Major Tindall
1885	Pvt John Ashcroft	1891	Sgt Bugler Tindall

APPENDIX

Victoria Challenge Cup –
Presented by J W Radcliffe Esq.
200,500 and 600 yards, 7 rounds at each, 200 kneeling 500 & 600 prone.

1887	Pvt Driver	1893	Sgt H Davis
1888	Sgt Wild	1894	Sgt Ellis
1889	Col Sgt Slater	1898	Pvt Walter Hamer
1890	Sgt Ellis	1899	Armour Sgt Taylor
1891	Pvt Jno Taylor	1900	Sgt Ellis
1892	Col Sgt Arnold	1901	Sgt C F Ellis

Officers Challenge Shield –

1888	Capt. H. Mc. L. Young & Lieut. J. Saville	1922	Lieut. D. W. Deakin
1889	Lieut. J. Saville	1923	Lt. Col. G. R. Newton
1890	Lieut. J. Saville	1924	Capt. J. A C. Taylor
1891	Capt. A. E. Wrigley	1925	Capt. H. R. C. Green
1892	Capt. A. E. Wrigley	1926	Capt. P. Stott
1893	Capt. W. Patterson	1927	Col. Gr. R. Newton
1899	Capt. Wm. Bagshaw	1929	Capt. H. H. Holness
1907	Capt. & Or. Mr. S. A. Thorp	1930	2nd Lieut. H. A. Wallace
1908	Capt. & Or. Mr. S. A. Thorp	1931	Lieut. Col. F. Hardman
1909	Lieut. H. M. Fort	1932	Lieut. T. S. Evans
1910	Capt L. C. Wilde	1933	Lieut. J. Brewer
1911	Capt. J. A Newton	1934	Lieut. H. Wallace
1912	Lieut. R. Fitton	1935	Lieut. F. H. Ashton
1913	Lieut. Colonel W. Patterson	1936	2nd Lieut. P. Mellodew
1921	Capt. J. A. C. Taylor	1937	Capt. T. S. Evans

Officers Challenge shield

By kind permission of the 10th Bt Manchester Regiment & 40/41st RTR Trustees

Regimental Challenge Cup – First presented in 1887
By kind permission of the 10th Bt Manchester Regiment & 40/41st RTR Trustees

Rifle Club Cup
Presented by J. B. Rowland Esq. Won
By Ensign John Greaves Septr. 4th 1872

By kind permission of the 10th Bt Manchester
Regiment & 40/41st RTR Trustees

Band Marksman Cup – First presented in 1898
Presented by Messrs. Butterfield Bros.
Oldham in Commemoration of Her
Majesty's Diamond Jubilee 1837 – 1897

By kind permission of the 10th Bt Manchester
Regiment & 40/41st RTR Trustees

Appendix 12 – Strength of the Oldham Rifle Volunteers

Information gathered from a combination of newspaper reports and returns held at Lancashire Record Office.

Year	Enrolled	Efficients	Leavers	Joiners	Total Since formation
4 Sept 1860	92				
1 Aug 1861	196				
11 Aug 1862	226				
1864	268	257			
1865	299	282			
30 Nov 1866	269				
1868	503	492			
30 Nov 1869	472	463	75	44	
30 Nov 1870	457	432			
30 Nov 1871	463	453			
1872					1421
1873	396	380		90	1510
30 Nov 1874	409	347		69	1579
30 Nov 1875	401	394		65	1644
30 Nov 1876	360	355		71	1715
30 Nov 1877	373		73	86	1801
30 Nov 1878	429	418		105	1906
1879	441		74	224	2130
1880	591	584	84	73	2227
1881	605	605	95	115	2340
1882	625		115	310	2649
1883	785	778	142	124	
1884	774	768	175	164	2940
1885	787	763	171	183	3124
1886	785		203	201	3325
1887	800	755	152	167	3492
1888	749				
1889	797	768	239	287	
1890	787	725	183	193	
1891	758	723	212	184	
1892	737	724	195	175	
1893	795	720	147	205	
1894	802	800			
1896	791	686			

History of Oldham Volunteer Corps 1798 - 1908

Year	Enrolled	Efficients	Leavers	Joiners	Total Since formation
1897	760	741			
1898	721	697			
1899	719	712			
1900	937	886			
1901	945	914			6077
1902	1045	982	182	163	6240
1903	880	875	252	127	6360
1904	856	850	212	188	6548
1905	775	773			6626
1906	819	772			

The volunteer year began in October from 1859-62, in December from 1863-71 and thereafter in November.

Appendix 13 – 6th Volunteer Battalion members who served in the South Africa War

Service with 1st Volunteer Service Company

Name	No	Comments
Bamford, Percy - Capt		Living at Wellington Rd. Volunteered as a Lieutenant.
Barr, JH - Sergeant	7170	Discharged in South Africa 1/4/1901 and joined the Imperial Military Railway. Seen May 1901 by Sgt Mulcaster at Bronker's Spruit as assistant Station Master earning £4 per week. Seen April 1902 by Pvt Stott at Pan employed as Station Master.
Bowden, George H	7175	9 Adelphi St, age 21.
Dolphyn, Walace	7129	8 Brook St
Emmott, William	7197	334 Manchester St
Kershaw, T	7181	Living at 26 Villa St. Discharged in South Africa 1/12/1900 and joined the Imperial Military Railway as a fitter.
Ogden, Handel	7179	150 Redgrave St. Cotton Spinner Piercer.
Taylor, A	7191	12 Stewart St
Taylor, P	7215	12 Stewart St
Wadsworth, T	7187	649 Ripponden Rd
Weston, R	7193	3 Ramsey St

Service with 2nd Volunteer Service Company

Name	No	Comments
Hardman, George W - Lt		Living at Waterhead. Son of Joseph Hardman, cotton spinner, Bangor Mill.
Dunkerley, Cyrus - Sgt	7211	Living at 59 Morton St. Brother of Fred. Mechanic. Age 23.
Jackson, H - Sgt	8244	Living at 53 Belmont St.
Mulcaster, J - Colour Sgt	2712	Living at 145 Radcliffe St. Previously served in South Africa. Joined the 6VB as Sgt Instructor from the 4th Battalion Manchester Regiment 1/10/1897.
Caley, Alfred - Cpl	7171	Living at 228 Shaw Rd. Packer in cotton mill. Age 20.
Street, JR - Cpl	7173	Living at 74 Middleton Rd
Dunkerley, Fred - Lance Cpl	7203	Living at 19 Dunkerley St. Brother of Cyrus.
Williams, F – Lance Cpl	8250	Living at 181 Coppice St.
Black, J - Bugler	7174	Living at 20 Fankhill St

Name	No	Comments
Andrew, Frank	8248	Living at 6 King St. Became ill with enteric fever hospitalised in Pretoria and returned later than rest.
Armstrong, G	7204	Living at 72 Glodwick Rd. Stretcher bearer. Remained in South Africa and joined the Mines Defence Force.
Ashworth, George W	7190	Living at 29 Franklin St. Age 21.
Bancroft, A	7217	Living at 4 Back Thomas St.
Bell, J	8245	Living at 162 Radcliffe St.
Bowman, J	7195	Living at 34 Franklin St.
Buckley, C	7176	7176. Living at 26 Higginshaw Rd
Buckley, Jas	8251	Living at 9 Behind 91 Siddall St.
Cash, R	7186	Living at 17 Woodstock St
Chadwick, James	7178	Living at 26 Higginshaw Rd. Engine Fitter. Age 19.
Colgan, J	7196	Living at 47 Stone St, Ordsall Lane, Salford.
Collier, S	8241	Living at 27 Broome St.
Conway, J	7194	Living at 172 Featherstall Rd.
Cubby, Joseph	7205	Living at 22 Knott St. Became ill with enteric and was hospitalised and returned later than rest.
Curran, J	8247	Living at 192 Shaw Rd.
Ebdon, J	7209	Living at 44 Robins St. Became ill with enteric fever hospitalised in Cape Town and returned later than rest.
Garland, H	7184	Living at 2 Barton St
Glover, A	7224	Living at 52 Cranbrook St.
Goodwin, George	7200	Living at 23 William St.
Greenhalgh, S	8243	Living at 101 Brierley St, Chadderton.
Halkyard, William	7219	Living at 142 Edge Lane Rd.
Hall, R	7206	Living at 28 Worcester St.
Hankinson, Thomas A	8238	Living at 45 Ray St.
Heron, JT	7189	Living at 103 Eldon St
Hibbert, John	8249	Living at 71 Chamber Rd. Iron Turner. Age 29. Remained in South Africa and joined the Mines Defence Force.
Holden, Ernest	7223	Living at 36 Morris St. Age 22.
Houlston, J	8240	Living at 36 Knott St.
Kiernan, John	8246	Living at 4 Edgar St.
Lane, E	7218	Living at 7 Stable St.
Lees, R	7202	Living at 132 Bower St.
Marcroft, J	7221	Living at 21 Howard St, Waterhead.
McConnochie, Adam	7198	Living at 84 Chadderton Rd.
Papworth, Philip	7207	Living at 76 Greenacres Rd.
Prescott, Arthur	7180	Living at 38 Widdop St. Worked at Derker Mills.
Rhodes, Eli	7185	Living at 57 Littlemore Lane.
Royle, H	7201	Living at 25 Napier St.
Schofield, T	7182	Living at 49 Chadderton Rd
Schofield, WH	7199	Living at 103 Barton St. Remained in South Africa and joined the Mines Defence Force.

APPENDIX

Name	No	Comments
Smith, E	8237	Living at 7 Davidson St.
Steeple, William	7188	Living at 24 Fletcher St, then Lyon Dam St.
Summersgill, HV	7208	Living at 5 St James St.
Tattersall, G	8252	Living at 7 Smith St.
Trevitt, Jim	8242	Living at 6 Mulliner St.
Walne, James	7213	Living at Oldham Rd, Bardsley. Age 29.
Waugh, Rodger	7214	Living at 16 Malton St. Age 29.
Whitehead, T	7177	Living at 52 Peel St.
Whittaker, Harry	7212	Living at 14 Church St.
Wood, JS	8253	Living at Clay St.
Wood, JW	7210	Living at 5 Sydney St.

Service with 3rd Volunteer Service Company

Name	No	Comments
Bailey, William - Colour Sgt	2883	41 Miners Street. Age 31. Married. Born Macclesfield. Joined the 6VB in Jan 1897 as Sgt Instructor from the 4th Batt Manchester Regiment.
Davies, W Cpl	8346	102 Webster Street
Byron, J Pvt	8342	209 West Street
Collins, C	8343	69 Southern Street
Goodwin, J E	8345	37 Miners Street
Smith, Edward	8347	49 Mortimer Street. Joined the Johannesburg Police.
Wolstencroft, J	8344	37 Miners Street

Service with 4th Volunteer Service Company

Name	No	Comments
Cheetham, John J – Lance Cpl	8396	Living at 102 Edward St. Spindle and fly maker. Age 26.
Barber, Herbert	8385	Living at 341 Featherstall Rd North. Labourer in iron foundry. Married. Age 28.
Bardsley, Joseph H	8394	Living at 15 Evelyn St. Iron planer. Married, age 30.
Belshaw, J J	8379	Living at 9 Chapman St
Clegg, W	8421	Living at 5 Court 2, Scott St.
Cole, G C	8420	Living at 8 Austerberry St.
Davies, G	8378	Living at 20 Cranbrook St.
Drinkwater, Ernest	8425	Living at 35 Whiteley St. Age 19.
Gilham, John	8386	Living at 10 Heyside. Cotton machine minder. Age 26.
Harding, Frank	8422	Living at 1 Campbell St. Labourer. Age 17.
Hardman, Charles	8457	Living at 42 Glebe St, Shaw. Cotton spinner. Age 20.
Harrison, W	8426	Living at 29 Parsons St.
Hoddy, W	8376	Living at 9 Stake Street
Hoyle, William	8393	Living at 108 King St. Machine Borer. Age 25.
Hunt, Benjamin	8424	Living at 13 Bower St. Age 21.

Name	No	Comments
Insull, J	8391	Living at 43 Garnet St
Marsden, J W	8389	Living at 164 Block Lane, Chadderton.
Mellor, E	8390	Living at 22 Cooper St. Could be Frank age 18 at this address
Mellor, Harry	8381	Living at 277 Rochdale Rd. Machine winder. Age 22.
Orris, P W	8419	Living at 22 Bower St.
Rhodes, Joseph	8395	Living at 36 Glebe Street, Shaw. Cotton mule piercer. Age 19.
Roebuck, W	8388	Living at 10 Eden St.
Seddon, John J	8382	Living at 5 Flora St. Machine minder in a cotton mill. Married, age 30.
Strandring, Eli F	8387	Living at 25 Simmon Street. Flyer Maker. Age 21.
Stott, Herbert	8418	Living at 43 Tamworth St. Apprentice machine fitter. Age 18.
Stott, S E	8383	Living at 24 High St, Shaw.
Taylor, A J	8384	Living at 108 Fraser St, Shaw
Taylor, Robert	8392	Living at 17 Leamington St, Watersheddings. Cotton Piercer, age 21.
Taylor, W	8423	Living at 17 Mordaunt St.
Turner, Harry	8377	Living at 21 Montgomery St. Iron moulder, age 19.
Winterburn, Fred	8456	Living at 19 Joseph St
Whyatt, William	8380	Living at 16 Mole St.

APPENDIX

Appendix 14 – South Africa War - Service with 23rd Company 8th Battalion Imperial Yeomanry

DLOY A Squadron (Oldham & Rochdale Troop) members who went to South Africa with 1st Draft

Name	No	Rank	Remarks
Kemp, George		Captain	Promoted Major. With the 23rd Company until 9/7/01. Lt-Col of 32 Batt IY from May to Nov 1902.
Heap, James Arthur Berry		Lt	Service in SA 11/2/00 to 20/2/01. Joined DLOY 20/1/00. Rochdale Troop.
Griffiths, William Henry	2159	Colour Sergeant	Service in SA 11/2/00 to Aug 1902. Living at Coronation Hotel, Oldham. Promoted to Lt on 12/12/1900, promoted to Captain on 15/5/1901. Appointed Commandant of 23rd Company on 23rd March 1901. Awarded Distinguished Conduct Medal. Joined DLOY 1/9/97.
Harrington, Arthur George	2746	Sergeant	Service in SA 11/2/00 to 10/6/01. Born in Sussex Age 32. Served previously in the Royal Horse Artillery until invalid out.
Miller, Richard	2710	Sergeant Farrier	Service in SA 11/2/00 to 5/7/01.Living at Brunswick Hotel, Ashton. Born in Oldham. Farrier by trade. Age 36. Joined DLOY 1/2/93.
Wilson, James	2700	Corporal	Service in SA 11/2/00 to 10/6/01.Born in Rochdale. Age 27. Promoted to Sergeant. Married to Alice Ann (nee Mills). Living at 22 Baillis Street, Rochdale. Joined DLOY 2/3/94.
Ashworth, Walter	2713	Trooper	Service in SA 11/2/00 to 10/6/01.Living at Horsedge St, Oldham 22 years old, butcher by trade.
Brierley, Ernest Joseph	2763	Trooper	

Name	No	Rank	Remarks
Brooks, Graham	2685	Trooper	Service in SA 11/2/00 to 17/6/01. Age 20. Born in Halifax. Clerk. Severely wounded in the neck near Pearston on 22 April 1901. Joined DLOY 25/2/98.
Brooksbank, Allen	2717	Trooper	Service in SA 11/2/00 to 25/7/01. Living at Curzon St, Ashton. 24 years old, a butcher by trade. Became ill on the journey home and recovered at Netley Hospital, Hants. Joined DLOY 12/1/97.
Casson, Samuel	2701	Trooper	Service in SA 11/2/00 to 10/6/01. Born Rochdale. Age 31. Promoted to Corporal. Married to Emma (nee Bancroft), living at Park Hill, Rochdale.
Clegg, John	2695	Trooper	Service in SA 11/2/00 to June 01. In D Troop. Manager at establishment of Mr Hugh Cooper, Hatter on Yorkshire St, Oldham.
Coulthard, Thomas	2698	Trooper	Service in SA 11/2/00 to 20/6/01. Born Clitheroe. Age 27. Promoted to Farrier Lance Corporal. Married to Ida (nee Porter). Living at 9 Butterworth Street, Rochdale. Joined DLOY 16/10/96.
Dransfield, James William	2718	Trooper	Living 7 West St, Lees. Married to Mary Ann (nee Brown). Worked as a bus driver between Oldham and Springhead for the firm R.Chadwick & Co.. Age 26. Died Kimberley 27/11/1900. Joined DLOY 12/11/96.
Halliwell, William	2687	Trooper	Service in SA 11/2/00 to 7/5/01. Born in Rochdale. Age 31. Surveyor by trade. Living at 53 Drake St, Rochdale.
Hargreaves, James	2696	Trooper	Service in SA 11/2/00 to 10/6/01. Born Rochdale. Age 20. Coachman by trade. Living at 17 College St, Rochdale.
Hollingworth, Frank	2684	Trooper	Service in SA 11/2/00 to 20/6/01. Born Ashton. Age 24.

APPENDIX

Name	No	Rank	Remarks
Jones, Ernest	2719	Trooper	Service in SA 11/2/00 to 3/1/01. Living at 21 Waddington St, Ashton. Wounded in the right shoulder and damaged right eye. 23/10/1900 at Hoopstad.. Invalided home.
Kay, Ernest Walter	2737	Trooper	Service in SA 11/2/00 to 16/6/01. Born Rochdale. Age 21. Promoted Sergeant and served with 32nd Batt IY from May 02. Joined DLOY 14/10/96.
Kershaw, Joseph Harrison	2712	Trooper	Service in SA 11/2/00 to 7/6/01. Living at Firs Ave, Failsworth. 21 years old. Traveller by trade.
Lewin, Frank	2686	Trooper	Service in SA 11/2/00 to 17/6/01. Born in Hull. Age 20. Draftsman by trade. Mother , Elizabeth, living at Bull green, Halifax. Joined DLOY 29/5/97.
Makin, Frederick Arthur	2711	Trooper	Service in SA 11/2/00 to 18/3/01. Living at Burlington St, Ashton. 25 years old, trade of Soda Water manufacturer. Joined DLOY 24/11/97.
Ormrod, Thomas William	2708	Trooper	Service in SA 11/2/00 to 10/6/01. Living at 25 Robinson Street, Ashton. Born in Hollinwood. Age 27. Coal Merchant by trade. Married to Ada (nee Ditchfield). Joined DLOY 25/9/94.
Pearson, Ernest	2688	Trooper	Service in SA 11/2/00 to 8/8/01
Rodgers, Gervase	2720	Trooper	Service in SA 11/2/00 to 10/6/01. Living at 224 Rochdale Rd, Oldham. Age 24. Insurance Agent. Originally from Ripley in Derbyshire.
Smith, Mathew	2697	Trooper	Service in SA 11/2/00 to 10/6/01. Born Rochdale. Age 26. Cab proprietor by trade. Married to Ada (nee Kershaw). Living at 18 Whitworth Rd, Rochdale.

Name	No	Rank	Remarks
Waterfield, Henry	2716	Trooper	Service in SA 11/2/00 to 10/6/01. In D Section. Living at Peter St, Oldham. Age 33. Born in Nottingham. Originally served for 12 years in 7th Dragoon Guards. Promoted Cpl July 1901. Signed on to serve again in October 1901 with 117th (Sharpshooters) Company IY and discharged in September 1902.
Whittaker, Charles William	2776	Trooper	Service in SA 11/2/00 to 20/4/01. In Gun section. Born Oldham. Living 62 Ripponden Road, Oldham. Age 28. Police constable in Hyde police. Horse fell whilst on service causing an injury known as 'Spanish back', discharged home.
Wild, John Brierley	2706	Trooper	Service in SA 11/2/00 to 10/6/01.Promoted to Corporal. Living at Waterhead. Joined DLOY 6/2/88 left 1906.

6th Volunteer Battalion members, who went to South Africa with 1st Draft

Name	No	Rank	Remarks
Priestley, Arthur Henry	2715	Trooper	Service in SA 11/2/00 to 10/6/01. Joined from the 6th VB Manchester Regiment. Auctioneers Clerk, Living at Malton St, Coppice, Oldham. Age 20. Acted as Lt Heap's orderly.

Oldham & Rochdale area civilians, who went to South Africa with 1st Draft

Name	No	Rank	Remarks
Brierley, Frank	2709	Trooper	Service in SA 11/2/00 to 10/6/01. Joined for the Boer war. Born Rochdale. Age 27. Brass Founder by trade. Married to Mary Ann (nee Holt).
Brooks, Walter	2690	Trooper	Service in SA 11/2/00 to 10/6/01. Born in Middleton. Age 36. Married to Annie. Living at 3 Bradshaw St, Heywood. Joined for the Boer war.

APPENDIX

Name	No	Rank	Remarks
Culeen, James Edward	2678	Trooper	Service in SA 11/2/00 to 4/12/00. Born in Oldham. Formerly served in the 17th Lancers. Theatrical Manager. Age 20. In No 4 Section. Joined for the Boer war.
Handley, William Walter	2691	Trooper	Service in SA 11/2/00 to 20/6/01. Born in Rochdale. Age 29. Plumber by trade. Joined for the Boer war. Married to Mary Jane (nee Halstead). Living at 3 Moss Street, Rochdale.
Rigg, Harvey	2703	Trooper	Service in SA 11/2/00 to 10/6/01. Born in Rochdale. Age 35. Schoolmaster by trade. Joined for the Boer war.
Travis, Charles Lee	2714	Trooper	Service in SA 11/2/00 to 10/6/01. Living at Burton St, Middleton. Age 22. Originally served in the Royal Navy, joined for the Boer war.

Relief Contingent for the 23rd Company IY (from Oldham area)

Name	No	Rank	Remarks
Chadderton, William Midgley	20497	Trooper	Member of 6VB Manchester Reg. Served 22/2/01 to 4/8/01. Born Chadderton. Age 28. Married to Florence Ann (nee Shepherd). Living at 8 Tin St, Featherstall Road. Spinner in cotton mill..
Finney, W	20500	Trooper	Civilian. Living at 14 Bloom St, Oldham.
Geary, Fred	20501	Trooper	Civilian. Living at West Hill, High Crompton. Born in Derby.
Greenwood, Joseph	23766	Trooper	Served 22/2/01 to 31/8/02. Civilian, born Royton, Oldham. Age 22. Tramway Inspector. Living at 31 Sydney St, Oldham.
Harrison, John JW	21367	Trooper	DLOY Trooper. Served 16/2/01 to 26/8/01. Living at St Georges Villa, Whitegate End.

Name	No	Rank	Remarks
Henderson, Robert	20505	Trooper	Civilian. Served 9/2/01 to 12/8/01. Born in Edinburgh. Living at 38 Spencer St, Oldham.
Horrobin, Albert	21370	Trooper	DLOY Trooper. Served in SA 16/2/01 to 15/5/01. Died at Heilbron of enteric fever 15/5/01. Born Chadderton. Age 23. Living 60 Stanley Road, Hollinwood. Engine tool maker.
Kershaw, Joseph Henry	20514	Trooper	Served in SA 16/2/01 to 31/8/02. Born Oldham. Age 20. Bricklayer. Volunteer in 2VB Lancashire Fusiliers.
Marsden, GH	20521	Trooper	Member of 6VB Manchester Reg. 104 Glodwick Road.
Mellor, Wilfred	21380	Trooper	Served in SA 16/2/01 to 25/4/02. Wounded 12/11/01. Born Saddleworth. Age 20. Previously served in 3rd Batt Grenadier Guards.
Mycock, Arthur Edgar	20528	Trooper	Civilian. Served in SA 10/3/01 to 8/9/02.Age 22
Richardson, Albert Ernest	20536	Trooper	Civilian. Served in SA 16/2/01 to 31/8/02. Age 20. Born Oldham. Living 49 Union St, Oldham. Sailor in Merchant Navy.

23rd Company Imperial Yeomanry in South Africa
(By kind permission of the Duke of Lancaster's Own Yeomanry Museum)

Appendix 15 - Officers of the Oldham Troop of the Duke of Lancaster's Own Yeomanry:

Name	Commissions	Notes
Ashton, Howarth	Cornet 7/11/63, Lt 12/7/69, Capt 15/3/73, Hon Major 1/7/81, Retires 20/7/87.	Born 1841 in Middleton. Oct 80 leaves Oldham troop
Bibby, Henry Leigh	2nd Lt 19/7/99, Lt 5/6/01, Capt 11/7/03	
Buckley, Robert Whitehead	Cornet 15/3/73, Lt 1/6/73, Capt 20/10/80, retires Feb 86	Born about 1849 in Oldham. Cotton Spinning business. Supernumery from 1883
Heap, James Arthur Berry	2nd Lt 20/1/00, Capt May 05	
Johnson-Ferguson, Edward Alexander James	2nd Lt 18/3/96, Lt 13/7/98	
Lees, Albert Ernest	2nd Lt 4/2/88, Lt 21/9/89, Capt 11/3/96, Major 21/9/01, retires April 06	Born Oldham about 1868. Cotton Spinning business.
Lees-Milne, Alec Milne	2nd Lt 16/11/01, Lt 6/1/04	
Platt, Fred	Lt 15/3/73, Capt 19/1/78, Hon Major 27/6/88, Retires 16/10/80	1878 left Oldham troop to take charge of another troop
Platt, James Edward	2nd Lt 8/8/78, Lt 20/10/80, Capt 22/8/83, Hon Major 22/8/88, resigns Feb 96	Of Platt Bros & Co. Living at Bruntwood, Cheadle
Wrigley, Arthur Edward	2nd Lt 16/5/00, Lt 6/1/04	Cotton Spinner of Lees & Wrigley, Greenbank Mills, Glodwick. Born about 1865, living at Werneth.

APPENDIX

Duke of Lancaster's Own Yeomanry – A Squadron officers and Honorary members. Oldham officers seated on chairs left to right are A.M.Lees-Milne, H.L.Bibby & J.A.B.Heap

(By kind permission of the Duke of Lancaster's Own Yeomanry Museum)

Appendix 16 - Time Line of Oldham Volunteers

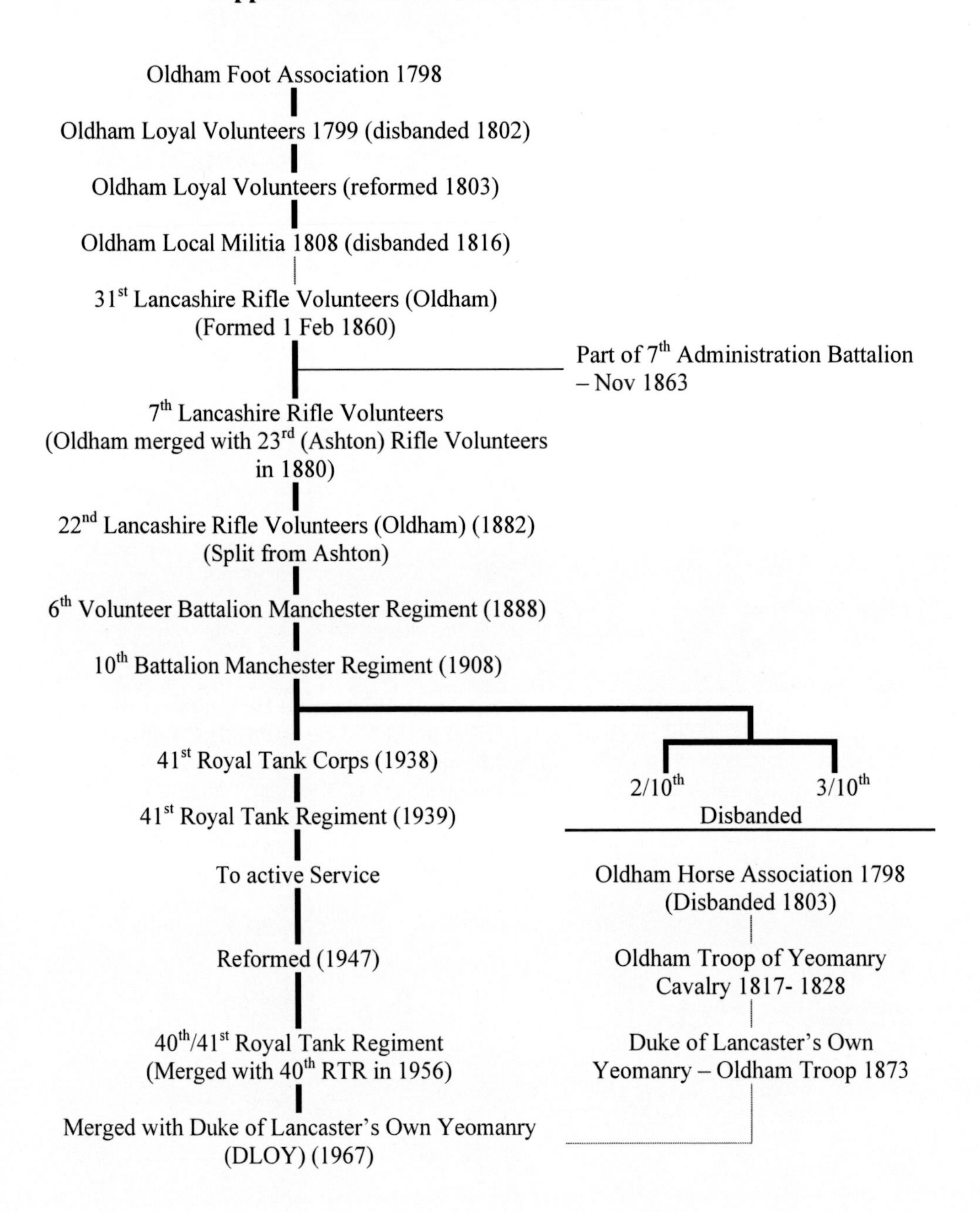

APPENDIX

Glossary and Abbreviations

CIV	City Imperial Volunteers
DEOVR	Duke of Edinburgh's Own Volunteer Rifles
DLOIY	Duke of Lancaster's Own Imperial Yeomanry
DLOY	Duke of Lancaster's Own Yeomanry
Enteric fever	Typhoid
IY	Imperial Yeomanry
Kop, Kopjes, koppie(s)	Hill or hills
LF	Lancashire Fusiliers
LRV	Lancashire Rifle Volunteers
MR	Manchester Regiment
NCO	Non commissioned officer
Nek	Mountain Pass
OLM	Oldham Local Militia
OTYC	Oldham Troop of Yeomanry Cavalry
RAMC	Royal Army Medical Corps
RB	Rifle Brigade
RFA	Royal Field Artillery
RTR	Royal Tank Regiment
Sangar	Stone wall or emplacement built by troops as a temporary protection
SJA	Saint Johns Ambulance
VB	Volunteer Battalion
VSC	Volunteer Service Company

Bibliography

Primary Sources

Chetham Library	Minutes book of 31st officers mess (A.7.78)
House of Commons Papers	1862 (3053) Report on condition of Volunteer Force in Great Britain, 1862
Lancashire Record Office	QSP Local Militia Returns, LN14 & LN22 rolls of LRV, LN11 Yeomanry returns
National Archives, Kew	Army Lists, Census Returns, HO, WO
National Army Museum	OLM Uniform (8212-68)
Oldham Local Studies	Rowbottoms Diary, Giles Shaw MSS, OLM Regimental Daily Orders, Oldham Directories
Standing Orders of OLM	Printed 1809

Newspapers: London Gazette, Manchester Courier, Manchester Gazette, Manchester Guardian, Manchester Times, Oldham Chronicle, Oldham Standard, Oldham Telegraph, The Times, Volunteer Journal for Lancashire & Cheshire, Wheelers Manchester Chronicle

Secondary Sources

Amery, L.S., *The Times History of the War in South Africa* (1909)
Barlow, L & Smith R.J., *Uniforms of the British Yeomanry Forces: 6. The Duke of Lancaster's Own Yeomanry* (Ogilby Trusts 1983)
Bastick, Desmond., *Trumpet Call: The story of the Duke of Lancaster's Own Yeomanry* (1973)
Beckett, Ian F.W., *Riflemen Form: A study of the Rifle Volunteer Movement 1859-1908* (Ogilby Trusts 1982)
Bonner, Robert., *Volunteer Infantry of Ashton-Under-Lyne 1859-1871* (Fleur de Lys 2005)
Brereton, John., *Chain Mail – The history of the Duke of Lancaster's Own Yeomanry 1798-1991* (Picton)
Bull, Stephen., *The Lancashire Rifle Volunteers, 1859-85* (Lancashire County Books 1993)
Butterworth, Edwin., *Historical Sketches of Oldham (1856)*
Foster, John., *Class struggle and the industrial revolution* (University Paperbacks 1977)
Gee, Austin., *The British Volunteer Movement 1794-1814* (Oxford University Press 2003)
Johnson, L.H., *Duke of Lancaster's Own Yeomanry Cavalry 23rd Company IY, record of incidents connected with the services of 1st contingent of DOLYC in South Africa*
Jooste, Cecilia P., *The Battle of Bergendal* (South African Military History Society Vol 12 No 4, 2002)
Law, Brian., *Oldham brave Oldham*
Marden & Newbigging., *Rough diary of the doings of the 1st Battalion Manchester Regiment during the South African War* (John Heywood, Manchester 1902)
Pakenham, Thomas., *The Boer War* (Abacus 1992)
Rawnsley, H. D., *Ballads of the War* (Dent 1900)
Read, Fergus., The Duke of Lancaster's Own Yeomanry: A Short History Compiled from Regimental and Other Records (Lancashire County Books 1992)
Ripley, H & Moodie, B., *Local Militia Buttons* (1994)
Wilson, H.W., *After Pretoria: The Guerilla War* (Amalgamated Press 1902)
Wylly, H.C. Colonel., *History of the Manchester Regiment* (Forster Groom 1925)